Endurance Running

Running is a fundamental human activity and holds an important place in popular culture. In recent decades it has exploded in popularity as a leisure pursuit, with marathons and endurance challenges exerting a strong fascination.

Endurance Running is the first collection of original qualitative research to examine distance running through a socio-cultural lens, with a general objective of understanding the concept and meaning of endurance historically and in contemporary times. Adopting diverse theoretical and methodological approaches to explore topics such as historical conceptualizations of endurance, lived experiences of endurance running, and the meaning of endurance in individual lives, the book reveals how the biological, historical, psychological, and sociological converge to form contextually specific ideas about endurance running and runners.

Endurance Running is an essential book for anybody researching across the entire spectrum of endurance sports and fascinating reading for anybody working in the sociology of sport or the body, cultural studies, or behavioral science.

William Bridel is an Assistant Professor in the Faculty of Kinesiology at the University of Calgary, Canada. His teaching and research focus on socio-cultural aspects of the body, sport, physical activity, and health. His research interests include: the emergence of ultra-endurance sports as forms of leisure activities; social and political aspects of health; sport-related pain and injury; and, gender, sexuality, and sport.

Jim Denison is an Associate Professor in the Faculty of Physical Education and Recreation at the University of Alberta, Canada. A sport sociologist and coach educator, his research primarily examines the formation of endurance running coaches' practices through a Foucauldian lens. Along with numerous book chapters and referred articles, he was co-editor of the *Routledge Handbook of Sports Coaching* (Routledge, 2013).

Pirkko Markula (Ph.D.) is a Professor of socio-cultural studies of physical activity at the University of Alberta, Canada. Her research interests include social analyses of dance, exercise, and sport in which she has employed several theoretical lenses ranging from critical, cultural studies research to Foucault and Deleuze. She is the previous editor of the *Sociology of Sport Journal*. She is the co-author, with Michael Silk, of *Qualitative Research for Physical Culture* (Routledge, 2011), co-author with Richard Pringle, of *Foucault, Sport and Exercise: Power, Knowledge and Transforming the Self* (Routledge, 2006), and co-editor with Eileen Kennedy of *Women and Exercise: Body, Health and Consumerism* (Routledge, 2011).

Routledge research in sport, culture and society

1 **Sport, Masculinities and the Body**
Ian Wellard

2 **India and the Olympics**
Boria Majumdar and Nalin Mehta

3 **Social Capital and Sport Governance in Europe**
Edited by Margaret Groeneveld, Barrie Houlihan and Fabien Ohl

4 **Theology, Ethics and Transcendence in Sports**
Edited by Jim Parry, Mark Nesti and Nick Watson

5 **Women and Exercise**
The body, health and consumerism
Edited by Eileen Kennedy and Pirkko Markula

6 **Race, Ethnicity and Football**
Persisting debates and emergent issues
Edited by Daniel Burdsey

7 **The Organisation and Governance of Top Football Across Europe**
An institutional perspective
Edited by Hallgeir Gammelsæter and Benoît Senaux

8 **Sport and Social Mobility**
Crossing boundaries
Ramón Spaaij

9 **Critical Readings in Bodybuilding**
Edited by Adam Locks and Niall Richardson

10 **The Cultural Politics of Post-9/11 American Sport**
Power, pedagogy and the popular
Michael Silk

11 **Ultimate Fighting and Embodiment**
Violence, gender and mixed martial arts
Dale C. Spencer

12 **The Olympic Games and Cultural Policy**
Beatriz Garcia

13 **The Urban Geography of Boxing**
Race, class, and gender in the ring
Benita Heiskanen

14 **The Social Organization of Sports Medicine**
Critical socio-cultural perspectives
Edited by Dominic Malcolm and Parissa Safai

15 **Host Cities and the Olympics**
An interactionist approach
Harry Hiller

16 **Sports Governance, Development and Corporate Responsibility**
Edited by Barbara Segaert, Marc Theeboom, Christiane Timmerman and Bart Vanreusel

17 **Sport and Its Female Fans**
Edited by Kim Toffoletti and Peter Mewett

18 **Sport Policy in Britain**
Barrie Houlihan and Iain Lindsey

19 **Sports and Christianity**
Historical and contemporary perspectives
Edited by Nick J. Watson and Andrew Parker

20 **Sports Coaching Research**
Context, consequences, and consciousness
Anthony Bush, Michael Silk, David Andrews and Hugh Lauder

21 **Sport Across Asia**
Politics, cultures, and identities
Edited by Katrin Bromber, Birgit Krawietz, and Joseph Maguire

22 **Athletes, Sexual Assault, and "Trials by Media"**
Narrative immunity
Deb Waterhouse-Watson

23 **Youth Sport, Physical Activity and Play**
Policy, interventions and participation
Andrew Parker and Don Vinson

24 **The Global Horseracing Industry**
Social, economic, environmental and ethical perspectives
Phil McManus, Glenn Albrecht, and Raewyn Graham

25 **Sport, Public Broadcasting, and Cultural Citizenship**
Signal lost?
Edited by Jay Scherer and David Rowe

26 **Sport and Body Politics in Japan**
Wolfram Manzenreiter

27 **The Fantasy Sport Industry**
Games within games
Andrew C. Billings and Brody J. Ruihley

28 **Sport in Prison**
Exploring the role of physical activity in penal practices
Rosie Meek

29 **Sport and Nationalism in China**
Lu Zhouxiang and Fan Hong

30 **Rethinking Drug Use in Sport**
Why the war will never be won
Bob Stewart and Aaron Smith

31 **Sport, Animals, and Society**
Edited by James Gillett and Michelle Gilbert

32 **Sport Development in the United States**
Edited by Peter Smolianov, Dwight Zakus and Joseph Gallo

33 **Youth Olympic Games**
Edited by Dag Vidar Hanstad, Barrie Houlihan and Milena Parent

34 **Safeguarding, Child Protection and Abuse in Sport**
International perspectives in research, policy and practice
Edited by Melanie Lang and Mike Hartill

35 **Touch in Sports Coaching and Physical Education**
Fear, risk, and moral panic
Edited by Heather Piper

36 **Sport, Racism and Social Media**
Neil Farrington, Lee Hall, Daniel Kilvington, John Price and Amir Saeed

37 **Football and Migration**
Perspectives, places, players
Edited by Richard Elliott and John Harris

38 **Health and Elite Sport**
Is high performance sport a healthy pursuit?
Edited by Joe Baker, Parissa Safai and Jessica Fraser-Thomas

39 **Asian American Athletes in Sport and Society**
Edited by C. Richard King

40 **Pierre Bourdieu and Physical Culture**
Edited by lisahunter, Wayne Smith and elke emerald

41 **Reframing Disability?**
Media, (dis)empowerment, and voice in the 2012 Paralympics
Edited by Daniel Jackson, Caroline E. M. Hodges, Mike Molesworth and Richard Scullion

42 **Sport and the Social Significance of Pleasure**
Richard Pringle, Robert E. Rinehart and Jayne Caudwell

43 **A Sociology of Football in a Global Context**
Jamie Cleland

44 **Gambling with the Myth of the American Dream**
Aaron M. Duncan

45 **Inclusion and Exclusion in Competitive Sport**
Socio-legal and regulatory perspectives
Seema Patel

46 **Asia and the Future of Football**
The role of the Asian Football Confederation
Ben Weinberg

47 **Football and Accelerated Culture**
This modern sporting life
Steve Redhead

48 **Researching Embodied Sport**
Exploring movement cultures
Edited by Ian Wellard

49 **Female Fans of the NFL**
Taking their place in the stands
Anne Cunnningham Osborne and Danielle Sarver Coombs

50 **Sport in Islam and in Muslim Communities**
Edited by Alberto Testa and Mahfoud Amara

51 **Endurance Running**
A socio-cultural examination
Edited by William Bridel, Pirkko Markula and Jim Denison

52 **Mega Events and Globalization**
Capital, cultures and spectacle in a changing world order
Edited by Richard Gruneau and John Horne

53 **Beyond Sport for Development and Peace**
Transnational perspectives on theory, policy and practice
Edited by Lyndsay Hayhurst, Tess Kay and Megan Chawansky

54 **Ethics and Governance in Sport**
The future of sport imagined
Edited by Yves Vanden Auweele, Elaine Cook and Jim Parry

55 **Skateboarding**
Subcultures, sites and shifts
Edited by Kara-Jane Lombard

Endurance Running

A socio-cultural examination

Edited by William Bridel, Pirkko Markula, and Jim Denison

Routledge
Taylor & Francis Group
LONDON AND NEW YORK

First published 2016
by Routledge
2 Park Square, Milton Park, Abingdon, Oxfordshire OX14 4RN

and by Routledge
711 Third Avenue, New York, NY 10017

First issued in paperback 2017

Routledge is an imprint of the Taylor & Francis Group, an informa business

British Library Cataloguing-in-Publication Data
A catalogue record for this book is available from the British Library

Library of Congress Cataloging in Publication Data
Endurance running : a socio-cultural examination / edited by William Bridel, Pirkko Markula and Jim Denison.
pages cm
Includes bibliographical references and index.
1. Running–Social aspects. 2. Marathon running. I. Bridel, William.
GV1062.E64 2016
796.42'4–dc23 2015017272

ISBN 13: 978-1-138-06785-1 (pbk)
ISBN 13: 978-1-138-81042-6 (hbk)

Typeset in Times New Roman
by Wearset Ltd, Boldon, Tyne and Wear

In memory of my grandmother, Barbara Wallace: a strong, caring, passionate, compassionate, and talented woman who instilled in me a love for the written word. Thanks, Gram.

William

Contents

Contributors

Mary Louise Adams (Ph.D.) is a Professor in Kinesiology and Health Studies at Queen's University, Canada. She is the author of *Artistic Impressions: Figure Skating, Masculinity and the Limits of Sport* (2011) and *The Trouble with Normal: Postwar Youth and the Making of Heterosexuality* (1997). Her current work investigates the cultural meanings of walking.

Jacquelyn Allen-Collinson (Ph.D.) is a Reader in the Sociology of Sport, and Director of the multi-disciplinary Health Advancement Research Team (HART) at the University of Lincoln, the United Kingdom. Jacquelyn is a qualitative sociologist with research interests in the sociological phenomenology of the body and sporting embodiment, particularly relating to distance running.

William Bridel (Ph.D.) is an Assistant Professor in the Faculty of Kinesiology at the University of Calgary, Canada. His teaching and research focus on socio-cultural aspects of the body, sport, physical activity, and health. His research interests include: the emergence of ultra-endurance sports as forms of leisure activities; social and political aspects of health; sport-related pain and injury; and, gender, sexuality, and sport. His work has appeared in various journals including *The Sociology of Sport Journal* and *Leisure/Loisir*. His current list of projects includes collaborations with national and provincial sport organizations, focused on inclusivity and diversity.

Kyle S. Bunds (Ph.D.) is an Assistant Professor in the Department of Parks, Recreation, and Tourism Management at North Carolina State University, United States. His work has appeared in journals such as: *Critical Studies in Media Communications*; *Communication, Culture, & Critique*; *Sport Management Review*; *Cultural Studies ⇔ Critical Methodologies*; and, *Review of Education, Pedagogy, and Cultural Studies*. His current research examines the intersection of sport and global water charities.

Laura Frances Chase (Ph.D.) is Associate Chair and Professor in the Department of Kinesiology and Health Promotion at Cal Poly Pomona, United States. She completed her graduate studies in the Cultural Studies of Sport and Leisure at the University of Iowa. Her published work focuses on issues of the body, physicality, and the social construction of fat in sport and exercise.

Jim Denison (Ph.D.) is an Associate Professor in the Faculty of Physical Education and Recreation at the University of Alberta, Canada. A sport sociologist and coach educator, his research primarily examines the formation of endurance running coaches' practices through a Foucauldian lens. Along with numerous book chapters and referred articles, he edited *Coaching Knowledges: Understanding the Dynamics of Performance Sport* (2007, AC Black) and was co-editor of *The Routledge Handbook of Sports Coaching* (2013, Routledge). In addition, Denison is the author of *The Greatest* (2004, Breakaway Books), the official biography of the Ethiopian running legend Haile Gebrselassie, and *Bannister and Beyond: The Mystique of the Four-Minute Mile* (2003, Breakaway Books), a collection of in-depth interviews with a wide-array of sub four-minute milers.

Michael D. Giardina (Ph.D.) is an Associate Professor of sport, media, and cultural studies in the Department of Sport Management at Florida State University, United States. He is the author or editor of 16 books, including *Sport, Spectacle, and NASCAR Nation: Consumption and the Cultural Politics of Neoliberalism* (with Joshua I. Newman; Palgrave Macmillan, 2011), which received the 2012 "Outstanding Book Award" from the North American Society for the Sociology of Sport and was named to *CHOICE*'s "Outstanding Academic Titles" list, and *Qualitative Inquiry—Past, Present, and Future: A Critical Reader* (with Norman K. Denzin; Left Coast Press, 2015). He is the current editor of the *Sociology of Sport Journal*.

Maylon Hanold (Ph.D.) teaches in the Sport Administration and Leadership masters program at Seattle University, United States. Her courses include sport sociology, sport leadership, human resources, and organizational behavior. From the perspective of physicality and embodiment, she explores endurance sports, leadership, and leadership development.

John Hockey (Ph.D.) is a sociological ethnographer at the University of Gloucestershire, the United Kingdom. He has research interests in sociological phenomenology and its application to sporting and occupational life. In 2010, at the British Sociological Association Conference he was awarded a Sage prize for sociological innovation, following a published paper on sensory phenomenology.

P. David Howe (Ph.D.) is a social anthropologist of sport in the School of Sport, Exercise and Health Sciences at Loughborough University, the United Kingdom. David is a leading figure in socio-cultural analysis of Paralympic sport. He holds a visiting professorship at Katholieke Universiteit Leuven, Belgium and an adjunct Professorship at Queen's University, Canada. Trained as a medical anthropologist, he is the author of *Sport, Professionalism and Pain: Ethnographies of Injury and Risk* (Routledge, 2004) and *The Cultural Politics of the Paralympic Movement: Through the Anthropological Lens* (Routledge, 2008).

Ryan King-White (Ph.D.) is an Assistant Professor of Sport Management at Towson University, United States. He has published widely on the cultural politics of sport and late-capitalism in journals such as *Sociology of Sport Journal* and *Review of Education, Pedagogy, and Cultural Studies*, as well as in numerous edited collections.

Pirkko Markula (Ph.D.) is a professor of socio-cultural studies of physical activity at the University of Alberta, Canada. Her research interests include social analyses of dance, exercise, and sport in which she has employed several theoretical lenses ranging from critical, cultural studies research to Foucault and Deleuze. While her work is based on qualitative research methods (textual analysis, participant-observation, interviewing, ethnography), she is also interested in methodological experimentation including autoethnography and performance ethnography. She is the previous editor of the *Sociology of Sport Journal*. She is the co-author, with Michael Silk, of *Qualitative Research for Physical Culture* (Routledge, 2011), co-author with Richard Pringle, of *Foucault, Sport and Exercise: Power, Knowledge and Transforming the Self* (Routledge, 2006), editor of *Feminist Sport Studies: Sharing Joy, Sharing Pain* (SUNY Press, 2005) and *Olympic women and the media: International perspectives* (Palgrave, 2009), co-editor with Eileen Kennedy of *Women and Exercise: Body, Health and Consumerism* (Routledge, 2011), co-editor, with Sarah Riley, Maree Burns, Hannah Frith and Sally Wiggins, of *Critical Bodies: Representations, Identities and Practices of Weight and Body Management* (Palgrave, 2007), and co-editor, with Jim Denison, of *Moving Writing: Crafting Movement in Sport Research* (Peter Lang, 2003).

Joseph Mills (Ph.D.) is currently an adjunct professor in psychology/sociology and kinesiology at St. Mary's University in Calgary, Canada. A former international endurance runner, his research examines the formation of high-performance coaches' practices and knowledge, the physically active body, and sport psychology through a poststructural lens.

Danielle Peers (Ph.D.) is a former Paralympic athlete, coach, and organizer who writes on the intersections of disability, sport, and social justice movements. Her chapter was funded through the Trudeau Foundation and Vanier (Social Sciences and Humanities Research Council) Scholarships. Danielle is currently a Banting Postdoctoral Fellow at Concordia University, Canada.

Marie-Josée Perrier (Ph.D.) is a Postdoctoral Fellow in Kinesiology at McMaster University, Canada. She works primarily in the field of sport and exercise psychology and disability, with her research interests spanning identity, behavior change interventions including messaging and mentorship, and narrative inquiry.

Richard Pringle (Ph.D.) is currently Associate Dean Postgraduate in the Faculty of Education, University of Auckland, New Zealand. His critical research interests span socio-cultural, pedagogical, and historical analyses of sport, gender, injury, and pleasure.

Holly Thorpe (Ph.D.) is a Senior Lecturer in Te Oranga School of Human Development and Movement Studies at the University of Waikato, New Zealand. She works primarily (though not exclusively) in the field of the sociology of sport and physical culture, with her research interests including gender, women's health, action sports, social theory, and qualitative methods.

Theresa Walton-Fisette (Ph.D.) an associate professor in the School of Foundations, Leadership and Administration at Kent State University, United States, focuses on investigations of power relationships and the ways those relationships are both resisted and maintained within sport and physical activity. In particular, she has examined media discourse of gender equality in sport, women's amateur wrestling, and elite distance running. More recently, she has investigated how high school girls navigate and understand their embodied identities. Her work has been published in the *Sociology of Sport Journal*, the *Women in Sport and Physical Activity Journal*, the *Journal of Popular Culture* and *Sport, Education and Society*.

Gavin Weedon is a Ph.D. candidate at the University of British Columbia, Canada. His research spans a broad range of somatic and communicative practices, from athletic labor migration and militarism to sport journalism and the academic publishing industry. His chapter in this collection is drawn from an ongoing project on the twenty-first century renaissance of physical culture.

Acknowledgments

William Bridel: I would like to take this opportunity to thank Dr. Penny Werthner, Dean of the Faculty of Kinesiology at the University of Calgary, for her tremendous interest in and support of this project, as well as my academic endeavors more generally. I would also like to thank Dr. Geneviève Rail and Dr. Mary Louise Adams for being incredible graduate supervisors; both have been pivotal in my development as a researcher and teacher. My family has always been a huge source of support—words cannot adequately express how grateful I am for your love and encouragement. Similarly, I am blessed to have an amazing group of friends who all inspire and influence me in different ways every day; special thanks to Marty Clark and Jose Perez who have *endured* countless conversations about this project. I offer my most sincere thanks to the scholars who have contributed to this book; it was a privilege and a pleasure to work with all of you. Finally, to my co-editors Pirkko and Jim: thank you for your guidance, your encouragement, your support, and your friendship; I look forward to many future collaborations.

Pirkko Markula: Coming from a small town, I would like to acknowledge my running club members who introduced me to running. While not always pleasurable, I continue to run on a regular basis. I would like to thank my first personal running coach who taught me how to lift my heels "over the stick" and land on my forefoot for increased efficiency and endurance. I also want to thank him for obtaining my first pair of Nike Free shoes before minimalist running became a fashion. Finally, I would like to thank my co-editors, William and Jim, who have made preparing this book an enjoyable and rewarding process.

Jim Denison: I would like to thank all the friends I have made over the 40 years I have inhabited the world of endurance running—as an athlete, a coach, and a researcher. Your influence is exhibited here in so many ways. And of course thanks to Pirkko for her enduring love and support. And hats off to William for all of your hard work.

1 Critical considerations of runners and running

William Bridel, Pirkko Markula, and Jim Denison

On Friday November 2, 2012, New York City Mayor Michael Bloomberg announced that the New York City Marathon—one of the largest in the world—would be cancelled due to the destruction left by superstorm Sandy and the subsequent cleanup efforts. While this decision received significant positive support in mainstream and social media it was also met with some resistance and anger, mostly from runners registered for the race, many of whom had already traveled to New York. Other participants were more understanding of the circumstances, yet remained firm in their desire to complete a marathon that weekend. As a post on an on-line running community board stated:

> In respect to those in need, cancelling the NYC Marathon was the right move. But for those of us who are running for causes or for others, we should finish what we started. We will do it like the old days where we run the necessary amount of times around Central Park to complete 26.2 miles.

Superstorm Sandy also evoked different, and sometimes, conflicting narratives regarding what have been constructed as other types of human endurance (i.e., dealing with adversity, suffering, and perseverance). Similar narratives about endurance emerged following the bombings at the Boston Marathon in 2013 vis-à-vis the city, its residents, and emergency services personnel, but also specifically the victims of the bombings, their families, friends, other runners in the event, and the running community globally.

Because the tragedies in New York and Boston involved elite and mass participation marathons, distance running was brought into the public discourse and as such, the narratives that emerged from the aftermath in New York and Boston raised a number of interesting questions about the place and meaning of running and endurance challenges like the marathon. However, running as a "test" of human endurance is not a new phenomenon.

A brief timeline of endurance running challenges in Western culture

According to Cooper (1998), organized footraces can be traced back to the early part of the 1800s in the United States. With increased industrialization and therefore both more leisure time and less demand for physical labor, the latter stages of the nineteenth and early part of the twentieth centuries saw the popularity of endurance challenges increase. Following the creation of the marathon as part of the inaugural modern Olympic Games in 1896, other marathons in the United States and Europe appeared. Not surprisingly, the popularity of endurance events waned through the Great Depression before virtually disappearing during World War II.

The 1950s saw some renewed interest in running but the size and constitution of endurance running events changed significantly when jogging and running as a leisure pursuit exploded in popularity in North America in the 1970s and 1980s (Cooper, 1998; Smith, 1998), a trend that has continued into the first two decades of the twenty-first century. Road races of varying distances sprung up for "weekend warriors" including the marathon—a distance that had in the past primarily been reserved for elite competition, not mass participation. The number of people finishing marathons tripled between 1980 and 2007 in the United States (Hoffman, Ong, & Wang, 2010). In 2013, it was estimated that 800 marathons were held around the globe with approximately a half million participants. The marathon, however, is far from the only form of endurance running.

The introduction and rapid growth of run/obstacle events like the Warrior Dash in 2009 and Tough Mudder and the Spartan Race in 2010, explored further by Weedon in Chapter 3, and the even newer Neon Run, Color Run and Run or Dye events have added new dimensions to the endurance sportscape. The Zombie Run, a 5 km fun run in which the "obstacles" are people dressed as zombies, and ultramarathons (any race longer than a marathon) are further examples of contemporary endurance challenges. According to Hoffman, Ong, and Wang (2010), participation in 100-mile runs in North America grew exponentially between 1977 and 1991 and in 2011 the number of events 50 km or longer held in North America tripled (Hanold, 2011). In parts of Europe, fell running has become popular, though far less so than road running (Atkinson, 2010; Nettleton, 2013). In short, elite athletes, neophytes, and (ostensibly) everyone else in between can now participate in a variety of endurance running events.

The growing interest in endurance running has also sparked the development of a body of academic literature, primarily in the natural sciences. From physiological, biomechanical, and nutritional perspectives scholars have sought to dissect and improve runners' performances. A number of scholars have also tried to determine what makes some runners, such as Kenyans, "better suited" for endurance running challenges (e.g., Bale & Pitsiladis, 2007; Epstein, 2014; Komi, Ishikawa, Ito, Locatelli, & Nicol, 2014; Larsen, 2003).

There is also a substantial exercise and sport psychology literature around running, with a particular (though not exclusive) focus on motivation. Through the use of primarily quantitative methods, researchers have suggested that people's motivations to run include improved physical fitness and health, better psychological health through the relief of tension and improved moods, improved self-image, the opportunity for social networking, personal and/or competitive achievement, and the development of an "athletic identity" (e.g., Clough, Shepherd & Maughan, 1989; Horton & Mack, 2000; Jeffrey & Butryn, 2012; Kilduff, 2014; Masters & Ogles, 2003; Summers, Machin & Sargent, 1983; Summers, Sargent, Levey & Murray, 1982; Ziegler, 1991).

Exercise and sport psychology scholars have also noted that people can become addicted to running (e.g., Summers, Machin, & Sargent, 1983). The over-prioritization of running, to the point it might be considered an addiction, has been referred to as obligatory running. Health policies and academic scholarship, nevertheless, continue to promote running as a way to alleviate the obesity epidemic arguing that the positives of running outweigh any potential negatives. Shipway and Holloway (2010), for example, reasoned that, "distance running has the potential to play a role in supporting and developing healthy lifestyles, and helping achieve government targets on physical activity and exercise" (p. 275).

Undoubtedly the bodies of literature on distance running in the physical sciences and sport and exercise psychology have made important contributions to the "how to" and the "why" of running but do so from an individual runner's perspective. However, as noted sport geographer John Bale (2004a) asserted, an "understanding of running cannot be achieved by simply looking at runners" (p. 9) without considering the cultural context in which running occurs. Bale also noted that the study of running as a body/cultural phenomenon has not been the focal point of the social sciences and humanities. His book, *Running Cultures: Racing in Time and Space*, filled that void by (without meaning to overgeneralize) interpreting running and its representations in different spatial and temporal contexts to examine the popularity of distance running. The existing socio-cultural work exploring distance running through a socio-cultural lens has since explored two main themes: mediated representations of runners and experiences of/meanings assigned to the "running body." In the following sections we draw out some of the main issues from this literature to further contextualize the sections and chapters comprising this book.

Reading runners in the media critically

Several socio-cultural scholars have interrogated the ways well-known middle- and long-distance runners are represented in various forms of media to examine the media's significant role in the reification of dominant ideologies. Such celebrated runners as Roger Bannister (Bale, 2004; Walton & Birrell, 2012), Haile Gebrselassie (Denison, 2007; Denison & Markula, 2005), Kelly Holmes (Hills & Kennedy, 2009), Tegla Loroupe (Mwaniki, 2011), Steve Prefontaine (Walton, 2004), Paula Radcliffe (Walton, 2010), Caster Semenya (Wells & Darnell, 2014) and a trio of female African runners (Chepyator-Thomson, 2005)[1] have been the subjects of critical media readings.

Several critical analyses of the mediated representations of runners reveal the "structures of dominance expressed around … the power lines of race, class, gender, and sexuality (and age, nationality, ability, religion, etc.)" (Birrell & McDonald, 2000, p. 4). This work reveals, for example, that the "innocent" reporting of facts actually serves to (re)constitute taken-for-granted ideas about gendered running bodies. In her project, Walton (2010) asserted that mediated representations of the British marathoner Paula Radcliffe in some ways served to reproduce stereotypical ideas about femininity, largely because the "tropes surrounding Radcliffe are familiar and comfortable: She participates in an individual sport, is thin, blond, white, and married to a man" (p. 290). But beyond this, Radcliffe's successes in international events were largely positioned in relationship to the failure of British male distance runners in the same time period. Walton argued that qualifying Radcliffe's success in such a way reproduces the popular belief that men's sport (in this case, distance running) is somehow more legitimate than women's sport, noting that, "even as Radcliffe represented British success, she concurrently represented British failure, by highlighting the lack of 'real' sporting representation that was ultimately male" (p. 291).

Mwaniki (2011) pointed to the stereotypically feminine representation of Kenyan long-distance track runner and marathoner Tegla Loroupe. The media stories emphasized her small physical stature, her penchant for shopping, and her "need" to find a man. Mwaniki also revealed that Loroupe was "framed as another typical elite Kenyan runner … [following] a pattern of discourse often seen regarding athletes from developing nations which trivializes athletic performance due to their assumed genetic predisposition or environmental essentialism" (p. 454). The "genetic disposition" narrative refers to the "natural," genetically-gifted black athlete (Chepatyor-Thomson, 2005; Denison, 2007; Denison & Markula, 2005; Mwaniki, 2011; Walton, 2010; Walton & Butryn, 2006) to explain the current dominance of East African distance runners. This ideological construction attributes their success entirely to their physiological advantage and not the outcome of "intention, government funding, coaching, or the help of scientifically derived training programs" (Denison & Markula, 2005, p. 315).

In addition to gender and race, scholars have discussed dominant notions about national identity (e.g., Bale, 2004b; Hills & Kennedy, 2009; Walton, 2010) and the use of runners' images to promote ideas about masculinity and consumerism (e.g., Walton, 2004). The analysis of British middle-distance runner Kelly Holmes by Hills and Kennedy (2009) brought together several ideologically constructed intersecting identities. They found that the British media had difficulty negotiating an acceptable identity for Holmes who tended to be not quite feminine, not quite British (she has a Jamaican father), not clearly heterosexual, and not quite young enough to serve as a national heroine despite winning two gold medals at the 2004 Olympic Games.

At the same time, some scholars have explored the subversion of gender norms in mediated representations of female runners. For example, Walton (2010) referred to the "sometimes contradictory" ideologies in constructions of

Radcliffe. Mwaniki (2011) noted that Loroupe was predominantly portrayed as a determined "amazing athlete" who dominated her opponents in international competitions with little to no qualification of her gender. According to Mwaniki, this should be looked at as a positive step forward as "generally such discourse usually frames men as the only athletes capable of such amazing feats of physical prowess" (pp. 452–453).

Chepyator-Thomson (2005) also highlighted the subversive potential emerging from mediated representations of three female African runners—Loroupe (Kenya), Nawal El Moutawakel-Bennis (Morocco), and Maria Mutola (Mozambique)—arguing that their running successes and the media stories about them contributed to positive social change. She highlighted how these runners' stories challenged traditional roles of women within the family, encouraged a rethinking of education for girls and women in Africa, and in certain scenarios served to challenge Islamic law, in particular around what was considered acceptable attire for women. Beyond mediated representations of female runners, in this book Chase (Chapter 5) traces the different ways women have challenged the exclusivity of distance running as a male preserve. And Walton-Fisette (Chapter 9) examines the different meanings that "endurance" has had in the life and subjectivation of "Lost Boy" Lopez Lomong, a Sudanese-born runner who currently represents the United States in international middle-distance running competitions.

Running bodies: meanings and experiences

In addition to the analysis of ideological constructions, socio-cultural research on running has focused on the body in one way or another. From an early interest in marathoning demographics (e.g., Curtis & McTeer, 1981), socio-cultural analyses of running have evolved into complex and nuanced readings of the running body to complement and challenge psychological and physiological research. This work can be loosely categorized into themes of bodily aesthetics, pain/injury and health, and relationships of the body to nature.

On running bodies and aesthetics

Changing one's body shape by losing weight, increasing musculature and/or shape, or becoming more physically attractive (Bridel & Rail, 2007; Chase, 2008; Major, 2001; Ogles, Masters, & Richardson, 1995; Smith, 2000; Summers, Machin, & Sargent, 1983; van Ingen, 2004) is often mentioned as a motivation for and outcome of running. This idea of modifying one's body by adhering to the disciplinary practices of endurance running such as training, diet, and recovery (Bridel & Rail, 2007) follows the bodily aesthetics of the archetype "distance running body": lean, muscular, toned, slight but strong.

While often constructed as primarily a concern for women, running as a way to obtain a more attractive body seems to cross gender lines. In his research on non-elite male runners in Britain, for example, Smith (2000) found that his participants related their physical appearance to running, some in terms of a youthful appearance and others in terms of maintenance or loss of body weight. It was clear that the bodies of the male runners became projects produced through activity: "[something] to be worked at through conscious management, maintenance and molding" (p. 198). Abbas (2004) pointed to a predominance of white male running bodies that fit the constructed ideal within the pages of *Runner's World* and other scholars have noted that female running bodies are also often represented as extremely lean (Chase, 2008; Hanold, 2010; Markula, 2000).[2]

For both men and women, attaining a body similar to the archetype distance running body could be considered a form of cultural capital since being lean aligns with dominant bodily ideals in Western society and is considered to be a representation of healthiness. For example, scholars examining LGBTQ running groups have argued that dominant bodily ideals (both in terms of aesthetics and notions of healthiness) seem to greatly influence participants' motivations for involvement (e.g., Bridel & Rail, 2007; van Ingen, 2004). Some scholars, however, have pointed to the incongruence between dominant representations of running bodies and actual running bodies.

Chase (2008), for example, undertook research on the Clydesdale running community. Through participant observation, interviews, and textual analysis informed by Foucault's ideas of the technologies of power and the self, she argued that larger bodies are subjected to scrutiny or surveillance and marginalization based on the narrowly defined ideal running body and the conceptualization that larger bodies reflect a lack of self-discipline. At the same time, the presence of larger running bodies, she observed, challenge dominant images of the ideal running body. Chase's work, along with Hanold's (2010) suggestion that female elite ultra-marathoners tend to be more focused on creating a functional body (i.e., one that is capable of sustaining the challenges of ultra-running) as opposed to one that fits a certain aesthetic, reveals the sometimes contradictory relationship between the representations of the running body in popular texts and people's lived experiences.

On running, "pain," injury, and health

Despite the visual representations of the archetype lean and sinewy successful distance running body (Johns & Johns, 2000), many runners state that they run for pleasure or personal achievement. Importantly, however, part of running's pleasure for many derives from the unquestioned belief that running should hurt and that "hurting" can, in fact, feel good. For example, Adam Goucher, an American distance runner, commented that for "something to hurt that bad and feel so good, it's just inexplicable." His statement reflects a common understanding of the relationship between running and the body. One has to be willing to experience some degree of suffering for success. Specific to distance running, Howe (2004) referred to this type of bodily sensation variably as "positive pain" and "Zatopekian pain" (after Czech runner Emil Zatopek who was legendary for completing incredibly demanding training regimes). According to Howe, positive pain is "a burning ache all over the body during and after the [training] session" (p. 86). Medico-scientific explanations of this type of pain refer to the concept of "adaptation" arguing that, "the purpose of physical training is to stress systematically the body so it improves its capacity to exercise.... If the stress is not sufficient to overload the body, then no adaptation occurs" but—and this is important—"if a stress cannot be tolerated, then injury or over-training results" (Fahey, 1998, paras i and iii). The idea of adaptation or positive pain is built into most runners' training plans as a way to improve their fitness and performance but there are other benefits as well.

Bale (2006) asserted that runners might view non-injury related pain as "the deposit, the investment, through which speed is extracted. Pain is a form of bodily or physical capital, a bearer of symbolic value" (p. 66). Such an understanding of pain is not specific to elite runners. Drawing from Foucault's concepts of discipline and surveillance, Bridel and Rail (2007) discovered that non-elite marathoners inevitably ended up injured. The authors suggested consequently that, "pushing the limits of the [non-elite] 'marathon body' is in line with dominant discourses of high-performance sport in that it is seen as a necessary means through which one would bring one's body to its optimal, functional state" (p. 135). Pain, thus, appears to be part of runners' identity or sense of self: the ability to endure pain, tolerate pain, and/or overcome pain (Bale, 2004a, 2006; Loland, 2006; Young, 2004). When coupled with the popular idea that endurance running is in some way about pushing the limits of the body, the taken-for-grantedness that one will "hurt" starts to make sense. Perhaps not surprisingly then in a book on endurance running, although discussed in different ways, ideas about suffering, pain, and injury appear in several chapters: Adams (Chapter 2); Hanold (Chapter 12); Hockey and Allen-Collinson (Chapter 15); and Markula (Chapter 6). In contrast, Perrier and Bridel (Chapter 13) and Pringle (Chapter 7) explore running-related enjoyment and pleasure.

To further examine the relationship between endurance (running) and suffering, Le Breton (2000) argued for a philosophical connection to seeking symbolic death. Intrigued by the fact that in addition to elite athletes "weekend warriors" were taking on different types of endurance challenges, Le Breton noted that much of this increased interest undoubtedly had to do with testing personal limits and willpower, but when taken to more extreme ends represented a symbolic flirtation with death. He argued that this was particularly true in a sociohistorical context where personal value is measured not by morality but rather by physical accomplishments. Perhaps paradoxically, the growth in popularity of endurance challenges has occurred within neoliberalism in which great value is placed on physical health and physical activity, such as running, as a health producing practice.

Already in the 1970s and 1980s, the jogging boom both reflected and reproduced running as a healthy endeavor with the ability to create a strong cardiovascular system, increase weight loss, and lower the risk for diabetes and other "weight-related illnesses." And running, as noted previously, continues to factor into government health promotion strategies and policies as a strategy to deal with the so-called obesity epidemic: to lose weight, put on a pair of running shoes and "just do it." As a result, several researchers have examined the meanings of running within the context of neoliberal politics of health.

Within a neoliberal social and political context, individuals are expected to be autonomous, self-governing, and act morally responsibly in all aspects of one's life including physical and mental health. In this context, the healthful self means self-empowerment, self-actualization, and discipline achieved through consumerism (King, 2006; Lemke, 2001; McDermott, 2007; Rose, 1999). Thus, in a neoliberal social and political context failure to take care of one's health is constructed not only as lacking in responsibility but, in fact, as a failure to live up to expectations of what constitutes a good citizen. It is in this context that the tremendous growth of non-elite participation in distance running has occurred and the ability to run farther or faster (or farther faster) has come to represent the successful disciplining of one's body and, therefore, achievement.

King (2003, 2006) used running events organized for charitable fundraising as a prime example of such health politics. She argued that in the mid to late 1980s the relationship of running to neoliberal agendas was further strengthened with the birth of a cultural phenomenon that connected physical activity and fundraising, especially the creation of the Susan G. Komen Breast Cancer Foundation's Race for a Cure. In these events, and others like them, people combined charitable fundraising with running using the individual pursuit of running to become a part of something bigger. But as King (2003) pointed out, the shift to "running for a cause" produced a new kind of American (or Western) citizen, one which combined the imperative for people to be responsible for their own health (through participation in physical activity, such as running) with the idea that personal giving was the way toward the cure for, in this case, cancer.

Placing the onus on individuals to "step up" renders the lack of corporate and government support for healthcare and health research more invisible, a central tenet and outcome of neoliberal governance. Such a neoliberal approach tends to understate (or ignore altogether) barriers or impediments to participation within the "anyone can run" ideology. In the Western world especially, the health benefits of distance running then are quite overstated since such benefits would mostly apply to middle- and upper-class individuals, who several scholars have noted are the primary participants in distance running at non-elite levels (Abbas, 2004; Curtis & McTeer, 1981; Serravallo, 2000; Smith, 2000). These alleged health benefits are further complicated by notions of pushing one's limits, a "no pain, no gain" mentality that tends to result in almost every (serious) runner experiencing at least one injury at some point.

Of course, the insidiousness of neoliberal tropes extends well beyond individual responsibility for health; several authors explore the relationship between neoliberalism and endurance in other ways in this book, in particular as related to capitalism and privatization. For example, Giardina, King-White, and Bunds (Chapter 8) interrogate narratives emerging from the Boston marathon bombings, the advent of #bostonstrong, and the commodification of tragedy. And

Peers (Chapter 10), drawing from some of King's ideas, frames one part of her critical analysis of inspirational endurance athletes in relation to the discourses and techniques of neoliberalism—corporate-charity collaboration specifically.

On the body, bodily experiences, and nature

The research that has focused on the aesthetics of the ideal running body, health, and pain/injury has largely made sense of different bodily experiences in running in relation to dominant ideologies or discourses. With this emphasis on the socially constructed running body, some researchers have lamented the disappearance of the material body. Nettleton (2013), for example, called for increased attention to embodied running experiences. Drawing heavily from the work of Bourdieu, she suggested increased consideration be given to what she coined "existential capital," a form of capital comprised of "visceral pleasures, corporeal resources, and a novel form of sociality" (p. 209). Scholars, like Nettleton, suggest that to ignore the biological and the sensorial nature of peoples' bodies and their experiences is to say that the body is not fundamentally biological and to slip into what has been called discursive essentialism (Best, 2007) or discursive determinism (Lupton, 1998). These critiques have led to numerous calls from scholars for a "carnal sociology" of the body, including the running body. In consideration of this, Hockey and Allen-Collinson (Chapter 15) undertake a sociological phenomenology to account for/make sense of different bodily sensations experienced in the context of distance running and Thorpe (Chapter 11), drawing from the work of feminist biologists and science philosophers, considers the inseparability of the biological and the social with a view to understanding female recreational runners' embodied experiences of amenorrhea.

The focus on the embodied experiences of runners by scholars has also brought in the consideration of nature—after all, a majority of distance running occurs outdoors. Borrowing from Ingold's concept of "taskscapes," Howe and Morris (2009) suggested that through different experiences in training, running bodies and notions of nature are actively co-produced, thus blurring the oft made distinction between the social and the natural. They considered natural spaces as a type of "shrine" that serves as a respite from running on roads or other man-made structures: "Natural spaces beyond those encountered in the daily routines of the running taskscape become places of pilgrimage and the act of training the body in those spaces serves to stimulate and encourage the runner to greater achievements" (p. 322). In his phenomenological ethnography, Howe (Chapter 14) extends the conversation about running taskscapes with a particular focus on the embodied habitus of elite middle-distance runners.

The relationship between bodies and nature has also been central to academic explorations of fell running. If nature serves as a form of pleasure in Nettleton's work, Atkinson (2010) offered a vivid description of space (as well as the participant base) in his ethnographic project on fell running, a type of running that occurs in various natural terrain. Atkinson observed less concern with finishing times, rankings, personal best records, and placements in events—all things that are often concerns for many runners—and a greater focus on the relationship between the body and nature. In this book, Hanold (Chapter 12) adds to the discussion about running and nature in her exploration of the way ultrarunners construct their bodily experiences in relation to the terrain over which they traverse in training and racing. Markula (Chapter 6) and Weedon (Chapter 3) read the nature–human body relationship more critically against the need to return to what is "natural" through endurance running.

Whether discussing running in relation to bodily aesthetics, pain/injury, or in relation to space, scholars in the social sciences and humanities have no doubt produced some excellent work that has wrested the body away from the exclusive domain of the physical sciences. This work has also offered interpretations of the meanings people find in running beyond simplistic psychological explanations focused on motivation. In its entirety, this literature reveals the influence of dominant social norms and values and relations of power on individuals' bodily experiences of running. For example, Mills and Denison (Chapter 4) unpack the privilege given to scientific discourses throughout the history of distance running coaching and Adams (Chapter 2), focusing on pedestrianism, discusses the discursive construction of "endurance" in the Western context and how physical endurance in particular has come to be valued.

Going the distance: what else can be learned?

In the spirit of C. L. R. James, Bale (2004a) questioned: "What do they know of running who only running know?" (p. 9). It is evident in the preceding review of the socio-cultural work on distance running as a popular endeavor for elite and non-elite athletes alike, that scholars have considered in different ways the relationship between individual runners and the cultural meanings of running. *Endurance Running: A Socio-Cultural Examination* is a collection of original, qualitative research that seeks to expand on Bale's (2004a) ideas and other published work on running as a social phenomenon.

The book is purposefully organized into three sections: *Running Beginnings*, *Running Because*, and *Running Bodies*. This in and of itself offers a new way of thinking about running from a socio-cultural perspective, a unique analytical structure to approach endurance running in multiple ways: the object of study, the types of research questions asked, the methodological approach, and the theoretical framework. Scholars here examine mass, elite, and disabled running/runners through the use of textual analysis, interviews, and personal experiences and with great theoretical breadth: Bourdieu, Butler, Deleuze, Foucault, Ingold, Lefebvre, poststructuralism, physical cultural studies, sociological phenomenology, and critical sport psychology. Such a comprehensive approach serves to reveal the ways that the biological, historical, psychological, and sociological converge to form contextually specific ideas about running and runners, nuances and complexities oft missing from strict (read experimental) cognitive/behavioral and physiological investigations.

The four chapters that comprise *Running Beginnings* consider the "histories" of different kinds of distance events as well as increased participation in endurance running. Adams offers a socio-historical account of nineteenth-century long-distance pedestrian events with a goal of historicizing endurance in relationship to other notions of endurance circulating in the same historical context and as its emergence as a prized athletic quality. Weedon analyzes the rather recent beginnings of obstacle course racing and mud runs but does so by looking to historical constructions of physical activity, the "outdoors," and urbanization and the similar narratives emerging in these "new" forms of endurance challenges. Mills and Denison provide insights into the development of knowledge about "endurance training," employing a Foucauldian lens to trace the formation of key concepts in contemporary endurance training. In the final chapter in the section, adopting a critical cultural studies theoretical perspective, Chase explores the experiences of women in distance running from the late 1960s through to today, with a particular focus on elite women's running, gender and cause-based running, and the creation of Athena divisions.

Running Because has an overall theme of exploring the "why" of *why run* or *why running?* However, in the spirit of this book, and the academic disciplines represented by the authors, these explorations go beyond celebratory accounts of running. Markula, drawing on Deleuze and Guattari's conceptualization of capitalism as a type of fabric, investigates the popularity of the minimalist running movement from the original design of the Nike Free shoes, to Christopher McDougall's best selling book *Born to Run* to scientific research debating the "naturalness" of barefoot running. Also drawing from Deleuze and Guattari, in his textual analysis of *Runner's World* magazine, Pringle contributes a polyvocal reading of the pains and pleasures of endurance running that seeks to move beyond the limitations of poststructuralist accounts of physical activity and explore the malleable relationship between the social and biological. Giardina, King-White, and Bunds turn to popular narratives about the 2013 Boston Marathon bombings, endurance, and terrorism in a so-called "post-racial" America, to provide an analysis of the meaning of running and running events in the larger context, as opposed to the meaning individuals make of their participation in running. Following in the tradition of using individual runners as an entry point to conversations about larger social issues, Walton-Fisette unpacks Lopez Lomong's story and the different experiences/meanings/constructions of endurance in his life, with a particular interest in considering identities as embodied processes. Turning a critical lens to narratives about three Canadian "inspirational endurance athletes" (i.e., Terry Fox, Steve Fonyo, and Rick Hansen), Peers applies supercrip critique and a more contextual genealogical analysis to illustrate enduring (and intersecting) forces of ableism, colonialism, and neoliberalism in the Canadian context.

Authors contributing chapters to the *Running Bodies* section explore different running populations, the experiences of and meanings assigned to running, and the potential relationships between popular discourses about endurance and individual lived experiences to gain more critical understanding about running and running bodies. Thorpe theorizes the body as both biological and socially constructed in an effort to understand amenorrhea as prevalent in the experiences of female recreational runners. Hanold provides insights into the way male and female ultrarunners make sense of endurance through the experiences of their bodies, but also the meaning ascribed to the spaces where ultrarunning takes place. Perrier and Bridel contemplate their own (very non-elite) involvement in distance running to engage in an interdisciplinary conversation about (their) running bodies and "identities" from micro (i.e., exercise and sport psychology) and macro (i.e., sociology) perspectives, ultimately calling into question the disciplinary rigidity that complicates interdisciplinary work. Howe, incorporating representational fiction, analyzes the culture of elite middle- and long-distance running and the "building" of high performance runners. In the final chapter Hockey and Allen-Collinson draw on autoethnographic/autophenomenographic data to explore the phenomenology of endurance while also considering the relationship between individual, sensorial experiences and socio-cultural context.

American poet T. S. Eliot wrote: "Only those who will risk going too far can possibly find out how far one can go." In a sense, this encapsulates much of how endurance running is popularly understood; be it a challenge against oneself or others to run the farthest or the fastest (or the farthest fastest) endurance running is about challenging one's limits. Each of the 14 chapters in this book, on its own, offers important insights about distance running historically and in contemporary times. But when taken up as a whole—the beginnings, the because, the bodies—we believe an even greater understanding of our longstanding fascination with the concept of endurance can be gained.

Notes

1 Please note that there are also excellent articles that have been published about Canadian sprinters Ben Johnson and Donovan Bailey (e.g., Jackson, 1998, 2004) and Australian 400-meter runner Cathy Freeman (e.g., Bruce & Hallinan, 2001; Wensing & Bruce, 2003), all of which add to accumulated knowledge about runners and running from a socio-cultural perspective.

2 Given the dominant representation of women's running bodies as extremely thin (as well as the physical demands of the sport), it is not surprising—yet nevertheless perturbing—that the prevalence of body related psychological disorders such as the Female Athletes' Triad, disordered eating, and exercise dependence are very high among women distance runners.

References

Abbas, A. (2004). The embodiment of class, gender and age through leisure: A realist analysis of long distance running. *Leisure Studies, 23*, 159–175.

Atkinson, M. (2010). Fell running in post-sport territories. *Qualitative Research in Sport and Exercise, 2*, 109–132.

Bale, J. (2004a). *Running cultures: Racing in time and space*. London, England: Routledge.

Bale, J. (2004b). *Roger Bannister and the four-minute mile: Sports myth and sports history*. London, England: Routledge.

Bale, J. (2006). The place of pain in running. In S. Loland, B. Skirstad, & I. Waddington (Eds.), *Pain and injury in sport: Social and ethical analysis* (pp. 65–75). New York, NY: Routledge.

Bale, J., & Pitsiladis, Y. (2007) *East African running: Toward a cross-disciplinary perspective*. London, England: Routledge.

Best, S. (2007). The social construction of pain: An evaluation. *Disability and Society, 22*, 161–171.

Birrell, S., & McDonald, M. (2000). *Reading sport: Critical essays on power and representation.* Boston, MA: Northeastern University Press.

Bridel, W., & Rail, G. (2007). Sport, sexuality, and the production of (resistant) bodies: De-/re-/constructing the meanings of gay male marathon corporeality. *Sociology of Sport Journal, 24*, 127–144.

Bruce, T., & Hallinan, C. (2001). Cathy Freeman: The quest for Australian identity. In D. Andrews & S. Jackson (Eds.), *Sport stars: The cultural politics of sporting celebrity* (pp. 257–270). London, England: Routledge.

Chase, L. (2008). Running big: Clydesdale runners and technologies of the body. *Sociology of Sport Journal, 25*, 130–147.

Chepyator-Thomson, J. R. (2005). *African women and globalization.* Trenton, NJ: Africa World Press.

Clough, P. J., Shepherd, J., & Maughan, R. J. (1989). Gender differences in non-elite runners. *Journal of Sport Behavior, 12*, 92–106.

Cooper, P. (1998). *The American marathon.* Syracuse, NY: Syracuse University Press.

Curtis, J., & McTeer, W. (1981). Toward a sociology of marathoning. *Journal of Sport Behavior, 4*, 67–81.

Denison, J. (2006). Inhibiting progress: The record of the four-minute mile. *Sport in History, 26*, 280–288.

Denison, J. (2007). The Haile Gebrselassie story: A biography of difference. In J. Bale & Y. Pitsiladis (Eds.), *East African running: Toward a cross-disciplinary perspective* (pp. 51–59). London, England: Routledge.

Denison, J., & Markula, P. (2005). The press conference as performance: Representing Haile Gebrselassie. *Sociology of Sport Journal, 22*, 311–335.

Epstein, D. (2014). *The sports gene: Inside the science of extraordinary athletic performance.* New York, NY: Penguin Group.

Fahey, T. D. (1998). Adaptation to exercise: progressive resistance exercise. In T. D. Fahey (Ed.), *Encyclopedia of sports medicine and science*. Retrieved from http://immv.sportsci.org/encyc/adaptex/adaptex.html.

Hanold, M. T. (2010). Beyond the marathon: (De)Construction of female ultrarunning bodies. *Sociology of Sport Journal, 27*, 160–177.

Hanold, M. T. (2011). Leadership, women in sport, and embracing empathy. *Advancing Women in Leadership, 31*, 160–165.

Hills, L., & Kennedy, E. (2009). Double trouble: Kelly Holmes, intersectionality, and unstable narratives of Olympic heroism in the British media. In P. Markula (Ed.), *Olympic women in the media: International perspectives* (pp. 112–131). London, England: Palgrave Macmillan.

Hoffman, M., Ong, J., & Wang, G. (2010). Historical analysis of participation in 161 km ultramarathons in North America. *The International Journal of the History of Sport, 27*, 1877–1891.

Howe, P. D. (2004). *Sport, professionalism, and pain: Ethnographies of injury and risk.* London, England: Routledge.

Howe, P. D., & Morris, C. (2009). An exploration of the co-production of performance running bodies and natures within "running taskscapes." *Journal of Sport and Social Issues, 33*, 308–330.

Jackson, S. (1998). A twist of race: Ben Johnson and the Canadian crisis of racial and national identity. *Sociology of Sport Journal, 15*, 21–40.

Jackson, S. (2004). Exorcizing the ghost: Donovan Bailey, Ben Johnson and the politics of Canadian identity. *Media, Culture and Society, 26*, 121–141.

Jeffery, K., & Butryn, T. (2012). The motivations of runners in a cause-based marathon-training program. *Journal of Sport Behavior, 35*, 300–320.

Johns, D. P., & Johns, J. S. (2000). Surveillance, subjectivism, and technologies of power: An analysis of the discursive practice of high-performance sport. *International Review for the Sociology of Sport, 35*, 219–234.

Kilduff, G. (2014). Driven to win: Rivalry, motivation, and performance. *Social Psychological and Personality Science, 5*, 944–952.

King, S. (2003). Doing good by running well: breast cancer, the race for the cure, and new technologies of ethical citizenship. In J. Z. Bratich, J. Packer, & C. McCarthy (Eds.), *Foucault, cultural studies, and governmentality* (pp. 295–316). New York, NY: SUNY Press.

King, S. (2006). *Pink ribbons, inc.: Breast cancer and the politics of philanthropy.* Minneapolis, MN: University of Minnesota Press.

Komi, P., Ishikawa, M., Ito, A., Locatelli, E., & Nicol, C. (2014). Specific muscle tendon architecture in elite Kenyan distance runners. *Scandinavian Journal of Medicine & Science in Sports, 24*, 269–274.

Larsen, H. (2003). Kenyan dominance in distance running. *Comparative Biochemistry and Physiology, 136*, 161–170.

Le Breton, D. (2000). Playing symbolically with death in extreme sports. *Body and Society, 6*, 1–11.

Lemke, T. (2001). "The birth of bio-politics": Michel Foucault's lecture at the College de France on neo-liberal governmentality. *Economy and Society, 30*, 190–207.

Loland, S. (2006). Three approaches to the study of pain in sport. In S. Loland, B. Skirstad, & I. Waddington (Eds.), *Pain and injury in sport: Social and ethical analysis* (pp. 49–62). New York, NY: Routledge.

Lupton, D. (1998). *The emotional self: A sociocultural exploration.* London, England: Sage.

Major, W. F. (2001). The benefits and costs of serious running. *World Leisure Journal, 43*, 12–25.

Markula, P. (2000). "'Gotta' do the marathon": Women's running as a truth-game. *Aethlon, xviii*, 89–106.

Masters, K., & Ogles, B. (2003). A typology of marathon runners based on cluster analysis of motivations. *Journal of Sport Behavior, 26*, 69–85.

McDermott, L. (2007). A governmental analysis of children "at risk" in a world of physical inactivity and obesity epidemics. *Sociology of Sport Journal, 24*, 302–324.

McDougall, C. (2009). *Born to run: A hidden tribe, superathletes, and the greatest race the world has never seen.* New York, NY: Vintage Books.

Mwaniki, M. (2011). Reading the career of a Kenyan runner: The case of Tegla Loroupe. *International Review for the Sociology of Sport, 47*, 446–460.

Nettleton, S. (2013). Cementing relations within a sporting field: Fell running in the English Lake District and the acquisition of existential capital. *Cultural Sociology, 7*, 196–210.

Ogles, B., Masters, K., & Richardson, S. (1995). Obligatory running and gender: An analysis of participative motives and training habits. *International Journal of Sport Psychology, 26*, 233–248.

Serravallo, V. (2000). Class and gender in recreational marathon running. Race, Gender and Class, 7(2); 96. Retrieved from http://proxy.bib.uottawa.ca:2078/pqdlink?did=494618281&sid=4&Fmt=3&clientI d=3345&RQT=309&VName=PQD.

Shipway, R., & Holloway, I. (2010). Running free: Embracing a healthy lifestyle through distance running. *Perspectives in Public Health, 130*, 270–276.

Smith, S. (1998). Athletes, runners and joggers: Participant-group dynamics in a sport of "individuals." *Sociology of Sport Journal, 15*, 174–192.

Smith, S. (2000). British nonelite road running and masculinity: A case of "running repairs"? *Men and Masculinities, 3*, 187–208.

Summers, J., Machin, V., & Sargent, G. (1983). Psychosocial factors related to marathon running. *Journal of Sport Psychology, 3*, 314–331.

Summers, J., Sargent, G., Levey, A., & Murray, K. (1982). Middle-aged, non-elite marathon runners: A profile. *Perceptual and Motor Skills, 54*, 963–969.

Van Ingen, C. (2004). Therapeutic landscapes and the regulated body in the Toronto Front Runners. *Sociology of Sport Journal, 21*, 253–269.

Walton, T. (2004). Steve Prefontaine: From rebel with a cause to hero with a swoosh. *Sociology of Sport Journal, 21*, 61–83.

Walton, T. (2010). Theorizing Paula Radcliffe: Representing a nation. *Sociology of Sport Journal, 27*, 285–300.

Walton, T., & Birrell, S. (2012). Enduring heroes: Hillary, Bannister, and the epic challenges of human exploration. *Journal of Sport History, 39*, 211–226.

Walton, T., & Butryn, T. (2006). Policing the race: U.S. men's distance running and the crisis of whiteness. *Sociology of Sport Journal, 23*, 1–28.

Wensing, E., & Bruce, T. (2003). Bending the rules: Media representations of gender during an international sporting event. *International Review for the Sociology of Sport, 38*, 387–396.

Young, K. (2004). Sports-related pain and injury: Sociological notes. In K. Young (Ed.), *Sporting Bodies, Damaged Selves: Sociological Studies of Sports-Related Injury* (pp. 1–25). Oxford, England: Elsevier.

Ziegler, S. (1991). Perceived benefits of marathon running in males and females. *Sex Roles, 25*, 119–127.

Running beginnings

2 "Astounding exploits" and "laborious undertakings"

Nineteenth-century pedestrianism and the cultural meanings of endurance

Mary Louise Adams

Over the past few decades, endurance sports have become increasingly popular amongst certain segments of the white middle classes. Marathons, once the purview of the uniquely tenacious and talented, are now common and crowded. According to Running USA, the number of marathon races in the United States grew from 300 in the year 2000 to 720 in 2011, and the number of finishers increased by 47 percent (Schexnayder, 2012). As marathons have become ubiquitous, events like Ironman triathlons, ultramarathons, and multi-day adventure races have become the new tests of physical distinction. Of all the possible ways to be physically active, of all the challenging things that people might choose to do with their bodies, what is it that makes long-distance endurance events the activity of choice for so many recreational athletes? And why are endurance events becoming longer and more difficult?

Sociologists have offered a variety of explanations for why endurance events have come to be popular in the current context. Writing about extreme sports, including truly exceptional endurance activities like trans-Atlantic swimming or rowing, Le Breton (2000) suggested that people who pursue such sports are looking for intensity of feeling, an opportunity to "play symbolically with death," but also the sacred (as opposed to religious) experience of being at one with the world. Le Breton wrote that these desires emerge in a social context in which "values are in crisis," and people are looking to validate and legitimate life. He said that the "physical limit has come to replace the moral limit that present-day society no longer provides" (Le Breton, 2000, p. 1). In an ethnographic study of Canadian triathletes, Atkinson (2008) saw the attraction to endurance sports in less metaphysical terms, suggesting that it is a conservative response to middle class malaise. He proposed that the participants in his research used triathlons as a solution to boredom, a way to distinguish themselves from others, or to be pegged as special. Atkinson suggested that recreational triathletes use their training to help them find both physical exhilaration and feelings of connection and community (Atkinson, 2008). The sport is a means of coping with and responding to a broader context in which social fragmentation has come to be the norm.

Other authors have also drawn the connection between endurance sport and the production of middle-class identities. In her work with women who run ultramarathons, Hanold (2010) talked about ultrarunning as a site in which white middle-class values become normalized. She argued that the sport gives women access to the specific kind of pleasure that comes of disciplining bodies and fulfilling neoliberal notions of success and empowerment. Bridel (2013) developed the neoliberal connection further in his research on Ironman triathletes. He was especially concerned with the ways that neoliberal notions of health as an individual responsibility and a sign of moral rectitude have animated the experiences of people training for and participating in Ironman events. In a context in which leisure-time exercise is promoted as a primary means of fulfilling one's role as a responsible, health-conscious citizen, the extensive training regime required for Ironman can mark participants as exceptionally good and conscientious—despite physical evidence, like injuries and stress, that such training may in fact not be good for their "health." Bridel suggested that neoliberal health discourses that emphasize self-improvement and discipline have helped to make possible the normalization of pain and injury among Ironman participants. They also shape broader conversations about what the pursuit of "better health" might look like and the extent to which people, in general, should be working on their bodies (Bridel, 2013).

Bridel's article conveys a sense of unease about the growing attractiveness of more extreme endurance sports and what their appeal might say about the pervasive neoliberal health frameworks through which they are experienced and read. This chapter is an attempt to provide historical context to his critique. My aim is to extend our understanding of the contemporary allure of endurance sport by historicizing not the sports themselves, which have been variously popular in different time periods, but the concept of athletic endurance. The assumption underlying this task is that bodies and their capacities mean different things in different contexts. As Cole (2000), in an overview of body studies in sport sociology, wrote: "Where, when and how bodies appear and how they are perceived are intimately bound to historically specific dynamics and pressures" (p. 439). My aim is simply to argue that endurance has referred to different physical capacities over time and, more importantly, that the cultural meanings of the concept have changed. This is an absolutely typical argument in historical and/or sociological studies of the body; yet, it is easily forgotten. In what follows, I look at the cultural meanings of athletic endurance by looking at pedestrianism, a sport that was hugely popular in English-speaking countries during the nineteenth century.

The term pedestrianism referred to any type of footrace—running or walking—over any distance. Today it is more commonly used to refer to long-distance walking than to running. The sport was among the first to take advantage of precise stopwatches, which, by the end of the 1800s, were reliable to one-fifth of a second (Hutchinson, 1996, p. 45). Accurate time-pieces meant records could be kept, and broken, and sensationalized; stopwatches made it possible for pedestrians to pit themselves against people whom they may never have seen nor met, and for narratives to be constructed about who was the fastest and, therefore, the best. But the sport was not standardized and the length and time of events varied greatly—as did the possible gains to be won from betting: London to York (200 miles) and back again in six days for a wager of 100 guineas; 23 miles in three hours for a bet of £10; 60 miles in 14 hours for a bet of 100 guineas; 300 miles in four days for 200 guineas (Thom, 1813).

In 1801, Robert Allardice Barclay, about whom we will hear more below, walked 90 miles in 21½ hours to win a bet of £5,000. He had lost four previous wagers, all made with the same man, totaling £6,000—more than four times the annual income of his (wealthy) family (Radford, 2001). Not surprisingly, public interest in the fifth wager and Barclay's walking challenge was unusually high. One Edinburgh newspaper claimed that the total amount bet on the outcome of Barclay's attempt was about £100,000 (Radford, 2001), a staggering amount of money at a time when laborers could only expect to make £50 in a year (Radford, 2001). According to Barclay's chronicler, Walter Thom, the pedestrian was

> so strong and hearty, and in fact so well, that he could have continued for several hours longer, and might have gone twenty or thirty miles further. Thousands of spectators on foot and on horseback, attended during the course of his walking, and he was loudly huzzaed, and carried on the shoulders of the multitude.
>
> (Thom, 1813, p. 108)

While early pedestrian events took place on open land or existing byways and roads, walkers eventually moved to specially designated outdoor tracks and then, during the 1870s, to indoor arenas. In these controlled environments they walked not just against the clock but also against each other. On both sides of the Atlantic, and in New Zealand and Australia, important pedestrian matches garnered international news coverage and drew thousands of spectators to venues that, at times, became so crowded the athletes feared for their own safety. The transformation of pedestrian events over the course of the nineteenth century—from individual outdoor endeavors to indoor head-to-head races— provides a frame through which we can see historical shifts in the meanings of endurance.

The plotline of a long-distance pedestrian event was generally quite simple: who kept moving and who did not, who moved the farthest in a given time. Reading news coverage of a pedestrian race, one encounters a cast of characters, an organized event, and *endurance* itself, the particular human capacity that pedestrian events were designed to make visible, to measure, to validate. What was it that people were celebrating when they fêted the long-distance walkers? What is sporting endurance? Why do sports tend to show off certain forms of physical endurance and not others? Which experiences, which understandings, which people are made visible, and which are obscured through the celebration of endurance as it is expressed through sport? How has the historical celebration of endurance in sport influenced or been influenced by understandings of endurance in other contexts?

This chapter is not a historical study of pedestrianism. A number of recent popular texts provide excellent descriptive histories of the sport (Algeo, 2014;

Curtis, 2014; Kastner, 2014, Radford, 2008). Instead, I discuss two examples from the history of pedestrianism that have helped me to think about endurance: Captain Robert Barclay's feat of walking 1,000 miles in 1,000 hours in 1809; and, the six-day walking matches that came to be the most important pedestrian events of the 1870s and 1880s. The contrast between the examples demonstrates shifts in the meanings of endurance and the kinds of ideological work that performances of endurance might have accomplished. The chapter concludes with a brief discussion of the meanings of endurance that circulate beyond sport.

Captain Barclay—the exceptional specimen

In June 1809, a Scottish landowner named Captain Robert Barclay Allardice of Ury walked 1,000 miles in each of 1,000 successive hours (about 42 days) for a wager of 1,000 guineas, a massive amount of money at the time. In successfully completing this task, Barclay established a legacy as one of the most famous walkers in recorded history. What was unique about his accomplishment was not just the time involved or the distance he covered but the fact that Barclay walked one mile an hour in *every* hour for 42 days. Barclay's task was not just to log miles, but to do so on very little sleep. He negotiated this requirement by walking the first mile towards the end of the first hour and the second mile at the beginning of the second hour and so on. Thus he was able to rest for 90 minutes between bouts of walking. As the days passed and it took him longer to walk each mile, these rest periods became shorter. But Barclay persisted and presented a fine figure to the massive crowds that gathered during the final portions of the trial. After his last mile, he was given a bath and put to bed. He slept for eight hours, woke and ate some gruel, and went back to sleep for nine more hours. What came next, according to one writer, was "the most remarkable circumstance attending [the match]…" After his 42-day trial and one long night of sleep, Captain Barclay awoke the next day in "perfect health and strength" (Obituary—Capt. Barclay Allardice, 1854, p. 81). He spent much of that day on his feet on the race grounds, and four days later, he joined his regiment at Ramsgate to set sail for the Netherlands.

The key contemporary source on Barclay is Thom's *Pedestrianism; or, An Account of the Performances of Celebrated Pedestrians during the Last and Present Century; with a Full Narrative of Captain Barclay's Public and Private Matches; and an Essay on Training* (1813). The book includes a long list of pedestrian records, a biography of Barclay, a reproduction of Barclay's training manual, and Thom's own account of the 1,000-hour trial, along with notes and diaries written by Barclay's attendants during the event. These notes provide records of Barclay's sleep and the foods he ate, and assessments of his physical condition. For instance:

> Thirty-second day.—One, morning: now much exhausted, and so stiff after resting that he could not rise without assistance; complained much of pain, and walked with great difficulty.—Three, morning: still worse; when he

> rested, the back tendons of his legs shrunk up, and the pain was excessive during the time of relaxing them, but his courage was unconquerable.—Five, morning: he now required so much time to walk, that he had little time to rest, and even great part of that, was taken up with rubbing his legs with the oil.
>
> (Thom, 1813, pp. 146–147)

The attendants' notes make evident the difficulty of Barclay's task. Over the six weeks he lost 32 pounds. After three weeks it was clear that he was suffering. His legs became swollen. He got a toothache. As the days pass, the records prepared by the attendants become longer and more detailed and begin to focus primarily on pain. By the 34th day Barclay needed help to get himself standing. The note for the 35th day said:

> Three, morning: his worst hour; pain excessive; could not rise, and was lifted up. To have seen him at this time, one would have thought that it would be impossible for him to go on, he was so debilitated and in such agony, but he was determined to complete the match at all risques.
>
> (Thom, 1813, p. 149)

On the 36th day in the late afternoon: "at this time, a spectator would have thought it impossible for him to go on another hour, but he persevered contrary to all expectation" (Thom, 1813, p. 150).

Thousands of people, from all classes, watched Barclay over the final days of his walk. They came to watch the drama, of course—would he be able to do it? They came to lay bets (total wagers, according to historian Peter Radford equaled the staggering sum of approximately five million pounds in today's currency). And they came to watch the spectacle of a man pushing the limits of human performance, pushing his body through pain and debility to accomplish a feat that had been thought impossible. The fact that he was able to do so underscored the general view that Barclay was not just *any* man—he was a remarkable exception. Thom (1813) tells us that Barclay was descended from "an ancient and honourable family" (p. 205). Commentary on Barclay's athletic achievements often noted his superior lineage, as in this quote from his obituary in *The Gentlemen's Magazine*:

> In early life he was much distinguished for the great bodily strength which had rendered many of his ancestors remarkable. Colonel David Barclay, the first of Ury, was one of the tallest, strongest, and handsomest men in the kingdom; his grandson was named the Strong; and the father of the late Captain Barclay was six feet high, of a handsome form, and a noted pedestrian … his ordinary pace was six miles an hour…
>
> (Obituary—Capt. Barclay Allardice, 1854, p. 80)

The entry for Barclay in the *Dictionary of National Biography* makes the same point: "Barclay's strength was inherited. His ancestor, the first Barclay of Ury, was one of the strongest men in the kingdom, and his sword, too heavy for ordinary men, was preserved in the family" (Stephen, 1885, p. 299).

Descriptions of Barclay inevitably remark on the "strong conformation of his body and his great muscular strength" (Thom, 1813, p. 206). Thom extended the point: "What might appear difficult or impossible to a man of ordinary frame, is to him quite easily accomplished" (p. 207). Barclay's strength, his ability to persevere and to overcome pain, his capability for endurance, signified not just his personal fortitude, but the superior capabilities of his ancestry and his class. Barclay was an outlier, an exceptional human specimen—so much so that he was the subject of an article in *The Eugenics Review* in 1962 (Bloomfield, 1962).

Nevertheless, Barclay did not rely solely on his hereditary talents. His athletic capabilities were also, Thom wrote, a product of modern scientific training practices—purging, sweating, special diet, massage, regulated physical activity. With the inclusion of Barclay's training instructions, Thom's book came to be seen as one of the most important training manuals of the early nineteenth century. While Thom extolled Barclay's exceptional capabilities, he also claimed that Barclay's training regime could do much to improve the performance of other men.

> It is not surprising that the art of training should be carried to a degree of perfection almost incredible; and that by certain processes, the BREATH, strength, and courage of man, should be so greatly improved as to enable him to perform the most laborious undertakings.
>
> (Thom, 1813, p. 226)

The "astonishing exploits" of well-known pedestrians could demonstrate "the infallible results of preparatory discipline" (Thom, 1813, p. 227). Even a "man of the ordinary frame," Thom claimed, could be trained to go "one hundred miles in twenty-four hours" (p. 227), an admirable goal, but one well below the exceptional Barclay's 110 miles in 19 hours and 27 minutes.

Thom concluded his book with an odd and racist little chapter entitled *The Physical Powers of Man* in which the reader is apprised of the racial philosophies that underpin his work. One learns, for instance, that man is not only the smartest of the all the "created beings," he is also the strongest, and that among men, those "under the influence of civilization" are stronger than "savages" (p. 252). Thom wrote about "American Indians" who could walk 60 miles a day for up to two months at a time (roughly the distance from one side of Canada to the other), a rather incredible accomplishment. Yet Thom was little moved by it. He argued that one must look to Britain to see truly "astonishing" feats of walking, like Barclay's 110 miles in 19 hours, or the effort of a Shropshire man named Glanville, who covered 142 miles in 29 hours (Thom, 1813). What else but racial and imperial logics could make a walk of 3,600 miles in 60 days fail to astonish? Thom's notion of endurance, represented first and foremost by the exceptional Barclay, but also by other English athletes, was as much about nationalism and colonial civilizing discourse as it was about breath and muscle and courage. By Thom's definition, endurance was part of the discourse of British athletic superiority (Walvin, 1987). Feats like Barclay's 1,000 mile walk were imbued with meaning by gendered discourses of patriarchy, colonialism, and class privilege and these, in turn, were reinforced by emerging scientific discourses about the body and its capacities. For Thom, endurance was a natural physical potential that resulted from good breeding and could be improved upon by science and by civilization, which was the well-bred pedestrian's natural habitat.

Six-day pedestrian matches, 1870s–1880s

In 1968, sport historian Lucas wrote:

> No more incredible sport event has ever taken place in New York's old Madison square Garden than that of six-day marathon running. Of all terrestrial creatures, the one animal officially having recorded the greatest feats of endurance running is man himself. The combination of muscle, lungpower, indomitable will, and powerful incentives is more than a match for any beast. No greater proof can be found than in some of the remarkable exploits of late nineteenth-century six-day marathon runners.
>
> (Lucas, 1968, p. 587)

By the latter decades of the 1800s, pedestrian matches had moved to indoor venues and were held on measured tracks. While there were many formats, the one that came to carry the most prestige was the six-day go-as-you-please match in which competitors could walk or run as they saw fit (Lucas, 1968), starting on Monday and finishing on Saturday, so as to avoid racing on Sunday. Lucas's quote above notwithstanding, news accounts suggest that six-day marathon runners were as likely to be walkers. American Edward Payson Weston, perhaps the most famous of the six-day racers, took to periodic bouts of running only late in his career. So committed were the top American pedestrians—Weston and an Irish immigrant named Dan O'Leary—to walking that they were scoffed at by the British press (Algeo, 2014).

In indoor matches, pedestrians—mostly men but women as well—would circle a track hundreds of times over a six-day event. The venues were often poorly lit and poorly ventilated. Each competitor had a small, furnished tent inside the arena in which to rest, change clothes, and eat. Competitors rested and ate as they saw fit. The prize went to the competitor who walked or ran the farthest distance in the allotted time. Six-day matches attracted thousands of spectators, men and women of all classes. Betting was vigorous. Newspapers ran regular columns on pedestrian events, sometimes on the front page. In the best matches, the winning distance could be more than 500 miles. In 1880, Frank Hart, an African American pedestrian from Boston broke the six-day world record by walking 565 miles, an average of 94 and a bit miles a day. Some pedestrians—including Hart—became wealthy and famous.

The distances covered in these six-day marathons are mind-boggling and yet the performances themselves must have been, for a good part of the time, less than exciting to watch, with the plotlines taking days to reach their climax and little significant skill on display. A correspondent for the *New York Times* had this to say while watching "the great international match" in London in 1878:

> The men went round and round something like the school of herring in the Brighton Aquarium, round and round, in groups, in twos and threes, in ones and twos, in threes and fours, round and round until one began to get giddy with watching them…

This writer was not the first to call the competitors "human machines" or note the tedium of their efforts ("Pedestrianism in London," 1878). Another journalist, even less appreciative, wrote:

> What particular gratification [the general public] derives from the spectacle of a usually unattractive-looking person in tights, doing only to excess what each of them is in the habit of doing in moderation every day of his life, is incomprehensible enough. One can only speculate on what drew people to watch these events.
>
> ("Walking as a vocation," 1870)

In his book *Pedestrianism: When Watching People Walk Was America's Favorite Spectator Sport* (upon which I have relied heavily for the discussion here), Algeo wrote that watching a pedestrian match would have been like watching a "NASCAR race in super-slow motion: hypnotic, mesmerizing, with the promise of imminent catastrophe" (2014, p. 95). While some walkers certainly did drop, such dramatic moments would not have been the norm. More typical would have been a withdrawal due to exhaustion; a pedestrian might have retired to his or her tent and simply not come back to the track.

Walking matches were among the first organized sports to come indoors, making the athletes visible to the audience in ways that had not been possible outside. Sitting in the stands, what would spectators have seen? They would have seen a small group of athletes, usually men, walking around a rolled dirt or sawdust track. The walkers wore a range of athletic and not-so-athletic clothing. Officials maintained order with the crowds and kept note of the laps. The walkers had assistants to help them with food and various methods of physical rejuvenation. Bands or other musicians were often brought in to provide additional entertainment. But the main attraction was the walkers themselves—those who were succeeding *and* those who were failing.

In the six-day matches, the physical deterioration of the competitors was a key part of the spectacle. Algeo (2014) cited a story from the *New York Times*, from 1878:

> "It was a sorry sight the last few hours of the week's walk," the *New York Times* correspondent wrote. "Haggard, dazed, staggering O'Leary, his arms

> no longer knitted in pedestrian form and braced with muscular strength, were limp and almost helpless. His legs were swollen. He went his miserable round in evident pain."
>
> Yet somehow, O'Leary still managed to keep walking, managed to keep the lead. It was as if his body were on autopilot. One spectator said he "seemed more like a machine than a man." It was a remarkable exhibition of endurance, but it was painful to watch.
>
> (Algeo, 2014, p. 96)

"Endurance" is Algeo's word, an interpretation, more than 100 years later, of the image presented by the journalist. What might it mean here? Stamina? Fortitude? Tenacity? Suffering? Good lungs? Good heart? In six-day pedestrian events, like most other activities that come under the heading of "endurance sport," a competitor's endurance was signified by the ability to keep going, to work through pain and boredom, and, importantly, to do so with very little rest. Pedestrian endurance involved some combination of the ability to walk or run a very long distance, at a good pace, while deprived of sleep. When Frank Hart broke the six-day record in 1880, his total rest time was 23 hours and 23 minutes, which, one is reminded by Algeo (2014), meant that he was moving for more than 20 hours a day for six days.

Not all were impressed by the drawn-out spectacle of increasingly weary and obviously pained walkers—and even less so when the walkers were women. In a 1999 article on "pedestriennes," Shaulis wrote about the contradictory and complex reception received by the women who were long-distance walkers. On the one hand they were celebrated by suffragettes and others who saw them as fine representatives of women's athletic potential. On the other hand, they were seen as immoral or as victims of cruelty and abuse (Shaulis, 1999). The *New York Times* cited the Philadelphia Medical Society, which had put forward motions of "unqualified condemnation of the barbarities now being inflicted upon women under the falsely-assumed name of 'exemplification of physical culture and pedestrianism,' but which simply consists in the systematic deprivation of natural sleep for long periods of time." *The Times* argued for regulation ("The women's walk," 1879). New York City aldermen discussed a proposal to ban women's pedestrian matches but it did not pass (Algeo, 2014).

While men's six-day races did not engender quite so much moral concern as women's did, they were also the subject of critique and comment. Critics called pedestrianism "sinful," "stupid," "cruel," "harsh," "barbaric," and "boring." Yet the sport continued to attract an audience through the 1880s. In terms of public appeal it was eventually replaced by non-stop six-day cycling events, the first of which was held in Madison Square Gardens in New York in 1891. Yet these too were considered by many to be ill-advised "brutal" events. In 1899, New York State legislators passed a law to put a limit on endurance events. In competitions longer than 48 hours, the athletes could perform for no more than 12 hours in any 24-hour period. It was a law that mandated sleep. The *New York Times* suggested that the law might increase the audience for long-distance cycling

> for the continuous accession of fresh riders to the track naturally means frequent bursts of phenomenal speed, and the public already seems to prefer this to the spectacle of a score or so of tortured, toiling men, whose steadily failing vitality shows itself in the very-depressing lines of their countenances and the feebleness of their movements.
>
> ("The six-day bicycle race," 1899)

Contextualizing the meanings of endurance

In each of the pedestrian examples, endurance is a term that captures the ability of an athlete to persist through long periods of exercise. What made these events somewhat different from other long-distance athletic trials is the necessity of a competitor performing with very little sleep. A successful pedestrian was someone who could manage without rest. While there is not the space to discuss them in detail here, there were many pedestrian records that were more extreme than the six-day races in this regard. For instance Ada Anderson walked 2,700 quarter-miles (675 miles) in 2,700 quarter-hours in 1878. That's one-quarter mile every 15 minutes for 28 days. The longest she could sleep would have been ten minutes at a time (Shaulis, 1999). The following year, a French walker named Exilda La Chappelle repeated the feat in Chicago. A story appeared in the *Chicago Daily Tribune*, after she had been walking for ten days:

> Thus far she has borne up under the ordeal very well, but Manager Davis has found it necessary to station men near the pillars which support the gallery, as, in her half-asleep moments, the Madame is apt to walk against them and injure herself. As soon as she reaches her dressing-room, after completing her quarter of a mile, she falls on the bed, and in an instant she is fast asleep.
>
> ("*Pedestrianism*," 1879, p. 5)

The drowsy pedestrienne, stumbling along a small track for a few minutes at a time, over and over, does not necessarily conjure the present-day image of an endurance athlete.

Anderson had been introduced to pedestrianism by a Welsh walker named William Gale. In 1877, Gale bettered Barclay's famous record by walking 1,500 miles in 1,000 consecutive hours around a measured track in London. A magazine report on Gale demonstrates the ambivalence with which some observers greeted such accomplishments. The writer lauds Gale's courage and determination before questioning the value of the exercise: "of what particular benefit it may be to the world at large it is utterly impossible to imagine" ("Feats of endurance," 1877, p. 808). Gale's next effort, a few months later, was a walk of 4,000-quarter miles in 4,000 consecutive ten-minute periods, a "dreary walk" lasting about 28 days. Again the issue of sleep was paramount, as the report makes clear:

> Men have on many occasions attempted walking feats which required a vast amount of physical endurance, and have failed from their utter inability to

> go without the natural quantum of sleep; but Gale has not only shewn himself to be possessed of the former, but to be altogether independent of the latter. This, however, instead of indicating 'pluck' merely, would rather seem to point to a peculiarity in the man's constitution; as there are doubtless many persons whose courage would enable them to perform the same or even a greater task, if, like Gale, they could walk about in a state of somnolency or semi-sleep.
>
> (p. 808)

The report concluded with a wish that "such exhibitions" would be given no further attention from the public, as they were undignified and needless and not befitting a "country which, we trust will ever pride itself on a nobler civilisation than that which is founded upon mere physical endurance" ("Feats of endurance," 1877, p. 808). The word "mere" flags the hierarchy of mind over body, the intellect over the physical, a binary that framed and helped to justify the relationship between the Empire and the "uncivilized" peoples who had been subjugated through projects of colonial expansion.

In *Orientalism*, Said (1977) described the ways that binaries like mind/body, intellectual/physical, civilized/savage helped to establish a concept of Europe as both distinct from and superior to the non-Western cultures over which Europeans were establishing their authority. Within Britain the mind/body binary also distinguished those who by necessity used their bodies for labor from those who did not, the former being devalued and the latter privileged by such acts of classification. In the 1870s, it was no longer gentleman like Barclay who were engaged in "feats of endurance" but men like William Gale, who made his living as a trainer. Gale was a small man, who, during his trial of 4,000-quarter hours, was described by one critic as "an aged-looking man of five-and-forty, undersized, with 'lack-lustre eye,' and decidedly 'bandy' [bow-legged]" ("Sickening spectacles," 1877, p. 559). The same critic likened Gale's endurance to the "determination of a dog" and the "never-ending movement of an over-worked horse" ("Sickening spectacles," 1877, p. 559):

> The London Omnibus Company possesses many an animal that never gives in, starts, when the door is banged, and sleeps standing at its stall. The 'sporting press' has got hold of a biped that does pretty much the same. William Gale can endure, but he does not look either a bright, or a very intellectual specimen of humanity.
>
> ("Sickening spectacles," 1877, p. 560)

Contrast this to the descriptions of Barclay as the measure of well-bred masculinity. And, remember too that the smaller Gale walked 1,500 miles in the same number of hours in which Barclay had walked 1,000.

What is the quality that is celebrated in sport as endurance and what has it signified? Barclay, the lone athlete, challenges himself in the open air; he structures the event; he is the focus of all attention. His capacity to endure is taken as a sign of his exceptional ancestry and his exceptional body. His achievements signify the superiority of British civilization and British masculinity. Sixty years later, Gale's more difficult feat is read, by at least one critic, as a clear sign of his inferiority and his failure to exhibit intelligence, the most vaunted quality of the urban industrial age.

The pedestrians competing in six-day races were performing in the same historical context as Gale, but their participation in head-to-head athletic competition meant that their capacity for endurance could be read through increasingly mainstream discourses of sport, athleticism, and competition. In the 1870s, athletes were more numerous and sporting events were popular entertainments, organized as much to sell tickets as to showcase athletic skill or capacity. One would think that shorter, more exciting contests might have served this purpose better than the week-long trials, but promoters surely organized events they assumed would capture the interest of the public and bring the greatest profit. However, in an era when most sports were still contested out of doors, the smoke-filled indoor arenas, the small tracks, the repetitive movements, the poor ventilation and artificial light, and the fact that the pedestrians were constantly under the gaze of spectators, might have been more likely to evoke the urban factory than the athletic field.

Press reports tended to focus on the most famous pedestrians or the front-runners. But for spectators in the arena, the story of the match was not just about those who remained standing. Like most sporting events, the six-day pedestrian races were a means of differentiating bodies. On the walking track, some of the "human machines" managed to keep walking and others broke down. In their successes, but perhaps more so in their failures, the pedestrians demonstrated the "limits of human endurance."

Among athletes, "the limits of human endurance" have stood as a goal to be reached, a record to be broken. Outside the sports arena, "the limits of human endurance" have signified the conditions of human suffering. For example, throughout the nineteenth century the limits of physical endurance were, to a great extent, the limits of capital. In the early part of the century, in slave economies, in systems of indenture, in factories and mines, overseers and employers pushed those limits with impunity. How hard and how far could workers be pushed, until they could no longer work? In *Capital*, Marx argued:

> in its blind unrestrainable passion, its were-wolf hunger for surplus-labour, capital oversteps not only the moral, but even the merely physical maximum bounds of the working-day. It usurps the time for growth, development, and healthy maintenance of the body. It steals the time required for the consumption of fresh air and sunlight. It higgles over a meal-time, incorporating it where possible with the process of production itself, so that food is given to the labourer as to a mere means of production, as coal is supplied to the boiler, grease and oil to the machinery. It reduces the sound sleep needed for the restoration, reparation, refreshment of the bodily powers to just so many hours of torpor as the revival of an organism, absolutely

> exhausted, renders essential. It is not the normal maintenance of the labour-power which is to determine the limits of the working-day; it is the greatest possible daily expenditure of labour-power, no matter how diseased, compulsory, and painful it may be, which is to determine the limits of the labourers' period of repose. Capital cares nothing for the length of life of labour-power.
>
> (Marx, 1867, Paragraph III.X.55)

In Britain, over the course of the 1800s, a series of Factory Acts eventually regulated hours of work. The Factory Act of 1850, for instance, limited the workday for women and children to ten and a half hours (Cook & Stevenson, 2014). How might people's work experiences—before and after such reforms—have colored the meanings that could be taken from celebrations of endurance in sport, the lauding of people who kept moving almost until they dropped? Algeo (2014) claimed that people of all classes attended the indoor pedestrian races. He wrote that it was not uncommon for some people to pay their 50¢ admission as a means to acquire shelter for a week. How would people who might have experienced unregulated and physically punishing employment conditions have read the voluntary body-breaking toil of the athletes? It is clear from the attendance figures that the six-day races were very popular, but attendance figures tell us nothing about what sense the average spectator made of what was happening on the track.

Final thoughts

As I was writing the first draft of this chapter, students in my graduate seminar were reading Steedman's wonderful *Landscape for a Good Woman*, a memoir about the author's working class childhood in South London in the 1950s (Steedman, 1987). One of the students—a competitive rower—wrote about a comment that Steedman makes about endurance: "I am an athlete in an endurance sport. But, I had never thought about endurance like that." The student was referring to a passage in which Steedman recounts the story of her grandmother being sent away to work as a domestic servant. Steedman describes an 11-year-old girl, standing on a train platform with a small metal trunk, waiting to be taken away from her family and all that she knows: "…I knew perfectly well what that child … had felt," Steedman writes:

> She cried, because tears are cheap; and then she stopped, and got by, because no one gives you anything in this world. What was given to her, passed on to all of us, was a powerful and terrible endurance, the self-destructive defiance of those doing the best they can with what life hands out to them.
>
> (p. 31)

It is of course too simple to say that the notion of endurance that Steedman presents here and the notion of endurance that motivates athletes are the same.

But it is also too simple to say that they have no metonymic or signifying relationship to each other. The endurance that Steedman points to is the tolerance of suffering that arises from material and emotional hardship, an endurance produced by capitalism, inequality, and deprivation, and grounded by long traditions of religious and moral teachings. Many spectators at the six-day matches, for instance, would have been familiar with the general Christian valuing of endurance, as in Romans 5:03, "We rejoice in our sufferings, knowing that suffering produces endurance, and endurance produces character, and character produces hope, and hope does not disappoint us, because God's love has been poured into our hearts." What I want to suggest here is simply that Christian understandings of endurance—implied in Steedman's narrative despite the fact that she does not really discuss religion—may have provided at least part of the cultural and conceptual framework that helped to make the ability to endure physical suffering a valued capacity in sport.

Out of all the ways to test a body, why test its endurance? Why the valuing of something as non-spectacular as the ability to keep walking (quickly) around an indoor track? There is nothing inherently valuable in the ability to push the body to its physical limits, to keep it moving or to break it down. In a culture organized differently—for example, the nineteenth-century factory floor—this capacity might simply be taken for granted. One can also imagine cultures—for example, the nineteenth-century labor movement—where this capacity might be reviled. What gave endurance its meaning was not simply physiological knowledge, which was remarkable in its absence from the sources I have used, it was—and continues to be—a range of discourses—religious, cultural, scientific, aesthetic—through which we come to know bodies. As the relationships among these discourses shift, the meaning of endurance has shifted with them.

Athletic skills and sporting events are highly symbolic forms of physical activity that have been designed by people who are variously located in specific historical and cultural contexts. The meanings that accrue to these activities—whether in terms of classificatory categories like race, nation, gender or class, or notions of exceptionalism, corporeality or social value—are not inherent in the physical activities themselves; they are attributed to them by people in accord with views of the world that are available to them. The meanings, the people, and the contexts can change. Historical and sociological analysis can help suggest why and how they might need to.

References

Algeo, M. (2014). *Pedestrianism: When watching people walk was America's favourite spectator sport*. Chicago, IL: Chicago Review Press.

Atkinson, M. (2008). Triathlon, suffering and exciting significance. *Leisure Studies, 27*, 165–180.

Bloomfield, P. (1962). Captain Barclay. *The Eugenics Review*, *54*, 25–28.

Brailsford, D. (1992). *British sport: A social history*. Cambridge, England: Lutterworth Press.

Bridel, W. (2013). Not fat, not skinny, functional enough to finish: interrogating constructions of health in the Ironman Triathlon *Leisure/Loisir*, *37*, 37–56.

Cole, C. L. (2000). Body studies in the sociology of sport: A review of the field. In J. Coakley & E. Dunnings (Eds.), *Handbook of sports studies* (pp. 439–460). London, England: Sage.

Cook, C., & Stevenson, J. (2014). *Longman handbook to modern British history 1714–2001*. London: Routledge.

Curtis, W. (2014). *The last great walk: The true story of a 1909 walk from New York to San Francisco and why it matters today*. New York, NY: Rodale Books.

Feats of endurance. (1877). *Chambers's journal of popular literature, science and arts (730)*, 806–808. Retrieved from http://search.proquest.com/docview/2597853?accountid=6180.

Hanold, M. T. (2010). Beyond the marathon: (De)construction of female ultrarunning bodies. *Sociology of Sport Journal, 27*, 160–177.

Hutchinson, R. (1996). *Empire Games: The British invention of twentieth-century sport*. Edinburgh and London, United Kingdom: Mainstream Publishing.

Kastner, C. B. (2014). *The 1929 Bunion Derby: Johnny Salo and the great footrace across America*. Syracuse, NY: Syracuse University Press.

Le Breton, D. (2000). Playing symbolically with death in extreme sports. *Body & Society. 6*, 1–11.

Lucas, J. A. (1968). Pedestrianism and the struggle for the Sir John Astley Belt, 1878–79. *The Research Quarterly, 39*, 587–594.

Marx, K. (1867). Chapter 10: The working day—Section 5. *Capital Volume I*. Retrieved from;www.econlib.org/library/YPDBooks/Marx/mrxCpA10.html#Part%20III,%20Chapter%2010.

Obituary—Capt. Barclay Allardice. (1854) *The gentleman's magazine and historical review*, Vol. XLII. 80–82. Retrieved from https://books.google.ca.

Pedestrianism. (1879, February 5). *Chicago Daily Tribune*, p. 5.

Pedestrianism in London. (1878, September 24). *New York Times*, p. 1.

Radford, P. (2001). *The celebrated Captain Barclay: Sport, money and fame in Regency Britain*. London, England: Headline.

Said, E. (1977). *Orientalism*. London, England: Penguin.

Schexnayder, CJ. (2012, February 28) *The marathon: more popular than ever*. Retrieved from www.stridenation.com/2012/2/28/2830407/the-marathon-more-popular-than-ever.

Shaulis, D. (1999). Pedestriennes: Newsworthy but controversial women in sporting entertainment." *Journal of Sport History*, *26*, 29–50.

Sickening spectacles (1877, November 8). *Truth*, pp. 558–560.

Steedman, C. (1987). *Landscape for a good woman: A Story of two lives*. New Brunswick, NJ: Rutgers University Press.

Stephen, L. (1885). Allardice, Robert Barclay. In L. Stephen and S. M. Lee (Eds.), *Dictionary of National Biography*, *Vol. I* (pp. 298–299). London, England: Smith, Elder & Co. Retrieved from http://en.wikisource.org/wiki/Allardice,_Robert_Barclay_(DNB00).

The six-day bicycle race. (1899, December 5). *New York Times*, p. 2.

The walking mania. (1879, March 31). *Hartford Daily Courant*, p. 2.

The women's walk. (1879, December 14). *New York Times*, p. 6.

Thom, W. (1813). *Pedestrianism; or, an account of the performances of celebrated pedestrians during the last and present century; with a full narrative of Captain Barclay's public and private matches; and an essay on training*. Aberdeen, Scotland: D. Chalmers and Co.

Walking as a vocation. (1870, September 24). *New York Times*, p. 4.
Walvin, J. (1987). Symbols of moral superiority: Slavery, sport and the changing world order, 1800–1950. In J. A. Mangan & J. Walvin (Eds.), *Manliness and morality: Middle class masculinity in Britain and America, 1800–1940* (pp. 242–260). Manchester, United Kingdom: Manchester University Press.

3 On the entangled origins of mud running

"Overcivilization," physical culture, and overcoming obstacles in the Spartan Race

Gavin Weedon

Mud running, known also as obstacle racing, is a twenty-first century enterprise that lays claim to ancient, premodern, and distinctively human beginnings. The growth of a mud running industry follows a recent and relatively straightforward history, beginning with the launch of the Warrior Dash in 2009 and the Spartan Race and Tough Mudder in 2010.[1] Notwithstanding their differences, these events share in comprising predetermined obstacle courses over, under, and through which paying participants travail, traipse, and traverse and, in doing so, become caked in the eponymous soil. The mud running industry, much like the obstacle courses on which it trades, charts a linear, progressive path of popularity and economic prosperity that in 2015 shows no signs of curtailing. *Outside Magazine* (Beresini, 2014) had described it as the "fastest-growing sport in the United States," and there are currently several world championships, run by respective companies and organizations, competing for participants, sponsors, and media coverage.[2]

While these developments lend themselves to an array of cultural and economic explanations for mud running's popularity, those at the forefront of industry developments suggest that mud running rekindles a far deeper, more fundamentally human history. According to Spartan Race co-founder Joe De Sena, the contemporary appeal of obstacle racing is due to its entwinement, and reconciliation, with an essential human nature. It is, he asserted, a profoundly

> HUMAN sport, very accessible, and the movements are what we have done for 1 million years on earth. It's authentic. We [humans] are a race, we are athletic in nature. At the end of the day that appeals in a big way to our consumers—so much so they share it.
>
> (as cited in Rodriguez, 2014, p. 17)

These movements—running, jumping, climbing, and crawling through dirt and over obstacles—are said to constitute mud running's "natural" authenticity, which, in De Sena's account, explains and produces its "cultural" popularity. The corollary is that mud running not only appeals to an "authentically athletic human nature" but is an exercise in somehow revisiting that nature, as embodied in the mythologized primordiality of mud. Running through mud becomes the source for not only regressing to a premodern past, but reinventing the self through an ascetic commitment to overcoming obstacles encountered within and beyond the course.

This chapter casts the history of mud running as not only or simply a re-emergent practice and growing industry with ancient or evolutionary beginnings, but as a quintessentially modern expression of physical culture with some renowned and revealing historical precedents. This is not to dismiss research in anthropology and evolutionary biology that explores questions of our athletic ancestry, such as Bramble and Lieberman's (2004) study of *Endurance running and the Evolution of Homo*. But to accept mud running as simply an expression of or realignment with human biological destiny, hunter-gather dexterity, or primordial mud and earth, as is purported by many event founders, would risk neglecting some of its most telling, controversial, and consequential roots and routes. I suggest in what follows that mud running is at least as much a recuperation of nineteenth-century physical cultural movements and movements practices concerning asceticism and nature, social Darwinist doctrines proclaiming innate human athleticisism, and fears about the enervating effects of urbanization and white-collar work (then diagnosed as "neurasthenia"), as it is a rekindling of ancient, premodern comportments or virtues. In late nineteenth-century Britain and North America, outdoor sport, health, and exercise practices were heralded as antidotes to the perceived "overcivilization" of young, middle-class boys, whose bodies and minds were deemed to be weakened by the ostensibly more cerebral labor and leisure of industrial capitalist society. A host of revitalizing projects, from playgrounds and parks to camping sites, along with the founding of enduring (and expressly virile) institutions such as the Boy Scouts and the Young Man's Christian Association (YMCA), were fostered during this era (Vertinsky, in press). In the same vein as its nineteenth-century forerunners, mud running can be seen as a kindred vision and practice for physical and social reform; one in which the heroic, corporeal act of "overcoming" obstacles and toiling through dirt is both an *expression and a critique* of the perceived ills of modern life.

The most authoritative account of mud running's history is currently conferred by health and fitness reformists-come-entrepreneurs, and Spartan Race co-founders, De Sena and Andy Weinberg. My attempt to join in writing mud running's entangled origins centers primarily on their Spartan Race, and begins with two books that are in effect manifestos designed to historicize and credentialize obstacle racing as a professional sport, as well as to realize the "Spartan Race vision" to "establish, own, and defend the #1 position in obstacle racing" (De Sena & Weinberg, 2012, p. 42). From this point of departure, I then consider the entwinement of De Sena's biography, athletic philosophy, and given history of obstacle racing, before historicizing mud running's "will to overcome" as entangled with nineteenth-century physical cultural movements, and their political and ecological enfoldings.

First, in my attempt to join in writing mud running's history, let's begin with De Sena's autobiography, *Spartan Up*!, and the scenes chosen by him and Weinberg to cast the ancient and contemporary geneses of the Spartan Race.

Spartan Up! a reformer's vision of ascetic excellence

Pittsfield, Vermont: A small northeastern town with a population of little over 500 people, just a few hours drive from New York City and the Canadian border. If New York City's Central Park was built to "heal the overwrought or decadent city dweller with a prophylactic dose of nature" (Haraway, 1989, p. 26; but see Gandy, 2003), then Vermont might be thought of as a haven or hinterland for those who fetishize after a more "authentic" and encompassing antidote to metropolitan life. "Vermont," as noted by Elizabeth Dugger (2000) in her adventure guide to the region, "is credited as the most rural state in the country," one where you'll likely come across "as many maple sugar makers as lawyers" (p. 2). Much of Vermont's appeal for residents and visitors alike is as a place of escape; somewhere to "feel alive" among the mountainous terrain and its many opportunities for athletic pursuits, be it skiing, snowshoeing, hiking, trail running, or cycling. In the spirit of adventure tourism, Dugger lauded Vermont as a place that "has always inspired independence, which may be why so many people feel that coming here is coming home to themselves at last" (p. 2). That independence is borne of sixteenth-century colonial struggles to which the French name Vermont (green mountain) and Pittsfield, like its eponym in nearby Massachusetts, are indebted.[3]

Pittsfield's rolling peaks have been home to Spartan Race co-founder De Sena since the early 2000s, where he and his family run a farm, a bed and breakfast, a general store, and since 2009, the Spartan Race headquarters. De Sena's 2014 book, *Spartan Up! A Take No Prisoner's Guide to Overcoming Obstacles and Achieving Peak Performance in Life*, is part biography, part proselytizing account of an ascetic lifestyle, part doctrine on the efficacy of an indomitable work ethic for success in all domains of life. It's a transformational tale of shifting and self-made fortunes that recounts De Sena's own triumphant journey: from the self-proclaimed "spoilt brat" growing up in Queen's, New York, whose entrepreneurial father was "focused 100% on business and making money" (De Sena, 2014, p. 26), to a financial and personal lowpoint following the Wall Street crash in the 1980s and his parent's divorce, to his eventual admission to Cornell University and the subsequent parlaying of "a pool-business into a job on Wall Street, a job on Wall Street into a small fortune and a small fortune into a 400-acre spread in the Green Mountains" (Brick, 2009).

Spartan Up! is full of fables and recollections that champion will power over circumstances, most of which are either drawn from De Sena's own experiences or vicariously indebted to him by grateful adherents. His accomplishments in extreme, endurance, and adventure sports (including an oft-cited week in which he completed the Vermont 100, the Lake Placid Ironman, and the Badwater Ultra marathon) are presented as precedents against which all other hardships are to be measured and overcome. The book's prologue, exemplary of this, opens with De Sena about to embark on the six-day Ukatak endurance race in Quebec, Canada, "in the dead of winter, the absolute coldest time of the year" (2014, p. xiii). Perilous conditions unravel thereafter: the "blast of the Arctic wind" put him and his team members at risk of death from hypothermia overnight (p. xvi); ropes needed for descending icy surfaces snapped; having the wrong skis and wax for their 60-mile cross country ski left the crew mired in snow that swallowed them waist high "like quicksand" (p. xvi); but they persevered through grit and "primal" (p. xiv) instincts, and lived to pen the story. De Sena heralded this experience as epiphanic: it taught him that challenging oneself to "accomplish more than you know you can is never stupid—it helps you know what you are capable of" (p. xix), even if, like him, you are "an average guy in an extraordinary situation" who "lived in New York City and had a desk job" (p. xvii). This story, pivotal to and emblematic of his given biography, serves to attest for the necessity and virtue of suffering at nature's behest in pursuit of one's goals.

Not satiated by these daring feats of endurance, in 2004 De Sena co-founded with Weinberg the Spartan Race's more esoteric predecessor and contemporary, the ominously titled Death Race. The Death Race is an untimed, unstructured event set on the grounds of De Sena's home in Vermont, designed "to either break competitors or inspire them" (De Sena, 2014, p. 10). All sorts of grueling and gruesome tales surround the Death Race, and its cultural currency in endurance sport circles is high—especially for the small fraction of participants who keep going for upwards of 70 hours and make it through to the end. With the help of groups of volunteers, De Sena and Weinberg instruct and oversee Death Race participants not only running, but "diving for pennies, eating onions, extracting stumps from the ground, carrying kayaks and tires for an ultradistance, lifting rocks for six hours, completing three thousand burpees—anything to try to make people quit" (De Sena, 2014, p. 11).[4]

De Sena's justification for all this, his motto and mantra, is that "you need to suffer" (2014, p. 18) to appreciate and to excel in life, and that in suffering lies a reconciliation, a realignment, with human destiny. This is where his athletic philosophy—and that underpinning the Death Race—becomes most conspicuously entwined with a broader historical, anthropological, socio-cultural, and political-economic diagnosis. In his words, "I believe that confronting these insane obstacles is the best way to rewire a human brain after years or even decades of coddling, predictability and excuses … [by] … encouraging people to get in touch with a more primal survival instinct or mechanism" (De Sena, 2014, pp. 11–12). De Sena's critique of modernity and modern life is that it has realized part of its promise; that "our post-modern Western culture" (De Sena & Weinberg, 2012, p. 49) and its specialized divisions of labor have made life simpler and easier, to the detriment of the physical and psychological functionality and dexterity deemed necessary for happiness and prosperity. Transformation of bodies and selves that have fallen prey to modern conveniences follows an ascetic encounter with nature. "To feel alive" is the promise and the premise of the Death Race, suffering the corporeal conduit, and nature the eternal bearer of redemption from a life contaminated by modern ills.[5]

Just as Dugger promised in her travel guide, then, Vermont's "sublime" appeal in the Death Race is its reinvigorating naturality, where pristine peaks are held to inhere and bestow a healing quality rendered necessary by the tumult of civilization. De Sena's short migration from New York to Vermont embodies, in these idealized terms, the regressive journey he believes all of us should be making, from city to wilderness, in order to return to a destined path, a primal mode of being, through physical abstinence, exertion, and endurance. "Coming home to yourself at last," as Dugger put it, is not so much a discovery as a renewal or revival of self, made possible—or rather made meaningful—by exertion in the wild, but is akin to Foucault's (1984) understanding of modernity as an "attitude" toward producing the self in which, as we will see, physical culture has long been implicated.[6]

The Death Race was and remains a niche event, limited in its appeal to those with the desire, and various resources and forms of capital, needed to commit to 60 or more consecutive hours of solicited endurance. Despite De Sena's insistence that "anybody could finish this race, but failure always comes when there's a lack of commitment" (as cited in Brick, 2009), he also recognized that something more widely accessible was needed in order to bring his philosophy to "the masses" (De Sena, 2014, p. 10). The proposed corrective would need to depart from the specialized demands of activities such as running or cycling in favor of an all-round "functional excellence." It would need to retain from its precursor an ethic based on personal will power, maximal effort towards overcoming obstacles within and out of the course, and sacrificial suffering in pursuit of a stronger, more dexterous, and so more "successful" body and mind. But it would need to do so on a sufficiently large scale in order to realize their vision of widespread physical and social reform. Obstacle racing is the sport, and the Spartan Race is the iteration that De Sena—leader among the self-proclaimed "Founding Few"—has been championing since 2009.

Invoking Sparta: biography, history, and entangled origins

Through the Spartan Race, De Sena has sought to craft an event and promote a sport in his own self-image, his own ruggedly authentic (auto-)biography, as well as that of ancient Sparta's virile and resolute citizen-soldiery. "[T]he Spartans," De Sena stated in recalling the process of naming his events,

> seemed to personify everything we stood for and everything we conspired against. They were strong, brave, resourceful citizens with no tolerance for bullshit. They were known far and wide for their ability to defeat much larger populations and military forces through force of will.
>
> (De Sena, 2014, pp. 23–24)

As well as a marketing strategy, likely influenced by the success of Zack Snyder's 2007 movie *300*, this invocation of ancient Sparta presents us with an anchoring point for the history and ethos of obstacle racing. Yet perhaps more tellingly, it also betrays and endorses a distinctively Western rendition of history that begins with the ancients of Greek civilization, moves through sequential stages of societal and athletic development (e.g., the renaissance, the reformation, Englightenment, industrialism), and finds in the present a state of decadence—of "overcivilization"—born of the perceived successes and excesses of modernity and modern life.

Hence, across De Sena's accounts, we can trace both a teleological history of the development of obstacle racing, and a nostalgic critique of that history for its apparently degenerative consequences. The former is illustrated in De Sena and Weinberg's "Timeline of Multisport Events" (2012, p. 19) which follows a single, ascendant path, beginning in 708 BCE with the ancient pentathlon at Olympia and thereafter incorporating, for instance, the scattered beginnings of triathlons up until the event's debut in the Sydney Games in 2000, and the development of marathons and ultra-marathons. Other events featured are notable for either sharing with the Spartan Race a functional (holistic) as opposed to specified fitness ethos and apparatus, or for having been professionalized or gained Olympic status in the past century. Despite internal rivalries (Keneally, 2012), they also acknowledge the founding of other mud running events, namely Warrior Dash (2009) and Tough Mudder (2010), at the culmination of a history spanning two and a half millennia. Rather than wait decades, let alone centuries to shift from ritual to record (cf. Guttmann, 1978), De Sena, Weinberg, and the rest of the Spartan Race's "Founding Few" are fast-tracking themselves into the annals of sporting history by association. And by drawing a teleological line of ascent that begins with the virility and tenacity of ancient Spartan lore, recruits the historical landmarks of "multi-sport" and professionalized athletic events, and culminates in the twenty-first century advent of an obstacle racing industry, they are at once mythologizing and credentializing the nascent sport of obstacle racing, and strategically endorsing a Whig history of Western (athletic) development.

The critical view of "Modern" society informs the regressive impulse in mud running. It claims that the divisions and specialization of labor that have accompanied and contoured the development of civilization, and of work and play, have detrimentally distanced us hominids from our hunter-gatherer ancestry. Thus civilization, despite its promise of progress, has resulted in "overcivilization." While the temptation might be to point this out as a contradiction or faultline, in the remainder of this chapter I want not to critique De Sena's philosophy or entwined history of obstacle racing so much as to rework and extend it, and to thereby historicize mud running as part of a lineage that is not acknowledged by him. Indeed, we do not need to hearken back over two millennia to ancient Sparta for analogous athletic philosophies and broader movements towards health, fitness, and social reform. In fact the Spartan Race, as with mud running more broadly, bears a closer resemblance to reform movements and movement practices and ecological upheavals heralding from late nineteenth-century Britain and North America than to those of its antiquitous eponym. What's more, and as we will see, De Sena is not the first self-proclaimed adventurer, reformist, or entrepreneur to uphold the afore-discussed ideals or to narrate a journey of transcendence and purification through embodied practice, and mud running is not the first physical cultural expression of natural sensibilities that harbors moral and biopolitical undertones.

"Overcivilization," functional fitness, and progressive era biopolitics

In the Progressive Decades (1890–1920) in the United States, industrialization, urbanization, and associated social and political changes were apace: nation-building and imperialism were matters of great public interest and political import; and Darwinism and Taylorism had become hugely influential among academics, politicians, managers, and reformers. The growth of physical cultural movements and of adventure-based "wilderness cults" (Nash, 2001), each of which share a great deal with the ethos and infrastructure of mud running as a somatic practice, are enfolded in this period of substantial political and ecological change.

Heightened concerns about the supposedly emasculating effects of civilization, especially for Anglo-Saxon boys, were rife in the Progressive Era. The growth of industrial capitalism and associated proliferation of middle-management jobs in fledgling corporations came to be seen as a source of physical enervation and, by discursive association, encroaching femininity and weakness. The concern was pronounced among middle- and upper-class parents who wanted to ensure that their sons would be (seen as) strong enough to inherit positions of power and authority at a time when "immigrant politicians, articulate suffragists, and powerful monopolists" were viewed as an imminent threat to the political, economic, and social status quo (Putney, 2001, p. 5). We find this attitude most overtly politicized in Theodore Roosevelt's "Strenuous Life" philosophy, a rhetorically deft marriage of athleticism and nationalism insistent that "a healthy state can only exist when the men and women who make it up lead clean, vigorous, healthy lives; when the children are so trained that they shall endeavor, not to shirk difficulties, but overcome them" (1899, cited in Briedlid, Brogger, Gulliksen, & Sirevag, 1996, pp. 377–378; see also Smith Maguire, 2008, p. 30). Roosevelt's own physical transformation "from a sickly house-bound teenager into the rough-riding, safari-going, big-stick wielding Bull Moose of legend" (Putney, 2001, p. 5) conveyed this aspirational model of masculinity, leadership, and colonial conquest to American youth. Overcoming adversity through ascetic grit and determination was a potent political and physical cultural trope then as now, though the appeal to cleanliness (as next to godliness), as opposed to the appeal of dirtiness in mud running, is a telling shift.

The proposed antidote to the "overcivilizing" of Anglo-Saxon Americans was, as Roosevelt embodied and encouraged, a healthy and manly dose of "articifical exercise, outdoor camping, and other methods of strengthening America's elite" (Putney, 2001, p. 4). In other words, an invigorating bout of exposure-to-nature for white male youth, intended to foster strength and survival skills during adolescence and, in the long term, to rescue and secure the future of the boy, American manhood, and the nation. Muscular Christianity was the most influential movement to implement these beliefs, and gained traction in North America after its mid-nineteenth-century diffusion from Britain (accompanied by its most renowned and enduring institution, the YMCA). These adventurous exercises in supposedly premodern and preindustrial labor and living were never meant to be necessitated by the boys in later life; they were rites of passage in pursuit of personal strength, moral hygiene, and national virility *en route* to wielding power in administrative positions. Physical exertion was viewed as a conduit for a kind of managerial excellence, and nature an invigorating resource in its service.

Echoes of this "overcivilizing" thesis are heard in mud running's opposition to specialized leisure such as (only) running or (only) cycling, and labor, especially the kinds of enervating, office-bound work that so alarmed Progressive Era politicians, pastors, and reformers. Whereas athletic practices and white-collar work are each held to be individualistic and isolating, obstacle courses require and engender collaboration, and are varied in the composition of respective courses and the physical demands of different obstacles. They are thus said to produce a more "functional," all-round fitness and dexterity, transferable to the "real world." The Spartan Race, as our example, comprises a series (or *trifecta*) of standardized, timed obstacle courses set at three distance and difficulty levels: The 5 km Spartan "Sprint," the 10 km Spartan "Super," and the 21 km Spartan "Beast." The obstacles in each course include climbing ropes, traversing balance beams, throwing spears at targets, navigating cargo nets, and other such assemblies of movement practice, bodies, and fitness technologies. This emphasis on variety and accessibility is a direct response to prevailing trends towards specialization.

In this way, mud running event founders are responding to one of the criticisms also made of nineteenth-century physical culture: That the "dullness of repetitive training" (Markschukat, 2011, 481) as prescribed by doctors, physicians, and reformists, would fail to maintain the enthusiasm of practitioners.[7] When De Sena and Weinberg (2012) declared their "desire to extend the exhaustion and exhilaration of extreme, adventure, and endurance racing to a million people who would never attempt many of the events the Founding Few had conquered" (p. 31), the twinned invocation of exhaustion *and* exhilaration is an attempt to harmonize the imperative of enduring pain and suffering in overcoming obstacles, and the existential, childlike pleasure associated with frolicking in dirt with friends and family. Together the aim is to incentivize exercise that is fun and fearsome, painful and productive. Indeed one of the most prominent tensions in the mud running industry is between asceticism and hedonism, as is broadly evident in the standardized, competitive, and rule-governed Spartan Race, and its more outlandish, playful, and parodic rival Tough Mudder.

Mud running's popularity suggests that "overcivilization" remains a concern for those who imply modern life to have become "too separate" from nature, and valorize practices—such as the Spartan Race—deemed to offset the enervating (and so "emasculating") effects of modern conveniences, "white collar" labor, and a life that is somehow "too easy." Just as managerial excellence was foregrounded by Progressive Era reformers, mud running is popular as a means of building "morale" among office co-workers, as has been the case for some time in adventure racing (Kay & Theberge, 2002). Obstacle courses also have related appeal as a material-metaphor for capitalism's ostensibly moral reward system, whereby success is directly proportionate to work ethic (Lamb & Hillman, 2015). Class, however, isn't the only, less still the central mode of distinction enacted in either mud running or Progressive Era biopolitics. For one of the most telling recuperations in mud running's ongoing historicity, we must focus our attention on nineteenth-century ideas about the division of labor, and their relation to evolutionism, progress, and human development.

Social Darwinism, adventure, and human nature

Mattelart (1997) described the prevailing discourse of late nineteenth-century Europe and North America as being based on a "biological paradigm," one that curiously "borrowed from political economy" (p. 54) in its production of evolutionary understandings of nature and society. In a "circuitous route" (p. 54), those theorizing the historical development of societies as one of teleological diffusion from a single origin, or cell, would in turn take from the life sciences advanced by the biological paradigm. This same period also witnessed a broad, related shift from cultural (and so malleable) to biological (and so inescapable) understandings of "race" and operations of scientific racism (Anderson, 2007). How are these developments related to the physical culture of the time, and in what ways are they implicated in mud running's genealogy?

Late nineteenth-century expeditions into "wild" nature, and their apparent necessity due to "overcivilization," indicated a significant fissure in the prevailing views on "race," human nature, and progress. Implicit in the notion of "overcivilization" is that the project of civilization, with its optimistic vision of science and reason as twinned beacons that would lead all of humankind to its destined ends, had been checked by the socio-political upheavals and associated physical ills of the time. It seemed that industrialization and rationality alone might not pave an unobscured path towards prosperity. The corollary that environmental nature might serve as an antidote to the afore-discussed ills of civilization for physical health held consequences for some of the keystone, racialized assumptions of eighteenth-century Enlightenment thought (Anderson, 2007; Goldberg, 1993). Specifically, the Enlightenment belief in teleological progress and human unity—that different "races" are simply at different stages of cultural development on the way to transcending their "wild" roots, but all will breach the immaturity of nature and divinity at some point—was challenged by the depleting effects of industrial capitalism for physical health. Putney (2001) bluntly summarized the dilemma facing Anglo-Saxon American parents concerned by "overcivilization" in the Progressive Era: "On the one hand they want to encourage primitiveness in their sons. On the other hand they want to deplore primitiveness in other cultures" (p. 6). How to advocate for nature-retreat exercises as manly and healthy in order to secure and retain virtue, prestige, and power for the individual and the nation, without conceding the discursively-constituted currency of a racialized taxonomy of difference? To put the dilemma another way, how to publicly recognize an affinity between virility and primitiveness—between strength and nature—while continually asserting the correlation of "closeness-to-nature," weakness, and inferiority?

The solution was manifest in social Darwinism, enjoying its heyday in the Progressive Era before being largely—or at least scientifically—discredited in the early twentieth century. Interpretations of Darwin's insights in *Origin of Species*, most (in)famously popularized as a social doctrine by Herbert Spencer, enabled the assertion that some "races" were in fact mired in their natures while others (namely white males such as those doing the interpretative work) can benefit from wild and rural exposures *en route* to civility (see Anderson, 2007).[8] The irony of Darwinism in this respect is that it dealt a wound to the conceit of human exceptionalism by positing a fundamental kinship between people and other animals (Haraway, 2008), yet inadvertently served to propagate a racial ideology by lending credence to the biological destiny of racially-segregated groups. The Enlightenment ideal of linear progress and uneven development among "races" toward a common, humanitarian end was challenged through this confluent emergence of evolutionary theory, and its uptake in accordance with the political, ecological, and nationalistic concerns of the now self-appointed "native" white American populous.[9] Thus an appeal of social Darwinism was that it leant ostensibly scientific credence to nature-retreats as a kind of treatment for "overcivilized" boys, without conceding the futility of civility as a racially-determined marker of natural superiority.

The popularity of adventure-sports in nineteenth-century Europe and North America, and the associated rise of "wilderness cults" (Nash, 2001)—also part of mud running's genealogy—are enfolded in these social, scientific, and political developments. As Ray (2009) documented, nineteenth-century wilderness adventure sports such as alpine climbing were "not just about communing with nature and testing the body. Rather, [they were] a direct response to social instability and nation-building during the Progressive Era" whereby, ironically, "American civilization could be advanced by 'going native' (Huhndorf, 2001)—practicing wilderness survival exercises, such as hunting, living 'off the land,' and eschewing modernity's conveniences" (Ray, 2009, p. 258). Ray called this the "corporeal unconscious" of adventure sports, a term denoting that contemporary risk and adventure sports culture "enacts many of these racial, gendered, and classist exclusions of the nineteenth-century wilderness movement" (p. 259), albeit in ways that enthusiasts might not necessarily recognize, express, or (want to) see themselves in. When the whiteness of adventure sports is recognized, it is often as an acknowledgement that enthusiasts are, predominantly, "white." What Ray highlighted to great effect is that adventure sports are themselves are invested with an attitude towards nature and the body, a "corporeal unconscious," that both echoes through De Sena's biography and the ascetic ethos of "overcoming obstacles" in the Spartan Race, and bears the trace of the historical, social, and political enfoldings in which these activities took shape.

De Sena and Weinberg's conviction that humans are an innately "competitive species" (2012, p. 18) is striking for its resonance with the social Darwinist doctrine that was so prominent in the Progressive Era. Indeed these two echo the claims of those (often misguided) health reformers of the time, such as Martin Luther Holbrook, who compelled the public to "[t]ake a part in your own evolution" (as cited in Whorton, 1982, p. 156) through a will to self-improvement; that is, through physical activity, nutrition, and hygiene. Moreover, De Sena and Weinberg lament the onset of civilization for producing widespread decadence and physical enervation, and proclaim the antidote to be a (re)turn to a "premodern" form of physical activity that has both a moral imperative and evolutionary significance; one in which exertion among dirt in pursuit of excellence is the "right" thing to do with one's body as individuals and as a species. And dirt, or mud, is discursively recruited here as virile and masculine, and as a challenge to those who quest after a renewed and revived sense of self, rather than for its associations with, for example, fertility and "Mother Earth." Mud in mud running becomes " 'the mud' of everyday life, the stuff that drags us down, or at least tries to" (De Sena, 2014, p. 6), *en route* to recovery, success, and above all, overcoming life's difficulties.

What bears emphasis is that the overt modes of exclusion (such as scientific racism) that informed those nineteenth-century adventure-based practices associated with social Darwinism, or the physical cultural philosophies and practices conjectured by hygienists, reformists, and politicians of the Progressive and Jacksonian Eras, are not simply mirrored in mud running. What prevails in events like the Spartan Race is a kind of relentless positivity that works to efface any "whining," pessimism, or contemplation that would impede the overcoming of obstacles, literal or metaphorical. The Spartan Race is infused with a philosophy through which unfettered will power and strong-mindedness can overcome all circumstances, however historically entrenched, physically inhibiting, psychologically traumatic, or culturally enforced. This philosophy is materialized by and through the infrastructure of the obstacle course itself: predetermined, linear, measurable, and so constituting—like so many other sports and physical culture practices—a misleadingly simplistic and egalitarian, and yet in a compelling sense individually empowering material metaphor for social life. It taps into a humanistic spirit of inspiration, a naturalistic ethic, and the all-conquering power of the will that is *en vogue* in late twentieth and twenty-first century fitness trends such as CrossFit (Herz, 2014), and foregrounded in the promotional strategies of leading apparel brands such as the Spartan Race's sponsor, Reebok, and Tough Mudder's commercial partner, Under Armour. It yearns for premodernity only in order to get back to a mythical future unencumbered by contouring culture, sedating technology, and specialized physical comportments. In doing so, De Sena, Weinberg, and those who harbor this worldview display "the uncritical tendency for 'civilised man' to reclaim a 'lost primordiality,' an otherness and origin that call up the wounds of 'alienation from nature' " (Anderson, 2007, p. 13).

Mud running histories yet to come

Keeping apace with the beginnings of mud running is a full-time endeavor. I am writing at a time of especial upheaval, one where the mud running moniker may be giving way to obstacle course racing, or obstacle racing, as part of a familiar design headed towards professionalization and perhaps even Olympic status. But that is the remit of the Spartan Race founders, and not one that is universally shared by other event owners and mud running aficionados.

As a case in point, two milestone broadcasts signpost different, though not necessarily antithetical paths that could inform mud running's future, and (re) define its history. On December 7, 2013, the NBC sports network televised the Spartan Race World Championships, an event that had taken place three months prior among the mountainous terrain of Killington, Vermont. On December 8 of the same weekend, Tough Mudder was the feature of MTV's *True Life* television series. The former development is a step towards realizing De Sena's vision for the professionalization and standardization of obstacle racing, and is supported and embodied by elite athletes such as Hobie Call, Amelia Boone, and Hunter McIntyre who vie for prize money and sponsorship in the Spartan Race, and other leading events, across North America. By some contrast, Tough Mudder's business model and promotional culture are built around "camaraderie" and teamwork, parodic, masculinist humor, and satirical suffering, as found in spectacular "obstacles" involving electricity and fire with names like "balls to the wall" and "trench warfare." True to entrepreneurial form, De Sena's take on Tough Mudder is not subtle:

> It's not timed, so it's not a race and not treated like a sport—it's more like a friendly get-together at a bar or a birthday party.... We do not define ourselves with mud; we define ourselves with obstacles, and our obstacles are not just going to electrocute people. There's nothing athletic about being electrocuted.
>
> (De Sena, 2013)

Here De Sena took a strategic stance on the tension between work and play, labor and leisure, and revised his view on mud in order to emphasize a competitive distinction.[10] Nonetheless, as is the case with most such rivalries, the events are quicker to stress their differences than all they hold in common, and Tough Mudder foregrounds the same "will to overcome" that characterizes the Spartan Race.

An alternative history might have sketched these more recent developments and rivalries endemic to the mud running industry, such as the controversy surrounding Tough Mudder's origins following the accusations, and subsequent court case, brought forward by the UK's 30-year-old Tough Guy event (Keneally, 2012). Or, given the focus on the Spartan Race here, there was also scope to plot links with CrossFit and other affiliated aspects of contemporary fitness culture in North America. I have instead sought to show that mud running's popularity is not simply an *en vogue* expression of American fitness culture, as if fitness and culture were themselves social abstracts. Nor is mud running simply an appeal to an authentically competitive and athletic human nature, although this narrative of transcendence and purification is, as De Sena recognized, clearly entwined with its contemporary appeal. Rather, it seems that mud running is premised on an attitude to bodies in and of nature recuperated from the nineteenth century, through which the dynamic of reclaiming and breaking with the past characterizes the spirit of modernity, the renaissance of (interest in) physical culture, and the *esprit de corps* of the focal practice. Perhaps it is this attitude—of breaking with and reclaiming the past, inventing new senses of self by redeeming ancient notions of what it means to be human, and seeking in nature a revitalizing antidote and an elemental adversary amid the ostensibly degenerative effects of modern life—that gives mud running its remarkable cultural currency in the early twenty-first century.

Notes

1 These were by no means the first commercial iterations of the mud running genre. For example, in Keneally's (2012) exposé in *Outside Magazine*, entitled *Playing Dirty*, he framed Tough Mudder's commercial success as a cut-throat capitalist heist at the expense of the United Kingdom's longer standing "Tough Guy" mud run, as well as detailing the enmity between event founders within the industry.

2 As with marathons and related endurance sports, the majority of heats feature not only competitive runners but a composition of participants—office workers, weekend warriors, locally-based running groups, curious researchers—whose motivations, intentions, and attire, are together more eclectic than their elite counterparts.

3 Both of the latter are so named after the 1st Earl of Chatham, William Pitt, whose reign as British Prime Minister preceded the chartering of Vermont's Pittsfield in 1781, before the drafting and ratification of the US constitution.

4 Further details about the Death Race, including its recent expansion, can be found at the morbidly intriguing youmaydie.com.

5 A similar argument is made by Le Breton (2000) in his stirring anthropology of extreme and endurance sports at the turn of the last century. Le Breton claims that these events are about the individual pursuit of meaning in a world where stable referents for identification are increasingly difficult to find.

6 Reading Baudelaire, Foucault (1984) proposed that "Modern man [*sic*]" is "not the man who goes off to discover himself, his secrets and his hidden truth; he is the man who tries to invent himself. This modernity does not 'liberate man in his own being'; it compels him to face the task of producing himself" (p. 42).

7 The concern, specifically, was that rational, task-oriented programs of physical culture prescribed by physicians and popular cultural sources would soon lead to boredom, even if the physical benefits were manifest (see Martschukat, 2011, p. 483).

8 This is not to absolve Darwin entirely. He was, as Mattelart (1997) has said, "a man of his time," a "subject of the Victorian empire" who had written of his travels on board the *Beagle* that "it is impossible for an Englishman to behold these distant colonies without a high pride and satisfaction" (p. 77).

9 Posthumanist scholars have suggested that this shift from cultural to biological modes of racial identification recasts the Enlightenment less as a project or a destined journey, and more as a reflexive question about what it means, and what it takes, to be human (Anderson, 2007; Foucault, 1984).

10 This tension found expression in the Spartan Race when, in 2014, the company announced that "elite heats" should not feature participants in unbefitting costume, inciting debate among aficionados as to the overarching ethos of the practice.

References

Anderson, K. (2007). *Race and the crisis of humanism*. London, England: Routledge.

Beresini, E. (2014, May 11). Obstacle course racing: The next Olympic event? *Outside Magazine Online*. Retrieved from www.outsideonline.com/1923871/obstacle-course-racing-next-olympic-event.

Bramble, D. M., & Lierberman, D. E. (2004). Endurance running and the evolution of Homo. *Nature, 432*, 345–352.

Brick, M. (2009, July 6). You created it, tough guy. So let's see you finish it. *New York Times*. Retrieved from www.nytimes.com/2009/07/07/sports/07deathrace.html?pagewanted=all.

Briedlid, A., Brogger, F. C., Gulliksen, O. T., & Sirevag, T. (1996). *American culture: An anthology of civilization texts*. London, England: Taylor Francis.

De Sena, J., & Weinberg, A. (2012). *You'll know at the finish line: A Spartan guide to the sport of obstacle racing*. Spartan Press.

De Sena, J. (2013). *Spartan Race Vs. Tough Mudder: Which makes you the bigger badass?* Retrieved from http://guycodeblog.mtv.com/2013/01/18/spartan-vs-tough-mudder/.

De Sena, J. (2014). *Spartan up! A take-no-prisoners guide to overcoming obstacles and achieving peak performance in life*. New York, NY: Houghton Mifflin Harcourt.

Dugger, E. (2000). *Adventure guide to Vermont (2nd Edition)*. New Jersey, NJ: Hunter Publishing.

Foucault, M. (1984). What is enlightenment? In P. Rabinow (Ed.), *The Foucault reader* (pp. 32–50). New York, NY: Pantheon.

Gandy, M. (2003). *Concrete and clay: Reworking nature in New York City*. Cambridge, MA: MIT Press.

Goldberg, D. T. (1993). *Racist culture: Philosophy and the politics of meaning*. Cambridge, MA: Blackwell.

Guttmann, A. (1978). *From ritual to record: The nature of modern sports*. New York, NY: Columbia University Press.

Haraway, D. (1989). Teddy Bear patriarchy: Taxidermy in the Garden of Eden, New York City, 1908–1936. In D. Haraway (Ed.), Primate visions: Gender, race, and nature in the world of modern science (pp. 26–58). New York, NY: Routledge.

Haraway, D. J. (2008). *When species meet*. Minneapolis, MN: University of Minnesota Press.

Herz, J. C. (2014). *Learning to breath fire: The rise of Crossfit and the primal future of fitness*. New York: Crown Publishing.

Huhndorf, S. (2001). *Going native: Indians in the American cultural imagination*. Ithaca, NY: Cornell University Press.

Keneally, S. (2013, November). Dirty playing. *Outside Magazine*.

Kumar, K. (2005). *From post-industrial to post-modern society* (Second Edition). Oxford, England: Blackwell.

Le Breton, D. (2000). Playing symbolically with death in extreme sports. *Body & Society, 6*, 1–11.

Martschukat, J. (2011). "The necessity for better bodies to perpetuate our institutions, insure a higher development of the individual, and advance the conditions of the race." Physical Culture and the formation of the self in late nineteenth and early twentieth century USA. *Journal of Historical Sociology, 24*, 472–493.

Nash, R. F. (2001). *Wilderness and the American mind* (4th Edition). New Haven, CT: Yale University Press.

Putney, C. (2001). *Muscular Christianity. Manhood and sports in Protestant America, 1880–1920*. Cambridge, MA: Harvard University Press.

Ray, S. (2009). Risking bodies in the wild: The "corporeal unconscious" of American adventure culture. *Journal of Sport and Social Issues, 33*, 257–284.

Rodriguez, M. (2014). *Obstacle race world: The state of the Mud Run business*. Copyright Melissa Rodriguez.

Smith Maguire, J. (2008). *Fit for consumption: Sociology and the business of fitness*. London, England: Routledge.

Stein, J. D. (2012, December 1). Extreme obstacle course races forge a bond in mud and guts. *New York Times*.

Vertinsky, P. (2002). The erotic gaze, violence, and "Booters with Hooters." *Journal of Sport History, 29(3)*, 387–394.

Vertinsky, P. (in press). Modernism and physical culture. In S. Ross (Ed.), *Routledge encyclopedia of modernism*. London, England: Routledge.

Whorton, J. (1982). *Crusaders for fitness. The history of American health reformers*. Princeton, NJ: Princeton University Press.

4 Charting the development of contemporary endurance running training theory

Joseph P. Mills and Jim Denison

It is widely understood that the modern sport we know today developed in the nineteenth century out of very specific historical circumstances (Andrews, 2000; Struna, 2001). Entering the nineteenth century the elite classes had become aware that extreme wealth awaited them if the inefficiencies of the past could be shaken off. However, the route to this extreme wealth through the processes of rapid industrialization and urbanization led to a host of social problems. Cramped living conditions, long working days, chronic hunger and malnutrition, poor sanitation, a de-skilled and disaffected labour force, and a society dominated by civil disobedience and disruption became the realities of life. Not only were these problems seen as unjust and dehumanizing, they also interfered with the creation of wealth. For the purposes of our analysis here, sport became seen as an activity that could reverse these problems and ensure that society remained on track to achieve its grand new aim: the unabashed pursuit of profit. For example, organized sport was used to teach the poor how to be productive and to give men a place to play to relieve their aggressive impulses (Burstyn, 1999; Coakley, 2009; Hobsbawm, 1975; Holt, 1989; Mangan, 1973). In this way, sport began to resemble work more and more. In other words, as one way for society to ensure the successful pursuit of profit, sport became increasingly characterized by mechanization, specialization, and efficiency. Thus by the last half of the nineteenth century the athleticization and industrialization of everyday life had become parallel and interconnected developments that underpinned the values of a maturing and stable capitalist society (Burstyn, 1999).

Further supporting and legitimating the rapid changes taking place in modern society was a new found belief in the power of science as the one arbiter of truth to provide "guaranteed" explanations about the world. For example, motor learning and control initially developed as a way of selecting the most suitable pilots for training in the U.S. Air Force during the World War II (Schmidt & Lee, 2005). Furthermore, as a direct result of the guarantees that science afforded modern society, individuals began to explore the limits of their potential and the pursuit of sheer performance across a number of realms intensified (Bale, 2003). Modern society adopted a general wonder at just how far (wo)man could progress—climbing Everest, walking on the Moon, exploring the Poles, and even running one mile in under four minutes all became "natural" obsessions.

So it was that science's assumptions aligned with society's new profit-driven, efficient, specialized, mechanistic, and performative aims and ambitions. These conditions began to form a number of complex interactions between the context of modernity, the power of capitalism, and the scientific knowledge of the body.

The growing competitiveness, commercialism, and appeal of sport in the twentieth century was also driven by heightened tensions rising out of an inhospitable West versus East Cold War climate. Within this climate success at the Olympics Games, for example, became much more important than fostering national pride; gold medals also vindicated and legitimized a nation's ideology. Victory in sport proved that a nation's entire constellation of foundational beliefs was not just supreme but legitimate and natural. In other words, sport was not just about athletes competing in global events: it was about competition between socio-cultural systems. And out of this context, the East led the way in terms of designing systematic and scientific approaches to sports training, leaving the West with no choice but to respond in equally systematic and scientific ways. So it was, according to Andrews (2008), that sport's rising political utility led to greater governmental oversight and accountability over athletes' and coaches' training practices. Thus, rather than being based on any inherent truthfulness, approaches to coaching and athlete development were actually the result of the *zeitgeist* of the modern era: a nationalistic outlook on the world that circulated rational and scientifically based knowledges, technologies, and institutions (Andrews, 2000). In other words, coaching became a political and scientific process with the intention of producing a specific performance outcome. In this way, sports coaching moved from a passionate pastime to a scientific process based around the co-ordination and integration of a series of pre-defined steps—a set of building blocks. In line with this sentiment, Huizinga (1972) observed, "an element of mechanization enter[ed] sport . . . [as] we see free youthful forces and courage reduced to normality and uniformity in the service of the machinery of rules of play and the competitive system" (pp. 115–116).

One sport that very clearly reflected the increased control of the coach over an athlete's preparation was endurance running. Accordingly, approaches to coaching endurance runners that might appear to be innovative or inspired by a coach's genius actually emerged out of a specific cultural understanding or definition of what effective endurance running coaches should do. To illustrate this point, we discuss in what follows six iconic endurance running coaches whose training methods have had a significant impact on the development of contemporary endurance running coaching. However, as we intend to make clear, when viewed through a socio-cultural/historical lens there was little that was original or pioneering about these coaches' training methods. Rather, their methods were more a result of the new scientific assumptions and profit-driven aims and ambitions that pervaded modern society in its progressive quests. All of which leads us to ask: how advanced and how authentically true is endurance running training theory? To answer this question, we begin the fashioning of our particular history of endurance running training, and an analysis of the coaches who played a significant part in the formation of this history, with the Swedish coach Gustav Holmer.

Gustav Holmer. By the early twentieth century the fastest endurance runners in the world were from Finland. Of particular note was Paavo Nurmi, the Flying Finn, who broke 22 world records and won 12 Olympic medals (nine gold). Nurmi's athletic career significantly developed during his military service, when indulged by his senior officers, he was allowed to take time from his military training to engage in sport training (Bourne, 2009). Nurmi was also known for his inventive training methods such as running in heavy army boots to develop his leg strength and running behind a train while holding onto the rear bumper to elongate his stride (Bale, 2003).

Frustrated by the Finnish supremacy in endurance running, the Swedish national coach, Gustav Holmer, visited Finland to observe Nurmi train. Following his observations, and in an effort to adapt Nurmi's understanding of training to the rugged Swedish forest landscape, Holmer devised a method of training that mixed hard and easy efforts. This mixing of running efforts came to be known as *fartlek* or speed-play. As a result, according to Mollet, a prominent Belgian track official who closely observed the development of fartlek, "a window was opened in the forest, and at the same time an idea of training emerged which one could classify as 'happy'" (as cited in Wilt, 1959, p. 97). But as Mollet also said, fartlek became a means by which the athlete could experience "severe training" (as cited in Wilt, 1959, p. 97). And as far as Mollet was concerned, the whole point about severe training was its impact on one's ability to run fast. As testament to this, under Holmer Sweden produced two athletes whose rivalry lowered the world mile record five times during the 1940s: Gunder Hägg and Arne Andersen.

Although the term speed-play implied that fartlek should be fun or joyous, in reality it was a harsh form of training. And importantly it was fartlek's harshness or toughness and not its playfulness that was credited for Hägg's and Andersen's success. Furthermore, the more important running efforts that made up a fartlek workout, that is the speedier parts, were rarely spontaneous. Rather, they were almost always organized around fixed and static markers or points within the forest (e.g., the top of a hill, a specific tree). Not only that, these harder efforts typically occurred on the smoothest surfaces of the forest that lent itself to faster, safer, and more efficient speeds. In Wilt's (1959), *How They Train*, a typical fartlek session of Hägg's was described in the following way:

> An uphill run, running on level terrain, a downhill run, a full speed 800 meter run on level ground, another uphill run, downhill relaxed running, full speed striding with mixed sprints on a level area and finishing with an uphill run of even speed.
>
> (pp. 27–28)

In other words, while fartlek training was supposed to be free and spontaneous, the hardest efforts were almost always measured and largely coach controlled—a physically demanding and controlled "spontaneity." Therefore, it is hardly surprising that today, fartlek is conceived by coaches in structured and controlled terms because, as in the case of Hägg and Andersen, the "real" running efforts are seen as needing to occur over a defined distance. Thus, the key point to emerge from Holmer's conception of fartlek training was that endurance running needed to be severe and physically demanding—a place for controlling man's aggression (Burstyn, 1999). As a result, the right way to train endurance runners began to form around a number of dominant social ideals (read capitalist) related to toughness, strength, and perseverance. In this sense, endurance running also began to resemble work as flogging oneself in the factory and in training became part of the same formation.

Dr. Woldemar Gerschler and Dr. Herbert Reindell. Despite the regulated nature of fartlek training, there was still a strong conception that it was unregulated. Or at the very least, fartlek training was seen as not being as controlled as training could be in an era where more and more aspects of life were becoming subject to control through the application of specific scientific principles. As a result, the pre-war scientist/endurance running coach Dr. Woldemar Gerschler, a Professor of Physical Education at Freiburg University, sought out scientific support for his coaching from the cardiologist, Dr. Herbert Reindell.

Working together, Gerschler and Reindell hypothesized that in running a hard effort for a set distance and time, an athlete's heart rate would rise to 170–180 beats per minute (bpm) and that he (they only worked with men) would be ready to run hard again once his heart rate dropped to 120–125 bpm. Thus, by manipulating the distance run, the interval of the recovery, the number of repetitions run, the speed of the run, and what took place during the recovery, a runner would experience a specific training effect. More specifically, they argued, through such regulated training efforts the expanded abilities or capacities of the cell and organ systems would enable the body to better process oxygen and so provide more energy: energy that in turn would propel the endurance runner to faster performances. And so it was that physiology began to shape endurance running coaches' understanding of how to train the endurance running body.

This form of training that Gerschler and Reindell "invented" became known as interval training because of the importance of the rest interval in bringing about the training effect. Importantly, Gerschler and Reindell "proved" the validity of interval training by improving the fitness of 3,000 Austrian soldiers who were preparing to fight in World War II (Thompson, *personal communication*). Thus, the key point to emerge from Gerschler and Reindell's conception of interval training was that endurance running training needed to be scientific. In this sense, endurance running training, alongside the workplace, entered the laboratory as more and more endurance running coaches' training protocols began to form around a bio-energetic conception of performance through an understanding of the body as a machine.

Percy Cerruty and Franz Stampfl. Percy Cerruty and Franz Stampfl were two of the most iconic endurance running coaches in the 1950s and 1960s. Stampfl coached Ralph Doubell, the 1968 Olympic 800m champion, but more significantly he was an advisor to Roger Bannister, the first person to run under four minutes for the mile. As an Austrian, Stampfl was significantly influenced by Gerschler's interval training methods. As such, he believed that an endurance runner's training should be based on a measured and precisely controlled progression of intense running. More specifically, Stampfl believed it was especially important to time his athletes' repetitions (Stampfl also only coached men) in order to monitor their progressions. Thus, an unequivocal emphasis or understanding of *cause-and-effect* (read quasi-scientific) began to take hold between the workouts a coach designed and his athletes' performances (Stampfl, 1955).

The great rival to Stampfl was the Australian coach Percy Cerruty, who coached a small band of male runners, most notably Herb Elliot, the world record-holder for both the 1,500 m and the mile and the 1960 Olympic 1,500 m champion. Cerruty's training plans were based on his philosophy of toughening the body in a natural environment, or what he referred to as stotanism (Cerruty, 1959). In a seeming contrast to Stampfl, for Cerruty endurance training should not be so coach controlled. Rather, running efforts should be more spontaneous, uninhibited, unfixed, and unregimented. In other words, the athlete should be able to discipline himself in training to tolerate the intense pain and discomfort that accompanied running fast and not worry about hitting specific times in training. In this overtly disciplined way, Cerruty was more concerned about the development of his athletes' state of mind, "their sporting conscience" (Phillips & Hicks, 2000, p. 19), and as a result rarely used a stopwatch to measure their progress.

Although Cerruty's training methods were intended to encourage athletes to be free and creative, in reality what they experienced in their training was an unrelenting discipline, so much so that many runners left Cerruty due to his overbearing nature, including John Landy, the second man to run under four minutes for the mile. Only through concentrated and focussed discipline to such physical demands could the endurance body be adequately "toughened" to cope with the demands of competition. Thus, although stotanism was Cerruty's philosophy that he developed from Greek history, it was very much a modern ideal designed to embody not just disciplined toughness, but sensitive self-sufficiency, independence and progress—by becoming stronger one became better (Sims, 2003). Thus, while Cerruty encouraged his athletes to read philosophy and poetry, his training program was infused with a series of overtly disciplining rules, such as no alcohol, no water with meals, no white bread, and no socializing after midnight (Sims, 2005). Accordingly, the key points to emerge from Stampfl's and Cerruty's conception of endurance running training was that despite their apparent originality and contrasting training philosophies—liberty versus constraint—in actuality their methods further extolled the virtues of different elements within the same overarching modernistic themes of progress through science, personal sacrifice, and *extremely* hard work (Phillips & Hicks, 2000).

Roger Bannister. Although Roger Bannister was an athlete best known for being the first person to run under four minutes for a mile, he was largely self-coached. On the verge of ending his running career following his disappointing fourth place finish in the 1,500 m at the 1952 Olympics, Bannister set himself *the* challenge of the twentieth century: to run the first sub-four minute mile. As an Oxford medical student, Bannister had limited time to train and so to compensate he increased the intensity of his workouts. However, by the end of 1953 Bannister still felt he lacked the requisite stamina to break four minutes. To help move his training forward he reluctantly sought the advice of Franz Stampfl, who coached his friend, Chris Brasher. Importantly, to run under four minutes Bannister had reasoned that he needed to be able to complete a workout where he averaged running 59 seconds for ten laps with a lap jog in between each repetition. With Stampfl's help, by the winter of 1954 Bannister was able to run every one of his ten repetitions in 61 seconds—a carefully measured progression. However, his progress soon stalled. Frustrated by this, Bannister took a rock-climbing holiday to Wales to escape the intensity of his training. Upon his return near the end of April he completed his ten repetitions in 59 seconds each. And on May 4 he ran 3:59.4.

In a historical analysis of Bannister's achievement, Kruger (2006) made the observation that while scientists had for the most part coached all the leading endurance athletes prior to Bannister (e.g., Gerschler and Reindell) Bannister *was* a scientist. In other words, while running under four minutes for the mile had been a realistic goal for many runners—Hägg and Andersen had lowered the world record from 4:06 to 4:01 between 1942 and 1944—it was specifically Bannister's scientific approach to endurance running training that enabled him to do it. Not only that, and perhaps more significantly, it wasn't any science that Bannister was an expert in: it was medicine.

Armed with his medical knowledge, Bannister began to control the volume and intensity of his workouts with great care and precision. Based on this rational approach, Kruger (2006) argued, Bannister was able to combine a number of precise training methods—interval training, time-trials, *and* rest—to ensure he was in peak physical condition on the day he needed to be. Thus, the key point to emerge from Bannister's approach to endurance running training was that through a more sophisticated application of science even greater control could be exercised over an athlete's progress and development. And it was in this scientifically controlled way, according to Kruger, that Bannister became recognized as an athlete who was truly ahead of his time.

Lev Matveyev. Similar to Bannister, Lev Matveyev was not strictly speaking an endurance running coach, but a sports training theorist. However, his work has arguably had a greater influence on the development of endurance running training theory than anyone before or after him. By the beginning of the 1970s, the athletes who had had the most global success in track and field were all from the Eastern Bloc. While much of this success has now been credited to systematic doping protocols, there can be no denying Matveyev's impact through his training model that came to be known as periodization (Matveyev, 1981).

To develop his model of periodization, Matveyev analyzed the performances and training of thousands of top Soviet athletes from a range of sports, such as track and field, swimming, and weight lifting. Included in Matveyev's theory was a wide and diverse range of topics, such as philosophy, sociology, aesthetics, ethics, biophysics, biochemistry, and tactics. However, the primary message that Western coaches took from Matveyev's model was that athletes' training needed to be divided and organized into *specific* periods of time, or cycles. Matveyev modelled his cyclical organization of athletes' training after the Soviet government's plans for yearly industrial production—an efficiency that was effective for its control.

A further influence on Matveyev was the publication in 1956 of Hans Selye's, *The Stress of Life*. This was a ground breaking text in which life was conceived as a process of adaptation stimulated by the specific circumstances of one's environment. And Matveyev saw no reason why these adaptive processes couldn't be structured and planned to produce the effects one desired. Thus, athletes' training cycles began to be broken into various series comprised of optimal volumes, intensities and densities each with specific adaptive aims. Moreover, this series of training cycles, according to Matveyev, could be calculated precisely in advance of an athlete's training year so that his or her peak fitness could be timed to coincide with the most important competitions of the year (e.g., the Olympic Games).

Briefly, within Matveyev's periodization model, a training year or *macrocycle* was divided into three smaller periods of time called *mesocycles*. The first of these mesocycles was further broken into two smaller phases, a general preparation phase that was characterized by a gradual increase in volume and intensity and a specific preparation phase that incorporated more specialized training designed to match the specific needs of an athlete's sport. This first mesocycle typically lasted between five and seven months, and was followed by the second mesocycle, the competitive period, that lasted approximately four months. The final mesocycle of the training year, which lasted between three and six weeks, focused on recovery and regeneration so that athletes would be ready to resume training at the start of the next macrocycle. Within each mesocycle there were also smaller periods of time that lasted anywhere from a week to ten days. These cycles were called microcycles and were further divided into specific categories of work ranging from "general" to "special preparatory" to "pre-competition" to "competition."

Thus, the key point to emerge from Matveyev's periodization model was that training needed to be structured in logically systematic ways based on the athlete's physical condition and the calendar year. In addition, prior to Matveyev, endurance running coaches had almost entirely focussed on the bio-energetic or physiological qualities of their athletes. However, following Matveyev, elements such as strength training, nutrition, and psychology were also seen as important for the coach to manage and control. As a result, the grip coaches held on their athletes through a scientific understanding of the body and performance tightened even more—which, given the West's critique of the East's state controlled regimes, was an ironic state of affairs.

Peter Coe and Harry Wilson. By the late 1970s and early 1980s, two endurance runners—Sebastian Coe coached by his father Peter and Steve Ovett coached by Harry Wilson—captivated the world because of their intensely competitive rivalry and their frequent interchanging of the mile world record. Building from Matveyev, both Coe and Wilson understood that the real potential of periodization lay in the ability to control the development of any bio-motor ability deemed crucial to performance. Thus, Coe and Wilson began to specify more precisely than any endurance running coach before, the *exact* physical qualities their athletes needed to improve in order to be successful.

For example, as a trained engineer, Coe believed he possessed an expertise in structured, systematic, and methodical thinking (Butcher, 2005). Accordingly, he organized his son's training program around the *specific* requirements of his events: 800 m, 1,500 m, and the mile. Thus, Sebastian underwent exact and isolated forms of strength training that his father believed met the biomechanical and physiological demands of running world record times. In addition, Coe carefully structured his son's workouts into bi-weekly cycles that corresponded to running repetitions at race paces that were both shorter and greater than his primary competitive distances of 400 m and 3,000 m (Horwill, 1991). It was in this way that Coe was preparing his son in a very pre-conceived and specific manner to have the requisite skills (e.g., speed and stamina) to become a world-class middle-distance runner.

Wilson also took a very pragmatic and analytical problems-based approach to designing Ovett's training that he based on the specific demands of the 1,500 m. For example, early in the training year, Wilson planned training that increased Ovett's aerobic capacities above all else. This was then followed by a pre-competition period that focused on developing Ovett's anaerobic qualities. Wilson also carefully planned periods of high volume interspersed with periods of low volume so that Ovett could recover before beginning another period of high volume training, a practice that came to be known as super-compensation. Crucially, if Wilson increased Ovett's training too sharply or too soon, overtraining could occur and his performances would decline. Or if he increased Ovett's training too slowly, the training effect would be limited and similarly Ovett's performances would be sub-par. In these carefully managed ways, Wilson continually alternated high and low bouts of training in *continued-progressively-increasing-cycles-of-super-compensatory-physiological-adaptations* to enable Ovett to experience the best physiological adaptations not just throughout the training year but throughout his entire career.

Thus, the key point to emerge from Coe's and Wilson's coaching was the need for a coach to determine the *specific* physical qualities that an athlete's training plan needed to cater for. In other words, endurance running training methods became even more sophisticated, more specialized and more concentrated around specifically *chosen* bio-energetic and bio-motor attributes. However, as we will discuss next in our conclusion, this aim for ever more sophisticated and precise approaches to training endurance runners has come at a cost. A cost, we will argue, that has had profound effects on both the development of endurance running coaches and their athletes.

Conclusion

What are today considered to be the dominant characteristics of society, and subsequently the "natural" and "normal" ways of being, are actually quite "new" to human nature, developing as they did out of a particular history associated with the advent of capitalism. For example, characteristics such as discipline, aggression, independence, rational thinking, self-control, and sacrifice can all be tied to the growth of individual responsibility and self-sufficiency that in turn was essential to the growth of capitalism. Unsurprisingly, as we have shown through our particular historiography of endurance running training, these characteristics infiltrated the development of contemporary endurance running coaching practices. As a result of this inherent naturalization, no other interpretation of endurance running training theory makes sense. Therefore, it is worth questioning the innovativeness of the coaches' training methods we have discussed in this chapter. Were they unique or pioneering methodologies? Or were they born from society itself: the obvious application of society's dominant ideals and prescriptions to and on the endurance running body? In other words, were all of these coaching icons just doing variations of the same thing: more science, more discipline, more toughness?

We believe these are important questions to ask about contemporary endurance running training theory because if so-called innovative or progressive approaches to endurance running training are really just variations of the same theme, where the same general points are made time and time again, then clearly we have not come very far with respect to our understanding of coach and athlete development. Consequently, it could be said that within endurance training theory today coaches are operating within an ever-decreasing circle of increasingly specific and narrower progressions (Mills & Denison, 2013). Or put differently, the framework within which endurance theory has seemingly progressed has in actuality remained fixed. Therefore, like the making of a rug that is confined by the width of its loom, all that can really be said to have changed with respect to coaching endurance runners over the last 150 years are the characteristics of the training principles, or threads, already inside the frame. And these threads repeatedly prove themselves as correct, or as the "best" threads to have in this rug, because, as we have just stated, no other interpretations of coaching endurance runners is seen as making sense.

In other words, endurance running coaches' frameworks for coaching, we would contend, have not significantly broadened at all in the last century and a half. They are static not progressive and this stasis could be said to be a reflection of the specific and very powerful discursive formation of endurance running coaches' knowledge of training theory (Denison, 2010). Thus, in spite of the ever increasing proliferation of books, conferences, seminars, articles, magazines, and blogs about endurance running, effective endurance running training can still be summarized in one sentence: the systematic energy conversion of the body via meticulously controlled and structured running efforts. As a result, the endurance body is known only in relation to scientific measurement and pain.

If the coach isn't controlling and the athlete isn't working, no one is progressing. And this is significant because as we have shown, there are no laws that state that this way of thinking is the only way to train endurance runners. Therefore, following our previous work (e.g., Denison & Mills, 2014), if we want to truly advance endurance runners' performances we need to begin by developing endurance running coaching methods without the handbrake of modernity on. More specifically, perhaps it is time to consider "endurance running coaching knowledges" outside of this framework and its dominant themes/threads?

We recognize that developing ways to coach endurance runners outside coaching's dominant modernist logic is a challenge due to the fact that we exist only in these societal relationships. But we believe it is at least worth wondering about other ways of training endurance runners. For example, what if endurance running coaches began to emphasize gentle *not* tough exercises and workouts, or uncontrolled and truly spontaneous *not* controlled and regulated workouts or awkward *not* efficient workouts? What if endurance running coaches began to imagine workouts inspired by something other than science, discipline, and hard work? For it is only through imagining advances (read knowledge) outside the loom, outside science's strict protocols and procedures, that true innovations in endurance running will occur.

References

Andrews, D. L. (2000). Posting-up: French post-structuralism and the critical analysis of contemporary sporting culture. In J. J. Coakley & E. Dunning (Eds.), *Handbook of sports studies* (pp. 106–138). London, England: Sage.

Andrews, D. L. (2008). Kinesiology's inconvenient truth and the physical cultural studies imperative. *Quest*, *60*, 46–63.

Bale, J. (2003). *Running cultures: Racing in time and space*. London, England: Routledge.

Bourne, N. (2009). *Fast science: A history of training theory and methods for elite runners through 1975*. (Unpublished doctoral dissertation). University of Texas, Austin, Texas.

Burstyn. V. (1998). *The rites of men manhood, politics, and the culture of sport*. Toronto, ON: University of Toronto Press.

Butcher, P. (2005). *The perfect distance: Coe and Ovett: The record breaking rivalry*. London, England: Phoenix.

Cerruty, P. (1959). *Running with Cerruty*. Los Altos, CA: Track and Field News.

Coakley, J. (2009). *Sports in society issues and controversies* (10th ed). New York, NY: McGraw Hill.

Denison, J. (2010). Planning, practice and performance: The discursive formation of coaches' knowledge. *Sport, Education & Society*, *15*, 461–478.

Denison, J., & Mills, J. P. (2014). Planning for distance running: Coaching with Foucault. *Sports Coaching Review*. *3*, 1–16, DOI: 10.1080/21640629.2014.953005.

Hobsbawm, E. J. (1975). *The age of revolution 1789–1848*. London, England: Weidenfeld & Nicolson.

Holt, R. (1989). *Sport and the British: A modern history*. Gloucestershire, United Kingdom: Clarendon Press.

Horwill, F. (1991). *Obsession for running: A lifetime in athletics*. Lancashire, United Kingdom: Colin Davies.

Huizinga, J. (1972). Man and the masses in America. In J. Huizinga (Ed.), *America: A Dutch historian's vision, from afar and near* (pp. 1–225). New York, NY: Harper and Row.

Kruger, A. (2006). Training theory and why Roger Bannister was the first four-minute miler. *Sport in History*, *26*, 305–324.

Mangan, J. A. (1973). *Physical education and sport: sociological and cultural perspectives; an introductory reader*. Oxford, United Kingdom: Blackwell.

Matveyev, L. (1981). *Fundamentals of sports training*. Translated by Albert P. Zdornykh. Moscow, Russia: Progress Publishers.

Mills, J. P., & Denison, J. (2013). Coach Foucault: Problematizing endurance running coaches' practices. *Sports Coaching Review*. *2*, 136–150. DOI:10.1080/21640629.2014.913871.

Phillips, M., & Hicks, F. (2000). Conflict, tensions and complexities: Athletic training in Australia in the1950s. *International Journal of the History of Sport*, *17*, 206–224.

Schmidt, R. A., & Lee, T. D. (2005). *Motor control and learning: A behavioral emphasis* (4th ed.). Champign, IL: Human Kinetics.

Selye, H. (1956). *The stress of life*. New York, NY: McGraw-Hill.

Sims, G. (2003). *Why die? The extraordinary Percy Cerruty, maker of champions*. Cambridge, MA: Star Bright Books.

Stampfl, F. (1955). *Franz Stampfl on running*. London, England: Herbert Jenkins.

Struna, N. L. (2001). Historical research in physical activity. In J. R. Thomas & J. K. Nelson (Eds.), *Research methods in physical activity* (pp. 203–217). Champaign, IL: Human Kinetics.

Wilt, F. (1959). *How they train: Half mile to six mile*. Los Altos, CA: Track and Field News.

5 Beyond Boston and Kathrine Switzer

Women's participation in distance running

Laura Frances Chase

On April 19, 1967, runner #261 lined up along with 741 other runners at the start of the Boston Marathon (Switzer, 2009). The temperature that historic morning hovered around 40 degrees Fahrenheit with snow, sleet, and bitterly cold wind. Many of the runners took refuge near the starting line in the high school gymnasium where the pre-race physicals were being conducted. K. V. Switzer, #261, started the race with the hood of her sweatshirt up, trying to keep warm and relaxed. She was disappointed she had to wear warm clothes over the pretty running outfit she had picked out, but she didn't want to perform poorly on this important day. As she moved along the course, Switzer removed the hood of her sweatshirt and ran comfortably along with several male friends, including her boyfriend, Tom, and her coach, Arnie. Soon after, she was spotted by a media truck and the news of a "girl" in the race spread rapidly. Several race officials began to taunt race director Jock Semple about a girl in his race. He was enraged and when he spotted Switzer he jumped out of the media truck and attempted to rip the numbers off of her chest. Semple was then tackled by Switzer's boyfriend, a former All American football player, the two landing in some bushes along the road. Switzer finished the race in four hours and 20 minutes with her numbers intact, but was disqualified by Semple and suspended for six months by the Amateur Athletic Union (AAU).

Mainstream media coverage of women's running, along with the bulk of historical work on women in distance running, has focused on the 1967 Boston Marathon exploits of Kathrine Switzer as a pivotal moment in the history of women's distance running (Cooper, 1992; Jutel, 2003; Plymire, 1997). Also on the Boston Marathon course that day was another woman, Roberta "Bobbi" Gibb. Gibb, however, was not a "numbered" runner in the race. She was, therefore, not an official participant and could not be disqualified, suspended, or even removed from the course. On that cold day, Gibb actually "finished" the race almost an hour ahead of Switzer (Pate & O'Neill, 2007) but Gibb had in fact become the first woman to complete the Boston Marathon when she did so a year prior, in 1966, in a time of 3:21:40.

So despite being the first woman to ever complete the race as well as finishing the 1967 race significantly faster than Switzer, Gibb received scant attention in the ensuing decades in comparison to Switzer. Her exploits merited a second page photograph and article headlined "Girl Finished Marathon" in the *Boston Globe* (Ralby, 1966) the morning after the 1966 race. This news article was followed the next day by an editorial noting that Gibb had finished "in a respectable time, to the chagrin of BAA officials" while cautioning that "this feminine initiative may trigger a sweeping counter-offensive" and concluding with the question, "Really now, is this really a man's world, as most women complain?" ("The Lady Also Ran," April 21, 1966, p. 14). To their credit, the *Boston Globe* did publish a subsequent letter from a male member of the public that criticized the editorial staff for "seek(ing) to destroy one moment of well-deserved glory" asking that they "give credit where credit is due" (Deslongchamps, May 5, 1966, p. 14). The May 2, 1966 issue of *Sports Illustrated* featured an article on Gibb (Brown, 1966) but outside of the *SI* article, *Boston Globe* editorial, and a few local newspaper sources and others that simply noted that Gibb was also on the course that infamous day, there was little publicity about Gibb at the time. This may be due in part to Gibb's own reluctance to challenge the AAU and BAA. Gibb said that if her participation caused any problem she just wouldn't run the race ("The Lady Also Ran," April 21, 1966, p. 14).

Despite her statements in 1966, in Gibb's 2011 memoir it becomes quite clear that she considered her running the Boston Marathon a subversive act that was critical to proving to the world that women could run the marathon distance. Gibb's achievements were recognized only much later by Boston officials and the running community. In 1996, the BAA listed Gibb as the unofficial Boston Marathon winner for 1966–1968 ("Celebrating Four Decades," 2015) and Gibb was increasingly included in local events commemorating women's inclusion in the Boston Marathon ("Marathon's Elite Women Runners," 1996).

It is important to note that, even though Gibb received only scant media attention relative to Switzer, Gibb was actually not the first woman to complete a marathon in the United States (Davis, 2012). That honor went to Merry Lepper when she completed the Western Hemisphere Marathon in Culver City, California in 1963. Lepper and her friend Lyn Carmen snuck into the Western Hemisphere marathon by hiding in some bushes near the starting line and running without official numbers in the race, just as Gibb would do almost two years later in the Boston Marathon. All this said, despite the earlier completions of U.S. marathons by Lepper and Gibb, Switzer's participation in the 1967 Boston Marathon generated unprecedented media and public interest in women's distance running and it was Switzer that would go on to become the face of women's distance running in the United States.

The emergence of women's distance running in the United States

The work of Cooper (1992), Plymire (1997), and Jutel (2003) explores the emergence of distance running in the 1960s and 1970s, with a particular focus on women's distance running. Their work details how distance running changed significantly in the 1970s, as large numbers of participants began to enter races, particularly the marathon, simply to participate and to be physically active. This shift to participatory running contributed to the gradual inclusion of a more diverse group of women in distance running, in terms of ability and performance. These three scholars also explore the role of increasing commercialization within the sport of distance running and the impact this had on women's involvement in the sport. Cooper's (1992, 1995) work, for example, highlights the important role of Avon Products, Inc. (Avon) in facilitating significant opportunities for women in distance running in the early years. Avon later became a major player in the cause-based charity fundraising movement (King, 2006). Jutel's (2003) work also briefly documents the role of Bonne Bell, Inc. (Bonne Bell), L'eggs, and Avon in sponsoring women's running events.

Jutel (2003) examines the ways in which certain runners, in particular Switzer, dominated media representations of female distance runners. Jutel (2007) also documents the ways in which certain female runners are remembered and others forgotten. She, along with numerous others, has highlighted many of the women who broke gender barriers in distance running events but remained relatively unknown, including: the legend of Melpomene at the 1896 Olympic Games in Athens (Jutel, 2003); Julia Chase at the 1961 Manchester, CT Turkey Trot (Plymire, 1997); Merry Lepper who completed the 1963 Western Hemisphere Marathon in Culver City, CA (Davis, 2012); and, Millie Sampson at the 1964 Owairaka marathon in New Zealand (Robinson, 2013).

These relatively unknown women stand in stark contrast to Switzer, whose running of the 1967 marathon with numbers (and the attack on and disqualification of Switzer), was singled out as the most important event in the history of women's distance running. Jutel (2003) details three major reasons why Switzer's run was seized upon as the pivotal moment in the history of women in distance running: (1) the very public nature of Switzer's performance; (2) the fact that Switzer fit the cultural ideals of femininity, allowing the distance running community to avoid transgression of traditional gender roles even as Switzer broke down barriers for women in distance running; and, (3) the blatant discrimination against female runners prompted a public response. A significant focus of Jutel's (2003) work is on how Switzer abided by gender norms and in many ways reinforced dominant notions of femininity despite her rule breaking (Jutel, 2003).

The remainder of this chapter examines selected historical experiences of women in United States distance running from the 1967 Boston Marathon onward, with particular focus on how women's experiences in distance running diverged from the experiences of male distance runners. Four significant movements or events that shaped women's involvement in running during this time period are explored, including: the corporate sponsorship of women's running/walking events; the acceptance of the women's marathon into the Olympic program; women's involvement in the development of cause-based endurance fund-raising events; and, the Clydesdale/Athena movement.

The corporate sponsorship of distance running

The 1967 Boston Marathon occurred near the beginning of a period of significant growth for marathon racing, and running in general (Cooper, 1992). Between 1896 and the mid-1960s most of the competitors in the marathon were what would be considered serious runners (Plymire, 1987) and most races were relatively small. The general consensus was that if you could not run well you should not run at all. The short cut off times embraced by many race directors reflected this philosophy. Men ran rather than jogged, and the AAU banned women from running races over a mile and a half.

As the numbers of distance runners grew throughout the late 1960s and the early 1970s, the singular focus on elite runners began to wane. A much wider range of participants began competing in distance running events. Prior to 1964 there had never been more than 300 competitors in the Boston Marathon. By 1968 there were over 1,000 competitors ("Boston Marathon History," 2015). As the numbers of distance runners grew, the number of marathons being contested in the United States also grew, from 40 at the end of the 1960s to almost 200 by 1977 (Cooper, 1992). According to Cooper (1998), "by the late 1960s the presence of fitness runners heightened differentiation in the marathon: the event now comprised two races" (p. 131). In the inaugural New York City Marathon in 1970 there were only 127 participants (126 men and one woman) but by the 1979 running of the NYC Marathon there were 11,533 participants (10,207 men and 1,326 women). In 2014, over 50,000 runners took part in the NYC Marathon ("New York City Marathon," 2015).

It was during the early 1970s that distance running started to become commodified, with corporate sponsorship beginning to shape the future of running (Plymire, 1997). Fred Lebow, director of the New York City Marathon, led the way in the commodification process. Lebow realized that a key to the success of the New York City Marathon lay in attracting a large number of competitors to the race and in the revenue their participation would generate (Cooper, 1992).

Lebow also recognized that increased numbers of participants could lead to additional revenue from corporate sponsors seeking to target their goods and services to distance running enthusiasts. Thus, Lebow decided to increase the numbers of marathon participants, regardless of their athletic ability. Cooper (1992) details how Lebow implemented a number of strategies to make the New York City Marathon more attractive to a larger number of runners. These strategies included: keeping the course open longer; recording the race times of all official finishers; and, providing commemorative medals and t-shirts for those completing the race. Finishers t-shirts, heavily adorned with race sponsorship logos, have become standard at most, if not all, races. This type of commodification fundamentally changed the marathon.

Although AAU rules still prevented women from running the marathon distance in the late 1960s and the IAAF did not officially sanction a women's marathon until 1979 (Sailors, 2012), some women were beginning to participate in marathon distance races because they believed women should have the same opportunities as men (Davis, 2012; Gibb, 2011; Switzer, 2009). In addition to the push from prospective women participants, the process of commercialization and the growing role of corporate sponsorship was also pushing the door open for women. In keeping with his desire to maximize race revenues, Lebow allowed women to compete in the first running of the New York Marathon in 1970 (Cooper, 1992). There was just one woman who entered the inaugural running of the NYC Marathon and she did not finish the race ("New York City Marathon," 2015). In 1971, five women started the race and four completed the race, with 19-year old Beth Bonner winning the women's title in 2:55:22.

In the fall of 1971, the AAU ruled that some women could compete in the marathon distance but the women must not be in the same exact race as the men (Switzer, 2009). The women would have a separate start and finish line or would not start at the same time as the men (Butler, 2012). But despite the progress made with the AAU, many female runners and Lebow were unhappy with the continued restriction on women's participation in the marathon. Several women and Lebow organized a protest against the AAU at the start of the 1972 race (Butler, 2012). Finally, in 1972 women were allowed to officially run the same marathon as the men.

As he was building the New York Marathon into one of the most popular and successful U.S. marathons, Lebow was approached by the public relations firm of S. C. Johnson & Son, Incorporated, about the creation of a women's marathon (Cooper, 1992). Given the reluctance in the early 1970s to have women and men compete in the same race, and a history of separate sport for men and women, this approach made sense. The problem was that Lebow wasn't sure there were enough women interested in competing in a women-only marathon. Instead, he pitched the idea of a shorter race. Lebow was a masterful promoter of the event. Despite his best efforts, which included taping flyers to light poles in Manhattan, the first Women's Mini-Marathon held in 1972 had only 78 participants and covered six miles. In 1977, cosmetics company Bonne Bell took over sponsorship of the Mini-Marathon and it became the Bonne Bell Mini-Marathon. Race organizers expected around 200 competitors but 2,231 women showed up for the race, including 17-year old high school student Lynn Jennings, who won the race in a time of 34:31 ("Start Strong," 2015). Jennings went on to win the event six times and placed second five times. The race continues today as the Tufts Health Plan 10K. The 2013 version of the race had almost 6,000 participants, including 18 women who had run the race for 37 consecutive years. While attracting a broad cross-section of the women's running community, the Tufts Health Plan 10K has also become an elite race attracting the best female runners from around the world. USA Track and Field has regularly designated the race as the United States 10K National Championship for women.

Jess Bell, chairman of Bonne Bell, Inc., was a pioneer in the field of corporate fitness. A marathoner himself and a member of the President's Council on Physical Fitness, Bell introduced fitness programs for employees of Bonne Bell in the 1970s (Baranick, 2005). Under his leadership, the company created on-site workout facilities for employees, including a track and a weight room, and also offered exercise programs for employees at both the firm's headquarters in Lakewood, Ohio and a production plant in Westlake, Ohio. Bell encouraged workers to work out, lose weight, and stop smoking by offering financial incentives. These programs were part of Bell's "Be Fit. Look Good" philosophy. Bell's first foray into sponsorship of distance running events was a community race between employees of the firm's headquarters and the production plant. But his role in the development of women's running events would prove even more significant than his pioneering efforts in corporate fitness.

Bell's decision to sponsor the Mini-Marathon in 1977 brought Bonne Bell to the forefront of the running boom with the first women-only race series in the United States. Bell actively recruited Kathrine Switzer to take charge of the Bonne Bell series (Switzer, 2009). Switzer was interested in the job with Bonne Bell if it could help her get distance events into the Olympics, but Jess Bell was unable or unwilling to pay her enough salary for Switzer to leave her job in New York. She described their interaction on the topic of her working for Bonne Bell in her book *Marathon Woman*:

> I sent Jess a proposal on his series idea, stressing state-of-the-art race organization, AAU sanctions, and professional public relations. It was more than Jess wanted to spend—he just wanted a celebration of women. Still, he offered me a job. Unfortunately, it was for less than I was making at AMF ... I got paid as a consultant and we let the job discussion drift.
>
> (Switzer, 2009, p. 310)

Thus, while Switzer never became a full time employee at Bonne Bell, she continued to be involved with the company's efforts to sponsor distance-running events for women.

Around the same time that Bonne Bell began sponsoring the Mini-Marathon, another cosmetics company appeared on the women's running scene (Cooper, 1995). Switzer pitched the idea of an international marathon for women and a women's racing circuit to Avon. Avon hired Switzer as a manager of special promotions with her primary job to run its already existing women's tennis futures circuit, with a secondary focus on creating running opportunities for women (Switzer, 2009). Avon's International Running Circuit for women was introduced in 1978 with the inaugural running of Avon Women's International Marathon in Atlanta, Georgia ("Avon Running," 2015). Switzer (2009) invited all of the top female runners in the world; 14 of the top 25 female runners showed up to compete. The next year the race was held in Germany and in 1980 the streets of London were shut down to accommodate the third running of the Avon Women's International Marathon. Avon expanded its racing circuit around the world, adding races in Brazil, Belgium, and Japan; it also expanded its women's racing series within the United States. The women who won local races qualified to participate at the next level, culminating in the Avon International Marathon. The Avon International Marathon and race circuit were designed to develop an international participation base in women's distance running that would help accelerate the addition of the women's marathon to the Olympic program (Switzer, 2009). However, despite all of these efforts and the enormous growth of women's running, women still struggled for acceptance at the highest level within the sport of distance running—the Olympics.

Women's Olympic Marathon debut

Throughout the 1960s and 1970s, the IOC consistently refused to allow the women's marathon onto the Olympic Program. And although the AAU began holding an AAU women's marathon championship in 1974 and the IAAF began sanctioning marathon distance races in 1979 (Hansen, 2012), the IOC continued to exclude the marathon for women at the Olympic Games.

The early exclusion of women was firmly rooted in the beliefs of the founder of the modern Olympic Games, Pierre de Coubertin. His efforts to exclude women from the Olympics continued throughout his presidency from 1896 to 1925; his failure to continue to exclude them ultimately contributed to his resignation (Teetzel, 2006). The exclusion of women from Olympic distance running events was reinforced by the well-documented media construction of the 800 m running event for women at the 1928 Olympic Games (Vertinsky, 2000). In 1928, the International Olympic Committee (IOC) had finally allowed women to run the 800 m race. But the widespread media coverage of the race depicted exhausted women collapsing on the track. The media's negative construction of this event led to the removal of the event in the next Olympics, and it did not reappear until the 1960 Rome Olympics. Although men had competed in the next longest event, the 1,500 m race, beginning in 1896, a 1,500 m event was not added to the Olympic program for women until 1972 (Sailors, 2012).

Despite growing pressure, due at least in part to the success of the Avon International Running Circuit, in July of 1980 the IOC deemed the women's marathon too controversial and decided to postpone a vote until the following February. The main reason cited was a lack of supporting evidence that marathon running was not medically dangerous for women (Switzer, 2009). The myth that long distance running or strenuous athletic exertion was dangerous for women was central to the IOC's reluctance to add certain women's events to the Olympic program (Sailors, 2012). The exclusion of women from Olympic competition in distance running, ski jumping, as well as team sports such as hockey and soccer, was often based on the perception of female frailty. Sailors (2012) cited additional factors affecting women's struggle to have distance events on the Olympic program. Sailors argued that concerns about female masculinity, and the belief that women were simply not interested in long distance running, also contributed to the IOC's reluctance to add distance-running events for women. Vertinsky's (2000) work studying older female runners addressed how women were once seen as too frail for any strenuous activity lasting more than a few minutes. The idea that long distance running was dangerous or risky for women continued to be perpetuated into the 1980s. Laurendeau's (2008) work on women's exclusion from ski jumping explains how "risk discourses operate to authorize and legitimate particular exclusionary practices" (p. 385). Women's participation in endurance running events, much like ski jumping, was and is shaped by completely illogical risk discourses that have resulted in women's exclusion from those events.

Concerns about sport interfering with women's femininity shaped the way many female runners were represented in mainstream and running media of the 1960s and 1970s (Jutel, 2003). Jutel's (2003) work provides a detailed review of the ways in which female runners, especially marathoners, were constructed as feminine in order to make running appear more acceptable for women. Fears about female runner's femininity were limiting women's opportunities to compete at the highest levels, including at the Olympic Games. Jutel (2003) described how important it was for Olympic inclusion that female runners maintained their femininity:

> The marathon was not the result of challenge so much as it was the result of conforming to gender expectations. The fortuitous convergence of visible gender conformity and injustice furnished the initial impetus; continued development hinged, however, on preserving expectations of femininity within a framework of resistance and diligence.
>
> (p. 34)

Jutel goes on to argue that Switzer became the focal point for women's right to run long distance races because Switzer did not upset the gender order.

Gradually discourses surrounding women and physical activity began to evolve. This evolution was impacted by scientific research that failed to demonstrate undue harm to women undertaking strenuous physical activity. Jutel (2003) suggested that one of the key players in this shift was physician and long distance running coach Ernst van Aaken. Van Aaken was in a unique position to address this issue as a doctor and a long time supporter of women's running. He was instrumental in refuting the medical discourses that viewed women as frail and women's participation in long distance running as dangerous. His efforts made it very difficult for race organizers, including the IOC, to continue to exclude women from competition. The American College of Sports Medicine (ACSM) also played a pivotal role in challenging these dominant discourses. In late 1979, ACSM recognized the scientific research and issued an opinion statement that read in part:

> It is the opinion of the American College of Sports Medicine that female athletes should not be denied the opportunity to complete in long-distance running. There exists no conclusive scientific or medical evidence that long-distance running is contraindicated for the healthy, trained female athlete. The American College of Sports Medicine recommends that females be allowed to compete at the national and international level in the same distances in which their male counterparts compete.
>
> (ACSM, 1979, ix)

Global resistance to women's participation in the marathon was beginning to wane as arguments supporting women's exclusion had been refuted by scientific research.

Although women's participation in distance running events had achieved fairly widespread acceptance by the early 1980s, time seemed to be running out to get the women's marathon added for the 1984 Los Angeles Olympic Games. However, shortly after the IAAF sanctioned the Tokyo International Marathon it recommended to the IOC that it allow the women's marathon. The combined efforts of Switzer and Avon, along with the IAAF support, culminated in the IOC's February 23, 1981 decision to allow the women's marathon (Switzer, 2009). With this principal goal achieved, the last Avon International Marathon for women was held in 1984 on the same Los Angeles course where the first Olympic Marathon would be contested just a few months later.

On August 5, 1984, 50 women lined up to start the first ever women's Olympic marathon at Santa Monica College near Los Angeles (Pattillo, 2014). Joan Benoit Samuelson, representing the United States, took the lead at mile three and never relinquished it. She won the race in 2:24:52, beating the second place finisher, Grete Waitz, by over a minute. Moran (1984, August 6), writing for the *New York Times* the following day, described Benoit's race:

> With a daring that successfully challenged the finest female distance runners in the world and an ease that surprised even herself, Joan Benoit took a calculated risk, ran away from the field after passing the three-mile mark, and won the first Olympic marathon for women.
>
> (Online)

It is difficult to measure the impact of Benoit's gold medal performance in the Los Angeles Olympics on women's distance running in the United States, but it is clear that in the ensuing decades many women in the United States took up the sport of running. Pattillo (2014), writing in *Competitor* magazine, described the perceived impact that Benoit's victory had on women in the United States:

> Although there were many women running pioneers and elite-level runners before Samuelson won gold, Joanie's stunning effort in Los Angeles that summer set about an energy wave that hasn't stopped 30 years later. In the wake of Joanie's victory came athletic empowerment, advancements in women's running apparel, Oprah running a marathon and inspired generations of women runners running for their goals and motivations.
>
> (Online)

It is important to note that the inclusion of the marathon for women in the Olympics did not signify full equality for female distance runners. There were no 5,000 m or 10,000 m races staged for women at the 1984 Olympic Games. The latter was added for the 1988 Games and the former was finally added in 1996 (Sailors, 2012).

Despite these lingering challenges, with the AAU, IAAF, and IOC allowing women to compete in marathon distance racing, there is no denying the landscape of women's distance running had changed significantly by the mid-1980s. Most distance running events now welcomed both men and women. With women's participation no longer limited to women-only competitions, distance running events had less appeal to corporate sponsors marketing specifically to women. As a result, elite women-only running events like the Avon International Running Circuit began to sputter in the mid-1980s. Avon attempted a return to women's running in 1998 with the creation of the Avon Running Global Circuit and Challenge (Wall, 1999). The Avon Global Circuit was intended to provide elite competition for the best 10 km female runners in the world, but was also designed to appeal to all levels of runners. Included with the Global Circuit races were a series of grassroots training workshops for new female runners. Avon proposed the series of 10 km runs, 5 km walks, and pre-race clinics that would bring women of varying running abilities together with a focus on fitness and health. The circuit was scheduled for 16 countries including Germany, Italy, Hungary, Argentina, Chile, Brazil, Venezuela, Panama, Mexico, Canada, Thailand, Malaysia, the Philippines, and the United States.

It appears that this comeback to women's running lasted only a few years. Little mention of Avon sponsorship of competitive running exists after the creation of the Avon Running Global Circuit in 1998. The IAAF noted on its website that Catherine Ndereba won the 2001 Avon Running Global Championship in Budapest ("Catherine Ndereba Captures," 2001). King (2006) mentions that there was a Avon Global Championship race in Bangkok in 2003. But after 2003, there is no mention of the Avon Running Global Championship or Circuit. Currently, Avon Running sponsors a Women's Run in Berlin with a 10 km and 5 km walk and run. This appears to be the only active Avon race. However, just as Avon seemed to shift out of sponsoring elite, competitive women's running events, their commitment to and involvement in more participation-based running and walking events seemed to grow. In the 1990s, Avon would become one of the leaders in promoting participation in endurance events for the purpose of cause-based fundraising.

Cause-based racing

Endurance events became a major site for charity or "cause-based" fundraising in the 1980s. In part fueled by the excitement associated with Joan Benoit Samuelson's gold medal marathon race in the 1984 Olympics, large numbers of people took up running and the opportunities to complete in endurance events grew exponentially. The running boom was part of the larger fitness boom that King (2006) talks about in her work, *Pink Ribbons, Inc.* Millions of people began to jog, go to the gym, and exercise alongside workout videos. Jane Fonda's video, *Workout*, became a top seller and sold over a million copies within a couple of years of its release (King, 2006). Home fitness equipment and videos became staples of the fitness industry. Many of these now-active people also began to enter races, particularly the marathon.

The origins of cause-based endurance events may be found in Terry Fox's Canadian Marathon of Hope in 1980, which combined endurance physical activity with cause-based fundraising (Jeffery, 2010). King (2006) suggests that there were several other events that also preceded the boom in physical activity-focused fundraising for charity, citing the March of Dime's WalkAmerica event as a prime example of combining physical activity and cause-based fundraising. The WalkAmerica event started in 1970 and is now one of the longest running activity-based fundraising events in existence.

Setting aside these early examples, it was really in the 1980s that cause-based endurance events began to take off. Three of the most well-known and successful programs started in the 1980s: the Susan G. Komen Race for the Cure, which started in Dallas, Texas in 1983; the American Cancer Society's Relay for Life in 1985; and the Leukemia and Lymphoma Society's Team in Training program, which started in 1988. These organizations provide trainers, training programs, and develop training communities specific to their fundraising efforts and associated physical endurance events. The creation of these programs has changed the face of endurance sport. These runners and walkers, who appear to be much more often women than men, form a large presence at many distance races. Although it varies by event and sponsor, one participant estimated that women comprised 90–95 percent of the participants in an Avon two-day walk staged in 2014 (A. Ryan, personal communication, April 5, 2015).

A slightly later entrant to sponsorship of cause-based endurance events, and as Avon's competitive women's running circuit faltered, the company began to focus on fundraising for women's health care issues. The first Avon Breast Cancer Fundraising three-day walk was held in 1998. In 2002, Avon moved to a two-day walk format that continues today (King, 2006). The Avon 39 is the only walking event format currently listed on the Avon website. Participants raise funds in order to participate in the event, in which participants cover up to 39 miles over two days ("Avon 39," 2015). In 2014, individuals were required to raise a minimum of $1,800 to participate in the event (A. Ryan, personal communication, April, 5, 2015). According to their website, the proceeds from the events are used to fund research and educational programs, promote awareness, provide breast cancer screenings, and assist individuals with breast cancer ("Avon 39," 2015).

The Leukemia and Lymphoma Society's Team in Training program has grown to become the largest marathon-training program in the world. In 2013, they celebrated the 25th anniversary of their first event, the 1988 New York City Marathon. As participation in cause-based fundraising has grown, even the Boston Marathon—considered one of the most prestigious distance running events—accepts participants who are running for various cause-based organizations. These cause-based runners are not required to the meet the challenging qualifying times that other runners must in order to participate in the race. The growth of cause-based fundraising has accelerated the overall democratization of endurance events.

Clydesdale and Athena running

As endurance events gradually came to accept women participants and cause-based fundraising, distance running was becoming democratized on another front. Large numbers of participants began to enter races, particularly the marathon, simply to participate and to be physically active (Cooper, 1992). This shift to participatory running contributed to the gradual inclusion of people with a wide range of ages, body types, sizes, and weights (Chase, 2008, 2012). Across the United States, running groups and organizations developed to serve this diverse group.

In the early 1980s, Joe Law, a statistician from Baltimore, spurred the Clydesdale movement after analyzing race times and body weight (Chase, 2008). He found that race times increased significantly for runners over certain weights and began actively lobbying race directors to add weight divisions in their events. In the ensuing two decades, a number of running organizations developed that were dedicated to advocating for weight divisions and providing weight divisions competition in distance running. The organizations include the New England Clydesdale and Filly Racing Federation, the USA Clydesdale and Filly Racing Federation, Team Clydesdale, and Run Big Chicago. In part because of pressure from these running groups and organizations, some races began to include categories for runners based on body weight to accommodate these bigger, fatter, and—sometimes—slower runners. These categories for runners based on body weight were commonly known as Clydesdale divisions for men and Filly or Athena divisions for women. Most of these weight-based running groups and organizations were or are primarily led by male runners (Chase, 2012).

In 1989, the Portland Marathon became one of the first races to add weight divisions (Chase, 2012). They have continued to offer five Clydesdale divisions for men (ranging from 185 to 300+ pounds) and three Athena divisions for women (ranging from 145 to 180+ pounds). In contrast to the variety of weight divisions offered for women at the Portland Marathon, most races with weight divisions offer multiple divisions for men but only one division for women. There are also often significantly less women participating in weight divisions in distance running events. For example, at the 2008 Portland Marathon, approximately 10 percent of the male runners (125 total) competed as Clydesdale runners while approximately 6 percent of female runners (32 total) were registered within the Athena division ("Portland Marathon," 2015). The Portland Marathon website lists incomplete race results from 2014 (only one division each for Clydesdale and Athena competitors was reported) while the registration area included five divisions for men and three divisions for women. There were nine male runners listed in the one Clydesdale division, but only four female runners listed in the sole Athena division ("Portland Marathon," 2015).

The Chicago Area Runners Association (CARA) provides a Clydesdale and Athena circuit for its runners. There are two divisions for Athena runners (155 to 169 pounds and greater than 170 pounds) and three divisions for Clydesdale runners (185 to 199 pounds; 200 to 224 pounds; and greater than 225 pounds).

CARA does not organize or provide races specifically for Clydesdale or Athena runners. Instead, CARA creates a virtual circuit consisting of specific running events and the results are reported to CARA (Chase, 2012). Thus, the races are not limited to Clydesdale or Athena participants, but the results from these races are used to calculate the standings in the Clydesdale and Athena circuits. In 2014, only 12 women participated in CARA Athena circuit while 33 men participated in the CARA Clydesdale circuit ("Clydesdale and Athena Competition," 2015). Similar to the Portland Marathon, more men than women compete in these Chicago area weight-based racing divisions.

Despite efforts of promoters and race organizers to include weight-based running divisions for women, women's place in Clydesdale running has often been on the sidelines. The lack of divisions for women is often attributed to a lack of women who want to participate in weight divisions (Chase, 2008). The reality is that while more women now participate in distance running events than men, more men choose to compete in weight divisions. The important question is why? Why are so few women willing to participate in Athena divisions? Many of the Clydesdale runners I interviewed for my research addressed how difficult it was to get women to participate in Athena divisions (Chase, 2008). Several men offered the theory that weight is a much less loaded issue for men than women. The men indicated they had no problems getting up on the scale in front of other runners. It seems that generally speaking, entering oneself into a Clydesdale category is not as problematic for men as is for women. Thus, while Athena categories have opened the door to meaningful competition for some female runners, many women have been unwilling to walk through that door.

Conclusion

Although women have now been formally participating in distance running events for five decades, the early efforts of women such as Julia Chase, Merry Lepper, Mildred Sampson, and even Roberta Gibb were largely undocumented and unnoticed by the running community. The bold actions of Kathrine Switzer and early race sponsors Bonne Bell and Avon did much to engender the participation of women in distance running and walking events. As women's distance running events proliferated, so did the women's running community.

The women's running community has grown to include a broad spectrum of women runners, including elite runners who are now offered nearly the same competitive opportunities as men, as well as recreational runners of various ages, body types, and running speeds, many of whom are involved in cause-based fundraising programs. While this chapter has examined how the growth of women's participation in distance running has been hampered by hegemonic notions of femininity, ideas about women's frailty, and notions of what constitutes an appropriate female running body, it has also addressed how women's increased participation in distance running challenged dominant ideas of femininity, helped disprove perceptions of women's frailty, and challenged dominant notions of the appropriate size or weight of female bodies.

References

American College of Sports Medicine (1979, Winter). Opinion statement on the participation of the female athlete in long-distance running. *Medicine and Science in Sports, 11*, ix.

Avon 39: The walk to end breast cancer. (2015). Retrieved from www.avon39.org/.

Avon Running Global Women's Circuit: History. (2015). Retrieved from www.coolrunning.com/ar/running_about_history.html.

Baranick, A. (2005, September 6). Jess Bell, executive of Bonne Bell, was fitness advocate. *The Cleveland Plain Dealer*, Metro Section.

Boston Marathon history: Participation. (2015). Retrieved from www.baa.org/races/boston-marathon/boston-marathon-history/participation.aspx.

Burfoot, A. (2007). The history of the marathon: 1976—present. *Sports Med, 37*, 284–287.

Butler, C. (2012, November). 40 years ago, six women changed racing forever. *Runner's World.* Retrieved from www.runnersworld.com/runners-stories/40-years-ago-six-women-changed-racing-forever?page=single.

Catherine Ndereba captures Avon Running Global Championship title. (2001, October 14). Retrieved from www.iaaf.org/news/news/catherine-ndereba-captures-avon-running-globa.

Celebrating two decades of women running Boston. (2015). Retrieved from www.26 2.org/initiatives/special-programs/40-years-women-running-boston/.

Chase, L. (2008). Running big: Clydesdale runners and technologies of the body. *Sociology of Sport Journal, 25*, 130–147.

Chase, L. (2012). Running with the masses: A history of the Clydesdale movement. *Journal of Sport History, 39*, 401–416.

Clydesdale and Athena Competition (2015). Retrieved from www.cararuns.org/en/Race/CARA-Runners-Choice-Circuit/Clydesdale-Athena/.

Cooper, P. (1992). The "visible hand" on the footrace: Fred Lebow and the marketing of the marathon. *Journal of Sport History, 19*, 244–256.

Cooper, P. (1995). Marathon women and the corporation. *Journal of Women's History, 7*, 62–81.

Cooper, P. (1998). *The American marathon.* Syracuse, NY: Syracuse University Press.

Davis, D. (2012). *Marathon crasher. The life and times of Merry Lepper, the first American woman to run a marathon.* Thomas Dunne Books. Retrieved from http://us.macmillan.com/books/9781466817104.

Deslongchamps, D. (1966, May 5). He saw her running [Letter to the Editor]. *Boston Globe*, p. 14.

Gibb, R. (2011). *Wind in the fire: A personal journey by Bobbi Gibb, the first woman to run and win at Boston.* Cambridge, MA: The Institute of Natural Systems Press.

Hansen, J. (Jan./Feb., 2012). The women's marathon movement. Retrieved from www.jacquelinehansen.com/wp-content/uploads/2012/01/M+B-xx-16-1w_pix-Hansen.pdf.

Jutel, A. (2007). Forgetting Millie Sampson: Collective frameworks for historical memory. *New Zealand Journal of Media Studies, 10*, 31–36.

Jutel, A. (2003). "Thou does run as in flotation": Femininity, reassurance and the emergence of the women's marathon. *The International Journal of the History of Sport, 20*, 17–36.

King, S. (2006). *Pink Ribbons, Inc.: Breast cancer and the politics of philanthropy.* Minneapolis, MN: University of Minnesota Press.

Laurendeau, J. (2008). "Jumping like a girl": Women's ski-jumping, risk discourses and discursive silence. *Pathways: Critiques and Discourse in Olympic Research, Proceedings* of the *9th International Symposium for Olympic Research, Beijing, China*, 382–390.

Lucas, J. (1976). A history of the marathon race—490 B.C. to 1975. *Journal of Sport History 3*, 120–138.

Moran, M. (1984, August 6). First women's Olympic marathon to Benoit. *New York Times.* Retrieved from www.nytimes.com/1984/08/06/sports/first-women-s-olympic-marathon-to-benoit.html.

New York City Marathon results: 1970–2014. (2015). Retrieved from http://web2.nyrrc.org/cgi-bin/start.cgi/mar-programs/archive/archive_search.html.

Pate, R. & O'Neill, J. (2007). American women in the marathon. *Sports Med, 37*, 294–298.

Pattillo, A. (2014, August 3). *How Joanie's '84 Olympic marathon victory energized women's running.* Retrieved from http://running.competitor.com/2014/08/news/samuelson-recalls-1984-olympic-victory_109740#CEYg7WBQsZIkJ2rR.99.

Plymire, D. (1997). *A moral exercise: Long-distance running in the 1970s.* (Unpublished doctoral dissertation). University of Iowa, Iowa City.

Plymire, D. (2004). Positive addiction: Running and human potential in the 1970s. *Journal of Sport History, 31*, 297–315.

Portland Marathon: Results and records. (2015). Retrieved from http://portlandmarathon.org/history/results-records/.

Ralby, H. (1966, April 20). Girl finishes marathon. *Boston Globe*, p. 2.

Robinson, R. (2013, July). Barrier breakers: Five early women runners to remember. *Running Times, 408*, p. 72.

Sailors, P. (2012). "Organically sound" Olympians: Gender and women's distance running. *Problems, possibilities, promising practices: Critical dialogues on the Olympic and Paralympic Games.* Eleventh International Symposium for Olympic Research, University of Western Ontario.

Start strong, finish stronger: Race history. (2015). Retrieved from www.tuftshealthplan.com/tufts10k/race_history/index.php?WT.mc_id=menu_history&WT.mc_ev=click.

Switzer, K. (2009). *Marathon woman.* Cambridge, MA: DeCapo Press.

"The Lady Also Ran…" [Letter to the Editor]. (1966, April 21). *Boston Globe*, p. 14.

Vertinksy, P. (2000). Eternally wounded women: Feminist perspectives on physical activity and aging or women's p(l)ace in the marathon of life. *Journal of Aging and Physical Activity, 8*, 386–406.

Wall, K. (1999). *Avon running global championship expected to draw record field from around the world; Top finishers to share richest women's 10K purse*. Retrieved from www.ontherunevents.com/news/~HDG0405.HTM.

Wellesley College. (1996). *Marathon's elite women runners defy spring snow to speak at Wellesley College* (Press Release).

Running because

6 Foot trouble

The minimalist running movement

Pirkko Markula

"Barefoot inspires a revolution in foot wear"

In 2004, Nike released its original Nike Free 5.0 V1 running shoe. That same year I began wearing them. Since then, minimalist shoe sales have skyrocketed making up about 15 percent of all U.S. running shoe sales in 2012. In addition, similar to many other Nike shoes, the Nike Free is popular everyday footwear—one running shoe internet site characterized it as "everyone's favorite coffee shop runner" (Click, 2013). Nike designers have responded to the amplified diversity of usage by modifying the original shoe several times; Nike Free model number 21 "The Flywire" hit the market in 2013 (Click, 2013). In addition, the Nike Free series has now expanded to include "trainers" designed specifically for fitness and exercise.

According to a Nike promotional video, the Free shoes are designed to mimic barefoot running. One of the original designers, Tobie Hatfield, is an avid barefoot runner who found most of his usual urban running routes unsuitable for barefoot running. Inspired by Stanford University track and field coach Vinnie Lananna, who advocated barefoot running for his athletes, Hatfield began to design a shoe that could protect the feet yet allow for more "natural" foot movement than "traditional" running shoes. The resulting design process had the support of several studies. First, Hatfield's concept was tested in the biomechanics labs at Nike's headquarters. A further "Nike campus" study videotaped a group of women and men wearing "pressure-measuring insoles taped to their feet" (Click, 2013). Finally, an "eight year extensive study … yielded the understanding of a 'natural' landing stride" and a consequent need for new running shoes "with minimal heel to toe offset, unconventional shape, and a super Phylon flexible outsole" (Click, 2013). The latter innovation, a flexible and articulated sole structure, was identified as the major breakthrough for the Nike Free design that was to further revolutionize the way running footwear was understood. Following their commercial success, the Nike Free can be identified as forerunners for Nike's recent turn to "natural design." They now feature as a part of Nike's "Nature Amplified Design Ethics" (for sport) for products that work "in harmony with the body moving." The campaign introduces technologically innovative designs that intensify the body's "natural" movement ability (insidenikerunning.com).

The emergence of the minimalist running shoe movement also coincided with the publication of Christopher McDougall's (2011) book, *Born to Run*: *The Hidden Tribe, the Ultra-Runners and the Greatest Race the World Has Never Seen*, a populist account of the Tarahumara Indians' ability to run long distances without getting injured. In his book, McDougall deliberated "natural" running as a solution to many problems in today's society. Although not an advocate of any particular footwear, McDougall's running "ethics" parallels Nike's nature amplified design ethics in its search for increased harmony with the "naturally" moving body. These intersecting moments have led me to ask: Why this pursuit for "natural" movement in this current age that is so characterized by sophisticated high technology? What is "revolutionary" about design or running that is close to "natural" movement?

To understand the concurrent adherence to "natural" (running) movement and technological innovation (such as the Nike Free shoes) I examine in this chapter the meanings of the minimalist shoe movement. I ground my reading on two major sources: McDougall's (2011) *Born to Run* and the scientific texts debating the pros and cons of "barefoot running," many of which are also referred to by McDougall. To further understand the desire for "natural running" in contemporary society, I draw from Deleuze and Guattari's poststructuralist conceptualization of the confrontation between smooth and striated spaces in capitalist society.

The fabric of minimalist running

While technology and "naturalness" or "nature" have sometimes been framed as polar opposites, with technology necessarily seen to be polluting what is "natural," Nike, through its design ethics, has clearly utilized the discourse of "naturalness" to create new technologies. Traditionally, technological innovations were intended to overcome the limitations and hardships created by "natural" conditions. Yet today, they are seen to enhance or enable "naturalness." To locate the heightened "naturalness" of minimalist running within the context of contemporary society, I employ Deleuze and Guattari's conceptualization of capitalism as a *striated space*, a type of fabric where two kinds of parallel elements, vertical (warp) and horizontal (weft), intersect. After detailing the elements of striated space, I discuss *smooth space* that Deleuze and Guattari found co-existing and often transforming the striated space.

Deleuze and Guattari (1987) understood capitalism as a striated space instituted by the State apparatus. The minimalist shoe movement, however, is not directly endorsed by any "State" such as the U.S. government. On the contrary, it is commonly thought of as a commercially driven phenomenon spearheaded by footwear companies such as Nike and Vibram, further boosted by the commercial success of McDougall's (2011) book. Nevertheless, the emergence of minimalist running has been made possible by neo-liberal capitalism operating within the United States. This space, according to Deleuze and Guattari, is organized based on the "technological model" that resembles the structure of "fabric." Such fabric is characterized by two kinds of parallel elements, vertical and horizontal, that intertwine. The vertical element (the warp) is fixed while the horizontal element (the weft) is mobile and passes above and beneath the warp. In other words, while such a fabric can have infinite length, its width is set. Such a fabric also has a clearly identifiable top and bottom. In this sense, the fabric's area is delimited and closed. This is the model, Deleuze and Guattari concluded, that can be said to define science, the art of governing people, and operating the state apparatus. In this space, also the body is primarily understood based on the principles of science that organizes it into an "organism." Deleuze and Guattari observed further that this fabric, literally and figuratively, integrates the body and its outside into a closed space.

The minimalist shoe, in a similar manner, incorporates the structure of fabric literally—for example, the "breathable" mesh weave lining the top of the Nike Free—and figuratively: it is inevitably an aspect of capitalist production riding on the popularity and visibility of running in (American) society. Following the fabric model, if the fixed element of the fabric of the minimalist movement is the commercialization of the running movement, the mobile threads are woven in several colors. Such a fabric could be constructed by intertwining the ideas of science, "naturalness," and technology. The Nike "Nature Amplified Design Ethics" could be seen as a sample of such a fabric. Its mobile, "revolutionary" principles—high technology design based on "natural" bodily movement—interweave with the fixed threads of profit making, commercial success, and scientific discovery in capitalism. In addition to the striated space, Deleuze and Guattari (1987) discussed smooth space, a different type of space that co-exists with the fabric-like capitalism.

Deleuze and Guattari (1987) contrasted the striated space with smooth space that, as infinite, open, and unlimited without a top or a bottom, is characterized by continuous variation. Deleuze and Guattari offered the image of "felt" as opposed to fabric (clearly organized by two interwoven threads) as illustrative of this smooth space. There are, however, many variations of textures between fabric and felt (e.g., crochet that has a clear starting point that can expand both vertically and horizontally). A smooth space, thus, does not exist in opposition to a striated space, neither does it offer a "liberation" from the confines of capitalism. Rather, "smooth space is constantly being translated, transversed into a striated space; striated space is constantly being reversed, returned to a smooth space" (p. 474). "The confrontations between the smooth and the striated, the passages, alternations and superpositions," Deleuze and Guattari observed, "are under way today, running in the most varied directions" (p. 481). They added that multinational companies potentially "fabricate" smooth spaces that become "quite independent of the classical paths of striation" (p. 491). For example, Nike, as primarily a footwear company, has enabled the development of the minimalist movement that, grounded on the idea of running without shoes, could be argued to undermine the sale of shoes. At the same time, capitalism continues to operate "by a complex qualitative process bringing into play modes of transportation, urban models, the media, the entertainment industries, ways of perceiving and feeling" (Deleuze & Guattari, 1987, p. 492). Many of these processes characterize the design story of the Nike Free shoe: its origin in the urban environment that is too hazardous for running in bare feet; its designer's perceived feeling for the need for unshod running in these environments; and its commercial success on the coat tales of the media frenzy surrounding McDougall's (2011) popularized tale of the "naturalness" of endurance running.

Following Deleuze and Guattari (1987), I am particularly interested in how a possible combination of striation and smoothing operate through the minimalist running movement: "how the forces at work within space continually striate it, and how in the course of its striation it develops other forces and emits new smooth spaces" (p. 500). Movements, such as minimalist running, provide possible spaces for change, reconstitution, or inventions when they confront obstacles or gain adversaries and supporters, but they can also be re-ordered into a classical form of fabric. McDougall's (2011) book, for example, could provide a possible innovative force to rethink endurance running. Although it was published after the launce of the first Nike Free shoe, it arguably put barefoot running into the popular consciousness. At the same time, as one part of the entertainment industry—the publishing industry—the book can also operate within the complex set of qualitative processes that striate capitalism. After all, barefoot running has elicited a passionate followership that vocally defends the minimalist style. Alongside the growing barefoot running community and the success of McDougall's book, the scientific interest on barefoot running has also intensified. While all aspects (or threads) of the minimalist movement operate quite simultaneously, I begin to examine its striation and smoothing in the popular media space before discussing the scientific findings around barefoot running.

Born to run within capitalism

Much of the general hype around *Born to Run* centers on the discovery of the secrets of the Tamahumara males who allegedly can run extremely long distances over a variety of terrains in bare feet. However, McDougall's (2011) book can be equally read to illuminate the American (ultra)distance running culture with the Tamahumara people serving as a justification for attempts to run distance races beyond the length of the marathon (26.2 miles). Thus, the book's subtitle, *The Hidden Tribe, the Ultra-Runners and the Greatest Race the World Has Never Seen*, although seldom cited, is more illustrative of its content, yet not equally as marketable as the beguiling *Born to Run*. In his book, McDougall placed the "underground ultra-running" movement in opposition to the marathon, that as he claimed, has been commercialized by increased sponsorship from shoe companies, prize money, marketing, and the media. In this sense, *Born to Run* could be interpreted as actively smoothing the striated space of capitalism (Deleuze & Guattari, 1987) to construct a type of felt instead of the weave of capitalist fabric.

It is natural to run long distances

Deleuze and Guattari (1987) envisioned a smooth space being constructed "by local operations" (p. 478). McDougall's (2011) personal quest for injury free endurance running, the reason he became aware of and interested in barefoot running, in many ways exemplifies local operations that can smooth out established ideas about endurance running. At the outset of his tale, McDougall does not appear to be born to run, quite the contrary. He is a journalist who reports on "semi-extreme sports" for *Men's Health* magazine. He is an aspiring marathoner, but a rather large man (6′4″), and he is continually injured. To try to cure his injuries, he visited several renowned medical doctors who specialized in running injuries only to be told that the human body, particularly his body, is not designed for running. Furthermore, his running technique, he was told, was inadequate, but changing it, as he learned, would likely come with other injury problems.

McDougall (2011) of course is not alone: running injuries are normal (eight out of ten runners get injured every year), a rate that the running shoe companies have been unable to reduce. Why, then, does McDougall continue to run against his doctors' advice? Because, he stated in his book, "There's something so universal about … the way running unites our two most primal impulses: fear and pleasure" (p. 11). Running, he added, provides stress relief and sensual pleasure before "you have sex" in your life (p. 12). Running, thus, must be universally human, a "natural" impulse and thus, a "natural" human endeavor. After establishing these "universal truths," McDougall concluded that while he did not love running when at the start of his book, he "*wanted* to [emphasis in original]" (p. 12). Briefly, the direction for his book crystallized into how to endure lots of running without injuries. This must be possible, McDougall hypothesized, because running is a natural impulse, a sign of joy. These principles serve as an unchanging guide for his journey from an injured wannabe Marathoner to a successful ultra-distance runner.

Deleuze and Guattari (1987) further defined smooth spaces as being characterized by "a direction" (rather than a dimension or metric determination) (p. 478). The direction, however, is not predetermined, but will constantly change "due to the variability of the goal to be attained" (p. 478). If operations in a smooth space necessarily involve changes in direction, the direction of McDougall's (2011) journey was firmly fixed on discovering the primal want for running that must be possible, for any body, without injuries. With undeviating commitment, characterizing the striated spaces of scientific truth, he traced the naturalness of endurance running linearly as evidenced by human evolution. Although the narrative itself does not proceed chronologically, McDougall marched in a set of experts to construct an evolutionary history of endurance running from Homo Erectus to Bushman endurance hunters and present day Kenyan runners. As a result, "The Running Man Theory" became verified by a triangle of experts: Americans Dr. Bramble (a biologist) and Dr. Lieberman (an evolutionary biologist), and South-African Louis Liebenberg, a mathematician and physicist, but "electrified by an insight into human evolution" (p. 234).

In this formation, Bramble proved that the erect position of Homo Sapiens enabled him to have an effective long running stride to eventually replace the Neanderthals. Lieberman added that humans as naked animals were able to evaporate excess running heat through the skin (instead of having to stop to pant it off like animals). As clear evidence of human's natural ability to run long distances without overheating, Bramble provided: "[we are] the only species in the world [that] has the urge to gather by the tens of thousands to run twenty-six miles in the heat for fun" (McDougall, 2011, p. 221). However, the two professors still needed evidence of the existence of hunting that, indeed, was done by running the game "to death." Thus entered Liebenberg who joined the Kalahari Bushmen who still practiced persistence hunting and who, according to McDougall (2011), stubbornly clung to the freedom and independence provided by traditional cultural practices instead of manual labor and prostitution offered by capitalist industrialization surrounding them. These persistence hunters, however, did not gather together to run in the heat for fun. Neither was their running uninterrupted or aimed at achieving a record pace. As Liebenberg observed: "the pace [during persistence hunting] wasn't too fierce; the Bushmen average about ten minutes a mile … but occasionally stop to study tracks" (p. 238). Although running during persistence hunting does not carry much resemblance to contemporary endurance racing, it provides evidence of humans' natural ability to run. As Lieberman summarized:

> humans really are obligatorily required to do aerobic exercise in order to stay healthy, and I think that has deep roots in our evolutionary history.… If there's any magic bullet to make human beings healthy, it's to run.
>
> (p. 168)

With the lineage of endurance running established, McDougall (2011) sought to find "tribes" whose traditional running practices were closer to endurance racing. He discovered the Raramuri (Tamahumara) in the deep isolated canyons of Barrancas, Mexico: they still "lived endurance running," running extreme distances injury free up to old age wearing only rubber sandals or rubber cut from used tires that they tied on the bottom of their feet. They ran in high altitude and difficult terrain, yet not to hunt. They appeared, not only unbelievably tough runners, but the kindest, happiest, healthiest, and most enlightened people. The Raramuri, McDougall revealed, had been persuaded to participate in organized ultra races (e.g., Leadville Trail 100) in the United States, but, despite their obvious success, had been disillusioned by the commercialized endurance running culture. As a result, they were unwilling to speak about the secrets of being able to run injury free. Undaunted, McDougall travelled, sponsored by *Runner's World* magazine, to meet representatives of the Raramuri to try to unravel the secrets of running-induced happiness. He, nevertheless, required intermediaries to actually have someone answer his questions. Here the anti-commercialization preferred by McDougall begins to weave together with sponsorship, organized running races, and elite professional runners that striate the potentially smooth space of "natural running." Namely, the story culminates in the ultimate ultra-running race, the

"Greatest Race," between the Raramuri and "underground American ultra-runners" who, for McDougall, epitomized "true" American running. The American "underground ultra-runners," were representatives of the "tribe of isolated outcasts, running for love and relying on raw instinct and crude equipment" (McDougall, 2011, p. 93) rather than for money and fame. This did not prevent them from being successful: besides McDougall himself, they were among the top ultra distance runners in America. To my reading, the Greatest Race demonstrated the incipient striation of a non-commercialized running space.

The notion of a clearly definable form for action, according to Deleuze and Guattari (1987), characterizes a striated space where there is a need for organization, measures, and properties such as an ultra-race with a clearly set course, time, and set of competitors. The Greatest Race, however, was to materialize in the desert like conditions of the Barrancas with rough terrain and demanding altitude conditions. While Deleuze and Guattari offered the "desert" as one metaphor for a smooth space, the inaccessible isolation of the Barrancas seemed to align with previously set requirements for extra challenging ultra races rather than smoothing out the dominant understandings for endurance running racing in America.

With these details, "natural" running as depicted by McDougall (2011), begins to turn into a fabric with the "naturalness" as a mobile horizontal thread intertwining with the fixed verticality of commercialized distance racing for White Americans who can choose to "live on the edge" to feel "happy," and/or become successful professional runners. Another horizontal thread for McDougall's running fabric, running bare feet, appeared alongside the Greatest Race.

It is natural and fun to run long distances bare feet

The underground ultra-running culture celebrated by McDougall (2011) embodies several further characteristics of smoothness (Deleuze & Guattari, 1987). It is filled with joy and haptic (feeling the body rather than visual) perception of the tactile qualities of the terrain.

McDougall (2011) observed that feeling joy is at the heart of successful endurance running. It was also the secret of the Raramuri's running triumphs. While the Raramuri runners did not directly talk about their experiences of running in his book, McDougall depicted these sentiments through a story from a 65-year coach Joe Vigil who discovered the Raramuri having "SUCH A SENSE OF JOY" (p. 91) at the Leadville race, one of the major American ultra-races. For Vigil, love and joy were the essential elements of the "natural" attitude for successful endurance running. McDougall summarized:

> The Tamahumara had never forgotten what it felt like to love running. They remembered that running was mankind's first fine art.... You had to love running, or you wouldn't live to love anything else. And like everything else we love—everything we sentimentally call our "passions" and "desires"—it's really an encoded ancestral necessity.
>
> (p. 93)

The "Tamahumara attitude," thus, was a barometer not only for winning races, but for running as natural ancestral heritage. Unlike the professional runners corrupted by "the American approach" ("business, not love"), the "amateur" ultra-runners embraced the "playfulness" and fun of "natural" running similar to the Raramuri.

This correct attitude for running was accompanied by a sensitivity to bodily feedback or as defined by Deleuze and Guattari (1987), haptic perception. For example, such runners operated by "feeling the trails" rather than following traditional training plans—an approach to running that, according to McDougall (2011), resembled art rather than sport. In addition, bodily fatigue and pain were repeatedly described as important feedback for the runner. However, an endurance runner was to learn to love these sensations and overcome them rather than treating them as warning signals for overexertion. McDougall asserted that if one pushes through fatigue and stress, one will find brand new strength and an entirely new, brave bodily world. For example, ultra-runner Lisa Smith Batchen advised runners to love "the Beast of fatigue, to learn to control it. To conquer it, you have to love it" (p. 95). The artistic approach to loving pain and fatigue did not exclude training and covering high mileage, albeit most of the time without a coach. Thus, ultra-running intertwined with traditional approaches to distance running (pain, fatigue, mileage, training), but it also exemplified many of the smooth qualities materializing in McDougall's defense for barefoot running.

It must be repeated that the Raramuri did not, in fact, run bare feet, but in sandals (huaraches) or cut off pieces of used tire that they tied to the bottom of their feet. Actually, McDougall (2011) himself ran in Nike Pegasus shoes. He, nevertheless, emphasized the haptic qualities of running bare feet: feet need to feel the terrain to transmit information to the brain, or as McDougall vividly put it: "Feet are sensitive, they are self-correcting devices. Covering feet with cushioned shoes turns off these smoke alarms" (p. 177). Various experts from medicine, physiotherapy, and exercise physiology further verified that if running is "natural," running bare feet is even more "natural." When shoes no longer block the pain, the runner's form also automatically improves: his back straightens and his legs stay squarely under the hips. McDougall's own form adjusted and he turned from more of a *heel striker* to a *mid/front striker* (landing on the front part of the foot instead of the heel). Somewhat contradictorily, he also described how he learned to run (with or without shoes) guided by his coach Eric Orton who believed that

> Everyone thinks they know how to run, but it's really as nuanced as any other activity … ask most people and they'll say, "People just run the way they run." That's ridiculous. Does everyone just swim the way they swim?… Learn it wrong, and you'll never know how good it can feel.
>
> (p. 180)

These "material" truths behind adopting barefoot running—human feet like a good beating and thus, we are designed to run without shoes—were complemented by broader social benefits of endurance running. McDougall estimated that the major problems of humanity such as violence, obesity, illness, and greed could be overcome if we all began running again:

> What if you could run for decades and never get injured … and log hundreds of weekly miles and enjoy every one of them … and see your heart rate drop and your stress and anger fade while your energy soared? Imagine crime, cholesterol, and greed melting away as a nation of Running People finally rediscovered its stride.
>
> (p. 99)

Although this sounds like a wonderful solution to the current ills of the world, from a Deleuzian perspective, McDougall's book does not necessarily smoothen the space of capitalism despite painting a picture of affection and haptic perception, of an intensive space of distances, and of bodily sensitivity deriving from desert conditions. Such a running space continues to be striated by long, measurable running distances and a body that is still organized through intense training and strict diet.

Although overtly critical of the running shoe industry, McDougall (2011) acknowledged Nike as a forerunner for the minimalist shoe movement. In this sense, Nike, as a multinational company, did fabricate a smooth space that has diverted "the classical paths of striation" (Deleuze & Guattari, 1987, p. 492) of endurance running. The book itself, nevertheless, continues to weave the fabric of capitalism: the mobile horizontal thread—"natural" running (reinforced by a number of scientific experts) preferable with bare feet—intertwines with the vertical warp of commercialism. "Natural" running occurs within the confines of racing, running technique, endurance training, proper diet, travel, and internet communication, all aspects of modern capitalist living. In other words, the haptic perceptions and feelings of the endurance running body actualize in the context of an organized ultra-race (culture), individual's responsibility for community building (for rather privileged and very successful people), and natural biological heritage. In McDougall's book, ultra-running exemplifies good living in the commercialized world: natural movement, a simple diet, and camaraderie combined with competitiveness and community building. Besides McDougall's popular text, the meaning of "natural running" is hotly debated in another space: the scientific community.

The fabric of barefoot running science

Although McDougall's (2011) book and barefoot running have their passionate followers, many scientists continue to debate the "hard facts" behind the benefits of shedding one's shoes. According to Ross Tucker, a regular blogger and sport scientist from the University of The Free State, South Africa, barefoot running is among the most discussed issues in the *Science of Sport* website that reports the latest scientific news on running and cycling. It is important to note that much of the sport science research on barefoot running focuses on the possible benefits of running in bare feet instead of "minimalist" footwear such as the Vibram 5 fingers (no sole cushioning) or Nike Free shoes (reduced cushioning). However, the debate regarding the advantages of both modes of running centers around the same issues and thus, to understand the link between "naturalness" and Nike Free technology in today's world, I highlight the main points in the sport science literature.

While acknowledging McDougall's (2011) contribution, the scientists approach each of the arguments for barefoot running by favoring evidence based on scientific testing rather than personal testimonies. They weave a fabric different from McDougall's commercial fabric of emotional personal experience. Their "technological model" (Deleuze & Guattari, 1987), where several mobile elements pass above and beneath the fixed strand of "scientific evidence," structures the running body as an organism to be protected from injury. In their recent meta-analysis, Tam and colleagues (2014) identified evolutionary biology, biomechanics for injury prevention, and improved running performance as the main scientific interests in barefoot running. The idea of running bare feet as the "natural" way of running is embedded within these mutually supporting themes.

The biomechanics of barefoot running: forefoot landing

Despite several "hues," the vertical threads of the scientific fabric around barefoot running are built for injury prevention. Runners' high injury rates serve as a starting point for several research articles (e.g., Lieberman *et al.*, 2010; Hall, Barton, Jones, & Morrissey, 2013; Murphy, Curry, & Matzkin, 2013; Lieberman, Davis, & Niggs, 2014). For example, in a series of experiments Lieberman provided an etiology for running injuries by classifying running shoes as "unnatural" and consequently, as the cause of injuries. His research, thus, acted as a principal grounding for the scientific fabric of barefoot running.

Having established endurance running as an integral aspect of human evolution (Bamble & Lieberman, 2004), Lieberman (Lieberman *et al.*, 2010), an avid barefoot runner, set out to scientifically prove the naturalness (and thus superiority) of barefoot running mechanics. He demonstrated that habitual adult barefoot runners used a forefoot landing whereas habitually shoed adult runners landed using a heel strike. Forefoot landing reduced the stress of impact or "the impact transient of the vertical ground reaction" (p. 531). With less stress on the body, Lieberman demonstrated, there are also less injuries most of which are a result of the collision between the foot and the ground. Arguing from an evolutionary perspective, he concluded: "If endurance running was an important behavior before the invention of modern shoes, then natural selection is expected to have operated to lower the risk of injury and discomfort when barefoot or in minimal footwear" (p. 533).

It must be noted that Lieberman's team did not test any runners with minimalist shoes. Nevertheless, in his later study on the Tamahumara Indians' footstrike variation, Lieberman (2014) found that in his sample of 23 minimally shod (traditional running sandals) runners, 70 percent used either a forefoot or mid-foot strike. Relying on previous research, Lieberman (2014) further asserted that 75–90 percent of shod runners tended to land first on their heels because the cushioning allows for tolerance of greater heel impact (see also Murphy, Curry, & Matzkin, 2013). Consequently, without the support provided by shoes, "habitually barefoot runners are more likely to land with either a forefoot strike (FFS) … or a midfoot strike (MFS)" (Lieberman, 2014, p. 86). He, thus, assumed that changing footwear automatically results in forefoot landing for most runners. Contrary to Lieberman, Tam and his colleagues (2014) concluded that "the suggestions that barefoot running is synonymous with forefoot striking is … inaccurate" (p. 350) because the strike pattern is related to running speed and running surface.

Since the groundbreaking study of Lieberman and colleagues (2010), as Tam and colleagues (2014) noted, "there has been something of a preoccupation with the foot strike" (p. 350) among the scientists studying the injury risk related to barefoot running. Verifying McDougall's (2011) earlier assertion, further studies have shown that a forefoot landing changes the biomechanics of running. There is greater plantar flexion of the foot (e.g., Ahn, Brayton, Bhatia, & Martin, 2014; Lieberman *et al.*, 2010) and knee flexion upon impact (e.g., Hall *et al.*, 2013; Lieberman *et al.*, 2010). As a result, the foot's plantar fascia is employed as a support system for the foot arch. The "stiffened" arches (Hein & Grau, 2014; Lieberman, 2014) then act as a shock absorption system. The altered mechanics of barefoot running also increases the eccentric work of the ankle but decreases the loading on the knee (e.g., Tam, Wilson, Noakes, & Tucker, 2014). This can improve the condition of some runners' knees, one of the most injury prone parts of a runner's body.[1] The combined changes in the kinematic chain tend to result in a shorter stride, which reduces shock attenuation (Mercer, Devita, Derrick, & Bates, 2013). Running bare feet also improves the sensory feedback from the feet and as a result, the runner is better able to feel the terrain, a fact also advanced by McDougall (2011).

In summary, the scientific research supports the idea that forefoot landing (not bare foot running per se) strengthens the feet muscles that have become "lazy" due to the use of shoes. It also reduces the impact transients to change the running mechanics and thus, reduces the stress on injury prone body parts. While the efficiency gain of barefoot (or minimalist shoe) running is debated, forefoot landing does tend to result in a shorter stride. In this discussion, the running body is carefully organized into a hierarchically structured organism (Deleuze & Guattari, 1987). The change in landing pattern stimulates an automatic response at all the layers of the organism without involvement of force by the body itself. Tucker's analogy of barefoot running as a medicine—"if you have a condition, take a drug. If you have an injury, take barefoot running" (June 6, 2011)—illustrates this type of understanding of the body. Tucker, however, questioned the lack of proper dosage, contra-indications, and exclusion criteria for barefoot running, not the idea of running as medicine.

Proponents of the barefoot/minimalist movement acknowledge, however, that most modern day runners are accustomed to shoes and thus, a sudden switch is likely to result in injuries, particularly in the foot and ankle where muscles are especially weak. Even if there is no immediate injury, the previously unused muscles tend to tire fast and thus, there is an increase of muscle pain and stiffness. Experts, such as Irene Davis who also featured in McDougall's (2011) book, recommended extreme care, even for experienced runners, when attempting the switch.[2] Tucker (June 6, 2011) echoed such cautions stating that smart training and gradual progression are the keys to successful and injury-free running in lightweight shoes.

Although injury prevention is the primary interest, the primary scientific evidence regarding the benefits of barefoot running focuses on the landing pattern. There is no definite evidence beyond the fact that running injuries have not decreased with the use of running shoes. Murphy and colleagues (2013) concluded their review: "there is no higher level evidence to support barefoot (or minimally supportive) running as a means of injury prevention, nor is there supporting evidence for shod running as a means of injury prevention either" (p. 1136). As a result, Vibram recently had to settle a $3.75 million lawsuit brought on by an unhappy customer claiming that Vibram's marketing was not supported by scientific evidence.[3] Vibram ended up refunding $94 to all of its customers due to this "deception." Deleuze and Guattari (1987) would observe that the capitalist fabric did not stretch when pulled by the minimalist running movement and relied on the vertical thread of science to keep its structure in place. Even Tucker, a scientist himself, found "scientization" claims limiting, rather than expanding the way to think innovatively about running stating that "perhaps the burden for scientific proof is just so high that a logical outcome [on benefits of barefoot running] can't be claimed" (May 15, 2014). Scientific studies have, nevertheless, indicated that the "landing" pattern changes with footwear change.

Natural running is for certain types of bodies

In his insightful blog series on minimalism, Tucker, generally, supported the idea that running barefoot considerably changes loading patterns and muscle activity compared to running with shoes. This is due to forefoot landing. He urged runners to try this themselves: within 50 m of running barefoot any runner will naturally shift toward forefoot landing, because landing on the heels hurts: "we 'feel' the ground more than we want to at first, and over time, we adjust our mechanics and shift to a forefoot landing" (June 6, 2011).[4] Tucker further claimed that a runner cannot actually control the landing cognitively and consequently, some will be unable to make a successful adjustment to barefoot running due to huge variations in the biomechanical response. For example, runners who continue to heel strike without shoe support may be unsuited to barefoot running.

Somewhat contradictorily, he stated elsewhere that foot strike is merely a result of otherwise good running form. One can have good form and land on the heel. However, although one can learn good running form, one is unable to learn a variety of landing foot strikes. The scientific studies, similar to McDougall's (2011) main thesis, support the premise of humans being "born to run" rather than endorsing humans "learning to run." If everyone is born to run naturally, then why cannot we all automatically employ the "efficient" forefoot landing? A question also presented by Tam and colleagues (2014) who looked for more scientific inquiry on learning the "skill" of running efficiently. However, including individual learning experience with the parameters of observable, measurable, and quantifiable scientific fabric might require widening, not merely lengthening, its structure. One further indication of the rigidness of the scientific fabric is Tucker's rejection of so-called "anthropological" justifications for barefoot running. According to him, to argue that we have run for millions of years on bare feet and thus, our bodies are unsuitable for shoes is the weakest argument for barefoot running. Such a statement is a gross generalization that ignores how running conditions and environment have changed, how runners have changed, and how our modern lifestyle differs from hunter-gatherer communities (March 17, 2011). Not proven in laboratory conditions, these conclusions do not fit within the tightly measured width of the scientific fabric. After confronted with the scientific logic of Lieberman's evolutionary biology, however, Tucker modified his view slightly but still called for "controlled" scientific studies instead of "historical comparisons" (June 6, 2011).

Conclusion

In this chapter, I surveyed the space occupied by the minimalist running movement within the striated space of (North American) capitalism. Generated by several forces—the Nike Free minimalist running shoe, McDougall's (2011) *Born to Run*, and the scientific research on barefoot running—there was a possible opening for smoothing the fabric by pulls from multiple directions.

Deleuze and Guattari (1987) observed that all spaces are continuously being transversed: striated spaces are altered into smooth, smooth spaces are reversed back into striation. Such a process is evident in the case of minimalist running. Nike, as a multinational company, might have begun to smoothen the striations about running with its Nike Free design concept and product. McDougall (2011) popularized the idea of minimalism, even without a major focus on barefoot running. With strong support by evolutionary biologist Lieberman, barefoot running also entered into the scientific community interested in distance running. These three forces, however, transpired as striations of the capitalist space. McDougall, openly critical of the commercialization of distance running in America (and Nike), smoothened the fabric more than the scientific community. He discussed runners' personal experiences, presented his own story, described local interactions, and dwelled on feelings and emotions associated with running long distances. The scientific space, instead, stretched only minimally to contemplate such issues as skill learning or evidence from evolutionary biology if contained within the strict limits of scientific testing. Unlike the scientists, who are limited to examinations of foot strike and the resulting kinematic chain (unable to even draw conclusions about possible injury rate changes), McDougall was not afraid to present ultra-distance running as a natural, and thus universal, human need that if fulfilled, will result in a better world. Nevertheless, as an answer to the ills of capitalism, ultra-running remains an individualized solution: as long as one is able to run long distances and have a good diet, social problems will be solved. While the characters of McDougall's book engaged with exotic marginalized peoples (the Raramuri, the Kalahari Bushmen), instead of aiming to improve these peoples' conditions, they sought self-fulfillment by visiting such places only to return to their middle-class American lives as happier consumers. Deleuze and Guattari (1987) might have recommended such localized solutions as a way of smoothing out the capitalist fabric. However, if the action is limited to changing one's behavior without problematization, for example, of the need of (middle class) Americans to overcome pain and engage in endurance running, it continues to improve individual "happiness" within the confines of capitalism. From a Deleuzian perspective, such action rides on the striations of the capitalist fabric rather smoothing it out.

In 2013, minimalist shoe sales were reported to "plummet": although increasing about 70 percent each month in the United States, they made up only 11 percent of all running shoe sales. Nike Free sales excluded, minimalist shoes constituted only 4 percent of U.S. running shoes sales (Douglas, March 13, 2013) inspiring some to declare "the minimalist trend" over (Douglas, May 13, 2013). In addition, counter developments like the "maximal shoe" Hoka One One now inhabit the market place to fulfill the needs of those runners, as identified by scientists like Tucker, who are seemingly unable to learn the forefoot technique needed for minimalist running.

Even intertwined within striations of weaved fabric, the minimalist movement continues to gain passionate followers of whose preferences we know very little. For example, although not a "zealot" of the minimalist running movement, I continue to wear my Nike Free shoes as a better option for the more uncomfortable "stability" shoes. Similar to the majority of runners in Hryvniak and colleague's (2014) study, a rare examination into the reasons for starting barefoot running,[5] I use them as a training tool to improve my running efficiency. To further identify smooth running spaces, the fabric of running research can include a wider variety of perspectives that smoothen the space of research to count, for example, for the possibilities and problems with skill learning, cultural conceptions of endurance running, running experiences in addition to those of successful ultra-racers, the role of minimalist running in everyday lives, or perceptions of minimalist walkers and exercisers. Such research can be one localized way to actualize a smooth space (of minimalist running) that is characterized by multiple directions enabled by technology, design, bodily techniques, and socio-cultural conditions.

Notes

1 Patellofemoral pain syndrome accounts for 20 percent of all running injuries (Murphy, Curry, & Matzkin, 2013).

2 Davis advised to begin with 30 minutes of barefoot walking before slowly starting with a one-minute jog followed by a nine-minute walk for 30 minutes. This is an extremely careful approach for runners with any experience.

3 Vibram five-fingered shoes were designed to strengthen the muscles in the feet and lower legs, improve rage of in motion the ankles, feet, and toes, stimulate neural function important to balance and agility, eliminate heel lift to align the spine and improve posture, and allow the foot and body to move "naturally." In a close look, these align with results from the scientific research, but do not ensure long term "health benefits" (Tucker, 2014).

4 "…natural running form is the form you adopt without any external input, or any conscious thoughts about how to run. It is the way you run when you simply run, not cognitive thoughts of how to position your arms, how to land how to lift the heel versus driving the knee forward—in the absence of all those instructions we run 'naturally.' I believe the natural way to run is the unadjusted one, but the best way to run is the modified natural" (Tucker, March 16, 2010).

5 The researchers did not define what they meant by "barefoot running" but seemed to include also minimally shod running.

References

Ahn, A. N., Brayton, C., Bhatia, T., & Martin, P. (2014). Muscle activity and kinematics of forefoot and rearfoot strike runners. *Journal of Sport and Health Science, 3*, 102–112.

Bramble, D. M., & Lieberman, D. E. (2004). Endurance running and the evolution of Homo. *Nature*, *432*, 345–52.

Click, C. (2013, March). The Complete Performance History of the Nike Free. Retrieved from http://ca.complex.com/sneakers/2013/03/the-complete-performance-history-of-the-nike-free.

Deleuze, G., & Guattari, F. (1987). *Thousand plateaus: Capitalism and Schizophrenia*, London, England: Athlone.

Douglas, S. (2013, March 13). Minimalism in the long run. What is the future for shoes? *Running Times*. Retrieved from www.runnersworld.com/barefoot-running-minimalism/minimalism-long-run.

Douglas, S. (2013, May 13). Sales of minimalist shoes plummet. *Runner's World & Running Times*. Retrieved from www.runnersworld.com/minimalist-shoes/sales-of-minimalist-shoes-plummet.

Hall, J. P., Barton, C., Jones, P. R., & Morrissey, D. (2013). The biomechanical differences between barefoot and shod distance running: A systematic review and preliminary meta-analysis. *Sports Medicine*, *43*, 1335–1353.

Hein, T., & Grau, S. (2014). Can minimal running shoes imitate barefoot heel-toe running patterns? A comparison of lower leg kinematics. *Journal of Sport and Health Science*, *3*, 67–73.

Hryvniak, D., Dicharry, J., & Wilder, R. (2014). Barefoot running survey: Evidence from the field. *Journal of Sport and Health Science*, *3*, 131–136.

Lieberman, D. E. (2014). Strike type variation among Tarahumara Indians in minimal sandals versus conventional running shoes. *Journal of Sport and Health Science*, *3*, 86–94.

Lieberman, D. E., Davis, I. S., & Nigss, B. M. (2014). Introduction: The past, present, and future of research on running barefoot and in minimal shoes. *Journal of Sport and Health Science*, *3*, 65–66.

Lieberman, D. E., Venkadesan, M., Werbel, W. A., Daoud, A. I., D'Andrea, S., Davis, I. S., Magn'Enie, R. O., & Pitsiladis, Y. (2010 January). Foot strike patterns and collision forces in habitually barefoot versus shod runners. *Nature*, *463*, 531–535.

McDougall, C. (2011). *Born to run: A hidden tribe, superathletes, and the greatest race the world has never seen*. New York, NY: Knopf.

Mercer, J. A., Devita, P., Derrick, T. R., & Bates, B. T. (20013). Individual effects of stride length and frequency on shock attenuation during running. *Medicine and Science in Sports and Exercise*, *35*, 307–313.

Murphy, K., Curry, E. J., & Matzkin, E. G. (2013). Barefoot running: Does it prevent injuries? *Sports Medicine*, *43*, 1131–1138.

Sneakerreport.com.

Tam, N., Wilson, J. L. A., Noakes, T. D., & Tucker, R. (2014). Barefoot running: An evaluation of current hypothesis, future research and clinical applications. *British Journal of Sports Medicine*, *48*, 349–355.

Tucker, E. (2014, May 12). Canadian refunds uncertain for Vibram "finger toe" shoes in US lawsuit. *Global News*. Retrieved from http://globalnews.ca/news/1325637/canadian-refunds-uncertain-for-vibram-finger-toe-shoes-in-us-lawsuit.

Tucker, R. (2010, March 16). Barefoot running and shoes Q & A Part 1. *The Science of Sport*. Retrieved from http://sportsscientists.com/2010/03/barefoot-running-and-shoes-q-a-part-1.

Tucker, R. (2010, March 16). Barefoot running and shoes Q & A Part 2. *The Science of Sport*. Retrieved from http://sportsscientists.com/2010/03/barefoot-running-and-shoes-q-a-part-2.

Tucker, R. (2010, March 17). Barefoot running and shoes Q & A Part 3. *The Science of Sport*. Retrieved from http://sportsscientists.com/2010/03/barefoot-running-and-shoes-q-a-part-3.

Tucker R. (2010, March 17). Barefoot running and shoes Q & A Part 4. *The Science of Sport*. Retrieved from http://sportsscientists.com/2010/03/barefoot-running-and-shoes-q-a-part-4.

Tucker, R. (2010, March 17). Barefoot running and shoes Q & A Part 5. *The Science of Sport*. Retrieved from http://sportsscientists.com/2010/03/barefoot-running-and-shoes-q-a-part-5.

Tucker, R., (2011, June 06). Barefoot running, shoes, and born to run. *The Science of Sport*. Retrieved from http://sportsscientists.com/2011/06/barefoot-running-shoes-and-born-to-run.

Tucker, R. (2013, May 16). A minimalism/barefoot fad and inconsequential footstrikes. *The Science of Sport*. Retrieved from http://sportsscientists.com/2013/05/a-minimalism barefoot-fad-and-inconsequential-footstrikes.

Tucker, R. (2014, May 15). The Vibram lawsuit, barefoot running and science perspective. *The Science of Sport*. Retrieved from http://sportsscientists.com/2014/05/vibram-lawsuit-barefoot-running-common-sense.

7 Disrupting identity

An affective embodied reading of *Runner's World*

Richard Pringle

In this chapter, I explore the pains and pleasures of endurance running via an affective analysis of *Runner's World*, a glossy magazine devoted to those who run long distances. My examination, rather than asking the more typical sociocultural studies questions (e.g., "what does this magazine mean?" or "how does this magazine contribute to the marginalization of certain individuals or groups?"), considers *Runner's World* as a "kind of actor with the power to affect its audiences" (Paasonen, 2010, p. 59). More specifically, I analyze how *Runner's World* evokes the corporeality of running and mobilizes various affects and emotions. I suggest that the mobilization of these divergent sensations and feelings work, in part, to produce an energized and embodied way of knowing that urges readers to run and, correspondingly, constitutes desire, running subjectivities, and interconnections. My aim, in part, is to present a different way of understanding or feeling running, one that sits aside from analyses that focus on select identity categories (e.g., female, male, straight, disabled) and/or critiques of running that center on discipline, docility, pain, and body image.[1]

Throughout the chapter I insert vignettes from my own embodied experiences of running. I do so in chronological order, starting from youthful memories of a body that was lean, fit, supple, and pain free, to more recent times and the associated confessions from "being" older, slower, and heavier. In this way I interweave my biography to tell a story about an aging body, running, and self. I do so, in following Coffey (1990) and Giardina and Newman (2011), who recognized the importance of bodies in the process of doing research. Coffey (1990) argued that the researcher's body and the body of others "are central to the practical accomplishments of fieldwork" (p. 59). She correspondingly explicated the complexities of the researcher's relationship to the field of inquiry and the importance of writing from an embodied reflexive position.

I understand embodied reflexivity, in part, via Deleuze's (1992) account of Foucault's notion of *dispositif* (often translated as an "apparatus" or "assemblage"). Deleuze explained in the first instance that an apparatus is "a tangle, a multilinear ensemble. It is composed of lines, each having a different nature.... Each line is broken and subject to *changes in direction*, bifurcating and forked, and subject to *drifting* [emphasis in original]" (p. 159). Deleuze suggested that to understand the complexities of a social apparatus it is important to untangle the lines (or curves, as they should not be assumed to be straight), of which he draws specific attention to lines of visibility—for example, what can be seen or not, depending on how light "falls, blurs and disperses" (p. 160), enunciations (which give rise, as examples, to laws, social movements, and literary genres), forces (or the workings of power), and subjectifications. Understanding "reality" as intersecting sets of apparatuses of which we belong and act within, allows a focus on the social and bodies as processes "of becoming" (p. 164), interconnected, fluid, and creative. Thus, Deleuze, in drawing from Foucault, refused the unity and stability of identity and offered a new way of understanding the body and its connections to others and things. Grosz (1994) explained that Deleuze conceptualized the body:

> ...in its connections with other bodies, both human and nonhuman, animate and inanimate, linking organs and biological processes to material objects and social practices while refusing to subordinate the body to a unit of a homogeneity of the kind provided by the bodies subordination to consciousness or to biological organizations.
>
> (p. 165)

Grosz, more succinctly, framed the body as an affective assemblage, through which she understood that affects were a means that allowed bodies, and other things, to come together, ricochet, or blur. It is within this respect that I reflexively interweave some of my own embodied accounts of running, to allow for possibilities of affective connections and for readers to gain insight into my interpretations of *Runner's World.*

For the record, I was a fan of the Olympics as a child and young adult, a harrier (cross-country runner) and inter-provincial track athlete until 14, and fair weather runner ever since. I typically only run for 30 minutes but have completed two half-marathons. Although I have run somewhat regularly for over 30 years, I do not consider it as a lifestyle nor do I consider myself as part of the running community. Running has nevertheless shaped my story of self.

I begin this chapter by proffering the notion, via link to relevant literature, that long-distance runners run for affective/emotional reasons. I then contextualize *Runner's World*, detail my theoretical and methodological tools for analyzing the magazine affectively, and, finally, present my findings.

> **9: We can be heroes**
> Edmund Hillary visited Tahunanui school in Nelson, Aotearoa New Zealand, when Rod Dixon[2] was a pupil. Dixon remembers Hillary saying that Mount Everest was not high enough to aspire to and, therefore, the pupils should dream bigger. When Dixon won an Olympic track medal he remembered Hillary's words of inspiration. I remember Dixon visiting Tahunanui School when I was nine. He looked like an athletic Beatle circa their 1967 look: tall, lean, black shoulder length hair, and moustache. We ran with him and jostled to get next to him or in front. We touched his

> bronze medal. It did not glisten in the sun, as one might have expected. He organized a school race. I won. As he shook my hand, he told me to join Harriers. I did. And dreamed of Olympic glory.

Understanding why runners run

Throsby (2013) observed that the defining characteristic of lifestyle sports as defined via media representations, is an apparent commitment to hedonism whereas endurance sports, such as long-distance running, are more likely to be epitomized via narratives of pain, suffering, and the deferral of pleasure. Bale (2006) similarly noted that good runners are those who can tolerate pain better than others—burning muscles, breathlessness, the sting of foot-strike—so that they run faster, longer, and harder than others. Yet such negative depictions of running do not resonate with how runners understand and are "moved" by running. So why do non-elite long-distance runners run?

In a provocative manner, I claim that distance running is not a purely rational pursuit. Indeed, runners often confess that friends and colleagues regard them as mad or crazy for running in the heat or cold and at peculiar times (Smith, 2000). I concede that some may claim to run long distances for rational reasons—such as with concerns for weight management, better physical health, or social benefits. Yet these reasons might be more imagined than real. The cardiovascular benefits of regular aerobic exercise, for example, are well documented and can (apparently) be gained through relatively moderate levels of movement: one does not need to run over 40-miles a week for "health," a distance that Collee (1990) suggests smacks of some form of fundamentalism. Conversely, I develop the argument that most long-distance runners run because they have developed an affective/emotional relationship with running. Runners talk of the sensual *joy* of running, the *freedom* of movement, the meditative *bliss*, the spiritual *gains*, the *guilt* of not running, the *connection* to the environment, *feelings* of worthiness, a *desire* for respect, and the *pleasures* of producing a physically attractive body (e.g., Bridel & Rail, 2007; Hanold, 2010; Major, 2001; Smith, 2000). With respect to the last point, one runner explained to Smith (2000) that "no-one wants to be a disappointment when they take their clothes off" (pp. 198–199).

Running as such can be understood as a technology for feeling good in a sensuous, quasi-moral, and embodied manner. Hanold's (2010) examination of female ultrarunning bodies supports this contention. She concluded that running produces a "neo-liberal notion of self empowerment" (p. 174) that allows female runners to feel "good about themselves" (p. 174) which, in turn, affirms their desire to run. Smith (2000) similarly noted that running brings middle-aged men the respect and admiration they seek, as their "patriarchal powers" allegedly decline with age, thus "their involvement may be a case of 'running repairs' to a threatened sense of masculinity" (p. 205). Bridel and Rail's (2007) research on male marathon runners (who self-identified as gay) similarly suggested that running provided a "sense of self-achievement and bodily satisfaction, connected to a stronger sense of self, of which being gay was very much a part" (p. 140).

These researchers position sex, gender, and sexuality as important factors for understanding why different runners run. Female runners, for example, feel empowered through running, mid-age males more masculine, and gay runners a more positive sense of (gay) self. Yet it also appears that the differing runners have similar motivations and experiences. Correspondingly, what the female, male, and/or gay runners do, how they are affected and affecting, appear to have much overlap. Perhaps, researchers' foci on seemingly stable and unitary forms of identity (i.e., notions of sex, gender, sexuality) highlight apparent "identity" differences rather than blur similarities? I do accept that identity politics can play a fruitful role in challenging various social inequities yet, at the same time and in a seemingly contradictory manner, I am also interested in disturbing identities and the possibilities of creating new ways of being or "line(s) of flight" (Deleuze & Guattari, 1987, p. 9) that offer possibilities for change and/or a refusal to be captured. An identity, as Markula (2006) noted, "is realized or found in a negative reflection to its binary opposition" (p. 31). An identity, accordingly, is constructed via assumptions of difference.

Drawing from Grosz (2011), I have become concerned about how bodies get "identified." Grosz, for example, advocated disturbing identity and thinking about other ways of conceptualizing humans, she explained why:

> If identity, social and political identities, identities that are understood either essentially or in terms of historically and socially specific constructions, are only possible to the extent that they are defined in opposition to others, those defined as different from oneself, then perhaps the very concept of identity, a hybrid or intersectional identity, may be problematic...
>
> (p. 101)

The potential "identity" problem being that when identification processes work to highlight differences, these differences can, at times, be used to justify social inequities and injustices (e.g., sexism, racism, ageism, homophobia). Yet I also recognize that identity differences are not inherently good or bad and that an understanding and celebration of difference (e.g., aging, sexualities, ethnicities) can be uplifting. Grosz (2011) relatedly observed, and I concur, that "'(d)isturbing differences' is a wonderfully ambiguous phrase" (p. 101).

In this admittedly complex manner, I have become interested in exploring how to do research that disturbs identities, or as Grosz (2011) questions: how to do research "to transform the ways in which identity is conceived so that identities do not emerge and function only through the suppression and subordination of other social identities" (p. 101)?

Hence my focus on what runners' bodies do and how they feel. As Grosz (2011) suggested "I am *not* what others see in me, but what I do, what I make, what I make myself, but also what I make of the world..." (p. 102). More specifically, I explore the act of running by focusing on runners' affects and emotions, as this reveals how they "feel" about running. The focus on affects/emotions offers a chance to blur boundaries between—and think differently about—bodies and identities.

To help negotiate the pains and pleasures of running, runners share strategies and training tips, and influence each other with motivational techniques and stories. One influential source, where such information is shared, is *Runner's World*. In the following, I introduce this magazine before analyzing how the magazine works affectively.

> **17: Runner's high**
>
> Seventeen and in Sydney on summer holidays. I'm seriously in love for the first time and wish I were back in Nelson with her. I check her photo one more time and lace my new running shoes. I put my nose into the insole and breathe deeply. The sun slides over the horizon and I run into the Manly beach twilight. Past shops, cafes, and bars. My legs feel light and smooth. I lengthen my stride and weave around those on the esplanade. I'm soon out of the crowds and heading towards North Head. It's effortless, I run and run and run.[3]

Introducing *Runner's World*

Runner's World has the largest global circulation of any running magazine. Its self-stated mission is to inspire and guide runners of all levels through "vivid story telling and expert advice" (Runner's World, 2014, para. 2). Its readers are claimed to be those who "view running as more than fitness, as a lifestyle" and the magazine aims to speak to their "passion, sparking a connection and sense of community with all runners…" (Runner's World, 2014, para. 2). The magazine has 18 international editions and an estimated circulation of over 1.5 million, with total readership of approximately 5.3 million. It also manages 14 websites, including its international editions and official Facebook, Twitter, and Instagram sites. The magazine informs potential advertisers that its readership is affluent, well-educated, and with an average age of 41 for females and 57 for males. Running, as Caudwell (2015) noted, is reflective and productive of middle-class cultural capital and associated embodied habitus.

The advertisements in *Runner's World* primarily promote running shoes, sportswear apparel, body and beauty products, and nutritional supplements, but also luxury products such as expensive cars and watches. The magazine's core topics focus on training and running techniques, motivational narratives, runner profiles, and upcoming events. It also devotes specific sections to injury and rehabilitation, beginners, and women.

Runner's World, given its self-stated mission, is concerned with affirming the value of running, inspiring runners, shaping bodies, and establishing connections. As such the magazine is in the business of managing affects/emotions. In order to understand how the magazine accomplishes this goal, and in paraphrasing Deleuze and Guattari (1987), we need to examine what *Runner's World* "can do":

> …in others words, what its affects are, how they can or cannot enter into composition with other affects, with the affects of another body … either to exchange actions and passions with it or to join with it in composing a more powerful body.
>
> (p. 257)

In the next section, therefore, I reveal my tools of analysis for understanding what *Runner's World* does.

> **21 on: Runner's dream**[4]
> I'm running. I'm fast, seriously fast. My stride lengthens. My knees pump high and my upper body smooth. The slope gets steeper. My feet barely touch the ground. Falling forward. Diving with outstretched arms. The air gives me support. I feel the lift. On the night wing: swooping, diving, and soaring. Sublime.

Tools of analysis

Critical studies of media representations of sport have tended to focus on ideological and political messages rather than the affective and corporeal dimensions. These ideological/political studies are typically concerned with issues associated with sexism, nationalism, racism, and ableism. Yet by bypassing the affective dimensions of media coverage there is a risk that these critical studies produce limited insight for understanding how sport media productions garner such popularity and, by default, "an understanding of the mechanisms associated with *how* the political messages are potentially inculcated amongst viewers" (Pringle, in press). Lyotard (1984) discussed the affective/political interface within texts by suggesting:

> What is important in a text is not what it means, but what it does and incites to do. What it does: the charge of affect it contains and transmits. What it incites to do: the metamorphoses of this potential energy into other things—other texts, but also … political actions.
>
> (Lyotard, as cited in Seidler, 2001, p. 133)

Following Lyotard, I suggest that the analysis of affect and emotions should be viewed as political, as these analyses lay at the heart of understanding motivations, desires, associated actions, and subjectivities, all of which play an important role in the production of various sets of power relations. Ahmed (2001) succinctly summarized that "emotions are crucial to politics" (p. 140).

The alleged "turn" to affect theorizings in the last decade has been regarded by Liljeström and Paasonen (2010) as a reaction to the limitations of poststructuralist theorizations and their associated focus on the semantic and symbolic; which, they suggest, has acted to marginalize analyses that consider the intersections between biology, affects, and energetic forces. The intersections of these three factors map surprisingly well onto the content of *Runner's World* with its associated discussion of biological knowledges of the running body (e.g., injuries, nutrition, training techniques, physiological adaptations), the circulation of affect via emotive photos and vignettes, and "energizing" articles designed to stir passions.

Most researchers distinguish between emotion and affect, "the latter referring mostly to a primary, non-conscious, bodily experience, whereas the former would indicate a more psychological, interpretive experience" (Ruberg, 2009, p. 514). Massumi (2002) more succinctly suggested that affect is autonomous but emotion is "owned and recognized" (p. 28). Affect, as Massumi illustrated, is typically understood as stemming from the body and *unconsciously* influencing how humans act/think/feel by inducing a particular state of being or intensity.

Yet not all researchers draw clear dividing lines between emotion and affect. Ruberg (2009), for example, deliberately used the "two words interchangeably" (p. 514) and Wetherell (2014) argued that although "affect belongs in the minuscule periods of time before consciousness is woken up in the body" (p. 13) it makes little sense to divorce affect "from everyday talk, discourse and meaning-making" (p. 13). She argued that attempts to study the preconscious workings of the mind make for a "methodological nightmare" (p. 14). Wetherell (2012), correspondingly, suggested that a blurring typically occurs between emotions and affects and subsequently promoted her concept of *affective practices*. A concept underpinned by the idea that affects may work unconsciously and can be somewhat chaotic but they are also associated with interrelated sets of patterns (e.g., feelings and thoughts, social relations, ways of being) and these patterns can be empirically studied. I have chosen to draw on Wetherell's understanding of the links between affect and emotion to analyze *Runner's World*, specifically because I consider how *Runner's World* "appeals directly to the senses, how it sways viewers (readers) somatically as well as symbolically" (Ott, 2010, p. 41), thus blurring affects, emotions and understandings.

My analysis is also underpinned by Deleuze's (1992) notion that we each belong and operate in various apparatuses. In this respect I regard running as an apparatus within which *Runner's World* and I, as a researcher and runner, exist within (see Markula, 2014). In following Deleuze's ideas, I attempt to untangle the lines of visibility, enunciations, forces, and subjectifications. I consider that the lines of visibility refer to the representational aspects of *Runner's World*—what is shown, reflected or hidden—representations (images and text) that have capacity to close down or structure available meanings, affects, and emotions. The lines of enunciations, in my analysis, link more specifically to the text, associated narratives, and use of language. In this respect, I am interested in analyzing how the magazine invites readers in through framing running, runners, and associated bodies as somehow desirable.

I consider the lines of force as productive (as similar to how Foucault understood power), correspondingly, I am interested in the lines of force that *Runner's World* produces, that is, the responses it evokes. For this analysis, I am particularly interested in the affective and emotional responses and, accordingly, how the text and images appeal to the senses, the unconscious, the aesthetic, and artistic. With respect to teasing out the lines of subjectification, I am interested in analyzing how the lines of visibility, enunciations, and force intersect, meld and potentially fold into the production of self. Markula (2006) drew from Deleuze, to suggest that this process of folding/subjectification is via thinking, reflection, and problematization yet I add that it is also through affective practices and thus an unconscious aspect is undoubtedly at work, even if only for split seconds, before the conscious mind starts thinking and reflecting.

Having revealed my approach for untangling and analyzing the lines associated with the *Runner's World*, I reiterate that this process is a tool for analysis, as in reality there is continuous interplay, melding, breaking, and morphing of these lines. As such, I regard these lines as "critical prompts" (Ott, 2010, p. 43) for reading *Runner's World*.

My method of analysis consisted of a close reading of various hard-copy issues of *Runner's World* published between 2013 and 2014 and via searches of the associated websites. MacDougall (2006) described careful reading as "more deliberate than seeing and yet more unguarded than thinking" (p. 7). My close reading, accordingly, involved reflecting on how the text and images made me feel and whether I was "moved."

> **35: Making a friend**
> A delegate at a conference presents her narrative on retirement from being a top runner. It's gripping. She talks of the joys of having a superbly fit body but also of discipline, pain, and failed dreams. At the end of the day, I talk to her about running and then invite her for a run. She pauses then turns to me seriously, looks me in the eye, "Ok," but then stipulates with a pointed finger "but we won't take our watches or race." I tell her self-effacingly, "If I can last 20 minutes in this heat, I'll be happy." She accepts. We run, talk, stop, stretch, run, sweat, laugh, walk. A new running buddy. It feels good.

Feeling *Runner's World*

Lines of visibility

The lines of visibility are concerned with what is shown, revealed, and hidden. In this section I pay particular attention to the photographs used in *Runner's World* but also note that there is a physical texture to the magazine that is of appeal. The paper is of high quality: it shines and is smooth to touch. In flicking through the pages of a copy of *Runner's World*, I am also hit by the kaleidoscope of bright colors. The shoe advertisements, at times, verge on the psychedelic; shoes and runners float in space, bright purples mesh with yellow, luminescent limes and blues. The vivid colors meld with the high-resolution photos of movement, to draw the senses in.

With respect to the competitive market of surfing magazines, Ford and Brown (2006) claimed that surfing is a visual culture and that the sensationalism of the photographs, are what "drives the purchase" (p. 33). Running magazines also exist in a competitive market with several different magazines on store shelves (e.g., *Trail Runner, Running Times, Women's Running, Fast Forward, Club Runner, Youth Runner, Men's Running, Distance Running*). High-definition color photographs are prominent in all these magazines. In contrast to surf magazines, however, the cover shot in *Runner's World* is not typically sensational but almost exclusively portrays a runner in action. The background is unimportant, often faded out, so the running space does not draw attention away from the central focus, that is, the running body. Women's bodies are on display at double the rate of men's bodies. Men typically have their shirts off and women reveal their toned mid-rifts. The bodies are typically thin, youngish (mostly under 35) and white and, correspondingly, reinforce biased views of the body beautiful.

The subjects of the cover shots also appear to enjoy running. Indeed, the women and men are characteristically smiling. More often than not, their eyes are looking directly at you, as such, they invite you to look back. The invitation is not sexual. Indeed, the facial expression does not suggest sexual availability, as Duncan (1990) noted about soft-core pornography and the associated "come-on" look (p. 31). Nor do the photographs invite the reader to gaze at a particular body part, such as the chest or legs, although I find myself drawn to the faces. The face, as "the prime organ of affect" (Tomkins, 1962, p. 224), reflects joy and excitement, and these positive emotions allow the reader to connect affectively with the athlete or, more specifically, with running. This affective connection reinforces the idea that running is "good" (i.e., running produces joy, fitness, health, and a good-looking body).

Once drawn inside the magazine, the reader finds many similar photographs. The majority of photographs are not posed, although some are clearly models (both male and female). These images typically depict runners in the act of running with looks of concentration, happiness, and satisfaction. Bodies remain on display—legs and torsos feature prominently. Although there are shots of a variety of bodies—aged, heavy, disabled—the majority of bodies are young and thin. Running is, thus, portrayed as beautiful and pleasurable but also as something that all bodies can do (if they desire to).

A regular double-page photo is titled "Rave Run" its focus is on the natural beauty of diverse spaces to run, such as deserts, mountains, forests, and rugged coastlines. The runner always pales in size to the scenes of sublime geography: a small female figure, for example, strides up the barren landscape of the Badlands heading towards a sun-drenched pinnacle, another effortlessly bounds up an escarpment overlooking the Italian coastline, and a bearded man barrels up Mt. Carmel highway, with Zion National Park as overwhelming backdrop. These images evoke feelings of freedom, awe, and envy (as in "it's so beautiful, I wish was running there"). A spiritual dimension is also conveyed—a connection to nature and something about the insignificance of individuals in nature. One of the runners, for example, claims that running in Zion has a "mythical feel" and that "the immensity of the rocks makes you feel so little. Yet ... so powerful and free…" (Pelchat, 2014, p. 7). In this way the magazine offers hints as to how the reader should feel when gazing on the image.

What is deliberately missing in the images, are photos of runners appearing tired, exhausted, anxious, or in pain. Thus, in contrast to Throsby's (2013) claim that running is represented via narratives of pain and the deferral of pleasure, *Runner's World* quixotically represents running as pain free, smooth, lean, spiritual, natural, good, immediately pleasurable, and sweat free. This representation, I confess, is somewhat energizing.

39: Interspecies running
He was six weeks old when I first saw him asleep in the pet shop. A black lab, border collie cross, with a white patch on his chest. When not more than a pup, he'd get the "sillies" in early evening and run as a fast as he could around the house, each lap he would turn and look at me with a look of excitement. We've been walking and running together ever since. The beach is his favorite running spot. He's now 11 and noticeably slower on the hills and even on the flat but still loves the freedom of running. He looks eagerly at me every morning, waiting for the nod.

Lines of enunciation

The lines of enunciation are concerned with the text, associated narratives, and use of language. Yet again I am not so interested in what the enunciations mean but what they evoke, arouse, remind, and affect. The larger words on the cover page, aside from the title, promote personalized invitations: "Your perfect plan"; "Best tips ever"; "Run strong, stay cool!"; "Get fit fast"; "Get fit, stay fit!" These invites resemble bad infomercials yet no doubt hail runners who want better fitness, greater motivation, and to be injury free. Yet a deeper call to runners (in an Althusserian sense) exists, it is a call that recognizes running as "a method for living a fuller life" (Willey, 2013, p. 16). Willey's (2013) editorial, for example, reveals running as an antidote to living inauthentic, disconnected, unnatural, digitalized lives. He quotes the words of cardiologist and recognized running philosopher George Sheehan, to emphasize his point:

> Running made me free. It rid me of concern for the opinion of others. Dispensed me from rules and regulations imposed from the outside. Running let me start from scratch. It stripped off those layers of programmed activity and thinking. Developed new priorities about eating and sleeping and what to do with leisure time. Running changed my attitude about work and play. About whom I really liked and who really liked me. Running let me see my twenty-four hour day in a new light and my lifestyle from a different point of view, from the inside instead of out.
>
> (as cited in Wiley, 2013, p. 16)

In contrast to the Foucauldian critique of competitive running—that it produces docile and disciplined bodies—*Runner's World* captures and promotes a different way of feeling (as opposed to knowing) running: running is freedom, is lifestyle, is worthy, is real. Running is portrayed as an alternative lifestyle or as a form of resistance to the shackles of a disciplined modern life. Fleshman's (2013) article title captures this sentiment: "To heck with science: Runners love numbers, but we can't measure, heart, grit, or passion" (p. 56). So to does her last sentence: "There is immeasurable power in the unmeasurable" (p. 57).[5] Another article title encourages runners to "Break the rules" (Hanic, p. 66). Advertisements also use this "alternative lifestyle sentiment" to sell products. An advert by Salomon, for example, tells readers that their clothing product allows one to "Run whenever and wherever you want" as they are "Designed for Freedom" ("Run whenever…," 2013, p. 84). An advert for Dick's Sporting Goods, in response to the Boston bombings, reinforces the iconoclastic aspect of running:

> Before Monday, April 15th, each runner had his or her own unique reasons to run. Ever since, defiant to our core and unified in our resolve, we also share one special reason to run.… Run for Boston.
>
> ("Run for Boston…," 2013, pp. 16–17)

The magazine represents and reaches out to anyone who runs or desires to run. Parent (2013a) informs that you can call yourself a runner "from the moment you begin" (p. 52). In other words, you do not have to run certain times or distances, you just have to run. A regular section in the magazine (Human Race) features articles about "regular runners doing amazing things." These human interest stories tell stories of Boston Marathon bombing victims who help each other train for the next marathon (May, 2014), a running club that helps troubled teens (September, 2014), a female immigrant from Ecuador who runs to motivate her pupils (October, 2013), and a pro-triathlete who returns from a horrific bike accident (August, 2013). These stories promote many letters to the editor with words of thanks, "for giving me hope" (Clark, 2013, p. 17) or with recognition that the words "hit me right in the heart" (Barber, 2013, p. 15). The letters are testament that readers are affected by the stories.

Given the magazine's commitment to promoting running as a lifestyle, it is not surprising that it has many articles on how to run, train, eat, and keep running even if in pain. With reference to pain and injury, words on the front cover invite readers to learn about "5 easy ways to recover faster," how to "beat the bonk," "5 ways to cure arch pain," "+8 foods that will heal you," and, how to "avoid injuries and stay motivated." *Runner's World*, accordingly, acknowledges that running long distances causes pain and injury. Although the magazine wants runner's to learn how to avoid injury, there is a sense that pain is inevitable and, correspondingly, a hint that readers should even feel good about this reality. Parent (2013b) for example, titled his article "Hurts so good" (p. 58) and stated, "if Eskimos have many words for *snow*, then so should runners for *pain*" (p. 60). At the same time, the magazine acknowledges, in a self-effacing manner, that there is a crazy or quirky dimension to running. Plenty of examples abound:

Sagal (2013), also known as the "road scholar" refers to his love of running as an "obsession" (p. 54), an article discusses the peculiar benefits of getting married on race day (Lori, July, 2014, p. 24), another titled "The maniac next door" (Balf, October, 2013, p. 88), celebrates Junyong Pak's eccentric training techniques, and Inman (2014) captured the vague insanity of running a marathon by defining it as:

> A popular form of overpriced torture wherein participants wake up at ass-o-clock in the morning and stand in the freezing cold until it's time to run, at which point they miserably trot for a god-awful interval of time that could be better spent sleeping in and/or consuming large quantities of beer and cupcakes. See also: masochism, awfulness, "a bunch of bullshit", boob-chafing, cupcake-deprivation therapy.
>
> (p. 73)

> **45: Running into trouble**
> Death of my father, my mother-in-law, shift to a new town to a new job, it's not what I expected. I start running seriously again. Therapy undoubtedly. I am soon fit, running hills and with speed. The pain in my ankle sharpens. I try to ignore it. I am told: "It's associated with too much exercise in an aging body". Ice, anti-inflammatories, autologous blood injections, eccentric exercises. No avail. Stop running hills ... then on the flat. Reduced to walking. I'm envious of others running. I don't feel good.

Lines of **force** *and subjectification: towards an untidy conclusion*

From a Deleuzean perspective, the lines of force refer to the workings of power and what gets "produced" through these workings. I suggest it is not hard to envisage how a critical researcher might interpret these lines of force in *Runner's World.* Concerns would likely be raised with respect to the overt celebration of thin white bodies, the disproportionate use of attractive female bodies on the covers, the acceptance of pain, and the magazine's seemingly apolitical stance towards issues of sexism, racism, ageism, and even the politics of terror. These concerns are all legitimate. Yet as already discussed, I have (ambiguous) reservations with how some critical researchers might study these issues in a manner that stabilizes identity categories and indirectly entrenches assumed differences between differing bodies. In other words, my concern is not with the research topic but with how "identities" might be conceptualized within the research process and how these conceptualizations might contribute or relate to identity problems.

Hence my current attempt to explore differing ways of knowing runners: a focus that can still be regarded as political as it allows possibilities for understanding bodies/people differently with scope for social change. I suggest, amongst many possibilities, that the lines of force within *Runner's World* evokes a passion and desire for running and an acceptance that regardless of age, ability or gender, that if you run, then you are a runner. In this manner, *Runner's World* encourages an affective connection or sense of "withness" between readers of the magazine, so that stories of other runners fold into the self to affirm the reader's story of self—as a runner. Ahmed (2004) uses the term "withness" with respect to an act of self-formation, often in a reparative sense, through emotional engagement with the experiences and stories of others. *Runner's World*, as such, is part of a broader apparatus, that I am enmeshed, that works to tidy and order the tangled lines to produce energy and desire. In my case, the production of energy and desire has me running once again.

> **50: Freedom**
> The four-year old pain in the Achilles has mysteriously gone. I no longer limp in the second set of tennis. Can it be? The tendon is not swollen, tender, red, painful. It's thin, white and healed. I tentatively run on the flat, I can feel the extra weight on my chest, abdomen. I take it slowly. I run on the beach. I like the sense of freedom. I feel good once again.

Final words

Runner's World represents running as an affective practice (see Wetherell, 2014). As enmeshed within a broader running *dispositif* (assemblage), the magazine allows runners to gain a sense of "withness" (Ahmed, 2004) with each other, the environment and running, to enhance a desire for running, and constitute running subjectivities. Although the pleasures of running are not presented in a sensational or intense manner, like the feelings of stoke in surf magazines (Booth, 2008), they are not deferred (Throsby, 2013) but immediately tangible and worthy. The representations of running offer the hope of freedom, well-being, enjoyment, a chance for embodied beauty, a sense of achievement, and even an alternative lifestyle, and, it is these various running pleasures that make the negotiation of running pain, injury, and breathlessness understandable and even enjoyable.

I accept that *Runner's World* is biased in its representations of runners yet suggest it primarily attempts to talk to anyone who desires to run: beginners, disabled, elite, youth, aged, women, men, queer, straight, and people of differing sizes, shapes, and ethnicities (yes … I acknowledge it is hard to escape identity categories). Its somewhat biased representation strategy, therefore, is not primarily an attempt to draw sharp lines between different types of bodies but an attempt to promote desire for running (and sell more copies). In this manner, the lines of force in *Runner's World*, and its associated inclusion or exclusion of differing bodies, is not predominantly associated with seemingly stable forms of identification (i.e., male, female, youth, aged) but is tied to the less tangible circulations of affects and emotions that can fold and enmesh to produce interconnected "running bodies."

With concern for disturbing identities, I hope my focus on running as an affective practice and with what *Runner's World* "does" (Deleuze & Guattari,

1987), sits in contrast to the many sociological analyses of sporting bodies that tend to read representations of bodies primarily through differences in gender, sexuality, appearance, race, or ability. Through focusing on affects/emotions I have aimed to illustrate the overlaps, similarities, and blurrings that exist between differing bodies rather than highlight the differences that can cement rather than disturb identity categories.

In tentative conclusion, I suggest that running should not be thought of as a practice for select "identities" (e.g., young, fit, thin, black/white bodies) but simply as an affective practice done by the bodies that run. By thinking of runners by what they do and their affects/emotions, there are possibilities for disrupting running identity categories so that runners do not just conceive of themselves, for example, as "white-runners" or "gay-runners" or "aged-runners" or "male-runners": identity categories that possibly constrain what individuals think they can or should do. In contrast, a focus on how runners' bodies come into being via what they do, the connections with other runners, the environment and affects/emotions allows for lines of flight and/or movement away from normalized identities and the associated focus on points of difference. My "utopian" idea is that a broader focus on the similarities of our affective/emotional lives, as opposed to a focus on the differences between what Deleuze calls molar categories (e.g., male/female, old/young, straight/gay), may allow a greater sense of empathy, tolerance, understanding and acceptance of the many "differences" we embody and perform.

Notes

1 Caudwell's (2015) work on running pleasures provided the key inspiration for my chapter. Her intimate autoethnographic embodied account of multiple and blurred running pleasures present running as simultaneously affectual, aesthetic, sensual, visceral, and playful.

2 Dixon gained bronze in the 1500m at Munich (1972) and won the 1983 New York marathon. As a nine-year-old I saw him race the epic 1,500 m at the 1974 Commonwealth Games where he placed 4th behind Filbert Bayi, John Walker, and Ben Jipcho. Bayi and Walker both broke the old world record in that race.

3 I learnt from a friend, only recently, that one definition of runner's high does not relate to a sense of euphoria but to an ability to run at speed/length without feeling tired. Once I heard this, I immediately remembered that warm Sydney evening and the effortless feel of the pace, fitness, speed, and, with hindsight, youth.

4 My favorite reoccurring dream always starts with running at speed and, if I am lucky, at some stage I become airborne and with complete control: the sensation is amazing. The link between running and flying is perhaps the feelings of freedom, open air, and speed.

5 Fleshman's point that running is not a science that can be measured but an emotional experience is reinforced, somewhat ironically, by the knowledge that she was U.S. champion over 5,000 m in 2006 and 2010.

References

Ahmed, S. (2001). Communities that feel: Intensity, difference and attachment. In A. Koivunen & S. Paasonen (Eds.), *Conference proceedings for affective encounters: Rethinking embodiment in feminist media studies*, Turku: The University of Turku School of Art, Literature and Music, Media Studies.

Ahmed, S. (2004). *The cultural politics of emotion*. Edinburgh, United Kingdom: Edinburgh University Press.

Bale, J. (2006). The place of pain in running. In S. Loland., B. Skirstad., & I. Waddington (Eds.), *Pain and injury in sport: Social and ethical analysis* (pp. 65–75). London, England: Routledge.

Balf, T. (2013, September). The maniac next door. *Runner's World*, pp. 88–97 and 119.

Barber, S. (2013, August). Words of encouragement. *Runner's World*, p. 15.

Booth, D. (2008). (Re) reading The Surfers' Bible: The affects of Tracks. *Continuum: Journal of Media & Cultural Studies*, *22*, 17–35.

Bridel, W., & Rail, G. (2007). Sport, sexuality, and the production of (resistant) bodies: De-/re-constructing the meanings of gay male marathon corporeality. *Sociology of Sport Journal*, *24*, 127–144.

Caudwell, J. (2015). Running for pleasures. In R. Pringle, R. Rinehart, & J. Caudwell, *Sport and the social significance of pleasure*. New York, NY: Routledge.

Clark, T. (2013, October). Moving forward. *Runner's World*, p. 17.

Coffey, A. (1999). *The ethnographic self: Fieldwork and the representation of identity*. Thousand Oaks, CA: Sage.

Colloo, J. (1990, April 22). A doctor writes. *Observer Magazine*, p. 8.

Deleuze, G. (1992). What is a dispositive? In T. J. Armstrong (Ed.), *Michel Foucault Philo sopher* (pp. 159–168). Hemel Hempstead, United Kingdom: Harvester Wheatsheaf.

Deleuze, G., & Guattari, F. (1987). *Capitalism and schizophrenia: A thousand plateaus* (trans. B. Massumi). Minneapolis, MN: University of Minnesota Press.

Duncan, M. (1990). Sport photographs and sexual difference: Images of women and men in the 1984 and 1988 Olympic Games. *Sociology of Sport Journal*, *7*, 22–43.

Fleshman, L. (2013, September). To heck with science. *Runner's World, pp.* 56–57.

Ford, N., & Brown, D. (2006). *Surfing and social theory: Experience, embodiment and narrative of the dream glide*. London, England: Taylor & Francis.

Giardina, M., & Newman, J. (2011). Physical cultural studies and embodied research acts. *Cultural Studies↔Critical Methodologies*, *11*, 523–534.

Grosz, E. (1994). *Volatile bodies: Toward a corporeal feminism*. Bloomington, IN: Indiana University Press.

Grosz, E. (2011). Differences disturbing identity: Deleuze and feminism. In M. Lijeström and S. Paasonen (Eds.), *Working with affect in feminist readings: Disturbing differences* (pp. 101–111). London, England: Routledge.

Hanic, J. (2013, September). Break the rules. *Runner's World*, pp. 66–71.

Hanold, M. (2010). Beyond the marathon: (De)construction of female ultrarunning bodies. *Sociology of Sport Journal*, *27*, 160–177.

Inman, M. (2014, July). The Dos and DO NOTs of running your first marathon. *Runner's World*, pp. 71–74.

Liljeström, M., & Paasonen, S. (2010). Introduction: Feeling differences—affect and feminist reading. In M. Lijeström and S. Paasonen (Eds.), *Working with affect in feminist readings: Disturbing differences* (pp. 1–28). London, England: Routledge.

Lori, M. (2014, July). Racing to the altar. *Runner's World*, p. 24.

Lyotard, J. (1984). Adrift. In R. McKeon (Ed.), *New York: Semiotext(e)/Foreign Agents Series*. New York, NY: Columbia University Press.

MacDougall, D. (2006). *The corporeal image: Film, ethnography, and the senses*. Princeton, NJ: Princeton University Press.

Major, W. F. (2001). The benefits and costs of serious running. *World Leisure Journal, 43*, 12–25.

Markula, P. (2006). Deleuze and the body without organs: Disreading the fit feminine identity. *Journal of Sport & Social Issues, 30*, 29–44.

Markula, P. (2014). The moving body and social change. *Cultural Studies↔Critical Methodologies, 14*, 483–95.

Massumi, B. (2002). *Parables for the Virtual: Movement, Affect, Sensation*. London, England: Duke University Press.

Ott, B. (2010). The visceral politics of V for Vendetta: On political affect in cinema. *Critical Studies in Media Communication*, 27, 39–54.

Paasonen, S. (2010). Disturbing, fleshy texts: Close looking at pornography. In M. Lijeström and S. Paasonen (Eds.), *Working with affect in feminist readings: Disturbing differences* (pp. 58–71). London, England: Routledge.

Parent, M. (2013a, September). "You're a real runner if…" *Runner's World*, pp. 52–55.

Parent, M. (2013b, May). Hurts so good. *Runner's World*, pp. 58–61.

Pelchat, J. (2014, September). Rave Run. *Runner's World*, p. 7.

Pringle, R. (in press). When the pleasurable is political: An affective analysis of viewing the Olympics. In R. Pringle, R. Rinehart, & J. Caudwell (Eds.), *Sport and the social significance of pleasure*. New York, NY: Routledge.

Ruberg, W. (2009). Interdisciplinarity and the history of emotions. *Cultural and Social History, 6*, 507–516.

"Run for Boston." (2013, July). Run for Boston. *Runner's World*, pp. 16–17.

"Run whenever." (2013, September). Run whenever and wherever you want. *Runner's World*, p. 84.

Runner's World. (2014). *Runner's World International Media Kit*. Retrieved from http://rw.runnersworld.com/mediakit/international/RunnersWorld_MediaKit_v5_sml.pdf.

Sagal, P. (2013, May). In her shoes. *Runner's World*, pp. 54–55.

Smith, S. (2000). British nonelite roadrunning and masculinity: A case of "running repairs"? *Men and Masculinities, 3*, 187–208.

Throsby, K. (2013). "If I go in like a cranky sea lion, I come out like a smiling dolphin": Marathon swimming and the unexpected pleasures of being a body in water. *Feminist Review, 103*, 5–22.

Tomkins, S. (1962). *Affect, imagery, consciousness*. New York, NY: Springer.

Wetherell, M. (2012) *Affect and emotion: A new social science understanding*. Los Angeles, CA: Sage.

Wetherell, M. (2014). Trends in the turn to affect: A social psychological critique. *Body & Society*. Published online July 21, 2014. doi: 10.1177/1357034X14539020.

Willey, D. (2013, May). A Sheehan revival. *Runner's World*, p. 16.

8 Boston Strong

Sport, terror/ism, and the spectacle pedagogy of citizenship

Michael D. Giardina, Ryan King-White and Kyle S. Bunds[1]

On April 15, 2013, two improvised explosive devices detonated at 2:49 p.m., near the finish line of the Boston Marathon. Three people were killed, and several hundred more were maimed or otherwise sustained serious injury. Two brothers, Dzhokhar and Tamerlan Tsarnaev, were implicated in the attack, which led to several days of chaos in the city as local, state, and federal law enforcement agencies mobilized to find the pair, who were still at large. Wall-to-wall media coverage across the spectrum of cable and network news gushed forth every conceivable storyline, backstory, and rumor concerning the identity(ies) of the potential bombers (as well as which state sponsor of terrorism may or may not have been "behind it"). Just a few days later, the two brothers engaged in a shootout with police that eventually led to Tamerlan being killed and Dzhokhar being apprehended; 30 charges were levied against him in federal court, including four counts for murder and one count for conspiring to use a weapon of mass destruction that resulted in the death of others (McPhee, Haskell, & Radia, 2013). On April 8, 2015, a jury found him guilty on all 30 charges; he was sentenced to death on May 15, 2015.

The bombing's immediate aftermath gave rise to nearly every choreographed American tragedy recovery behavior. While the authorities combed through hours of surveillance tape (as well as video taken on smartphones and other digital devices by those in attendance at the marathon) looking for the as-yet unknown perpetrators of the crime, both traditional and social media outlets provided countless articles, features, photos, videos, and more of the heroes who "ran toward the danger" (Alba, 2014). Fans of the National Hockey League's Boston Bruins provided an emotive Star Spangled Banner sing-along prior to the team's first home game after the attacks (Greenberg, 2013). The One Fund was erected as the official platform for people to donate money to the victims of the bombings. *Boston Strong*, a seemingly tireless retread from Lance Armstrong's *Livestrong* brand, became "a handy shorthand for defiance, solidarity, and caring. In its ubiquity, 'Boston Strong' present[ed] a united front in the face of threat" (Zimmer, 2013, para. 1). All of this was done (largely) as a coping mechanism for a shock to the American psyche, and was generally in keeping with the way the country has reacted to other shocking events over the last few decades.

Put differently, the attributes associated with modern American culture were ever present in the moments following the bombing: the U.S. media spinning this event as evidence of the strength of character Americans singularly possess? Check. A sporting event where everyone tearfully sings the national anthem as a show of solidarity? Check. The opportunity taken to rebrand the city and utilize corporate philanthropy wherein American citizens could "consume" their goodwill without having to do anything but swipe their credit card (King, 2006)? Check.

In this chapter, we offer a critical look back on the events that took place at the 2013 Boston Marathon, as well as the governmental, sporting, and public responses to it. To this end, we hope to offer a complex, and oftentimes necessarily hypocritical, reading of the city's lockdown that we characterize as a type of disaster capitalism (Klein, 2008). In so doing, we demonstrate how disaster capitalism is still utilized to brand the city post-bombing. We further posit that this choreographed response is not surprising as it helps manage our role as citizen consumers and the city's role in the aftermath of the event. At the same time, we read the spectacle pedagogy (Garoian & Gaudelius, 2008) of citizenship—that is, the "performative visual codes of the media, fueled by corporate, global capitalism, which manufacture our desires and determine or political choices" (Denzin, 2014, p. 242)—as it relates to the bombing. We continue by reading this narrative over and against the narrative arc that played out with respect to Mebrahtom "Meb" Keflezighi, the Eritrean-born American long-distance runner who in 2014 became the first American man to win the Boston Marathon since 1983. We highlight how his victory (re-)animated debates on "being American" at an event in which the very notion of citizenship had been put into contestation just a year earlier.

Pedagogies of citizenship: learning to accept a city on lockdown?

On September 11, 2001, terrorists flew planes into the World Trade Center in New York City and the Pentagon in Washington, D.C., an event that substantially impacted both national and international relationships and understandings about citizenship and national identity. Indeed, the nation came together as a strong community providing support and compassion for those in need, and in particular a strong sense of loyalty to *our* country. Yet, "there is a dark side to this newfound call for unity. Notions of community are now organized not only around flag-waving displays of patriotism but also around collective fears and an ongoing militarization of visual culture and public space" (Giroux, 2003, p. 4). To give but one example, images of planes crashing into the Twin Towers became a mediated spectacle that is still utilized by media companies, particularly Fox News, as the *raison d'être* for global interventionism in the Middle East. For Denzin (2014), this mediated form of jingoistic patriotism, grafted onto the backs of horrific disaster, serves as "an insidious, ever-present form of propaganda in the service of cultural imperialism" (p. 242).

More broadly speaking, Klein (2008) reminds us that catastrophic events such as this are often opportunities to reshape and (re-)mold public sentiment. In our current political economic condition of neoliberalism, what it means to be an American citizen is largely propagated by the media, corporations, global capitalism, and, especially for our purposes here, by a growing fear or resentment of "Others." Sandlin, Schultz, and Burdick (2010), in fact, go so far as to state that neoliberalism has become a *pedagogical force* "that transcends economic concerns to shape human consciousness according to the desire of the market" (p. xxiv). In our case, it is one that especially "speaks to the issues of racial inequality under post-9/11 forms of democracy" (Denzin, 2014, p. 250). In this context, citizenship becomes "expressed and achieves meaning through public discourse … the recurring themes, images, and appeals concerning ideal citizenship constitute an identifiable rhetorical form" (Murphy, 2003, p. 194). This we see in the representation of immigrants, who routinely get defined either as heroes or role models who can be placed on a pedestal to be emulated (e.g., Albert Einstein, Nikola Tesla, John Muir, Sergey Brin, Jerry Yang, Hakeem Olajuwon), or as those who fail to roll up their sleeves and put in the necessary work to become successful. Here we are thinking of, for example, the offensive popular-political representation of Mexican immigrants, especially those produced in the American southwest. Regardless, the rhetoric around (neoliberal) citizenship has come to be located squarely at the individual level; if an individual fails, it is his or her fault, not the fault of the system or community (Edwards, 2014).[2]

After 9/11, the general tenor of popular-political discourse in the United States was strongly situated in a fear of terrorism that has been "a financial winner for the (National Security) Complex" (Engelhardt & Dispatch, 2013, para. 15). According to Engelhardt and Dispatch (2013), this occurred through the commercial success of television shows such as *Homeland*, *NCIS*, and *CSI* that display constant mediated images of an inevitable dystopian future. In addition, more than $75 billion is annually put into the U.S. intelligence community's coffers. Yet despite numerous violent events that took more lives than the Boston Marathon bombing, such as Sandy Hook where 20 children and six adults at Sandy Hook Elementary School were murdered by Adam Lanza, or the 2007 Virginia Tech shooting of 32 people by student Seung-Hui Cho, it is generally agreed upon that the Boston Marathon bombing was the "first major terror attack on U.S. soil since 2001 (9/11)" (Holman, Garfin, & Silver, 2014).

It is perhaps not surprising that an act of violence carried out by two Muslim immigrants was granted the imprimatur of the "first" post-9/11 terrorist attack despite other events such as the ones listed above.[3] In a world of fear, where "foreign" people of color are quick to be labeled as terrorists, where military drone killings have become justified, where people are tortured and imprisoned at will without rights, and where spectacle pedagogy exists, and where American citizens are constantly inundated with visual justifications for the fear that grows the military-industrial-entertainment complex, the lockdown that followed the Boston Marathon bombing *felt natural*.

Almost immediately after the explosive devices were detonated on Boylston Street, the country turned its collective attention on Boston, as networks and 24-hour cable news channels went into overdrive to cover the event. Rumors ran rampant, but beyond stories focusing on survivors and a tick-tock of the day's unfolding tragedy, all that remained was idle speculation over what happened—until the night of April 18, when the suspected bombers were involved in a gunfight and car chase in a Boston suburb. While Holman and colleagues (2014) found that the media coverage alone was enough to cause individuals across the United States to experience stress related trauma, the next morning, Boston came to a stand still. Literally. At 8:05 a.m. on April 19, the following advisory was released: "Boston police and Massachusetts Gov. Deval Patrick (D) are now urging all residents of Boston to stay inside, doors locked, and not open the door to anybody but uniformed police with ID" (quoted in Weber & Terbush, 2013, para. 11). In addition, the people of Boston's western suburbs "Watertown, Newton, Waltham, Belmont, Cambridge and the Allston-Brighton neighborhoods of Boston [were instructed] to stay indoors and all mass transit were shut down" (AP, 2013). For hours, few besides law enforcement officers were seen on the streets of the city, who were (essentially) allowed to enter any home they chose to sweep for Dzhokhar (who was still at large).

Chief Dan Linskey, head of special events and the man who handcuffed Tamerlan Tsarneav, defended the decision to put the city on lockdown as being analogous to "a winter weather advisory" in that people were not "arrested for going to work." The *American Prospect*'s E. J. Graff (2013), who found himself amidst the lockdown in Cambridge, Massachusetts, agreed with the analogy, positing, "What we have here is a metro-region-wide snow day without the snow."[4] While this is true to an extent, no winter weather advisory that we can recall has ever involved armored police vehicles and members of nearly every law enforcement agency sweeping the streets. Undoubtedly, images of the heavily armored vehicles, low-flying helicopters, Humvees, S.W.A.T. teams, and snipers moving about a major American city are unnerving, but importantly for our purposes here, few in the mainstream media questioned these tactics (opting instead for outright praise). Moreover, no one reportedly refused the sweeps, and the sweeps ultimately did not actually work in apprehending Dzhokhar. In fact, Dzhokhar was apprehended *after* the lockdown was lifted, which led Marc Tracy of the *New Republic* to remind us,

> The problem with the lockdown, as a matter of principle, isn't that it could have prevented us from capturing Tsarnaev alive. Rather, the way Tsarnaev was captured alive is further suggestion that life in America is a Constitutionally-codified experiment, and that the worst time to suspend experiments is when you don't have all the answers.
>
> (quoted in Sullivan, 2013, para. 3)

Which is to say, the aftermath showed, as Tracy argues, that sequestration of individuals and liberty to freely move about one's community were not only unconstitutional but also ineffective.

When Dzhokhar Tsarnaev was eventually brought into custody, youth drunkenly (literally and figuratively) took to the streets of Boston chanting "U.S.A., U.S.A.," thanking and cheering for the law enforcement members that hours earlier had grossly restricted their freedom. The following day, David Ortiz, a fan favorite from Major League Baseball's Boston Red Sox, gave the following speech prior to the first game played in Fenway Park following the bombings:

> All right, all right Boston. This jersey that we wear today, it doesn't say Red Sox, it says Boston. We're gonna' thank you [Boston] Mayor [Tom] Menino, Governor [Deval] Patrick, the whole police department, for the great job that they did this past week. This is our fucking city, and nobody is gonna dictate our freedom—Stay Strong!

Ortiz was given a standing ovation by the crowd at Fenway Park for his statement. As the year progressed, *Boston Strong* became an enduring (some might say unending) slogan in the city. The Red Sox victory in that year's World Series became all-too-easily attributed, at least partially, to the bombings (i.e., the much-promoted idea that the team was brought closer together to the city). The World Series championship parade paused while the players symbolically placed the World Series trophy on the Marathon finish line. Social media posts from friends and relatives in the area were constantly punctuated with *Boston Strong* throughout the year. Boston busses would display *Boston Strong* on their LED banners for months after the marathon. Finally, (now former) Mayor Menino even rolled out a new bike network plan that was said to "improve the quality of life for every Bostonian and help keep Boston strong by improving our health, our air quality, and reducing congestion on our city streets" (quoted in Dufor, 2013, para. 3).

In the aftermath, the Red Sox organization (and other local media outlets, such as NESN), have done their best to celebrate and memorialize Ortiz's act as a seminal moment in the city's "healing" process. Ironically, Ortiz made his statement when just a day prior the American Law Enforcement system *did* dictate the presumptive freedoms of everyone in the city. As a further paradox, Ortiz, a Dominican man-turned-U.S. citizen, projected his speech act at two kids, Dzhokhar and Tamerlan Tsarnaev, who grew up in the city of Boston and held permanent resident status since 2007[5]—a fact that was seemingly lost on everyone.

Looking back on general responses to Ortiz and the de facto celebration if not normalization of a form of martial law with a critical perspective, we were reminded of Queen Amidala's statement in the third *Star Wars* prequel—"so this is how liberty dies … with thunderous applause"—in response to Emperor Palpatine celebrating the "security" afforded by the creation of the First Galactic Empire. In this instance, the lockdown of the city, the decision to not grant Tsarnaev his Constitutionally-protected rights before interrogation, and the accompanying pleasure and monetary benefit of corporations profiting from the sale of #BostonStrong material served as a strong example of how people accepted the lockdown to some degree and came out in support of the tactics. Not only were liberties taken away for "security" reasons after a relatively small terrorist attack, but as the report on the Boston Marathon bombing shows, "Thousands of officers self-deployed, showing up without being asked—and thus not receiving the intel and direction needed to actually help during the manhunt" and "Once the younger Tsarneav was located in the Watertown boat, more than 100 officers again self-deployed—eventually firing hundreds of bullets at the boat where the unarmed terror suspect was hiding despite never being ordered to do so" (Lowery, 2015). To put it more bluntly, Shalev (2013) observes the following:

> Of course, the killing of three precious people and the injury of dozens of others are a painful tragedy and an unforgiveable crime. Of course, the disruption of an iconic marathon in the heart of one of America's proudest cities is a significant event that warrants the full attention of the media and the justice authorities. Of course, Americans are justifiably concerned that after the first street bombing, others may follow. But this was not 9/11, the Bombay bombings, or the Beslan slaughter of children, also carried out by Chechen terrorists. It wasn't the Bali nightclub bombings, the downing of Pan Am 103 over Lockerbie or the destruction of the federal building in Oklahoma. And it didn't come close even to the Tel Aviv Dolphinarium carnage, the killing of students in Maalot or the murder of 39 Palestinians in the Cave of the Patriarchs in Hebron.
>
> Therefore, in terms of cost-benefit analysis, from the evil terrorist's point of view, the Boylston Street bombings and their after aftermath can only be viewed as a resounding triumph. If the primary goal of terror attacks is to instill fear and intimidate people, to influence governments and to attract world attention, then the Boston bombers have probably succeeded beyond their wildest dreams.
>
> (para. 5–7)

Shalev is not alone in rendering this appraisal. The senior editor of *Hot Air*, for example, opines along similar lines:

> You don't want people milling about in a park when there's a guy with a suicide vest, guns, and ammo on the loose. But then, murder suspects are on the loose all the time in big cities and nothing shuts down for them, even though in theory they're just as likely to go out in a blaze of nutty glory among a crowd. If you're an aspiring terrorist, knowing that you can shut down a city for a day must be encouraging.
>
> (para. 4)

Indeed, as Northwestern University law professor Eugene Kontorovich (2013) wrote, the Tsarnaevs:

> succeeded in turning Boston, America's cradle of liberty, into a prison. Just when we had gotten used to obscene lines and searches at airports as the

> price we pay for safety, the lockdown of Boston illustrates the extent to which civil liberties are at stake in the war on terror. Since 9/11, there has been an ongoing debate about the protection of the rights of suspected terrorists. But today's events show that its is not just the civil liberties of terrorists at stake, but also those of millions of innocent civilians.
>
> If Boston is "closed" for just six hours, that is 175,000 man days of functional house arrest; roughly as many as would be required to keep everyone in Guantanamo confined for a year or two. No doubt the police overreaction will be severely criticized in coming days, but largely on policy grounds, not civil rights grounds.
>
> (para. 1–2)

In retrospect, many concerned with civil liberties, regardless of political affiliation, would likely agree that the lockdown of a major U.S. city posed numerous challenges to and enunciated a particular fealty toward the security state as arbiter of law and order, even a law and order that went wildly above and beyond that which we had seen in recent history to capture two suspects in a crime. In this regard, Giroux (2013) has surmised that:

> Lockdown as a policy and mode of control misrepresents the notion of security by reducing it to personal safety and thereby mobilizing fears that demand trading civil liberties for increased militarized security. The lockdown that took place in Boston serves as a reminder of how narrow the notion of security has become in that it is almost entirely associated with personal safety but never with the insecurities that derive from poverty, a lack of social provisions, and the incarceration binge.

As Denzin (2014) instructs and Giroux (2013) details in the quote above, these fears of safety that have come to control citizenship and action in the post-9/11 world are defined largely by race and social status. Discussing the nationwide hysteria about Muslims, Giroux (2013) stated:

> the American public has been schizophrenically immersed within a culture of fear and cruelty punctuated by a law-and-order driven promise for personal safety, certainty, and collective protection that amounted to a Faustian bargain with the devil, one in which Americans traded constitutional rights and numerous civil liberties for the ever expanding presence of a militarized security and surveillance state run by a government that has little regard for human rights or the principles of justice and democracy.
>
> (para. 1)

Giroux (and many other critics), however, does not articulate that lockdown culture is what Americans *have seemingly come to expect, if not welcome*. To question its use, let alone criticize it, has to some become conflated with being *un-American*. Often overlooked in the complex web of narratives surrounding the aftermath of the bombings was the spectacle pedagogy of citizenship that engulfed not only the Tsarnaevs—who despite being raised largely in Boston were almost universally hailed as "Chechen terrorists" in the majority of press accountings—but also the winner of the 2014 Boston Marathon, Meb Keflezhigi, and how his victory once again brought to the fore lingering concerns with who gets to "count" as an American in the historical present.

Meb Keflezighi, the Tsarnaevs, and learning to be an "American"

In this section, we turn our attention to Meb Keflezhigi, the Eritrean-born American long-distance runner who won the 2014 Boston Marathon.[6] Keflezhigi's story is that of a typical immigrant success that fits with the long lasting image of pulling oneself up by his or her bootstraps (Edwards, 2014). As a child in the late 1980s, Keflezhigi (popularly referred to as "Meb"), his mother, and his nine siblings fled war-torn Eritrea, initially landing in Italy before settling in Southern California. Keflezighi was successful both on the track and in the classroom at UCLA before going on to win a silver medal at the 2004 Olympic Games (May, 2014). Although the biggest feat of his career was winning the 2014 Boston Marathon, Meb had already been cast as suspect, as someone who was not "really" American, well before his name was thrust into the popular lexicon for his stunning victory. Upon winning the 2009 New York City marathon and becoming the first American man to do so since 1982, CNBC sports business reporter Darren Rovell (now of ESPN) referred to Meb as only "technically American" and proclaimed him "a ringer who you hire to work a couple hours at your office so that you can win the executive softball league."[7] The trend of mobilizing the specter of citizenship inward against "the Other," of using it to cavil one's achievements, reveals the contested nature of citizenship debates in the contemporary United States (especially in a post-9/11 context). As Hoberman notes, Keflezighi's case raised the question of "who gets to represent the country," and in what capacity (quoted in Kolata, 2009). Yet although Keflezighi represented individual enterprise and success (e.g., winning major marathons, an Olympic medal), quoted Christian scripture on his official website (a stark contrast to the "fear" of Islam that invades the purview of many American stories of international foreign involvement), and can otherwise be viewed as an immigrant success story, the waters remain(ed) muddy for him.

Keflezighi's case is clearly not the only one in recent memory, nor is Rovell's statement an outlier in the American media. From several recent examples, we spotlight two, although somewhat different from marathon running. We have, nevertheless, chosen these because the racial and ethnic dynamics at play are illustrative of the larger discourse of citizenship currently operative within the United States.

As our first example, we point to contestations over Nina Davuluri, an American-born Hindu of South Asian descent from Syracuse, New York, after she was crowned Miss America in 2013. As Muhopadhyay (2013) wrote in

The Nation, Davuluri's historic victory was blanketed by "angry, post-9/11 racial hatred" that saw the Twitterverse and commentariat refer to her as, among other things, an "Indian," "a foreigner", and an "Arab" (all three of which are incorrect) (para. 2). Similarly, and over the course the last eight years, we've witnessed the far-Right in America refer to President Obama as "some combination of terrorist sympathizer, socialist, Marxist, Afro-Leninist, Muslim, anti-American, and more," language which signals a concerted effort to actively "Other" Obama, "to negatively construct his blackness as a visual if not visceral threat to the nation" (see Giardina & Bunds, 2013, p. 415).[8]

Along these lines, Miller (2006) has remarked that

> We are in a crisis of belonging, a population crisis, of who, what, when, and where. More and more people feel as though the *do not* belong. More and more people are *seeking* to belong, and more and more people are not *counted* as belonging.
>
> (p. 1)

This much is painfully clear to any consumer of U.S. media culture over the last decade or so. As Sanli (2011) asked:

> who is excluded from the public sphere by being excluded from the means of representation and political discourses, which characteristics of society are excluded, and what are the repercussions of such exclusions, and what kind of cultural consumption is privileged and which forms are relegated to the banal or unimportant?
>
> (p. 282)

In the present moment, the discourse around (or against) "immigrants" is once again front and center, from political debates in Congress to popular new television shows such as *Fresh off the Boat.* In other words, talented and successful immigrants such as Meb still face an uphill challenge in gaining acceptance for who they are and what they do—even when they have extraordinary talent that can be seen as representative of American exceptionalism (Edwards, 2014).

As a second example, we quote the filmmaker Haimy Assefa (2014) who, writing for CNN, locates herself alongside Keflezighi in a struggle for who and what has come to count as prevailing signifiers of Americanness. She stated:

> I was born in Ethiopia, raised in Oklahoma and Colorado, and ended up in Brooklyn, New York. Coming to America from Ethiopia, a place where black and white were only colors that had little to do with race, I had to learn English, and also the language of identity. In America, I was black.
>
> (para. 1)

Assefa's story is also the story told by the Nigerian novelist and McArthur Genius Grant recipient Chimamanda Ngozi Adichie (2009), who described her first encounter with being African in America when attending college in the United States:

> I must say before I moved to the U.S. I, I didn't consciously classify myself as African, but when I moved to the US when the topic of Africa came up, people turned to me, even though I knew nothing of places like Namibia. But I did come to embrace this new identity and have come to define myself as African.

Adichie, who classifies herself as Americanah, suggests that while all experiences are different, the continent of Africa and many geo-locations around the world come to be represented by a single story, one that is (often) incorrect. This is especially the case for those who come from places with a troubled political history. In the present context these single stories become another way of saying the Middle East or Africa.

The performative iterability (Butler, 1990; Walton-Fisette, this book) instantiated on and through Assefa and Adichie (and scores more like them) being made and re-made in the language of (a particularized form of) American identity, or, rather, being made black, or "Other," quite clearly reveals "the complexities of the individual experiences that inform our identity" (Assefa, 2014, para. 6). At the same time, this "Othering" also establishes the *boundaries* of cultural citizenship in the United States. This was evident in the cases of both the Tsarnaev brothers and Keflezighi. Cole (2014) has argued that "The Tsarnaev Brothers … seemed to confirm the worst prejudices of the anti-immigrant crowd," with many opining that they were "apparently haunted by the horrors of Chechnya's fate, and attracted by Chechnya nationalism in, at one time or another, both its secular and radical Muslim guises" (para. 3). The brothers were easily "Othered" because they were from a religion that has become post-9/11 shorthand for terrorism, and a geographic location that many would associate with international conflict if not acts of terrorism itself. However, Cole continues, both "showed promise and initiative. Tamerlan had real talent as a boxer. Dzhokar got into college. They could have built productive lives in their new homeland" (para. 4). That they didn't, however, could not have been known in advance, nor was it a foregone conclusion that would be the case. Importantly, Cole goes on to articulate the Tsarnaevs' biography to that of Keflezighi's, noting that Eritrea, much like Chechnya, has gone through violence and rebellion, with a president, Isaias Afwerki, who has been accused of supporting terrorist groups. Of course, this shared fact should not allow us to deign anything more about Keflezighi than it should the Tsarnaevs. Yet to see it play out, Keflezighi and the Tsarnaevs became effectively cut from the same cloth: both have faced questions over being deemed "American enough" in the prevailing level of popular discourse on American identity, *even as the Bible-quoting Keflezighi was crossing the Boston finish line to heroic chants of "USA! USA."* The point that Cole is making here is not, of course, that Keflezighi and the Tsarnaevs were the same, but rather that it did not matter that they weren't same in the eyes of many.

Three years after Keflezighi won the New York City Marathon, *Time* magazine found it necessary to run an article titled "What does it take to be American? Why Meb Keflezighi may rekindle that debate." In the piece, Keflezighi diplomatically stated the obvious:

> I'm a first generation immigrant, but you have to bear in mind—for somebody else who lives in America, where did their grandparents come from? It's a melting pot. They may have immigrated from somewhere else, whether it's the Netherlands, or Sweden, or wherever else.
>
> (quoted in Gregory, 2012, para. 4)

The author of the piece, Gregory, later states how whiteness becomes sutured into the discussion of Keflezhigi's "Americanness": "We've seen with the rhetoric surrounding Barack Obama and his ancestry, if a name or face doesn't sound familiar to a segment of 'real'—code word translation 'white'—America, its very Americanism is called into question" (para. 6). Gregory's interpretation lends credence back to the idea that an individual must have the "correct" characteristics in order to be considered the "right" type of immigrant.

After winning the Boston Marathon, Keflezighi and the Tsarnaevs were once again the subjects of conjoined debates concerning what we mean by American identity. Kohn (2014) reached the core of the debate:

> Keflezighi and the Tsarnaevs: Which of them is more American? Because it turns out that while the geography of our nation is fixed, our identity is treated as malleable—and, especially for immigrants and people of color, *revocable*.
>
> What makes someone an American? It's a profoundly complicated and rich question for us, our identity having been forged out of many strands—some willingly incorporated, others against their will, over generations and generations. But what seems to emerge from the Keflezighi/Tsarnaev example is the ephemeral nature of American identity.
>
> After all, Dzhokhar Tsarnaev is a naturalized American citizen and his brother had a green card and reportedly hoped to naturalize. Keflezighi is also a naturalized citizen of the United States. On paper, at least, Dzhokhar Tsarnaev and Meb Keflezighi are the same as far as citizenship goes. But not in terms of fitting the popular conception of what is "an American." When the Tsarnaevs were identified, the *Washington Post* wrote: "With their baseball hats and sauntering gaits, they appeared to friends and neighbors like ordinary American boys. But the Boston bombing suspects were refugees from another world—the blood, rubble and dirty wars of the Russian Caucasus," hinting at the idea that the Tsarnaevs resembled dangerous wolflike immigrants in sheepish American clothing.
>
> (paras. 5–7)[9]

According to Kohn, rather than portraying the brothers as disaffected youths violently rebelling against their city (or life in general) similar to, for example the

Columbine High School shooters in the late 1990s, the Tsarnaev's "American-ness" is written out of the story. Meb's American-ness, in turn, is written into—or like in Rovell's article, out of—the story.

By way of a conclusion: consuming security/consuming identity

We have read numerous articles critical of the lockdown. Some poked fun at the American (over-)reaction to the bombings, others were critical of the critiques. Far more celebrated the Bruins' national anthem, Ortiz's speech, and the decision to have the lockdown. *Nevertheless, there has been a lack of critical discussion about why two kids "from" Boston would want to terrorize Boston.* One of the lone examples of such questioning was taken up in a *Rolling Stone* magazine cover story, "The Bomber: How a Popular, Promising Student Was Failed by His Family, Fell into Radical Islam and Became a Monster." Authored by award-winning investigative journalist Janet Reitman (2013), the piece became a subject of much public backlash despite the fact that questioning the reasons for turning to terrorism does not mean excusing it.[10] The article frames Dzhokhar in the following way:

> He had been a captain of the Cambridge Rindge and Latin wrestling team for two years and a promising student. He was also "just a normal American kid," as his friends described him, who liked soccer, hip-hop, girls; obsessed over *The Walking Dead* and *Game of Thrones*; and smoked a copious amount of weed.... [The brothers] were Muslim, yes, but they were also *American*—especially [Dzokhar], who became a naturalized U.S. citizen on September 11th, 2012.

At the same time, Reitman posits, both brothers were becoming largely disaffected with their increasing familial and financial difficulties in their increasingly gentrified neighborhood (e.g., their father took ill, the family went on public assistance again—food stamps—for the first time in five years, their parents later divorced and returned to Russia separately). Gravitating toward religion and/or Chechnya, as Brian Glyn Williams argues, was an act of "classic diasporic reconstruction of identity" (quoted in Reitman), in which immigrants who feel isolated or out of the mainstream turn back to their country of origin to (re-) claim a particular identity. This story appears not unlike the ones seeing immigrants in Britain and France (among other countries) attempt to join ISIS in the Middle East as a means of finding a "place" to call home.[11] Raising questions concerning the radicalization of the Tsarnaevs (if indeed that is the best way to frame it) is not the only difficult item on the agenda.

We have to raise additional questions about the role of Americans in the way that the Boston tragedy became so readily commodified and consumed by so many people. And that includes *us*. On October 2014, after all our critique of those five days in April 2013, one of us, with his family, participated in

Touch-a-Truck event near our home.[12] Touch-a-Truck is an exhibition where vehicles from fire trucks, to police cruisers, and hospital helicopters make grand entrances and children pay a small fee to be able to sit in them to have their photos taken. We photographed our two children in the various machines and bought hamburgers and hot dogs. The proceeds from the event went to the Ericka Brannock Fund—a branded fundraising site for those who were inspired by her story. She lost both of her legs in the Boston bombing and was the last patient injured that day to leave Beth Israel Deaconess Medical Center. Roughly 18 months later, on November 9, 2014, Ericka walked for the first time with the aid of prosthetic legs. However, after doctors discovered a bacterial infection, she endured two more months off her feet to walk again onto the set of the hit television show *The View*. Later she threw out the first pitch at a Baltimore Orioles baseball game. Hers is one hell of a story—a story of tragedy, of triumph, of endurance, of spirit. Yet to look around the event, one had to wonder: was this also the triumph of branded philanthropy? Was this proof of the successes (and excesses) of a militarized and corporatized culture? We were supporting a charitable fund drive, for example, without questioning why the brave Brannock and/or all of the other victims host fundraisers at an international sporting event instead of being covered by the state.

Elavsky suggested that: "The logics of our contemporary media culture impel the reproduction of the spectacle that not only implicitly instructs us how to interpret news 'events' but also obscures 'the impact of spectacle culture and its underlying ideology on social relations'" (Garoian & Gaudelius, 2008, p. 24). As the story above demonstrates, Boston Strong continues to "carry the day"; the Tsarnaevs are easily caricatured as evil foreign terrorists; law enforcement are heralded for their protection despite constraints imposed on civil liberties in the act of so doing. The victims/survivors become but another image in the re-writing of the city's historical memory, and life proceeds apace. But this is only so because we let it, because we lack a critical media literacy and language to problematize the context of social relations in which such events transpire.

It is, thus, no surprise to us that in its aftermath, the Boston bombing is turned into a commodified event without history. It is, thus, no surprise to us that the perpetrators of this heinous crime were so easily caricatured as foreign enemies of the state. It is, thus, no surprise to us that Keflezighi, despite training as a runner for his entire life in the United States, saw his achievements undermined by questions of his "Americanness." This is the new normal of American identity politics, of living under the specters of terrorism and neoliberalism—of commodifying everything, including tragedy. The narrative seems to start: we'll bring an entire global city to a standstill to find two criminals who inflict damage to its psyche and cause physical harm to several hundred people under the auspices of terrorism, but major issues that affect millions of urban residents (largely due to, for example, government neglect, patterns of disinvestment, and racism) must only be spoken of in hushed tones. The narrative seems to continue: we'll turn tragedy into goods to be bought and sold, so long as it's a tragedy we can sell (e.g., breast cancer, 9/11). The narrative seems to conclude:

"the Others" are still—will always be—suspect, even when they win the Boston Marathon (or Miss America. Or even the Presidency). This is a truly depressing plot that portends a dangerous future void of history. If the spectacle of citizenship that so enraptured the Boston Marathon bombings and its aftermath, as well as all other such terrorist events, is allowed to sustain America's imagination, then, we believe, we have truly failed—whether as scholars, consumers, or citizens of a democratic society. If the racial politics of citizenship in the present moment is "largely a matter of advertising, commercials, and the media" (Denzin, 1996, p. 319)—a matter of cultural pedagogy insofar as it informs our understandings of who gets to "count" as American—then surely the script must change. And it is up to us to rewrite it.

Notes

1 This is an equally co-authored chapter. Portions of it are drawn from King-White's (2014) presentation titled, " 'This is our fucking city', or is it? Disaster capitalism and the loss of rights in national tragedies," which was presented at the 10th International Congress of Qualitative Inquiry in Urbana, Illinois.

2 The issue of citizenship played a key role in the framing of the 9/11 hijackers. While only one of the hijackers had overstayed his student visa, reports and Senate testimony suggested that four of the hijackers were citizens that had overstayed their visas (Farley, 2013). According to Farley (2013), this opened a decade of debate on immigration and who should be allowed into the country, even on the level of student visa.

3 Before the Tsarnaev brothers were profiled as the suspects, social media wrongly accused Sunil Tripathi as the suspect while instantaneously stating that the suspect was "not white" (Safi, 2013).

4 Indeed, everyone that we know personally who lives in Boston relayed that they gladly stayed in their homes, watching the scene develop on their television screens or via Twitter/Facebook/social media. In that moment, we were obviously glad for their safety, too.

5 According to official reports, Dzhokhar was born in Kyrgzstan, and Tamerlan in what is now Kalmykia, a North Caucasus area of Russia. Both held permanent resident status in the United States at the moment of their act.

6 We are not concerned with the technical specificities of Meb's win, and how other American runners, such as Ryan Hall, may or may not have factored into a particular strategy that could have assisted him in winning the Boston Marathon. If you are interested in such a narrative, see Johnson (2014).

7 Rovell apologized in print the following day after public outcry stemming from his (mis)characterizations of Keflezighi.

8 For a similar discussion of cultural citizenship, albeit in a much different context, see Daniel Burdsey's work on Mo Farah.

9 Kohn (2014) is careful to point out later in her piece,

> I'm not saying we should embrace the Tsarnaev brothers as examples of patriotic Americans. Of course not. But to deny their American-ness not only rejects our core values but perpetuates a dangerous blind spot about the realities of homegrown terrorism.
>
> (para. 10)

10 *Rolling Stone* came under considerable pressure for publishing a cover story on Dzhokhar Tsarnaev that arguably presented him in celebrity overtones. Numerous retailers declined to sell that particular issue of the magazine, while others (such as

BJ's Wholesale Club, which is headquartered in Massachusetts) decided to forego carrying any future issues of the magazine as well.

11 By some estimates, nearly 600 British citizens have joined ISIS in Syria and Iraq, including many teenage girls looking to "fit in." For more see Kachroo (2015).

12 This is King-White talking.

References

Adichie, C. (2009, October 7). The danger of a single story. TEDTalks. Retrieved from www.youtube.com/watch?v=D9Ihs241zeg.

Alba, M. (2014, April 14). At Boston bombing, strangers ran toward chaos, not away from it. *NBC News*. Retrieved from www.nbcnews.com/storyline/boston-bombing-anniversary/boston-bombing-strangers-ran-toward-chaos-not-away-it-n78376.

Assega, H. (2014, April 23). Meb Keflezighi is American, and so am I. *CNN*. Retrieved from www.cnn.com/2014/04/22/living/african-black-identity-meb-keflezighi/.

Cole, J. (2014, April 22). Triumph of the immigrant American spirit: Meb Keflezighi and the Boston Marathon. Truthdig. Retrieved from www.truthdig.com/report/item/triumph_of_the_immigrant_american_spirit_meb_keflezighi_and_the_boston_mara.

Denzin, N. K. (2014). A critical performance pedagogy that matters. In R. Rinehart, K. Barbour, and C. C. Pope (Eds.), *Ethnographic worldviews: Transformations and social justice* (pp. 235–252). New York, NY: Springer.

Edwards, J. (2014). The good citizen: Presidential rhetoric, immigrants, and naturalization ceremonies. *American Communication Journal, 16*, 43–51.

Elavsky, C. M (2010). How you gonna save y/our soul? Tempering corporate identity in a global age. *Cultural Studies⇔Critical Methodologies, 10*, 175–186.

Engelhardt, T., & Dispatch, T. (2013, February 5). *Alternet*. The nefarious ways 9–11 turned America into a lockdown state. Retrieved from www.alternet.org/civil-liberties/nefarious-ways-9-11-turned-america-lockdown-state.

Giardina, M. D., & Bunds, K. S. (2013). Performing blackness: Barack Obama, sport, and the mediated politics of identity. In D. L. Leonard & L. Guerrero (Eds.), *African Americans on television: Race-ing for ratings* (pp. 414–433). Santa Barbara, CA: ABC-CLIO.

Giroux, H. A. (2013, May 6). Lockdown, USA: Lessons from the Boston Marathon manhunt. *Truthout*. Retrieved from http://truth-out.org/opinion/item/16175-lockdown-usa-lessons-from-the-boston-marathon-manhunt.

Giroux, H. (2003). Terrorism and the fate of democracy after September 11. In N. K. Denzin and Y. S. Lincoln (Eds.), *9/11 in American Culture* (pp. 4–8). Walnut Creek, CA: AltaMira Press.

Gregory, S. M. (2012, July 6). What does it mean to be American? Why Meb Keflezighi may rekindle that debate. *Time*. Retrieved from http://olympics.time.com/2012/07/06/what-does-it-take-to-be-american-why-meb-keflezighi-may-rekindle-that-debate/.

Holman, E. A., Garfin, D. R., & Silver, R. C. (2014). Media's role in broadcasting acute stress following the Boston Marathon bombings. *Proceedings of the National Academy of Sciences of the United States of America, 111*, 93–98. doi: 10.1073/pnas.1316265110.

Johnson, R. (2014, April 22). American strong: The untold story of American teamwork and how Ryan Hall helped Meb Keflezighi win Boston. *Let's Run*. Retrieved from www.letsrun.com/news/2014/04/untold-story-american-teamwork-ryan-hall-helped-meb-keflezighi-win-boston/.

Kachroo, R. (2015). ISIS Girls: Syria-bound teens' families struggle with blame. *NBC News*. Retrieved on April 12, 2015, from www.nbcnews.com/storyline/isis-terror/isis-girls-families-teens-thought-struggle-whos-blames-n331116.

Klein, N. (2008). *Shock doctrine: The rise of disaster capitalism*. New York, NY: Henry Holt and Company.

Kohn, S. (2014, April 22). What the Boston Marathon winner and bombers have in common. CNN. Retrieved from www.cnn.com/2014/04/22/opinion/kohn-boston-marathon-american/.

Kolata, G. (2009, November 2). To some, winner is not American enough. *New York Times*. Retrieved from www.nytimes.com/2009/11/03/sports/03runner.html.

Kontorovich, E. (2013, April 19). The American Athens becomes a prison city. *The Volokh Conspiracy*. Retrieved from http://volokh.com/2013/04/19/the-american-athens-becomes-a-prison-city/.

Lowery, W. (2015, April 3). 7 key takeaways from the long-waited Boston Marathon bombing report. *Washington Post*. Retrieved from www.washingtonpost.com/news/post-nation/wp/2015/04/03/7-key-takeaways-from-the-long-awaited-boston-marathon-bombing-report/.

May, P. (2014, April 21). A year later, it's old glory in Boston. New York Times. Retrieved from www.nytimes.com/2014/04/22/sports/meb-keflezighi-an-american-wins-boston-marathon.html.

Mukhopadhyay, S. (2013, September 18). Miss America Nina Duvuluri is not a symbol of progress. *The Nation*. Retrieved from www.thenation.com/article/176258/miss-america-nina-davuluri-not-symbol-progress.

Murphy, T. A. (2003). Romantic democracy and the rhetoric of heroic citizenship. *Communication Quarterly*, *51*, 192–208.

Sandlin, J. A., Schultz, B. D., & Burdick, J. (2010). Understanding, mapping, and exploring the terrain of public pedagogy. In J. A. Sandlin, B. D. Schultz, and J. Burdick (Eds.), *Handbook of public pedagogy: Education and learning beyond schooling* (pp. 1–6). New York, NY: Routledge.

Safi, O. (2013, April 20). 10 essential points about the Boston Marathon bombers, Islam, and America. *Religion News Service*. Retrieved from http://omidsafi.religionnews.com/2013/04/20/10-essential-points/.

Sanli, S. (2011). Public sphere and symbolic power: "Women's voice" as a case of cultural citizenship. *Cultural Sociology*, *5*, 281–300.

Sullivan, A. (2013, April 19). The shutting down of Boston, ctd. The Dish. Retrieved from http://dish.andrewsullivan.com/2013/04/19/the-shutting-down-of-boston-ctd/.

Zimmer, B. (2013, May 12). "Boston Strong," the phrase that rallied a city. *Boston Globe*. Retrieved from www.bostonglobe.com/ideas/2013/05/11/boston-strong-phrase-that-rallied-city/uNPFaI8Mv4QxsWqpjXBOQO/story.html.

9 Lopez Lomong

Enduring life

Theresa Walton-Fisette

The Republic of the Sudan has endured one of the longest and deadliest civil wars of the twentieth century, almost continuously since becoming independent of Egypt and Great Britain in 1956. One chapter of this traumatic history created a group of refugees, dubbed the "Lost Boys of Sudan," who gained global media attention beginning in the late 1980s into the early 2000s. In 2005, a peace agreement was signed leading to South Sudan's independence in 2011, but sadly not to the end of violence and disputes over resources. Throughout this time, tens of thousands of children, primarily boys, became separated from their families. While the stories of many ended brutally and tragically, some of those who survived ended up in refugee camps, the largest of which, Kakuma, holds more than 100,000 refugees in the northwest corner desert of Kenya, near the South Sudan border.

Lopepe Lomong was born in 1985 to Awei Lomong and Rita Namana, in the small village of Kimotong. Lomong and his family are of the Buya people. His village had no running water or electricity and his family lived as subsistence farmers. Lomong lived in Kimotong until he was six years old when he became one of those Lost Boys. In this chapter, I explore the notion of endurance as it applies throughout Lomong's life, centered on his experiences with running. This examination allows insight into the meaning of endurance—both on and off the track. For Lomong, distance running as a sport and as an occupation is a source of joy and privilege. This stands in contrast to the common view of running itself as a painful activity. Having endured multiple hardships and displacements in his life, Lomong demonstrates the importance of considering adaptability as a component of endurance. I explicate Lomong's story and experiences using Butler's (1993, 1999) performativity theory. Most especially I am interested in understanding identities as embodied processes by examining the central role of the body in Lomong's subjectivity. To do this, I conducted two extensive email interviews with Lomong. I also consider his 2012 autobiography written with Tabb, as well as mainstream media representations of Lomong.

Theoretical grounding

Butler has offered critical cultural theorists another way in approaching the concern between individual agency and social constraint. "The interrelation between oppressive identity norms and the possibilities for resistance to such norms are opened up in (identity) performance" (Allen, 1998, p. 460). It would be impossible to think we are, however, each performing our identities—our gender or our race, our roles as academics, athletes, our "selves"—in completely conscious ways. This is the nature of "social" construction—we are not the sole authors of the meanings and performances of our selves or the changes and meanings of resistance that our actions might incur. Neither is it possible for us to completely "know" ourselves and our social constructions, because we are embedded in it. Thus, while identities are performative, identities are not "artiface[s] to be taken on or taken off at will" (Butler, 1993, p. x).

Butler drew from Austin, who put forth the idea of speech act theory, whereby a "performative is an utterance that enacts or produces that which it names" (Allen, 1998, p. 462). Yet, Butler reformulated the idea of the performative using the work of Derrida so that "the performative utterance becomes a derivative citation rather than a founding act by an original subject" (Allen, 1998, p. 462). In other words, each "performance" of our identities always and already comes from the cultural context within which we are becoming ourselves—derivative citations. This allows for a full understanding of cultural construction and our embeddedness within cultural contexts. This recasts the performative as a "citation" of cultural norms that make a performance "successful" or not, conforming or resistant. As Butler (1993) wrote, "performativity cannot be understood outside of the process of iterability, a regularized and constrained repetition of norms" (p. 95). Iterability refers to the repetition of cultural performances, which reinforces the norms that they uphold, or as identities are individualized, how those changes get taken up (cited) by others to become new norms. "A citation will be at once an interpretation of the norm and an occasion to expose the norm itself as a privileged interpretation" (Butler, 1993, p. 108). This creates moments of possible subversion, whether or not such subversions are successful. Indeed some citations unwittingly reproduce the norms they seek to subvert.

Importantly, performativity

> is not a singular "act" or event, but a ritualized production, a ritual reiteration under and through the force of prohibition and taboo, with the threat of ostracism and even death controlling and compelling the shape of the production, but not determining it fully in advance.
>
> (Butler, 1993, p. 95)

Social expectations are enforced through this ritualized production, shaping individual identities in the social interaction. Thus, performativity is the way "subjects are called into being from diffuse social quarters, inaugurated into sociality by a variety of diffuse and powerful interpellations" (Butler, 1997, p. 160).

Nevertheless, at the same time, since it is necessary for norms to be reiterated by individuals to continue as norms, this means we are also never completely determined by them. So, we see the struggle in identity, meaning, and social power, for as Butler (1993) argued, "Identity categories are never merely descriptive, but always normative, and as such, exclusionary" (p. 50).

Given that identity categories are normative and exclusionary, one of the concepts of Butler's performativity that is particularly helpful here is cultural survival. Cultural survival is "an obligation whereby the subject is obliged to emerge within certain webs of power/knowledge, such that the process of subjectification is necessarily complicit in sustaining those dispositifs" (Bell, 2008, p. 395). In other words, through surviving the subject sustains the social arrangements. In this chapter, I examine the various dispositifs—meaning the various institutional, physical and administrative mechanisms and knowledge structures—which enhance and maintain the exercise of power within the social body, which have shaped the life and being of Lopez Lomong. Perhaps because of the extremes of his contexts, his adaptation in performativity make the very dispositifs themselves more visible—not just for understanding Lomong, but the particular ecologies from which he becomes.

The context of Sudan: Lomong's early years

The continuous war in Sudan has killed more than two million civilians and displaced another four million. Many of the refugees from Sudan escaped to neighboring countries: Ethiopia to the east; Kenya to the southeast; Uganda to the south; the Democratic Republic of Congo to the southwest; and, the Central African Republic to the west. Before splitting into separate countries, Sudan was the largest African nation with more than 600 ethnic groups subdivided by skin color, language, religion, and geography with 70 percent of the 41-million population Sunni Muslim. After a peace agreement in 2005, South Sudan seceded on July 9, 2011, although Sudan has initiated significant episodic violence against South Sudan through to 2015.

Geographical barriers within the country led to distinctly different cultures in northern and southern Sudan—particularly slowing the spread of Islam to the south, allowing the ethnic groups of the south to retain their cultural and social heritage, politics and religion, which is quite diverse with a large and socially significant Christian influence, some Muslim and many indigenous religious practices. Of the various ethnic groups, the Ninka are the majority at just 15 percent of the population. Due to the long and deadly civil war there is a large diaspora of South Sudanese to Ethiopia, Kenya and Uganda, as well as more recently a small number of refugees into Europe and North America. South Sudan suffers some of the worst health indicators in the world, such as high infant mortality, maternal mortality, very few hospitals and surgeons, and lack of clean and available drinking water. The long civil war has also meant a lack of strong infrastructure and social institutions, such as sewage systems, roads, transportation, schools, etc. (World Health Organization, 2014). Lomong was born and raised through his early years in this context. Lomong's first major life transition happened when he was abruptly and violently separated from his family at six years of age.

Boy soldiers: kidnapped by the SPLA

In 1991, while attending an outdoor Catholic church service with his family, soldiers of the Sudan People's Liberation Army (SPLA) came into Kimotong, forced all of the adults to the ground, and took all of the boys. Lomong was put in the back of a covered truck, the intense heat weakening many of the boys and making them sick. They were eventually transported to a soldier training camp. Lomong experienced his first ever ride in a motorized vehicle that day. When Lomong did not return, his family believed him to be dead. Lomong, in turn, had no idea what happened to his family. He recounts how his mother held on to him so hard as he was ripped from her arms (Lomong, 2012). While this marks what Lomong labels the end of his childhood, in it we see the beginning of the changing contexts of his life that demanded cultural survival. Bell (2008) has argued for examining cultural survival because "the notion of the unviable subject at the limit of economy of law brings us quickly to the question of human violence, where survival indexes forms of every day violence as well as genocidal killing" (p. 397). And within Lomong's life we see a road of violence and hardship for most of his childhood, but also cultural survival and adaptation.

The SPLA kidnapped the boys to try to train them as boy soldiers for the liberation of South Sudan. The people of Lomong's home village and other rural areas were not agitators in the civil war, however, there was no way for them to be neutral. Each side of the conflict used violence to try to force their participation. Several of the boys in these "training camps" died from the sand that was added to their food, the harsh conditions, and neglect. As Lomong described in a press conference before the 2012 Olympic Games in London:

> By the third or fourth day I noticed that not all the children got up when it was time to eat our one meal of the day," he remembers. "At first I thought these boys were sleeping in. Looking closer I noticed that these sleepy boys did not stir at all. They were dead. I'd never seen a dead boy before. I wanted to cry, but I didn't dare. Instead I sat and stared, horrified, wondering if it would be me soon.
>
> (Brown, 2012, p. 14)

Some of the stronger boys adapted to become accepted within the rebel group. In this context, the boys developed strategies of adaptation and survival. For those who did not, the consequences were death.

Kakuma: becoming an orphaned refugee

After several weeks in the training camp with very little food and harsh conditions, three older boys from church helped Lomong to escape during the night. The boys thought they were headed home, but after running for three nights they found their way to Kenya, where border patrol gave them food and water and brought them to the growing refugee camp, Kakuma. Lomong was among more than 20,000 child refugees from Southern Sudan, mostly boys, often referred to as the Lost Boys because they were separated from their families. The term Lost Boys, in common usage by journalists and aid workers by the 1990s, references the lost boys of Peter Pan.

In understanding Lomong's escape we must consider that any analysis of relations of power and the potential contestations of them are deeply ethical. This links the question of survival to the question of violence—one can perhaps avoid violence by becoming a certain way or to resist that way and risk violence. In this context, Lomong could have been one of the boys to gain certain power within the SPLA, risking the violence but relative strength of that, or to escape as he did, facing the dangers of being without food or water in a dangerous environment so young. As unimaginable as these choices seem, however, the alternative was certain death, as Lomong watched many of the boys in captivity die.

At six years of age Lomong's chances of being strong enough to become a rebel fighter were slight. However, without the help of the older boys, he also may not have made the arduous trek to Kakuma, showing our reliance on one another in our survival. Lomong (2012) described the scene when they were found by Kenyan border patrol:

> I looked closely at the faces of my three angels. Each of them looked like a runner who falls across the finish line, completely exhausted, with nothing left to give. That's what the Kenyan border felt like. It felt like stumbling across the finish line of the longest most grueling race in the world. I can only imagine how I looked to them. My clothes, my Sunday best shirt and shorts just a few weeks earlier, were now shredded. What little material remained was caked with dirt and blood.
>
> (p. 30)

Lomong knew that without the older boys, he might never have survived the soldier training camp or the dangerous journey to Kenya.

Lomong spent the next ten years in Kakuma, a camp divided and organized by ethnicity and nationality. Lomong lived in the Equatorian section, the region of south Sudan. However, as the Buya people were so small in number, Lomong learned Swahili at Kakuma and lost the Buyan language. Lomong recounts how he created a family with the boys with whom he shared his shelter. They looked out for each other, shared and protected their rations. In regard to responsibility, Butler has asked what makes us interested in the other? Or, the inter-human question of, "what is responsibility?" Bell (2008) reminds us that "the disorientation occasioned by loss reveals an indebtedness, an exposure; the intensely personal experiences of grief indicates the extent to which we are sustained by others; we can be 'undone' precisely because we require others for our own personal existence" (p. 401).

This becomes particularly salient in a refugee camp and for boys like Lomong without their traditional families and with no country of belonging. According to Lomong (2012):

> First and foremost, I learned what it meant to be a refugee. From the moment I stepped into Kakuma, I became a boy without a country. A refugee camp is a kind of a no-man's-land. No one lives there by choice. You end up in a place like Kakuma when you have no better option. Everyone who lived there just wanted to go home.
>
> (p. 34)

In the absence of culturally framed social ties, the boys created their own for their comfort and survival. In an email interview, Lomong wrote:

> Building and embracing what others may see as unconventional 'families' was how I survived many of the ordeals of my childhood. While I learned many fundamental morals and values from my birth family, I really matured with my family in Kakuma. That is where I felt like I moved into adulthood.

Lomong spent most of his childhood raising himself along with other boys. They learned the ways of the camp and created a life with the camp as the main context of their lives. Older boys taught younger boys and Lomong matured through those roles

Lomong knew boys who simply gave up living this life—unable to adjust, too lost without their families, afflicted with deep depressions, and the stress associated with such violent dislocation. With no one but the other boys to care for them, many of these boys would eventually die. Lomong (2012) wrote,

> I also had to adjust to the fact that death was a regular part of life. In Kakuma, boys got sick and died every day. Whenever a boy died, we always said malaria got them. They may have died of starvation, since food was hard to come by, especially after famine struck Kenya and the UN cut our food ration in half, but we didn't talk about that. We also didn't want to think that they may have died from the unsanitary conditions at the camp … I lost many friends in this way.
>
> (p. 38)

Lomong wrote about his experiences waiting once a week in anticipation for when the aid workers would dump their garbage and the boys would scavenge for food. His camp family would work together to protect what they found to share with each other. Because Lomong was only six years old when he came to

Kakuma he accepted this life as normal. As he wrote, "I never thought that life was unfair because I had to eat garbage. Instead, I looked at the scraps of food from the dump as a blessing" (p. 38). Again, he demonstrates that relations of power in our performativity are not only political but ethical. Given that we are sustained within our relations, it speaks not just to power, but also to the vulnerability of our relations, and therefore our being.

Lomong used sport as one of the distractions to make life meaningful and to give a focus to his days, particularly soccer, which was hugely popular with the boys at the camp. Because there were so many boys who wanted to play, the older boys created a system where to gain access to the game players had to run the perimeter of the camp—30 kilometers (about 18 miles). Lomong became one of the faster boys to complete the run in order to get more time on the soccer field. At the same time, Lomong enjoyed running: "When I ran, I did not think about conditions in the camp or the hunger in my belly. Running was my therapy, my release, my escape from the world around me" (p. 55). Lomong did not yet think of running as a sport. As he explained: "Running in Africa was a means of survival, transportation, and necessity. Running saved me from a life of slavery as a child soldier. It was also how we got from one place to another in Kenya" (Email interview).

However, in 2000, Lomong began hearing buzz around Kakuma of something he had never heard of—the Olympics. He had no idea what it was, but when presented with the opportunity to go to a house five miles from the refugee camp to watch the Games on television, he agreed. He used the only money he had, five schillings, to pay for the privilege of watching the Games. This was Lomong's first experience not only with the Olympics, but also with television. What he saw was Michael Johnson winning the 400m run. He wrote: "Watching people run on television was a revelation for me. Never before had I thought of running as a sport" (Lomong, 2012, p. 54).

Inspired, Lomong imagined himself as an Olympic athlete, running for the United States. For Lomong, he felt that this first Olympic experience shifted his expectation that there might be a life for him outside of Kakuma. He never considered this before because, "from the day I arrived at Kakuma, the camp defined my world. I thought I would always live here, because I never saw anyone leave" (Lomong, 2012, p. 57). His changed mindset meant he responded differently and made decisions he might not have otherwise made when given opportunities.

Lomong also found a place with the Christian workers and services at the camp, taking advantage of the meager educational offerings in Kakuma. This connected with Lomong's shifted mindset as he felt God had a plan for him, noting,

> God himself had brought me to Kakuma. I always thought He must have had a reason for bringing me here. Now I had it. Now I knew where my destiny lay. Michael Johnson opened a wider world to me. By God's grace, I would go there.
>
> (p. 57)

Lomong had been raised Christian by his parents and although the context and environment were much different, this provided some continuity in his identity as well. As indicated, his beliefs about his purpose and the meaning of his life are deeply tied to his religious beliefs and practices. Indeed, he described his baptism as the moment he became a man. The priest who baptized him gave him the name of Joseph. Lomong wrote:

> Second Corinthians 5:17 says that if anyone is in Christ he is a new creation. All the old things have passed away and everything is made new. That verse came true for me that night. I was a new boy with a new name.... *This is who I am. I am Joseph, a follower of Jesus, trustworthy and hardworking. I am no longer a lost boy. I am a brand new man* [emphasis in original].
>
> (p. 49)

His belief in God being with him has continued strongly throughout his life and has been a means of connection and continuity in his identity in vastly different contexts. As Lomong expressed it:

> My spirituality may be a little different than most Catholics or Christians. Rather than placing importance on going to church my faith has always been very integrated with every part of my journey. God has been present through every step of my journey and I certainly would not be alive without his hand on the events that have happened in my life. I coped with many of the challenges of life in the military prison and the refugee camp by holding on to the idea that God had a purpose for me beyond what I was suffering through at the moment.
>
> (Email interview)

Thus, for Lomong, his spiritual life is deeply tied to his physical life and the way that he has endured his many transitions.

In Lomong's process of actualization, we see his choices as potential "solutions" to the problems of cultural survival which he faced. As such, we can see his performativity within the ecologies of which the possibilities of being are produced/chosen. As Bell (2008) has argued, "whatever is sustained, is sustained by elements that not only pertain to it but are concerned with it" (p. 406). The concern makes the subject a component in the ecology. Therefore, for Lomong, he becomes himself through and with all of the aspects of his ecology—his created family, his physical activity, his spiritual life, and the many hardships he faced.

United States: immigration and settlement

In 2001, Lomong won an essay contest organized by the Catholic Christian Charities. Despite only having slight grasp of English, his winning essay was written in that language; his Kakuma family helped him to translate and his essay was selected. He became one of the small number of refugees from Kakuma relocated to the United States. Barbara and Robert Rogers of Tully, New York sponsored him. Robert Tully saw a flier at their church, looking for families for refugees from Southern Sudan. Lomong became the first of five boys whom the Rogers adopted. Once again, Lomong shifted to a dramatically different ecology with dispositifs unknown and to some extent unimaginable to him. Bell (2008) proves useful here once again:

> The experience of the subject in its activity of self realization (in its relevance to other things and as other things are relevant to it) has to be considered an achievement, an actualizing of potential in particular situations, the extension of the concept of experience … means that a reformed subjectivist principle remains.
>
> (p. 406)

We see this process at work as Lomong becomes a "runner" within the context of the United States. Lomong ran long distances in Kakuma, but it did not carry the same meaning.

We "are" not just our physical embodiment and abilities, including athletic abilities, but also our performance of ourselves, which as we see in performativity are citations of meaning defined within our particular ecologies. Running opened up a social world of care to support Lomong in such a vast cultural transition. He started running for Tully High School soon after his arrival in the United States, his first time experiencing running as a sport. As Lomong explained:

> I never thought of running as a sport until I came to the US. When I came to the US I started to realize that running could be a very exciting sport and most importantly it placed me in the hands of a very supportive coach and team. Coach Paccia from Tully HS and my teammates were such powerful supporters as I learned to fit in to this new country and new way of life. I learned to run for joy in the US.
>
> (Email interview)

Before that his running was geared toward surviving, transportation, or in the sporting world, making it onto the soccer field. While running for competition was new, and had to be learned, Lomong already was a "runner" to the extent that he regularly engaged in that activity and looked to do it for a sense of familiarity in the United States. Lomong described his feeling for running at a 2012 press conference: "Running is part of me. Running saved my life, and running is the thing that actually kept me going for 10 years in a refugee camp" ("Lomong a warrior," 2012, p. 3C). Indeed in his first days, Lomong asked where to run his customary daily 30 kilometers. The Rogers, of course, were taken aback by such a request, uncertain of the length of 30 kilometers and further, whether their new 16-year-old son really meant to go nearly 19 miles. They called their good friend, Jim Paccia, the track and cross-country coach at Tully High school. A runner himself, he met Lomong along the route after Lomong had already run about 12 miles. Paccia could not keep up. Lomong (2012) has described the physical experience of this first run:

> It felt good to run again. The air rushing into my lungs seemed heavier, more humid then what I'd lived with in Kenya. At the same time, I discovered I could run harder without losing my breath. Only later did I learn that I'd spent my entire life in high elevations. Syracuse sits at only 380 feet. I felt like I could run forever here and never grow tired.
>
> (pp. 96–97)

The physical act of running brought a comfort of familiarity in a completely foreign context, an entirely new dispositif, for Lomong (2012):

> Running set me free from all my worries and cares. I did not think about how someone had made a mistake in placing me in this home and how they would show up soon to take me away. Instead I lost myself in the feel of my feet against the smooth pavement and the flow of air rushing past my body.
>
> (p. 97)

Running provided a grounding in a world where little else made sense to Lomong—from electric lights, to hot and cold indoor plumbing, to the rapid fire English being spoken all around him, to being able to be a child again, rather than an adult responsible for himself. As he noted,

> I ran again the next day. And the next and the next. Running was about the only thing familiar for me in America. I had to learn everything else from scratch. In some ways, I was like a toddler because I knew nothing about the most basic elements of life here.
>
> (Lomong, 2012, p. 98)

As a high school student, Lomong won the state cross country meet twice, and in his senior year placed well enough in the Foot Locker National High School Championships for college recruiters to be interested. However, his SAT scores were not high enough to qualify him for a scholarship at a National Collegiate Athletic Association (NCAA) university right out of high school. Instead, Lomong selected Norfolk State University, in Norfolk, Virginia. He wanted someplace warm after his time in New York. He did not join the cross-country team, focusing his first semester on academics. His adopted brother, Dominic, graduated at the same time and they went to Norfolk together. Barbara Tully made clear to Lomong that academics and a college degree were non-negotiable. Nevertheless, while at Norfolk Lomong was encouraged by a friend, who ran for Norfolk, to transfer to a school that could help him develop his running talent. With his friend's encouragement, Lomong selected Northern Arizona University (NAU).

While at NAU, Lomong went on to have a successful running and academic career under the tutelage of Coach John Hayes. He won the NCAA 1,500 m and 3,000 m runs (indoor). He earned third place at the 2007 NCAA cross-country championships. He graduated with a degree in Hotel and Restaurant Management in 2009. Lomong chose his studies and pursued his running success with the idea in mind to put both to use helping address the needs of South Sudan. As he wrote:

> The lost boys of Sudan made the news back in 2001, but people have short memories. The more successful I am as an athlete as a former lost boy, the more people will talk about where I am from and the greater focus I can put on the needs of South Sudan. Then, with my education from NAU, I can lead the way in doing something.
>
> (Lomong, 2012, p. 142)

Importantly, Lomong did not feel this as pressure, rather, related to his spirituality, he felt his path was guided by God. He described his feelings before winning the NCAA Indoor Championship 1,500 m run:

> None of this made me feel greater pressure as I lined up for the 1,500 meter final. Pressure is trying to make the UN food allotment stretch for thirty days. Pressure is watching friends die of malaria and wondering who in camp will be next. Pressure is writing an essay that will determine your entire future in a language you do not know. A footrace, even a championship race, did not make me feel pressure.
>
> (Lomong, 2012, p. 142)

Lomong's lifelong experiences and personal adaptability allowed for his resilience, not only in the major shifts in his life and the dispositifs in which he became himself, but in dealing with the stressors of high-level athletic competition. As Lomong clearly points out, for him competitive running, even at the most elite levels, even as an international talent, was not a source of pressure and stress, but of joy. He wrote:

> Outside I put on my game face. Sunglasses on, stern look of determination on my face, I looked ready to dominate. Inside, I wore a huge grin. How could I not smile? Although this was the biggest race of my life up to this point, I did not run for my life.... Today I ran for pure, absolute joy. My past set me free to enjoy the present moment, and I planned to enjoy it to the fullest. No man ever felt so blessed by God as I did in that moment.
>
> (Lomong, 2012, p. 141)

Lomong demonstrates many of the predictable qualities and resources that allow people to adapt with resilience to new and unknown dispositifs. Carlson, Cacciotore, and Klimek (2012) studied risk and protective factors for unaccompanied refugee minors, like Lomong. Among protective factors are "high intelligence, easy temperament, good coping and problem-solving skills, female gender, and faith in a higher power or a religious orientation" (p. 262). Creating social bonds, as has been a clear pattern with Lomong, furthers his ability to adapt and adjust through the many, and sometimes difficult, transitions of his life and his performance of his own identity.

The Olympic Games: representing the United States

In 2008, Lomong made the Olympic team in the 1,500 m run, along with two other immigrant athletes, Leonel Manzano (born in Mexico) and Bernard Legat (born in Kenya). Lomong's far-fetched dream from watching Michael Johnson win gold had become a reality. While Lomong's dream did not have a fairy tale ending as he failed to qualify for the finals, his journey had taken him a nearly impossible distance. His story became well known and highly mediated throughout the world, especially when the United States Olympic team, in all sports, selected Lomong to be the flag-bearer. In this moment, and in Lomong's own thoughts about his purpose, we see an important point made by Anand (2000) about the possibility of tapping into otherwise limiting or constricting identities for one's own tactical purposes.

Anand (2000) has focused on the agency of Tibetans, within a culture often depicted as being destroyed by the Chinese government and/or modernization and reminds us with his focus on agency: "In such pessimistic scenarios, what is ignored is the creative potential of Tibetan people themselves to adjust and survive in a changing world" (p. 271). We see this form of cultural survival at work within Lomong's performativity. Lomong strategically deploys his cultural production as a Lost Boy, which accords considerably more sympathy—playing perhaps on a culture who grew up on a stream of Disney movies with orphaned characters—than immigrants from other nations and circumstances, particularly others from African nations, even African nations with considerable political and social issues (Walton, 2012).

The United States government has been roundly criticized globally for not doing its fair share in regard to crises in African nations, and further, has capitalized on and fomented those crises. Yet, Lomong has been able to use a constraining, but sympathetic, social construction as a Lost Boy to try to create social change. This began on a global scale with his exposure as the flag bearer for the United States at the 2008 Olympic Games in Beijing, as China was supporting the oppressive Sudanese government. Meanwhile, much of the world's attention was being drawn to the continued violence and genocide in Sudan, at this time within the Darfur region. Lomong deployed the sympathy toward the Lost Boys to shed light on this continued violence. As one reporter wrote of Lomong's press conference before the Opening Ceremonies:

> In a half-hour monologue here on Friday, just 10 hours before he was to carry the flag, Lomong told a tale of grief, endurance, redemption and

> almost unimaginable hardship that captures in human terms every aspect of the Darfur tragedy.
>
> (Boswell, 2008, p. E1)

In 2012, Lomong made the Olympic team in the 5,000 m run. He finished 10th in the finals. He joined Lagat (4th and a five-time Olympic medalist) and Galen Rupp (7th) for the United States' team. At the 2012 Games, more than 40 Olympians on the U.S. squad were foreign-born—the understanding of their "belonging" in the United States is another fruitful area of research. As one reporter commented, reflecting a potential change in attitude toward immigrant athletes,

> More than 40 Olympians on the U.S. squad are foreign-born, and that's particularly fitting because immigrants contribute so much to our national culture and character. The great genius of America is that it draws newcomers from all over the world who are particularly resilient, talented and tenacious.
>
> (Roberts, 2012, p. B7)

Humanitarian: making a difference

Lomong's humanitarian work had begun before the 2008 Olympic Games in Beijing with his return to Kimotong in December 2006. Seeing the conditions that he came from, and how vastly his life had changed, made Lomong want to do what he could to make things better in Southern Sudan, and in Kimotong. He first worked on building and funding a school in Kimotong then worked with Sudan Sunrise to build a Catholic reconciliation church with the help of Muslim university students from Darfur.

He has also been working with 4 South Sudan, a non-governmental organization, focused on clean water, education, health care, and nutrition. He partnered with them to have a greater impact given that they have nearly a thousand people working already within Sudan. In this way, all of his fundraising efforts actually go to Southern Sudan. In the summers of 2013 and 2014, Lomong organized five teams to run in the 197-mile Hood to Coast relay to raise money for World Vision's clean water initiative in Southern Sudan, raising $250,000 in 2013 and over $565,000 in 2014 ("LO Olympian Lomong," 2013; Andrews, 2014). The course goes from the top of Mt. Hood, near Portland, Oregon, to the town of Seaside on the Oregon coast. Lomong enlisted honorary leaders for each team, including three-time Olympian and United States Congressman Jim Ryun, and world record holder and Olympian Ashton Eaton in 2013 ("LO Olympian Lomong," 2013).

Lomong has made clear that he sees his running ability as a gift to give him a public platform to draw attention to the humanitarian needs of his birth country. As he noted in an interview ahead of the Beijing Games:

> When we were in Africa, we didn't know what was there for us as kids—we just ran. But God was planning all of this stuff for me and I didn't know.

> Now I'm using running to get the word out about how horrible things were back in Sudan during the war. Right now, similar terrible things are going on in Darfur; people are running out of Darfur, and I put myself in their shoes.
>
> ("Running in God's Games," 2008, p. 15)

Lomong used the media attention he got for running and particularly for carrying the flag for the United States team in 2008 to make his voice heard. He was a lead member of Team Darfur, an international peace group working to try to bring an end to the genocide in that region of Sudan. According to one media report:

> Later, given the world media stage, Lomong took the chance to get a little political. "As athletes, we need to send the message to the government not to kill or bomb and to China to stop [supplying arms to the Sudanese Khartoum regime] because those guns are not to defend the country, but to kill innocent people," Lomong said.
>
> (Gross, 2008, p. C6)

Some media commentators also indicated that the selection of Lomong as the flag bearer was a political statement by the United States athletes who selected him. For example, some writers recognized the selection of Lomong by team captains as a political statement that could elude censure:

> China, after all, not only helps to arm Sudan but has used its place on the UN Security Council to water down every resolution on Darfur in order to protect its interests. So as much as anything, as inspiring as Lopez Lomong's story is, this was about a group of American athletes actually standing up and saying something, and it was as refreshing as it is rare.
>
> (Vaccaro, 2008, p. 9)

Or, as another writer phrased it: "And now, he was here, on this night of wonder, a human symbol in the most symbolic of all ceremonies" (Shelton, 2008, p. 1C). In this way, Lomong was able to be the ambassador for his own humanitarian efforts while also allowing a more resistant perspective from a team that was tightly constricted in what they were permitted to say about China and the Games being hosted in Beijing.

Concluding remarks

> The abstraction "performativity" has captured the interest of many theorists; it is an abstraction that has, through that interest (the ecology it has created/has been created for it), constituted what we might think of as a domain, viz. a sustained attitude and sensitivity in theorizing.
>
> (Bell, 2000, p. 407)

Indeed, critiques of performativity also sustain it by according it value. In this way, it has become a productive concept. While Butler originally developed this concept to deconstruct and explicate the social construction of gender, the use of performativity reaches beyond gender.

In this chapter, I have developed an analysis of the performativity of Lopez Lomong in the very different ecological contexts within which he has become. In this way, we can understand endurance, not just in terms of an ability to run long distances at certain speeds, but we also can consider endurance more broadly in how Lomong has lived and survived his many dislocations and adaptations. Nearly every media account of him recounts his story of endurance, following the same basic narrative. For example,

> It has taken Lomong so many footsteps, and so many incarnations, to make it here. He was the kid who was ripped from his mother's arms, the kid who grew up hungry in a refugee camp, the kid who once gazed upon his own grave. He was born in Sudan, raised in Kenya and adopted by the United States.
>
> (Shelton, 2008, p. 1C)

Of course, for Lomong himself this is a continual process, as we understand identity as the "incessant and repeated action" whereby the body, rather than as a "factual ground upon which we might project images of our own devising, the substance of the body is itself a product of shifting and conflicting notions" of identity (Cohen, 1998, p. 485). Thinking of our performed identities in this way is particularly powerful when considering athletics, where certain of our identities are physically performed. At the same time, while Lomong's life has moved on, he is also asked to continually recount his story, solidifying his past into his present.

In the becoming of Lopez Lomong, we see his shifting performances throughout the extremely different dispositifs in which he becomes a part and performs his identity. It goes beyond labels, such as becoming a runner or being Buya or Sudanese or American, to our everyday choices and day-to-day lives. Through the incessant and repeated actions of who we are, or rather, who we are always in the process of becoming, we create ourselves through those actions and choices. Importantly, those choices and actions, or performances, happen within the contexts we are collectively actively constructing and at the same time, we are individually being constructed through and by. For Lomong, then, he contributed to each of the dispositifs in which he was embedded: in Kimotong with his family as a boy; in Kakuma with his family of other boys as a refugee; in the United States with his family, the Rogers and all of their other children; as a member of his high school and college track and cross country teams; as a member of the United States Olympic teams; and, as a humanitarian, etc. At the same time, each of those contexts and relationships made him who he is and contributed to his performances of his own identity. Lomong's life offers an understanding of endurance far beyond the simple understanding of him as an endurance athlete and an elite middle-distance runner. Indeed, his life, experiences, and perspectives help us to rethink both endurance and what it means to endure when it comes to competitive distance running.

References

Allen, A. (1998). Power trouble: Performativity as critical theory. *Constellations, 5*, 456–471.

Anand, D. (2000). (Re)imagining nationalism: Identity and representation in the Tibetan diaspora of South Asia. *Contemporary South Asia, 9*, 271–287.

Andrews, M. (2014, Sept. 4). Hood to Coast to the Sudan. *The Beacon*. Retrieved from http://upbeacon.com/2014/09/04/hood-to-coast-to-the-sudan/.

Bell, V. (2008). From performativity to ecology: On Judith Butler and matters of survival. *Subjectivity*, 25, 395–412.

Boswell, T. (2008, Aug. 8). Where once he was lost, now he is found. *Washington Post*, p. E1.

Brown, O. (2008, Aug. 8). The boy left for dead wants end to trauma; London 2012 interview. Kidnapped at six by Sudan soldiers, Lomong had to run for freedom. *The Daily Telegraph*, pp. 14–15.

Butler, J. (1993). *Bodies that matter: On the discursive limits of "sex."* New York, NY: Routledge.

Butler, J. (1997). *Excitable speech: A politics of the performative*. New York, NY: Routledge.

Butler, J. (1999). *Gender trouble: Feminism and the subversion of identity* (2nd Edition). New York, NY: Routledge.

Carlson, B. E., Cacciatore, J., & Klimek, B. (2012). A risk and resilience perspective on unaccompanied refugee minors. *Social Work, 57*, 259–269.

Cohen, S. R. (1998). Performing identity in the *Hard Nut*: Stereotype, modeling and the inventive body. *The Yale Journal of Criticism, 11*, 485–505.

Gross, M. (2008, Aug. 10). Lomong's eloquent statement. *Sunday News* (Lancaster, PA), p. C6.

LO Olympian Lomong running Hood to Coast for charity. (2013, Aug. 22). *Lake Oswego Review*. Retrieved from http://portlandtribune.com/lor/52-sports/159926-lo-olympian-lomong-running-hood-to-coast-for-charity.

Lomong, L. (with M. Tabb). (2012). *Running for my life: One Lost Boy's journey from the killing fields of Sudan to the Olympic Games*. Nashville, TN: Thomas Nelson, Inc.

Lomong a "warrior inside." (2012, June 15). *USA Today*, p. 3C.

Roberts, S. V. (2012, Aug. 5). Olympic dream born in Africa, fulfilled with USA on his chest. *Washington Post*, p. B7.

Running in God's games. (2008, Aug. 16). *The Irish Times*, p. 15.

Shelton, G. (2008, Aug. 9). The lost boy finds a home, and himself. *St. Petersburg Times* (Florida), p. 1C.

Vaccaro, M. (2008, Aug. 9). From Sudan slave to US flag bearer. *New York Post*, p. 9.

Walton, T. (2012). Developing catachrestic sport histories: Toward a critical biography of elite distance runner Sydney Maree. *Journal of Sport History, 39*, 123–138.

World Health Organization. (2014, May). South Sudan: Health profile. Retrieved from www.who.int/countries/ssd/en/.

10 Enduring disability, ableism, and whiteness

Three readings of inspirational endurance athletes in Canada

Danielle Peers

Canada is not a country famous for celebrating endurance athletes. Yet, an endurance runner from the early 1980s named Terry Fox was voted Canada's greatest hero in 1999 and the second greatest Canadian of all time in 2004 (Terry Fox Foundation [TFF], 2014a). Fox was awarded these and many other honors despite never having won a marathon or competed in the Olympics. Rather, he was a man with an amputation who tried to run across Canada to fundraise for cancer research.

Fox is one of three heroized Canadian endurance athletes experiencing disability[1] who embarked on highly publicized fundraising marathons in the 1980s. Collectively, they won Canadian Newsmaker of the Year (2014) five out of seven years: Terry Fox (1980, 1981), Steve Fonyo (1985), and Rick Hansen (1986, 1987). Canada's infatuation with these three endurance athletes[2] did not end in the 1980s. Fox and Hansen, in particular, continue to hold privileged places in the Canadian national imaginary. In this chapter, I first introduce these three athletes by reading how mainstream national media, as well as each of the three athletes' websites and biographies, portray each athlete and his social effect. In the second section, I read these popular representations, collectively, through the supercrip critique: a pre-existing theoretical framework developed by disability and sport studies scholars (e.g., Berger, 2008; Clare, 2009; Hardin & Hardin, 2004) for understanding the characteristics and effects of inspirational disability representations. In the third section, I offer a more contextualized and historicized reading of each of these figures and their effects: a reading I developed as part of my genealogical doctoral project.

Inspirationally enduring disability

In this section I introduce Fox, Fonyo, and Hansen to demonstrate the reoccurring claim that these athletes have inspired Canadians with and without disabilities to overcome barriers in pursuit of their dreams.

Terry Fox. In 1980, a young recent amputee and cancer survivor, Terry Fox, began his Marathon of Hope: an 8,860 km (5,505 mile) fundraising run across Canada from the Atlantic Ocean in Newfoundland to the Pacific Ocean in British Columbia. In so doing, Fox became a nation-wide celebrity and an inspirational hero to thousands of Canadians. According to his biographer, Scrivener (2014b), Fox was inspirational because "he showed there were no limits to what an amputee could do. He changed people's attitudes towards the disabled, and he showed that while cancer had claimed his leg, his spirit was unbreakable" (para. 4). Fox came to symbolize the strength of the Canadian spirit and the ability of ordinary Canadians to accomplish great things (Coupland, 2005; Scrivener, 2000). Less than two thirds of the way across Canada, Fox was airlifted back to his British Columbia home due to cancer's return. Fox died of cancer less than a year later.

Fox's memory lives on through an annual fundraising marathon and through his numerous awards. Fox was twice named Canadian newsmaker of the year and once Canadian athlete of the year. He was the youngest person to be named as a Companion to the Order of Canada—Canada's highest honour (TFF, 2014a). Fox has become a quintessential Canadian icon, appearing on Canadian money, stamps, and passports. He has had countless schools, roads, and awards named after him, as well as a coast guard ship and a mountain. To date, over $650 million has been raised for Cancer research in Fox's name (TFF, 2014a).

Steve Fonyo. In the spring of 1984, an 18-year-old British Columbian amputee and cancer survivor, Steve Fonyo, began his cross-Canadian cancer fundraising run: The Journey of Lives. Fonyo set out "to do what Terry Fox had been unable to do … to run from the Atlantic to the Pacific, a battle against weather, an unforgiving landscape and a physical handicap" (Adams, 2010). Fonyo completed the journey in 14 months, raising $14 million.

Fonyo spent most of his run in Fox's shadow, often perceived as a brash and uppity copycat (Chivers, 2009; Saddy, 2013). As Fonyo surpassed where Fox had left off, and in particular as he successfully navigated the massive Rocky Mountains, he started to be treated as an inspirational hero in his own right: a tenacious overcomer of physical and geographical obstacles. Of the moment when Fonyo completed his Journey, Canadian news anchor Mansbridge proclaimed:

> it was a moment of magic, and a moment you will see spread across the newspapers of this land tomorrow morning, and it will be a moment of history in Canadian books for years and years to come.
>
> (in Adams, 2010)

Indeed, Fonyo was immediately met with significant national press and numerous awards and accolades. He replaced Fox as the youngest person to be named to the Order of Canada, and a Vancouver beach was renamed in his honor. Fonyo, unlike Fox, however, would not be destined for the history books. He was almost entirely discredited and forgotten within a decade of his run (Chivers, 2009; Saddy, 2013). As headlines of Fonyo's inspirational feats were replaced with those of drug use, violence, and imprisonment, he was transformed from a symbol of inspiration to one of desperation.

Rick Hansen. From 1985 to 1987, another British Columbian man—Rick Hansen—wheeled 40,000 km (24,855 mile) across 34 countries in his Man in

Motion Tour ("Rick Hansen," 2014). His purpose was to raise funds for curing spinal cord injury, to change attitudes about disability, and to inspire people to believe that "if you dare to dream, anything is possible" (Rick Hansen Foundation [RHF], 2009a, para. 1). Unlike Fox or Fonyo, Hansen was already a world-class athlete prior to embarking on his tour, having won six Paralympic medals in wheelchair racing, and 19 international marathons ("Rick Hansen," 2014). Hansen was also a personal friend and wheelchair basketball teammate of Terry Fox, and often mentioned Fox as the inspiration for his tour (Scrivener, 2000).

Although not as widely or intensely celebrated as Fox, Hansen has remained in the spotlight as an inspirational Canadian. Hansen was named a Companion to the Order of Canada, was twice named Canadian Newsmaker of the Year, and has several roads and schools named in his honor. Unlike either Fox or Fonyo, Hansen's spinal cord fundraising continues to this day in his role as a leader of the RHF. More recently, Hansen was one of the final five inspirational torch-bearers for the 2010 Vancouver Olympics opening ceremonies. Shortly thereafter, he embarked on a fundraising and media tour (this time flying, not wheeling) to commemorate the 25th anniversary of his Man in Motion Tour. During the tour, Hansen awarded medals to local "difference makers" across Canada: people who were inspired to do as Hansen had, to "turn tragedy into triumph," and who "courageously followed their dreams, and inspired others to bring positive change to the world" (RHF, 2014a "stories of inspiration," para. 1).

Enduring ableism through inspirational disability

The above-described inspirational representations of Fox, Fonyo, and Hansen can be read as part of the pervasive supercrip story: a hyperbolic mainstream media representation of hyper-able disability that scholars have argued has negative impacts on disability communities and social movements (Clare, 2009; Hardin & Hardin, 2004). Below, I highlight three interrelated critiques of supercrip stories and apply this critical framework to analyze the representational strategies used around Fox, Fonyo, and Hansen.

Undervaluing accomplishments

Several scholars have argued that supercrip stories undervalue the accomplishments of the people they celebrate by focusing on disability than their achievements (Hardin & Hardin, 2004; Silva & Howe, 2012). For example, disability sport stories are frequently placed in the "human interest" newspaper sections, rather than in the sports section (Berger, 2008; Tynedal & Wolbring, 2012). The media campaigns of disability sports organizations also tend to devalue the achievements of disabled athletes (Silva & Howe, 2012). The official 1996 Paralympic motto, for example, was: "the Olympics is where heroes are made. The Paralympics is where heroes come" (Steadward & Peterson, 1997, p. 8). Read through the supercrip critique, this connotes that some Olympians are heroic because of their extraordinary athletic accomplishments, but all Paralympians are heroic simply for enduring disability and participating (Peers, 2009; Silva & Howe, 2012).

News stories of Fox, Fonyo, and Hansen also centered on how each acquired, endured, and overcame their disabilities, not their athletic feats. Fox, for example, ran nearly a marathon a day for 143 consecutive days, yet the vast majority of his media coverage appeared in the "Family" section of the Toronto Star (Scrivener, 2000). Fox himself was vocal about how his athletic accomplishments were consistently undervalued by the media, most notably when reporters refused to recognize his non-traditional running gait:

> It's not a walk-hop, it's not a trot, it's running, or as close as I can get to running, and it's harder than doing it on two legs. It makes me mad when people call this a walk. If I was walking it wouldn't be anything.
>
> (in TFF, 2014b, para. 4)

Although Fox understood the athletic feat of endurance running as pivotal to the meaning of his Marathon of Hope, reporters found the run-walk distinction as irrelevant to the real story of how Fox endured and overcame both illness and disability.

Fonyo ran over 7,900 km in 14 months yet the vast majority of the coverage either focused on his disability, or (unfavorably) compared him to Fox (Chivers, 2009). It was not until he managed to cross the massive Rocky Mountains that his athletic accomplishments—to some degree—were acknowledged (Saddy, 2013). Furthermore, although Fonyo ran far further than Fox through far more difficult terrain, he was far less celebrated. Fox overshadowed Fonyo, I argue, not because of his greater athletic performance, but because of his performance of gracious and tenacious disability overcoming.

Hansen wheeled 50 to 70 km per day over a two-year stretch, with very few rest days (Canada's Sports Hall of Fame, 2015): an athletic feat that is rarely mentioned in media accounts of the Man in Motion Tour (e.g., CBC, 1985a, 1985b). Most accounts do not mention Hansen's many Paralympic medals and international marathon wins to contextualize his incredible feats of endurance. More commonly, the opening couple of sentences reveal that "Rick Hansen was crippled in a car accident when he was 15, crippled but not defeated" (CBC, 1985b). From the perspective of the supercrip critique, I conclude that stories of enduring disability trump stories of the athletic accomplishments of these endurance athletes.

Raising expectations

The inspirational stories that often highlight achievements of exceptionally talented, trained, and physically able athletes have been critiqued for creating unrealistic expectations for all people experiencing disability (Longmore, 2003;

Withers, 2012). As Darcy (2003) argued, "the elite athlete's attitude that if you want to do it you can, no matter what," might work for some athletes, "but for the majority of people with disabilities this is not their lived experience" (p. 747). Some people face far greater physical, social, political, and financial barriers than others, some of which are either not surmountable, or surmountable only at great personal cost. Supercrip images, Longmore (2003) asserted, can be used as "a weapon to blame handicapped people who have not proved their worth by cheerfully 'overcoming'" (p. 130).

Fox, Fonyo, and Hansen each contributed to the imperative of disability overcoming by parroting the very inspirational discourses used to describe them. Fox, for example, repeatedly declared: "I'm not special … I just wish people would realize that anything's possible if you try" (TFF, 2014b, para. 1). Hansen similarly used his pedestal to argue that "just because you've had a spinal cord injury or other disability, doesn't mean you can't be successful in business, or family life … so long as you have the heart and desires" (Hansen in CBC, 1985b). Journalists and fundraisers ran these quotes ad nauseum, and often extrapolated to point toward those who did not simply overcome. As Scrivener (2000) declared: "[Fox] didn't blame anyone … he didn't expect special privileges," including increased accessibility or disability income (p. 35). Further, "he showed that you can live with cancer, you can be productive. Part of his legacy was to show you don't go to your room and hide" (p. 255). Thus, just as disability scholars have suggested, inspirational celebrations are never far removed from judgment aimed at those who do not, or cannot, simply overcome barriers in order to achieve such success.

Although Fonyo also parroted inspirational overcoming narratives during his run, he later came to represent the other side of the inspiration/underachiever divide. As his legal troubles emerged, Fonyo was widely scorned in the media for not overcoming these obstacles. The diatribes against Fonyo often used his own inspirational language including claims that he could "overcome" his addictions and make something of his life if he would only set his mind to it ("Honoring their legacy," 2011). Thus, through both their celebratory and scornful discourses, the mainstream media reproduced the imperative of disability overcoming.

Medicalizing and depoliticizing disability

The third critique is that supercrip stories represent disability as a tragic medical problem in individual bodies, as opposed to a social-structural problem of systemic oppression and marginalization (Hardin & Hardin, 2004; Withers, 2012). Clare (2009) argued, "supercrip stories never focus on the conditions that make it so difficult … I don't mean medical conditions, I mean material, social, legal conditions.… The dominant story about disability should be ableism, not the inspirational supercrip crap" (p. 2). The critics argue that stories of individual overcoming veil the socio-political structures that actively marginalize and exclude those with non-normative embodiments. This veiling perpetuates ableist structures and attitudes, undermines disability activist claims, and perpetuates life-effacing violences, poverty, and isolation faced by people experiencing disability (Clare, 2009; Longmore, 2003).

The medicalization of Fox, Fonyo, and Hansen is apparent in the focus on their impairments, but also in each athlete's focus on curing disability and illness. Such a focus reproduces the seemingly benevolent (yet eugenic) imperative to eradicate disability from society (Clare, 2009; Withers, 2012). It also constructs the medical-industrial complex as a savior rather than one of the greatest causes of direct and indirect violence for disabled people (e.g., institutionalization, experimentation, sterilization) (Withers, 2012). Further, these athletes' discourses of medical salvation are rarely tempered with discussions of more social strategies for increasing the life chances of those experiencing disability.

One exception to the above is that Hansen, Fox, and Fonyo have discussed the social impact of negative attitudes towards disability. One of Hansen's explicit marathon goals, for example, was "to raise awareness of the potential of people with disabilities" (RHF, 2009a). Undoubtedly, attitudes that equate disability with total inability contribute to isolation and marginalization. However, the sole focus on individual attitudes tends to efface the social structures that reproduce inequality and ableist attitudes (Withers, 2012). Further, raising awareness through overcoming near-impossible obstacles arguably puts the onus back onto individuals to overcome unfair social barriers instead of challenging governments to rectify barriers. Finally, the use of activist language by these athletes undermines politicized struggles to effect more radical, systemic change (CBC, 1987; Spade, 2011). The most glaring example of this is RHF's (2014b) call to action: "more needs to happen so that one day we can achieve a fully inclusive world where the wheelchair is obsolete." This implies that all disabled people will somehow be fully included in society through medically and eugenically wiping out all spinal cord injury.

In sum, the supercrip critique is useful for analyzing Fox, Fonyo, and Hansen's media representations because it unpacks how seemingly positive inspiration stories can negatively impact the life chances and social movements of people experiencing disability.

Enduring white supremacy, nationalism, and eugenics

In this final section, I offer a more historically contextualized, genealogical reading of Fox, Fonyo, and Hansen. This reading goes beyond the somewhat one-size-fits-all and disability-focused supercrip perspective that, while offering a social critique, tends to present a universalized interpretation of the negative impacts of contemporary inspirational stories. Through my genealogical analysis, I will demonstrate how the inspirational treatment of Fox, Fonyo, and Hansen was tied to Canadian histories of white settler colonialism, nationalism, eugenics, and neoliberalism. As a consequence of this, I argue, the celebration of these figures tends to perpetuate significant economic and political inequality for disabled, racialized, and colonized Canadians.

Genealogy was developed by French philosopher Michel Foucault (1980) as a deeply archival method of critique that "allows us to establish a historical knowledge of struggles and to make use of this knowledge tactically today" (p. 83). It provides much more complex retellings of the different power relations, discourses (e.g., different knowledge used to define race or Canadian nationalism), and subjectivities than do traditional, linear histories. In my genealogical doctoral dissertation, I studied over 200 archival documents (including Canadian Acts of Parliament, transcripts of political debates, academic journals, and newspapers), along with over 75 secondary historical sources, in order to trace the emergence of inspirational and physically fit disability from Canadian Confederation (1867) to contemporary times. The arguments I make herein draw from the penultimate chapter of my dissertation.

I begin my discussion below by demonstrating that the 1980s phenomenon of heroizing three fundraising disabled endurance athletes did not emerge out of nowhere. There are specific historical conditions—including discourses and power relations—that had to be in place to make this phenomenon possible and intelligible to Canadians, and that are, in turn, reproduced through the emergence of inspirational disability. The first of these conditions is the emergence and celebration of physically fit disability in Canada.

Physically fit disability and eugenics

Sport and physical exercise for people experiencing disability in Canada emerged during World War I (McKenzie, 1918; Wall, 2003). Such programs and practices were explicitly developed as techniques for rehabilitating injured soldiers, as well as for assisting in the state-supported project of eugenics. Eugenics is the nineteenth and twentieth century project of trying to improve the racial quality of future populations (McLaren, 1986). It was practiced through (often publically funded) programs for supporting the life and reproductive opportunities of certain "desirables" while curtailing the life and reproductive chances of "non-desirables" (McWhorter, 2009). The most famous examples of eugenic programs are forced sterilization laws in North America and the Holocaust in Germany.

The guiding logic behind eugenic programs was biological racism (Foucault, 1997; McWhorter, 2009). By the turn of the twentieth century the notion that there were separate "races" or species of humanity was replaced by an understanding that there was only one human race with some members thereof having evolved faster than others. The most developmentally advanced humans were understood to be able-bodied upper class Western Europeans with white skin. The increased supremacy of white people and the faster evolution of the human race, it was believed, would result from Europeans passing on their superior developmental traits through sexual reproduction. People with darker skin were conceptualized as less evolved (and thus more animalistic) and were thought to pass on their evolutionary "primitiveness" to their offspring. Similarly, those born with pale skin but understood to have congenital or development disabilities were conceptualized as racial throwbacks threatening to degenerate white populations back to earlier (and lesser) forms of human existence. Their sexual reproduction thus threatened both human evolution and the supremacy of "whites." Eugenics, at its heart, was about protecting and supporting white supremacy, and to do so, social programs had to target and curtail the sexual reproduction of "racial throwbacks," both those with darker skin and congenital disabilities.

Schools played a pivotal role in helping to identify, target, and sexually segregate those deemed degenerate (McLaren, 1986). Early Canadian public schools were explicitly designed and celebrated as "a place of observation, a kind of 'Sorting House'" for Canada's youth (MacMurchy, 1907, p. 7). Due to the capacity of surveillance, and the gathering of youth with peers of similar developmental age, it enabled the quick recognition and removal of the "feeble-minded" and other racialized and disabled "degenerates" who seemed to develop less quickly than their peers. Once identified, these "degenerates" were sent to lifelong sex-segregated institutions where their reproduction could be stopped.

Physical education was celebrated as a particularly efficient eugenic sorting mechanism for schools, and thus for society. According to the Nova Scotia Journal of Education (1917), physical education classes were introduced between the wars as "a practical eugenics, which shall assist in the elimination of mental deficiency and preventable physical deformity" (p. 37). McKenzie (1909) argued that physical activity had enormous curative effects on youth with acquired (i.e., not racially degenerate) disabilities. He argued that such curative effects on white disabled boys could help to identify (and thus institutionalize) defectives who were fundamentally (i.e., racially) affected by "mental dullness, backwardness, arrested development or feeble-mindedness" (p. 210) and thus, could not be cured by physical activity. Physical fitness was considered a marker of racial fitness: a way to distinguish white disability from racial degeneracy.

Based on such racial assumptions, sport and exercise programs for (mostly) men with acquired physical disabilities boomed between the World War II and the mid 1970s, including the birth of the Paralympic Movement. Over this same period, institutionalization and forced sterilization of "degenerates" was on the rise, hitting their peaks in the 1950s and 1960s. In the late 1960s, however, Canada began to rebrand itself not as a superior white nation, but rather as a nation of superior Western tolerance: a compassionate, inclusive, and tolerant welfare state (Thobani, 2007). This led, for example, to the "liberalized," theoretically de-racialized, Immigration Act of 1968. Further, in the era of the United Nations' (1975) declaration of disability rights, forced sterilization was repealed in both Alberta and British Columbia, followed by the closing of many institutions in the 1980s (Jongbloed, 2003). In effect, the explicitly eugenic treatment of those deemed "degenerates" was no longer consistent with Canada's new self-image of compassionate tolerance. In this (barely) post-eugenic context of national tolerance, three Caucasian, physically fit male endurance athletes with minimal, acquired disabilities came to be national heroes and icons.

The fundraising-athon and colonialism

In the 1970s and beyond, benevolence, compassion, and tolerance were celebrated as signs of Canada's Western moral superiority: a trope that replaced explicit claims of white supremacy throughout North America (McWhorter, 2009; Thobani, 2007). As King (2006) argued, philanthropy was another way that Western moral superiority was constructed and reified in this period (King, 2006). Successful national fundraising-athon campaigns, she demonstrated, served to construct the moral value of the marathoner, the benevolence of each donor and, by extension, the moral superiority of the nation. She traced how fundraising-athons were first used by Western countries to raise funds to help impoverished "third world" (often racialized) countries. By the late 1970s, however, fundraising-athons came to be ubiquitously used by private disability charities in the United States, as a way for non-disabled Westerners to benevolently contribute to the dream of a future without disability.

Cross-Canada fundraising-athons, by the 1980s, were a weekly affair (Scrivener, 2000). Because of Canada's size, they offered a hyperbolic, media-worthy, spin on fundraising. They also, I argue, imbued the athlete-fundraiser with a host of exalted characteristics tied to auto-mythologies of Canadian exploration and colonization. Thobani (2007) described such auto-mythologies:

> tales of pristine rivers and virgin mountains … of harsh winters and wild forests … abound in the national imaginary, as do the stories of individual perseverance and triumph over nature. The forces of nature that shape the land are represented as also shaping the national character, cultivating a pioneering spirit and a noble perseverance in these subjects … as [Canadians] celebrated their mythologized relationship to the land, colonial violence was faded into insignificance … the relationship of the settler was constituted as primarily to the land, emptied of Aboriginal life.
>
> (pp. 59–60)

The cross-Canada disabled marathoner, I observe, is often celebrated through such colonial auto-mythologies, in particular for their "noble perseverance" over disability and over the vast and wild Canadian landscape, as well as its harsh climate. Fonyo's marathon, for example, was popularly narrated as "a battle against weather, an unforgiving landscape and a physical handicap" (Adams, 2010). Fox's discursive connection to Canada's natural obstacles was so great that a mountain was named in his honor (TFF, 2014a). Furthermore, Fox was also often constructed in relation to Canada's harsh climate, how: "he ran through ice storms and summer heat, against bitter winds of such velocity he couldn't move," (Scrivener, 2014b). A movie of his accomplishments was named *Into the Wind* (TFF, 2014a). Heroizing Fox and Fonyo through their climate-based perseverance harkens back to a paragraph in Canada's immigration legislation—between 1910 and 1952—which prohibited "immigrants belonging to any race deemed unsuited to the climate or requirements of Canada" ("Immigration Act," 1910, p. 218). Early biological race theorists posited that the harsh

Northern European climate had accelerated the development of whites in relation to southern, dark skinned others (McWhorter, 2009). I argue that such white supremacist discourses of climate tolerance continue to inform the heroic imagery of contemporary cross-Canada runners like Fox and Fonyo.

The connections between cross-Canada marathoners and European explorers are strengthened by the symbolism of the specific route Fox and Fonyo chose to run. Running eastward from Vancouver to Halifax is the shortest route between the two oceans: it hits all the biggest fundraising cities and places the predominant winds at the runner's back (Scrivener, 2000). Fox and Fonyo, however, both chose a harder, less lucrative, yet more patriotic route. They started in St. John's, Newfoundland—the place where European's first "discovered" North America—then ran westward, like the explorers before them, towards Vancouver, British Columbia.

Notably, Hansen also chose to finish his tour with an east to west cross-Canada journey. More explicitly, Hansen helped Canadians construct themselves as a model of superior Western tolerance, inclusion, and morality as compared to "backward" non-Western societies. In Hansen's words: "every country we travel through just reinforces more that [Canadians] are a very, very fortunate people … I think we should all sit back and be thankful for what we have" (CBC, 1985a). Not surprisingly, China became the ideal "Other" for Canadian comparison. One CBC reporter argued: "in a country where the handicapped are still often left without help … Hansen says he hopes his determination will help the Chinese to change their attitude towards the handicapped" (CBC, 1986a). In this way, Hansen not only assured Canadians of their moral superiority, but also served as a benevolent white savior helping to civilize and enlighten the (racially and morally) less progressive Chinese people.

When read together, I argue that Fox, Fonyo, and Hansen's marathons were each celebrated partially as neo-colonial journeys of noble white perseverance, enlightenment, and supremacy. Each symbolic reconquering reproduces automythologies of noble exploration, and naturalizes white settler claims to the land while effacing a national history (and present) of horrific colonial and eugenic violence.

Terry Fox: ordinary anti-separatist whiteness

Fox did not become a national icon simply because of this colonial imagery and journey. There were other important factors, which took time to fully form. Journalists, politicians, and the public remained largely indifferent to Fox for the first two and a half months of his four and half month run (Scrivener, 2000). Fox was especially ignored as he ran through the highly populated French-speaking province of Quebec. He became increasingly vocal about his disdain and intolerance for their growing separatist movement, their culture, their language, and their ambivalence to him. He wrote: "apparently they can't speak English. Maybe they also don't get cancer" (in Scrivener, 2000, p. 94). As he crossed from Quebec to Ontario, a cancer fundraiser named Vigars capitalized on this disdain, selling Fox through the "circus-like" atmosphere of the freakshow (p. 93) mixed with the inspirational discourses of ordinary Canadianness and national unity. Although Fox refused to wear any corporate logos, he ran with a map of a unified Canada and a maple leaf on his shirt. In a time of rampant Quebec separatism and anti-Quebec sentiment, this map and maple leaf would have been the most important logos of all.

Fox was used to sell the unified Canadian nation-state more than cancer research. His various tributes and monuments speak to this. Scrivener (2000) wrote that after Fox's death, "his run, like Canada's motto, would be from sea to shining sea" (p. 6): a much more nationalist and unifying tribute than the literal reality that he would run from sea to Thunder Bay, Ontario. Fox's Thunder Bay monument, similarly reads: "Terry Fox inspired an entire generation of Canadians … it was through his strength and commitment that they were united as they had never been united before" (as cited in Chivers, 2009, p. 86). The monument "was designed, joining east with west, proudly displaying all provincial and territorial coats-of-arms" (Scrivener, 2014a). His memorials, Chivers (2009) noted, use Fox's transCanadian run to reaffirm the naturalness of a united nation-state. This despite the fact, she continued, that Fox's failure to pass into Western Canada could have just as well been used to symbolize the many federal failures of the era to fully incorporate and appease both east and west.

Ontario marketers and journalists played up Fox's symbolism of a united Canada, but also increasingly profited by constructing him as an ordinary Canadian with "a handsome face, perfect teeth and curly hair, and … one [amputated] leg" (i.e., middle class, white, non-degenerate, Anglophone, and an Anglo-Saxon national). Although ordinariness may seem like a step backwards for a hero, Thobani (2007) argued "the figure of the national subject is … exalted above all others as the embodiment of the quintessential characteristics of the nation and the personification of its values, ethics, and civilizational mores" (p. 3). Further, the ordinary Canadian has been widely theorized as a discourse that refers to, while invisibilizing, the assumption of whiteness, particularly when the phrase is used to contrast and demean "special interest groups" and their demands for equality and social change (Brodie, 1995). Constructing Fox as an ordinary Canadian, thus, distanced him from degenerate (racialized) disability as well as activist disability-related "special interest" groups. Fox was ordinary, in part, because "he didn't blame anyone … he didn't expect special privileges" (Scrivener, 2000).

This production of Fox's inspirational ordinariness was accomplished through describing, at length, his normal middle-class childhood, his "down-to-earth, solid and dependable" family, and his suburban home with a carved moose on the mantel and velvet pillows under plastic (Scrivener, 2000, p. 14). His biographer introduced Fox in the following manner:

> Terry saw himself as an ordinary person, average in everything but his determination. His tastes were simple. He loved sports, and admired two hockey players in particular.… He was close to his family. He appreciated pretty girls and enjoyed inspirational poetry. He was a loyal friend.

> He worked hard for everything he achieved. He was touched by the spontaneity of small children. He believed in national unity, and was puzzled by the efforts of the province of Quebec to separate from Canada.
>
> (Scrivener, 2000, p. 9)

In the above quote, Fox's ordinariness is produced through his superior white work ethic and loyalty, his caring white family, his love for the great (white) Canadian sport of ice-hockey, his simple middle class-yet-intellectual tastes, his heteronormative desires and cares, and his disdain for Quebec.

Fox's inspirational ordinariness thus imbued him with celebrated national characteristics of whiteness, and—importantly—projected his characteristics and accomplishments onto other Canadian nationals. Ordinary (Anglo)Canadians could strengthen their own identification with these same characteristics. They could further exalt themselves as a caring, compassionate, and tolerant people for the very fact that they were heroizing a disabled person. This heroization of Fox ballooned over the remaining two months of his run, multiplying upon Fox's death in 1981. Canadian flags flew at half-mast when he died. The CTV national news anchor, Lloyd Robertson, reported:

> to me he embodied the best of the Canadian spirit. We are a generous people, fair-minded, not stridently patriotic, but deeply proud of our country. And we're courageous when we have to be—just like him. He was our hero. He was one of us—a true-grit Canadian.
>
> (as cited in Scrivener, 2000, p. 228)

As Robertson articulated so clearly, what Canadians loved and love most about Terry Fox is that he assures ordinary Canadians of their superior white work ethic, generosity, humility, and courage. Further, Fox serves to reproduce discourses about the superior, compassionate, and tolerant Canadian culture, while effacing histories of colonialism and eugenics and undermining movements for structural equality. Perhaps above all, in an era marked by Quebec separatism, and followed by Aboriginal land claims, Fox reaffirms both the supremacy and the legitimacy of the united Anglo-Canadian nation-state.

Steve Fonyo: Fox's shadow

Three years after Fox's death, Fonyo sought to retrace and complete Fox's cross-Canada route from Newfoundland to British Columbia. Despite sharing the same route, similar amputation, and past illness, Fonyo was never embraced with the same patriotism and exaltation as Fox (Chivers, 2009). In a 1985 Maclean's article, for example, Fox is posthumously described as "a gifted athlete, university-educated and articulate man of easy charm" (i.e., an intelligent, physically superior middle class white Canadian), while Fonyo is designated as "a grade ten dropout who has difficulty expressing himself," and a brash, uppity, and uncouth immigrant (Tierney quoted in Chivers, 2009, p. 89). Fonyo, unlike Fox, could never pass as an ordinary national. He was too under-educated and poor to pass as middle class. His Hungarian immigrant parents were too Eastern European to be considered entirely white or to be imagined as partaking in superior Western morality. In addition, Fonyo's struggles with school and his inarticulate speech colluded with his immigrant status leading numerous journalists to pathologize Fonyo as having inferior intelligence and learning disabilities (i.e., degenerate disability) (Saddy, 2013). He may have been athletic, but he was not entirely intelligible as physically (and racially) fit. Despite rampant racialization and pathologization of Fonyo, by the time he made it through the difficult Rocky Mountains to Vancouver Fonyo was subject to some measure of inspirational overcoming discourses and accolades (Chivers, 2009).

Compared to Fox, however, such accolades are quite minimal. Fonyo has no commemorative statues, coins, or mountains to his name. He is the namesake of only two roads and a beach ("Steve Fonyo," 2014). To my knowledge, he has never been credited with "inspiring an entire generation" or for "uniting a country" (Chivers, 2009, p. 86) despite the fact that Fonyo actually did manage to run "from sea to shining sea" (Scrivener, 2000, p. 6). Rather, he was constructed as an unnatural Canadian, and after his fallout with the law, as unCanadian: an immigrant, an outsider, a wasted life, and a degenerate. Fonyo not only ran in Fox's shadow, he was constructed as the dark, racialized antithesis to Fox's shining white heroism.

Rick Hansen: neoliberal disabled hero

When Rick Hansen wheeled across the world (1985–1987) in his Man in Motion Tour, he was constructed—like Fox—as a white, physically fit Canadian with an acquired disability. His whiteness was constructed largely through silence. Unlike Fonyo, no one wrote about where Hansen's parents were from or how well he had done in school. He seemed to have an ordinary past other than the (constantly narrated) accident that broke his spinal cord. In short, Hansen was too racially fit to be compared to Fonyo.

Hansen also differed from Fox in ways that impacted their political effects. First, Hansen's tour was devoid of national unity discourses. Rather—as discussed above—his travels spoke to the moral superiority of the Canadian nation compared to non-Westerners. The second difference was that Hansen's campaign was much more influenced by the techniques of neoliberalism: some of which Fox fought adamantly against. Spade (2011) argued that neoliberalism is a political, economic, and discursive shift characterized by increasing "privatization, trade liberalization, labor and environmental deregulation, the elimination of health and welfare programs" (pp. 33–34). The generalized effect of neoliberalism, he argued, is "an over-all upward distribution of wealth and drastically decreased life chances for poor people" including a grossly over representative proportion of racialized and disabled people (p. 34).

The most notable example of neoliberalism within Hansen's Man in Motion Tour is his rampant use of corporate sponsorship. This neoliberal tactic of intensive corporate-charity collaboration was so new in Canada that the Canadian Broadcasting Corporation (CBC) (1986b) spent an entire investigative reporting segment explaining Hansen's use of it. The reporters explained how the symbiotic relationship of charitable sponsorship works. They displayed the names of multinational supporters (McDonalds, Nike, Esso, Ford), whose large logos are plastered across Hansen's clothing, wheelchair, and van in exchange for logistical and personal financial contributions. This use of sponsorship is in sharp contrast to Fox, who was adamantly anti-logo and believed that no one should make money off of cancer (Scrivener, 2000). Hansen, unlike Fox, had no ethical quandary with profiting off of charity. The CBC reporter (1986b) continued: "[Hansen] says the arrangement between him and his corporate sponsors is not only necessary, it's good: for him, for them, and ultimately for disabled people." Such arrangements continue to profit Hansen, who makes upwards of $350,000 per year through the RHF charity, and recently donated his name to his charity for a $1.8 million tax receipt (Baines, 2012). Further, the neoliberal Mulroney Government of the late 1980s used Hansen as a neoliberal poster-child for the Canadian meritocracy to further argue for the public good of privatization. Of note, the Mulroney Government donated $1 million to Hansen in the midst of massive neoliberal austerity cuts to disability supports and services (CBC, 1987).

Enduring inspiration

I began this chapter by introducing three disabled Canadian endurance athletes who are popularly represented as inspirations for all Canadians to overcome life's obstacles. I followed by applying the supercrip critique to these inspirational stories and outlining the disabling effects of such seemingly positive portrayals. Inspiration contributes to the enduring forces of ableism through downplaying accomplishments, creating unrealistic expectations, and depoliticizing disability through medicalization.

The more contextual, genealogical analysis that I developed in the final section offered some insight into why such figures emerged and their different impacts upon a wide range of subjects and social forces—not all of which are obviously related to disability. Based on my reading, Fox, Fonyo, and Hansen, collectively, served to exalt Canadian nationals for their superior perseverance: a mythological white quality that—along with the myth of meritocracy—continues to justify political and economic inequalities, particularly in relation to racialized and pathologized populations (Thobani, 2007). Their heroization also served to exalt Canadians for their superior (white) Western morality, which not only served as a politically correct rearticulation of white supremacy but also enabled Canadians to ignore, and reproduce "the 'actual inequality and exploitation' that disabled people in Canada ordinarily experience" (Chivers, 2006, p. 82). Such spectacles of benevolence and tolerance effaced and/or justified numerous state violences of the 1980s to present, including: immigration laws that refuse entrance to disabled subjects; neo-eugenic practices of incarceration and birth control that target disabled, poor, racialized, and Aboriginal populations; and, neoliberal austerity cuts that further impoverish, criminalize, institutionalize, and threaten the survival of racialized, pathologized, and colonized people in Canada. The inspirationalization of physically fit, white, disabled male endurance athletes, thus, helped to immunize privileged, white Anglo-Canadians against activist attempts to challenge the enduring violence and uneven distribution of life chances that characterize the "unified" settler colonial nation-state of Canada.

Notes

1 I use the term *experiencing disability* to refer to a range of biological, psychological, social, and political phenomena. I also use the terminology of those I am citing, including the politically correct *persons with disability*, and the explicitly political *disabled person*.

2 The term *running* continues to define marathons and other endurance events that have long been inclusive of athletes who use enabling technologies such as single-leg prostheses (e.g., Fox and Fonyo) and manual wheelchairs (e.g., Hansen). Thus, although all three can be understood as *endurance runners*, I use the less ableist and more inclusive term *endurance athletes*.

References

Adams, C. (2010). Steve Fonyo's run for life. Retrieved from http://claudeadams.blogspot.ca/2010/03/steve-fonyos-run-for-life.html.

Baines, D. (2012, October 31). Rick Hansen "donated" rights to his name to his foundation. *Vancouver Sun*. Retrieved from www.vancouversun.com/business/Rick+Hansen+donated+rights+name+foundation+received+million+receipt/7473401/story.html.

Brodie, J. (1995). Politics on the margins: Restructuring and the Canadian women's movement. Halifax, Canada: Fernwood Publishing.

Canadian Broadcast Corporation. (1985a). Hansen meets Pope John Paul II in Rome [Video file]. Retrieved from www.cbc.ca/archives/categories/sports/exploits/rick-hansen-man-in-motion/halfway-around-the-world.html.

Canadian Broadcast Corporation. (1985b). The start of the man in motion tour [Video file]. Retrieved from www.cbc.ca/archives/categories/sports/exploits/rick-hansen-man-in-motion/the-start-of-the-man-in-motion-world-tour.html.

Canadian Broadcast Corporation. (1986a). Hansen scales the Great Wall of China [Video file]. Retrieved from www.cbc.ca/archives/categories/sports/exploits/rick-hansen-man-in-motion/hansen-scales-the-great-wall-of-china.html.

Canadian Broadcast Corporation. (1986b). Rick Hansen's and corporate boosters [Video file]. Retrieved from www.cbc.ca/archives/categories/sports/exploits/rick-hansen-man-in-motion/corporate-hansen.html.

Canadian Broadcast Corporation. (1987). Is Rick Hansen Man In Motion Tour doing more harm than good [Video file]? Retrieved from www.cbc.ca/archives/categories/sports/exploits/rick-hansen-man-in-motion/doing-more-harm-than-good.html.

Canada's Sports Hall of Fame. (2015). Rick Hansen. Retrieved from www.sportshall.ca/stories.html?proID=329&catID=all&lang=.

Canadian newsmaker of the year. (2014b). Wikipedia. Retrieved from http://en.wikipedia.org/wiki/Canadian_Newsmaker_of_the_Year.

Chivers, S. (2009). Ordinary people: Reading the transCanadian Terry Fox. *Canadian Literature, 202*, 82–94.

Clare, E. (2009). *Exile & pride: Disability, queerness, and liberation* (2nd ed.). Cambridge, MA: South End Press.

Coupland, D. (2005). *Terry*. Vancouver, Canada: Douglas and McIntyre.

Darcy, S. (2003). The politics of disability and access: The Sydney 2000 games experience. *Disability & Society, 18*, 737–757.

Foucault, M. (1980). Two lectures. In C. Gordon (Ed.), *Power/knowledge: Selected interviews and other writings, 1972–1977* (pp. 78–108). New York, NY: Pantheon.

Foucault, M. (1997). *Society must be defended.* New York, NY: Picador.

Hardin, M., & Hardin, B. (2004). The "supercrip" in sport media: Wheelchair athletes discuss hegemony's disabled hero. *Sociology of Sport Online, 7*. Retrieved from http://physed.otago.ac.nz/sosol/v7i1/v7i1_1.html.

Honoring their legacy. (2011). *Van4um*. Retrieved from http://memebee.com/vancouver/viewtopic.php?f=2&t=28701.

Immigration Act, Statutes of Canada. (1910, c. 27). Retrieved from http://eco.canadiana.ca/view/oocihm.9_07184/2?r=0&s=1.

Jongbloed, L. (2003). Disability policy in Canada: An overview. *Journal of Disability Policy Studies, 13*, 203–209.

King, S. (2006). Pink ribbons, inc.: Breast cancer and the politics of philanthropy. Minneapolis, MN: University of Minnesota Press.

Longmore, P. K. (2003). *Why I burned my book and other essays on disability.* Philadelphia, PA: Temple University Press.

MacMurchy, H. (1907). *Feeble-minded in Ontario*. Toronto, Canada: Office of the Feeble-minded. Retrieved from https://archive.org/details/feeblemindedinon1907onta.

McKenzie, R.T. (1909). *Exercise in education & medicine*. Philadelphia, PA: W. B. Saunders.

McKenzie, R.T. (1918). *Reclaiming the maimed.* New York, NY: Macmillan.

McWhorter, L. (2009). *Racism and sexual oppression in Anglo-America: A genealogy.* Bloomington, IN: Indiana University Press.

Nova Scotia Journal of Education. (1917). *8*, 37–41.

Peers, D. (2009). (Dis)empowering Paralympic histories: Absent athletes and disabling discourses. *Disability & Society, 24*, 653–665. doi:10.1080/09687590903011113.

Rick Hansen. (2014). *Wikipedia*. Retrieved from http://en.wikipedia.org/wiki/Rick_Hansen.

Rick Hansen Foundation. (2009a). Media release. Retrieved from www.marketwired.com/press-release/24-years-ago-the-rick-hansen-man-in-motion-world-tour-began-964184.htm.

Rick Hansen Foundation. (2014a). The Hansen effect. Retrieved from www.rickhansen.com/About-Us/About-Rick/The-Hansen-Effect.

Rick Hansen Foundation. (2014b). What we do. Retrieved from www.rickhansen.com/What-We-Do.

Saddy, G. (2013, October 1). Arrested developments: The Steve Fonyo story. *Vancouver Magazine*. Retrieved from www.vanmag.com/News_and_Features/Arrested_Developments_The_Steve_Fonyo_Story?page=0%2C0.

Scrivener, L. (2000). *Terry Fox: His story*. Toronto, Canada: McClelland and Stewart.

Scrivener, L. (2014a). The legacy of Terry Fox. Retrieved from www.terryfox.org/SchoolRun/legacy_story.html.

Scrivener, L. (2014b). The marathon of hope. Retrieved from www.terryfox.org/TerryFox/The_Marathon_of_Hope.html.

Silva, C. F., & Howe, D. P. (2012). The (in)validity of *supercrip* representation of Paralympian athletes. *Journal of Sport and Social Issues*, *36*, 174–194. doi: 10.1177/0193723511433865.

Spade, D. (2011). Normal life: Administrative violence, critical trans politics, and the limits of the law. Brooklyn, NY: South End Press.

Steadward, R. D., & Peterson, C. J. (1997). *Paralympics: Where heroes come*. Edmonton, Canada: One Shot Holdings.

Terry Fox Foundation. (2014a). Honours. Retrieved from www.terryfox.org/TerryFox/Honours.html.

Terry Fox Foundation. (2014b). Quotes from Terry. Retrieved from www.terryfox.org/TerryFox/Quotes_from_Terry.html.

Thobani, S. (2007). Exalted subjects: Studies in the making of race and nation in Canada. Toronto, Canada: University of Toronto Press.

Tynedal, J., & Wolbring, G. (2013). Paralympics and its athletes through the lens of the *New York Times*. *Sports*, *1*, 13–36. doi: 10.3390/sports1010013.

United Nations. (1975). Declaration of the rights of disabled persons. Retrieved from www.ohchr.org/EN/ProfessionalInterest/Pages/RightsOfDisabledPersons.aspx.

Wall, A.E. (2003). The history of adapted physical activity in Canada. In, R. D. Steadward, G. D. Wheeler, & E. J. Watkinson (Eds.), *Adapted physical activity* (pp. 27–44). Edmonton, Canada: University of Alberta Press.

Withers, A.J. (2012). *Disability politics and theory*. Black Point, Canada: Fernwood.

Running bodies

11 "My hormones were all messed up"

Understanding female runners' experiences of amenorrhea

Holly Thorpe

Within the sports science community, it is widely acknowledged that female athletes face a unique set of health risks related to hormonal changes as a result of rigorous exercise regimes and restricted diets. In 1992, the American College of Sports Medicine coined the term the Female Athlete Triad to illustrate the three separate but interrelated conditions of bone mineral loss, disordered eating, and amenorrhea (chronic loss of menstruation). In 2014, the IOC research group renamed this phenomenon to Relative Energy Deficiency Syndrome (RED-S) to better account for the complexity involved, and the fact that male athletes are also increasingly affected.[1] Research over the past two decades has shown considerable variation of the risks of the Triad (or RED-S) to women across sports, with aesthetic activities such as ballet, and weight-bearing sports such as long-distance running, showing the highest prevalence (De Souza *et al.*, 1994; Beals & Manore, 2002; Harber, 2011). While the health risks for sports women have been well documented, recent endocrinological research is revealing similar health concerns among female exercisers, particularly those who are engaging in rigorous exercise regimes and restricting their caloric intake. Research from the Penn State Women's Health and Exercise Laboratory, for example, states that four out of five exercising women experience mild reproductive abnormalities (De Souza *et. al.*, 1998), and up to 46 percent of recreational runners develop oligomenorrhea (infrequent menstruation) or amenorrhea (De Souza *et al.*, 2010).

According to sport and exercise scientists, the hormonal changes associated with the Triad can lead to long-term damage to women's bone, cardiovascular, and reproductive health (De Souza *et al.*, 2010; Harber, 2011; Warren & Perloth, 2001). For De Souza *et al.* (2010), "heightened awareness among physically active women and raising awareness among athletic trainers, coaches, physical therapists and other health care professionals about the Female Athlete Triad, is essential to promote healthy exercise practices among girls and women" (p. 502). Similarly, Wheatley *et al.* (2012) proclaimed that the growing rate of secondary hypothalamic amenorrhea among young physically active women should be considered a "public health issue" (p. 10).

Interestingly, much of the scientific research on the Female Athlete Triad, and particularly concerns about amenorrhea and bone health, has focused on competitive and recreational female runners (e.g., Cockerill, Nevill, & Byrn, 1992; De Souza *et al.*, 1998). Yet the relationship between women's running practices and hormonal and reproductive systems are rarely critically examined in professional, public, or research texts. Arguably, we cannot understand the complex relationship between women's exercise practices and biological functioning without recognizing that there are many other social (e.g., media, peer group, medical "knowledge," broader health discourses) and psychological (e.g., body image, exercise addiction, personality) factors that influence women's relationships with their moving bodies. Thus, in this chapter I focus on female runners' lived experiences of hormonal changes, and particularly amenorrhea, as a result of their exercise and dieting practices. More specifically, I seek to understand how these women are actively exercising power in their everyday bodily practices, and their interactions and embodied responses to various medical and mediated discourses about the "healthy" female body. I will first explain the bio-cultural research approach toward understandings of the female exercising body before focusing on female runners' experiences of exercise and hormones, and particularly amenorrhea, and their relationships with food and exercise. I draw from the work of Nikolas Rose to further understand how these runners make meanings of biomedical knowledge of hormonal changes and regulated exercise.

Toward bio-cultural understandings of the female running body

Over the past two decades, feminist sport scholars have provided theoretically rigorous and empirically nuanced insights into the various forms of power operating on and through women's moving bodies. An area of particular strength has been examinations of the effects of dominating discourses—medical, mediated, and educational—on women's relationships with their bodies, and particularly body image concerns and feelings of dissatisfaction (e.g., D'Abundo, 2009; Duncan, 1994; Dworkin & Wachs, 2009; Kennedy & Markula, 2011; Maguire & Mansfield, 1998; Markula, 1995; McDermott, 2011). In particular, there has been a significant body of literature on women's exercise experiences, with some focusing on the role of the media in the discursive constructions of the exercising body (e.g., Dworkin & Wachs, 2009; Kennedy & Markula, 2011). A growing number of scholars are focusing specifically on the experiences of female runners—their motivations, fears, risks, and the pains and pleasures of such highly disciplined exercise and dietary practices (e.g., Allen-Collinson, 2011; Cronan & Scott, 2008; Hanold, 2008, 2010; McGannon, Johnson, & Spence, 2011).

Despite a move toward more embodied ways of knowing the exercising female body, there remains little space in contemporary feminist sport scholarship for women's moving bodies as "simultaneously composed of genes, hormones, cells and organs—all of which influence health and behavior—and of culture and history" (Fausto-Sterling, 2005, p. 1495). Despite a few noteworthy exceptions (e.g., Hargreaves & Vertinsky, 2007; Heywood, 2011; Jette, Vertinsky, & Ng, 2014; Markula & Kennedy, 2011; Wells, 2010), the biological dimensions of athletic women's bodily and embodied experiences have been largely ignored or purposefully overlooked in most critical sport scholarship. Certainly, there were good reasons for such silences.

Biological explanations have long been used (often far too successfully) to support inequalities in sport and exercise based on race, gender, sexuality, class, and age (Vertinsky, 1987, 1990, 1994). Thus, feminist historians and sociologists of sport were right to adamantly reject pseudo-scientific essentialist biological explanations used to support discriminatory practices and exclusionary discourses (Vertinsky, 1987, 1990). But while anti-biological approaches were politically necessary at the time to challenge the naturalized maleness of sport, such dualist approaches are now limiting our attempts to develop more complex and nuanced understandings of women's embodied and bodily sporting experiences.

In this chapter I attempt to bring biology, and particularly hormones, back into conversations about the athletic female body in sport and physical culture in non-reductionist and non-determinist terms. In so doing, I take inspiration from "new materialist" feminists and philosophers of science, such as Birke (1999, 2003), Frost (2011, 2014), Grosz (1994), Roberts (2002, 2003, 2007), and many others, who are helping us "think differently about biology, culture, sex, and gender" (Fausto-Sterling, 2003, p. 124), and working to "refigure" the dynamic relationship between biology and culture (Frost, 2014). I strongly concur with Birke (1999) who argued that, while feminists "must certainly reject" the kinds of biology that have been used as "an excuse for discriminatory practices, and exclusionary discourses," "rejecting biological processes altogether by ignoring or omitting the biological body does not help," but rather serves "indirectly to reinforce biological determinism" and to "marginalise the embodied experience of those whose voices are not heard in science" (p. 175). In this chapter, I create space for female runners' previously silenced voices to provide a feminist analysis of their experiences of exercise and hormones.

Female runners' relationships with food, exercise, and the body

To understand female runners' experiences of their biological *and* social bodies, I conducted semi-structured interviews with ten women who self-identified as having experienced amenorrhea as a result of their exercise and dietary practices.[2] I was interested in the experiences of both female athletes and non-athletes, and thus conducted interviews with four competitive runners and six committed exercisers, all of whom run on a regular basis. Participants ranged from 18–50 years old, and all were middle-class professionals or students living in New Zealand at the time of the interviews.

Each of the ten interviews was deeply affective and affecting, with all of the participants revealing their past or present experiences with body image concerns, disordered eating practices, and exercise addictions, to varying degrees. Many of my participants commented on disruptive relationships with their bodies, exercise, and food (e.g., Amanda, Renee, Gabby, Melissa). Renee's explanation exemplified many of these sentiments:

> ...when I stopped bingeing and purging, it was like I replaced that with the running. At the beginning it was a form of weight control, and then it just sort of got mashed up in my brain because, yes it was "oh my gosh if I don't go for a run I'll get fat," but at the same time I did feel really good afterwards. So it was that mix. But if I didn't manage to go, it would be this huge guilt and it could send me off on a spiral of bingeing...
>
> (Renee)

Renee's comment reflects one of the dominant themes emerging from the interviews: self-discipline and the sense of control gained via their embodied and bodily practices. Gabby, for example, admitted that she initially started regulating her diet and exercising vigorously as a response to "having rough ... relationships with my friends" and "that whole identity thing" during her late teens and early twenties. Continuing she explained, "I couldn't control a lot of the things that were happening at the time, but the one thing I could control was what I ate and how I exercised. It made me feel quite powerful ... people started noticing [and] I liked it". Gabby also pointed to her increased athleticism that she gained through her running—another prominent theme that emerged from the interviews. The runners also discussed the physical, social, and psychological pleasures and pains of exercise and dieting. For example, Amanda explained:

> If I knew I wasn't going to exercise, I would cut down my food intake or conversely, if I knew I was going to be able to exercise I might allow myself to eat more. It was always an equation going on in my head.... The food was a reward for exercise, and the exercise was the reward for having eaten. If I had a day without exercise, I would get really antsy, and ... I really felt like I could feel fat starting to grow.
>
> (Amanda)

These types of comments mirror the findings from various other projects on women's relationships with their bodies, exercise, and eating (e.g., Berman, Kerr, & De Souza, 2005; Cole, 1998; D'Abundo, 2009; Duncan, 1994; Dworkin & Wachs, 2009; Heywood, 2011; Markula, 1995). Heywood (2011) explained in her biocultural analysis of female athletes disordered eating practices that both sporting and everyday cultures are "obsessed ... with control of the unruly body" (citing Bordo, 1993, p. 149), and for anorexics, control over hunger and the body often has moral implications. Citing Goodin (2008, p. 281), Heywood added: "the experiences of hunger, which involves physical pain and suffering, is transformed into a feeling of self-efficacy, power and achievement that constitute[s] a sense of heroic selfhood" (p. 125). Gabby, for example, called herself "an extreme health nut" and "thought it was a positive, good thing ... you'd go out for a run ... and you feel really good."

Despite many differences among these women's experiences, throughout all of the interviews there was a high level of contradiction and ambivalence about medical knowledge and intervention. The women in this study were negotiating different subject positions in their desire to address their current disordered eating and exercise practices, and in their reflections upon past bodily practices. For example, many of the women also spoke of the pleasures of running: "I loved the isolation of running … it was also a very physical sensation…" (Amanda); "I just love it [running] … and I don't think I can survive without that, my own time" (Trish); "the running team manager at school noticed me and invited me to join the team. For me, there was a lot of prestige associated around that" (Heather).[3] But elsewhere in the interviews, most also revealed their motivations to run for aesthetic reasons, or as Ainsley admitted, "running is just the best vehicle for getting rid of fat."[4] Similarly, Amanda explained: "I definitely had some sort of resistance to fat. I liked the feeling of being able to make my body do what I wanted it to, and look the way I wanted it to. Running did things for my shape that nothing else could."

As a result of highly restrictive eating and regimented exercise practices, all of the women in this project had either been medically diagnosed with amenorrhea, or diagnosed themselves based on personal research into their symptoms. At the time of the interviews, five of the women were actively trying to create or maintain changes to their lifestyles, four were not, and the oldest participant was reflecting on her past experiences with amenorrhea during her 20s and early 30s. Interestingly, five of the women in this project described their addiction to exercise, and particularly to running, as a "drug" (Dunning & Waddington, 2003; Sachs & Pargman, 1979). While some continued to proclaim their reliance upon running as a "positive addiction," others acknowledged the detrimental effects of their dependence (Allen-Collinson, 2003; Cole, 1998). For example, Trish admitted that "just to get *that* drug, I would make the conscious decision to go out and run with a terrible injury, knowing that I was going to be completely screwed the next day," and Heather described running as "a gateway drug to something a lot worse." Here, Heather is acknowledging her running regime as intimately connected to the disordered eating practices and body image issues that consumed her teenage years, and saw her admitted to several eating disorder clinics before she eventually quit running as part of her prescribed program to recovery. Unfortunately, it is beyond the scope of this chapter to do justice to the sociological, psychological, and biological complexities of these female runners' experiences of amenorrhea. Thus, in the remainder of this chapter I focus on how female runners with amenorrhea make meaning of, and negotiate, the various discourses and different forms of embodied, mediated, and medical knowledge about the "healthy" female body.

Negotiating multiple "knowledges" of the amenorrheic running body

Each of my participants admitted that they had ignored their loss of menstruation for some time, with some actually celebrating the absence. However, at some point in their lives, and for various reasons (e.g., injury, parental or partner concerns, desire to have a child), each of them had sought information about their changing bodies from various sources, including their peers, family members, the Internet, books, and various health professionals. Many of my participants admitted to using the Internet to search for possible answers to their questions, but described becoming frustrated with the lack of clear information and conflicting messages.[5] Most of the participants in this study had also visited their General Practitioners and then, disappointed with the lack of empathy and/or understanding, sought further specialist advice from gynecologists and/or endocrinologists. In pursuing knowledge about their internal bodily functions, these women entered a long, frustrating, and often expensive process of elimination, typically beginning with a pregnancy test, then a series of blood tests to measure levels of testosterone, estrogen, and other hormones produced by the pituitary gland. Many also underwent imaging and ultrasound tests, and bone density scans. According to my participants, most medical professionals offered only pharmaceutical solutions, such as the oral contraceptive pill or other hormonal treatments. Only a few recommended lifestyle changes.

I draw upon the work of Rose (2007a, 2007b) to help explain how female runners make meaning of biomedical knowledges about their bodies, and particularly their hormonal changes as a result of highly regulated exercise and dieting practices. Extending Foucault's (1991) work on biopolitics, Rose (2007b), argued that developments in biomedicine, particularly new techniques of testing and practices of visualization, treatment and self-management, are not simply changing our relation to health and illness, but are also changing "the kinds of human beings we take ourselves to be" (p. 13). In his own words,

> We are increasingly coming to relate to ourselves as "somatic" individuals, that is to say, as beings whose individuality is, in part at least, grounded within our fleshy, corporeal existence, and who experience, articulate, judge and act upon ourselves in part in the language of biomedicine.
>
> (Rose, 2007a, p. 26)

In contrast to many sociological critics who argue that we are entering a period of "new biological and genetic determinism," Rose (2007a, p. 8) is much less pessimistic. He believed we are seeing the emergence of a "novel somatic ethics" that is "imposing obligations yet imbued with hope, oriented to the future yet demanding action in the present":

> ... on the one hand, our vitality has been opened up as never before for economic exploitation and the extraction of biovalue.... On the other ... our

> somatic, corporeal neurochemical individuality has become opened up to choice, prudence, and responsibility, to experimentation, to contestation, and so to a politics of life itself.
>
> (Rose, 2007a, p. 8)

Rose (2007a, 2007b) has offered some fascinating insights into how contemporary technologies of biopower are contributing to new kinds of ethical decisions and somatic subjectivities. I am particularly interested in his discussions regarding new reproductive technologies and their implications for women's (and men's) lives and imagined futures. Although Rose rarely focuses on gender per se, his work remains highly relevant for the "feminist imperative" of "transcend[ing] the dualism between nature and culture" (Gunnarsson, 2013, p. 3). Indeed, some feminist scholars are building upon and extending Rose's work to rethink the relationship between the biological and social body. Fullagar (2008, 2009), for example, drew upon a feminist governmentality perspective to examine the discourses that shape women's experiences of anti-depressant medication. In so doing, she offered fresh insights into the "gendered nature of somatic individuality" (Fullagar, 2008, p. 335). In the remainder of this chapter I take inspiration from Rose, and feminist scholars such as Fullagar, to examine athletic women's somatic experiences of amenorrhea.

According to Rose (2007b),

> In an age of biological prudence, where individuals … are obliged to take responsibility for their own medical futures … micro-technologies … are … blur[ring] the boundaries of coercion and consent … [and] transform[ing] the subjectivities of those who are counseled…
>
> (p. 15)

Indeed, through their interactions with new biotechnologies, some of the women in this project came to understand their "somatic selves" (Rose, 2007a) as hormonally deficient, which lead to a questioning of their authenticity as women. Heather, for example, revealed: "I was starting to become quite self-conscious that I didn't have my period, and I didn't feel like I was a woman if that was not going on." Similarly, Gabby spoke of her fears when she and her husband decided to start trying for a child: "my hormones were all messed up … I worried I wouldn't be able to conceive … that I wasn't a real woman … if I couldn't give him a baby…." For some women, this new biomedical knowledge evoked feelings of shame, guilt, and fears about the damage they were doing to their bone and reproductive health (see Fullagar, 2008). Not surprisingly, this was having a considerable impact on these women's "everyday relationships with others, and importantly themselves—their self-worth, their identity as women, mothers, workers, partners and their past and future selves" (Fullagar, 2009, p. 403).

Critical engagement and alternative knowledges

While medical knowledge and new biotechnologies are shaping women's subjectivities and affective relations with their bodies, the women in this project were not "passive recipients of expertise" (Fullagar, 2009, p. 391). As Rose (2007b) noted, biomedical power is certainly not a one way affair, rather "it entails a dynamic set of relations between the affects of those who council and of those of the counseled" (p. 15). Interestingly, all of my participants were highly critical of their interactions with medical professionals. They described their confusion, frustration, and even anger with medical professionals who refused to "really listen" to them, or see the "bigger picture" (Ainsley). For some, such as competitive long-distance runner Melissa, this offered justification to ignore medical advice:

> when I go to the doctor … and they're like "don't run as much," I try to explain that I'm training, we run every day, that's just what we do, and they just look at me like I'm frigging mental … it's like "you just don't get it, you're not going to be able to help me." So yeah, I just got straight out of there [the doctors office] and went "fuck it." And then you forget about it and time goes on, and you're like "oh yeah, it [menstrual cycle] still hasn't come back."

For others, such as Ainsley and Renee, their interactions with medical doctors prompted them to actively seek specialists with more holistic ways of knowing, and/or to pursue alternative health options (e.g., acupuncture, Chinese herbs). Ainsley was concerned by her experiences with medical professionals who "are just so quick to give you something that will mask it, as opposed to actually deal with the problem, or find out why it's happening," and took a proactive approach toward her own recovery: "you just have to rely on your own knowledge, you've got to be motivated to find it out for yourself." Similarly, Renee became frustrated by doctors who "just treat the chemical, the physical bits," and sought out treatment with a Chinese herbalist because "it is much more holistic … it looks at your emotions, what's going on psychologically, and if you want, spiritually as well."[6] Pike (2005) found similar attitudes among female rowers who became frustrated by medical doctors lack of understanding of the sporting culture, "incompetent diagnoses and over-reliance on drug prescription," and thus sought out "non-orthodox" health care options which were often considered "more empowering in terms of active involvement of the client in the treatment process" (p. 201). Thus, despite the power of medical knowledge to define "facts" and "truths" of women's biological bodies (often further reinforcing essentialist assumptions about female inferiority and natural weakness), there is always the potential for women to "problematize expert knowledge" (Markula, 2011, p. 71) and consider alternative ways of knowing their bodies (Jette, Vertinsky, & Ng, 2014; Pike, 2005).

Some women described receiving their diagnosis and medical advice as very upsetting, with one participant revealing that it caused her to have "a bit of a meltdown" (Renee). Yet others described feelings of empowerment through the process of gaining new knowledge about their biological bodies. For example, Ainsley enjoyed researching this topic and was fascinated to learn "how much hormones control everything in your body." But even though women engaged with information from various sources, ultimately biomedical knowledge and technologies continue to make amenorrhea thinkable in certain ways that are shaping the recovery practices and limiting the subject positions available to women (Fullagar, 2009).

Doing "what" with knowledge?

According to Rose (2013), "Knowing life at the molecular level has been intrinsically related to an enhanced capacity to act upon it at that level": Put simply, "it is not just to know, but also to do" (p. 6). After consulting with medical professionals, each of the women in this project admitted to feeling an increased need to act upon their "condition." However, at the time of their interviews, the participants in this study were negotiating different subject positions in their responses to mediated and bio-medical knowledges about the "healthy" female body. In so doing, their responses ranged from rejection and resistance to acceptance of medical advice and efforts to create lifestyle changes. Some interesting differences were observed between competitive athletes and recreational runners as a result of the different discourses operating on and through their bodies. Interestingly, the recreational runners were more willing to create lifestyle changes, with the competitive runners more likely to ignore or actively resist medical forms of authority and truth. For example, when a doctor asked Ainsley, a highly competitive runner, to "cut back" on her running and eat a little more, she replied matter-of-factly, "no, actually I can't." Continuing, she admitted that if she were trying to start a family, then perhaps she would consider this, but "at the moment … I don't want to change anything…." In so doing, Ainsley was prioritizing her coach's expert advice over that of medical professionals who, in her opinion, did not fully understand her quest (and responsibilities) as an athlete. Others, such as Trish, who is a successful marathoner and tertiary-level physical educator, revealed the difficulties of creating change even with access to such information. In her words, "I teach this stuff, [but] I blatantly ignored my own advice…. I knew that I was just a complete hypocrite in terms of what I taught and what I practiced myself." Despite being "pulled up on it quite a bit by students," Trish tended to "sort of laugh and brush it off" because "I didn't really care, I was just so focused on my performances." As this quote suggests, there is a tendency for female athletes to develop a short-term perspective on their bodies and prioritize sporting cultural discourses and respect their coaches' advice over medical knowledge provided by non-sporting specialists. Parallel to fitness instructors, who in Markula's Foucauldian analysis struggled to resist powerful discourses of the body, health, and beauty despite critical awareness of their operations (Markula & Pringle, 2006), Trish continued to negotiate her identity within the powerful discourse of sport performance.

According to Heywood (2011), those female athletes suffering from "anorexia athletica"—restricting calorie intake, disturbed body image, use of purging methods, binge eating, and repeatedly exercising beyond the requirements for good health—are affected by both the "athletic culture that says 'leanness equals performance', and … from the dominant culture that say[s] leanness equals beauty and even morality" (p. 128). Heywood further identified four discourses affecting female athletes' relationship with their bodies: (1) in many sports, a lean body enhances performance; (2) "real" athletes have a low body-fat percentage; (3) the "real" athlete will always push farther than others in terms of self-sacrifice, both in workouts and during practices; and, (4) part of this "pushing farther" is developing a global-attribution style that completely conflates the athlete's sense of self with her performance and identity as an athlete (p. 136).

The female athletes in this study all justified their eating and exercising practices as necessary for achieving their sporting goals and admitted that these behaviors were typically normalized within their (elite) sporting communities. Each of the competitive runners in this study also discussed their "ideal race weight" as playing a significant role in their decisions about their exercise and eating practices. For example, Melissa revealed some contradictions in her reading of the very thin endurance running body as both "horrible" and yet also desirable: "If I have the skinny runner body, I know I'm fit to race, and I'm probably going to perform well," before adding, "if somebody tells me [that] I 'look healthy' … it sends sirens off in my head. The term healthy means you look … not fit, you're not ready to race. If I hear that … it sends me into a spiral of bingeing, purging, and training harder than ever" (Melissa).

Some of the athletes also acknowledged their self-disciplining, -punishing, and even masochistic behaviors.[7] For example, Trish revealed: "I've been through phases of time when I've had a really destructive relationship with exercise, and often it's been when I've been unhappy. And that's been my coping mechanism, going out and thrashing myself on the road." Melissa also admitted that, "you're beating yourself up all the time, but it feels good." Each of the athletes proudly described having "a good work ethic" which they applied to their training and to their efforts to control the internal functioning and external performances of their bodies. Similar to Heywood's (2011) suggestions, some also attributed moralistic value systems to their disciplined regimes in contrast to the broader population who, according to Melissa, "need to exercise more anyway." Not dissimilar from the Ironman triathletes in Bridel's (2013) work, many of the participants in this project internalized neoliberal health discourses, particularly "the notions of individual responsibility, the use of leisure (non-work) time for self work and (albeit to an extreme end) anti-obesity messages" (p. 37).

Heywood (2011) made an interesting comparison between women with anorexia and female athletes with "anorexia athletica" arguing that the latter are often able to "get away with it." That is "they escape social sanction and stigmatizations because they are using their body in functional, seemingly adaptive ways that enact the heroic narrative of sport" (p. 127). This certainly became evident in my interviews with the competitive runners who, when prompted, all admitted that they often use their sporting goals and achievements to justify (to themselves and others) their highly regimented eating and exercise practices. For example, Ainsley admitted

> that's how I justify it to my mum … she often questions why I'm doing this or that, and asking me, "Is that in your program? Does [name of coach] know you're doing that [running and going to the gym]?" I say "yeah, it's on my program. *I have to do it.*"

Later in our conversation she acknowledged: "When you're competing, and you have certain goals to achieve, that's more acceptable to people."

But when Amanda stopped competing, she found that her family and members of the local community would occasionally challenge her for being "a bit selfish" and "extreme" in her exercise practices. Trish had similar responses from her family when she continued her highly disciplined training regime despite retiring from elite competition:

> Mum pulls me up on it all the time now, because I say "I'm going to do my training," and she says "what are you training for?" Then I think, "oh it's actually not training, it's just probably my routine." It's my lifestyle. But I'm questioning it a bit more now as I'm getting further away from competitions. [My partner] has also sort of made me accountable to things like rest days…

For Trish, the challenges being posed by her mother and partner have prompted her to ask new questions of her running and dieting practices. However, for those female athletes, such as Melissa and Ainsley, who are still deeply embedded in high performance running culture, and focused solely on their athletic achievements, family (and medical) concerns tend to be dismissed.

If the competitive runners in this study tended to ignore or reject medical knowledge in favor of sporting discourses, many of the recreational runners had accepted the advice from medical authorities as "truth" and were actively attempting (though often struggling) to create change. In so doing, however, they were making ethical decisions in their engagement with medical knowledge. Of the six recreational runners, two used hormonal pharmaceutical treatments, and three were seeking to create lifestyle changes. According to Dr. Stella Milsom, a New Zealand endocrinologist who has been involved in this broader study, the latter is considerably more difficult. In contrast to many of her colleagues, rather than offering reproductive drugs to her amenorrheic patients who wish to become pregnant, Milsom encourages them to first work towards creating lifestyle changes by reducing their exercise load and increasing their daily caloric intake. Yet she admitted that most of her patients resist her advice, opting instead for treatments that require little effort or discipline other than the consumption of a pill. Milsom's approach and her patients' resistance is an example of what Rose (2007b) referred to as the "entangling [of] the ethics of the different parties involved" (p. 15).

While most of Milsom's patients opt for pharmaceutical solutions, three of the women in my project were adopting a proactive approach to creating lifestyle changes. For example, Renee explained:

> I've grown up in a medical household ... I needed to know how things were working physiologically. But to adjust it and to treat it, I prefer to do it more naturally ... less chemicals and more holistically ... I'm not just going to put a Band-Aid on the problem, I actually want to get rid of it. So I've stopped running, I don't go to the gym anymore, and I'm going to a counselor.

Despite her medical upbringing, Renee was drawing upon her own research, embodied and lived experiences, and studies in social work to critically engage with and respond to the medical advice she had received.

Yet creating such lifestyle change is difficult, and we must understand the experience of recovering from amenorrhea, much like recovery from depression, as "always in process, a site of struggle..." (Fullagar, 2009, p. 402). For example, Gabby admitted to occasionally "sneak" running, and then feeling guilt afterwards:

> I know you pay a lot of money to see these specialists, but a few times I'd say [to the doctor/to her husband], "oh no I'm not really doing anything," but you are actually running or whatever. Just because you think they're being a bit extreme...

Gabby struggled to make meaning of the conflicting medical and social discourses around the healthy female body and, as with most of the participants in this project, occasionally found herself paralyzed by these mixed messages:

> I was really torn between the information and advice coming from my endocrinologist and then the stuff I was reading in the magazines.... One of them is telling me to stop exercising and dieting because its damaging my health, the other is showing all these really skinny beautiful women and saying we should be doing more exercise. I found this really confusing ... and still do actually.
>
> (Gabby)

As this quote suggests, Gabby experienced a contradiction between the mediated messages about the good neoliberal "healthy" female body as one that exercises regularly and carefully regulates and restricts her diet (Duncan, 1994; Dworkin & Wachs, 2009; Markula, 2001), and medical discourses emphasising the health risks associated with "relative energy deficiency," and encouraging individual responsibility (Safai, 2003, 2013; Thing, 2012). Such contradictory messages prompted Gabby to occassionally question, and momentarily resist, the medical expert's advice.

According to Novas and Rose (2000), in the age of biomedicine, clinical "risk" increasingly figures in the formation of selfhood, as well as our hopes and fears for our own and our families future subjectivities. As previously suggested, some of my participants were experiencing regret, and even guilt, for the potential long-term damage they may have done to their future bodies. Some expressed fears of osteoporosis and fertility issues later in their lives. For example, Renee admitted to "feel[ing] really terrible for what I had done to my own body … exercising in that way, purging in that way." She described these feelings as "the lowest of the low" and the moment in which she came to the realization that, "if you're going to change things, you need to take care of yourself." As a result of her proactivity and lifestyle changes, however, Renee was able to imagine a new, more positive somatic future for herself:

> Until recently, I really did not care that I did not get my period.… But the more I learn about the damage I have done, the more I worry about how all of my bingeing and exercising might have compromised my ability to have a baby … what I want now is much more beyond just being thin. I feel like I'm getting over it, like I'm tired of it. It's like this thing that you try to control, but it sucks the life out of you.

Perhaps not surprisingly, it tended to be those women who had decided they wanted to have children in the near future who were more willing to accept medical advice and attempt to create the lifestyle changes necessary to regain their menstrual cycle. Most of the other women in this study also admitted that the readiness to have children might be the only trigger for them to address their disordered eating and/or exercise addictions. Some women, such as Melissa, who were not interested in having children, were concerned about their bone health, but did not see it urgent enough to alter their highly disciplined training regime and restricted dieting practices.

Concluding thoughts

In an age of biomedicine, athletic women's internal functioning is increasingly rendered visible (and thus, governable) by new technologies. Yet not all women are docile bodies within such operations of power. The somatic ethics being practiced by female runners diagnosed with amenorrhea vary considerably, ranging from "compliance with biomedical explanations, to resistance against expert forms of authority and truth" (Fullagar, 2009, p. 403). Indeed, the women in this study are exercising agency through their refusal to passively accept medical advice, with some seeking alternative approaches to improve their health. Arguably, health and medical professionals, and those in the sport and exercise sciences, would do well to consider their patients and/or participants embodied, ethical, and socio-psychological responses to medical and scientific technologies for health and/or performance enhancement. The women in this project diagnosed with amenorrhea demonstrated their agency and resistance to medical knowledges and technologies in a plethora of ways, some of which might not be anticipated by those delivering such advice or utilizing such technologies.

Yet even those that pursue a pathway to recovery are still positioned within "a network of professional surveillance and authority..." (Fullagar, 2009, p. 403) that renders many self-policing (Ussher, 2004). Medical knowledge continues to affect these women's somatic subjectivities and understandings of their bodies in the past, present, and future. Moreover, we cannot separate medical discourses from dominant social messages within sporting cultures and broader society. As illustrated in this chapter, competitive and recreational female runners are negotiating multiple, and often conflicting, discourses about the "healthy," attractive, performing body, which influence their relations with their biological bodies, and their desire and/or ability to address their own or others concerns for their long-term health and well-being. But, as feminist "new materialist" scholars are careful to remind us, women's biological bodies are not purely discursive formations, or "historically specific products of power relations, linguistic practices, and cultural beliefs" (Frost, 2011, p. 75). For Birke (1999), the inner, physiological body, and the outer social body are "coterminous, not separable" (p. 174). Thus, a challenge facing socio-cultural scholars interested in developing more multi-dimensional understandings of the running body is how to recognize biological bodies "not only as they are formed by the forces of language, culture and politics, but also as they are formative" (Frost, 2011, p. 7). Arguably, feminist "new materialist" scholars have much to offer those of us seeking more nuanced understandings of the dynamic relationship between biology and culture, and women's bodies, health, identity, and subjectivities.

Notes

1 It is important to note that the renaming remains controversial and highly political, with some researchers claiming that it is based on a misunderstanding of the Female Athlete Triad (De Souza *et al.*, 2014).
2 Amenorrhea can be classified as primary or secondary. Broadly, primary amenorrhea refers to girls whose menstrual cycles have not begun by age 16, and secondary amenorrhea refers to previously menstruating women who have an absence of menstrual periods for at least three consecutive cycles. Nine of the participants in this study had experienced secondary amenorrhea, with one having been diagnosed with primary amenorrhea.
3 Narratives about running as pleasurable have also emerged in other socio-cultural research on running (e.g., Allen-Collinson, 2011; Cronan & Scott, 2008; Hanold, 2008).
4 Runners in other socio-cultural research have also discussed the relationship between running and bodily aesthetics (e.g., Markula, 1995; McGannon, Johnson, & Spence, 2011).

5 For further discussion, see also Fullagar, 2008.
6 Participants in other socio-cultural research have similarly discussed seeking out "non-traditional" treatments (e.g., Jette, Vertinsky, & Ng, 2014).
7 Similar ideas emerged in research previously done with Ironman triathletes (Bridel, 2010) and female ultrarunners (Hanold, 2008).

References

Allen-Collinson, J. (2003). Running into injury time: Distance running and temporality. *Sociology of Sport Journal, 20*, 331–350.

Allen-Collinson, J. (2011). Running embodiment, power and vulnerability: Notes toward a feminist phenomenology of female running. In E. Kennedy & P. Markula (Eds.), *Women and exercise: The body, health and consumerism* (pp. 280–290). London, England: Routledge.

Beals, K., & Manore, M. (2002). Disorders of the female athlete triad among collegiate athletes. *International Journal of Sport Nutrition and Exercise Metabolism, 12*, 281–293.

Berman, E., Kerr, G., & De Souza, M. J. (2005). A qualitative examination of weight concerns, eating and exercise behaviors in recreational exercisers. *Women in Sport and Physical Activity Journal, 14*, 24–38.

Birke, L. (1999). *Feminism and the biological body.* Edinburgh, United Kingdom: Edinburgh University Press.

Birke, L. (2003). Shaping biology: Feminism and the idea of "the biological." In S. Williams, L. Birke, & G. Bendelow (Eds.), *Debating biology: Sociological reflections on health, medicine and society* (pp. 39–52). New York, NY: Taylor and Francis.

Bordo, S. (1993). *Unbearable weight: Feminism, western culture, and the body*. Berkley, CA: University of California.

Bridel, W. (2013). Not fat, not skinny, functional enough to finish: Interrogating constructions of health in the Ironman Triathlon. *Leisure/Loisir, 37*, 37–56.

Bridel, W. (2010). *"Finish … Whatever it takes": Considering pain and pleasure in the Ironman Triathlon: A socio-cultural analysis* (Unpublished doctoral dissertation). Queen's University, Kingston, Canada.

Cockerill, I., Nevill, A., & Byrne, N. (1992). Mood, mileage and the menstrual cycle. *British Journal of Sports Medicine, 26*, 145–150.

Cole, C. L. (1998). Addiction, exercise and cyborgs: Technologies of deviant bodies. In G. Rail (Ed.), *Sport in postmodern times* (pp. 261–276). Albany, NY: State University of New York Press.

Cronan, M., & Scott, D. (2008). Triathlon and women's narratives of bodies and sport. *Leisure Studies, 30*, 17–34.

D'Abundo, M. (2009). Issues of health, appearance and physical activity in aerobic classes for women. *Sport, Education and Society, 14*, 301–319.

De Souza, M. J., Arce, J. C., & Metzger, D. A. (1994). Endocrine basis of exercise-induced amenorrhea. In D. M. Costa & S. R. Guthrie (Eds.), *Women and sport: Interdisciplinary perspectives* (pp. 185–210). Champaign, IL: Human Kinetics.

De Souza, M. J., Miller, B. E., Loucks, A. B., Luciano, A. A., Pescatello, L. S., Campbell, C. G., & Lasley, B. L. (1998). High frequency of luteal phase deficiency and anovulation in recreational women runners: blunted elevation in follicle-stimulating hormone observed during luteal-follicular transition. *Journal for Clinical Endocrinology and Metabolism, 83*, 4220–4232.

De Souza, M. J., Toombs, R. J., Scheid, J. L., O'Donnell, E., West, S. L., & Williams, N. I. (2010). High prevalence of subtle and severe menstrual disturbances in exercising women: Confirmation using daily hormone measures. *Reproductive Endocrinology, 25*, 491–503.

De Souza, M. J. *et al.*, (2014). Misunderstanding the Female Athlete Triad: Refuting the IOC Consensus Statement on Relative Energy Deficiency in Sport (RED-S). *British Journal of Sports Medicine*, doi:10.1136/bjsports-2014–093958.

Duncan, M. C. (1994). The politics of women's body images and practices. Foucault, and Panopticon and *Shape* magazine. *Journal of Sport and Social Issues, 18*, 48–65.

Dunning, E., & Waddington, I. (2003). Sport as a drug and drugs in sort: Some exploratory comments. *International Review for the Sociology of Sport, 38*, 351–368.

Dworkin, S. L., & Wachs, F. L. (2009). *Body panic: Gender, health and the selling of fitness*. New York, NY: New York University Press.

Fausto-Sterling, A. (2003). The problem with sex/gender and nature/nurture. In S. Williams, L. Birke, & G. Bendelow (Eds.), *Debating biology: Sociological reflections on health, medicine and society* (pp. 123–132). New York, NY: Taylor and Francis.

Fausto-Sterling, A. (2005). The bare bones of sex: Part 1—Sex and gender. *Signs, 30*, 1491–1527.

Foucault, M. (1991). Governmentality. In G. Burchell, G. Gordon, & P. Miller (Eds.), *The Foucault effect: Studies in governmentality* (pp. 87–104). Hemel Hempstead, United Kingdom: Harvester Wheatsheaf.

Frost, S. (2011). The implications of new materialisms for feminist epistemology. In H. E. Grasswick (Ed.), *Feminist epistemology and philosophy of science: Power in knowledge* (pp. 69–83). Dordrecht, Netherlands: Springer.

Frost, S. (2014). Re-considering the turn to biology in feminist theory. *Feminist Theory, 15*, 307–326.

Fullagar, S. (2008). Sites of somatic subjectivity: E-scaped mental health promotion and the biopolitics of depression. *Social Theory and Health, 6*, 323–341.

Fullagar, S. (2009). Negotiating the neurochemical self: Anti-depressant consumption in women's recovery from depression. *Health: An Interdisciplinary Journal for the Social Study of Health, Illness and Medicine, 13*, 389–406.

Goodlin, S. (2008). Being anorexic: Hunger, subjectivity, and embodied morality. *Medical Anthropology Quarterly, 12*, 274–296.

Grosz, E. (1994). *Volatile bodies: Toward a corporeal feminism*. Bloomington and Indianapolis, IN: Indiana University Press.

Gunnarsson, L. (2013). The naturalistic turn in feminist theory: A Marxist-Realist contribution. *Feminist Theory, 14*, 3–19.

Hanold, M. T. (2008). *Ultrarunning: A Foucauldian analysis of female body experiences in high level performance* (Unpublished doctoral dissertation). Seattle University, Seattle, WA.

Hanold, M. T. (2010). Beyond the marathon: (De)construction of female ultrarunning bodies. *Sociology of Sport Journal, 27*, 160–177.

Harber, V. (2011). The young female athlete: Using the menstrual cycle as a navigational beacon for healthy development. *Canadian Journal for Women in Coaching, 11*, 1–11.

Hargreaves, J., & Vertinsky, P. (2007). Introduction. In J. Hargreaves & P. Vertinsky (Eds.), *Physical culture, power and the body* (pp. 1–24). London, England: Routledge.

Heywood, L. (2011). Hunger, emotions and sport: A biocultural approach. *Symplokē, 19*, 119–142.

Jette, S., Vertinsky, P., & Ng, C. (2014). Balance and biomedicine. How Chinese-Canadian women negotiate pregnancy-related "risk" and lifestyle directives. *Health, Risk and Society, 16*, 494–511.

Kennedy, E., & Markula, P. (2011). *Women and exercise: The body, health and consumerism*. London, England: Routledge.

Maguire, J., & Mansfield, L. (1998). "No-body is perfect": Women, aerobics, and the body beautiful. *Sociology of Sport Journal, 12*, 424–453.

Markula, P. (1995). Firm but shapely, fit but sexy, strong but thin: The postmodern aerobicizing female body. *Journal of Sport and Social Issues, 30*, 29–44.

Markula, P. (2001). Beyond the perfect body: Women's body image distortion in fitness magazine discourse. *Journal of Sport and Social Issues, 25*, 158–179.

Markula, P. (2011). "Folding": A feminist intervention in mindful fitness. In E. Kennedy & P. Markula (Eds.), *Women and exercise: The body, health and consumerism* (pp. 60–78). London, England: Routledge.

Markula, P., & Kennedy, E. (2011). Beyond binaries: Contemporary approaches to women and exercise. In E. Kennedy & P. Markula (Eds.), *Women and exercise: The body, health and consumerism* (pp. 1–25). London, England: Routledge.

Markula, P., & Pringle, R. (2006). *Foucault, sport and exercise: Power, knowledge and transforming the self*. London, England: Routledge.

McDermott, L. (2011). "Doing something that's good for me": Exploring intersections of physical activity and health. In E. Kennedy & P. Markula (Eds.), *Women and exercise: The body, health and consumerism* (pp. 197–226). London, England: Routledge.

McGannon, K., Johnson, C., & Spence, J. (2011). "I am (not) big … It's the pictures that got small." Examining cultural and personal exercise narratives and the fear of fat. In E. Kennedy & P. Markula (Eds.), *Women and exercise: The body, health and consumerism* (pp. 101–120). London, England: Routledge.

Novas, C., & Rose, N. (2000). Genetic risk and the birth of the somatic individual. *Economy and Society, 29*, 485–513.

Pike, E. C. J. (2005). "Doctors just say 'rest and take Ibuprofen'": A critical examination of the role of "non-orthodox" health care in women's sport. *International Review for the Sociology of Sport, 40*, 201–219.

Roberts, C. (2002). A matter of embodied fact: Sex hormones and the history of bodies. *Feminist Theory, 3*, 7–26.

Roberts, C. (2003). Drowning in a sea of Estrogens: Sex hormones, sexual reproduction and sex. *Sexualities, 6*, 195–213.

Roberts, C. (2007). *Messengers of sex: Hormones, biomedicine and feminism*. New York, NY: Cambridge University Press.

Rose, N. (2007a). *The politics of life itself: Biomedicine, power, and subjectivity in twenty-first century*. Princeton, NJ: Princeton University Press.

Rose, N. (2007b). Molecular biopolitics, somatic ethics and the spirit of biocapital. *Social Theory and Health, 5*, 3–29.

Rose, N. (2013). The human sciences in a biological age. *Theory, Culture and Society, 30*, 3–34.

Sachs, M., & Pargman, D. (1979). Running addiction: A depth interview examination. *Journal of Sport Behavior, 2*, 143–155.

Safai, P. (2003). Healing the body in the "culture of risk": Examining the negotiation of treatment between sports medicine clinicians and injured athletes in Canadian intercollegiate sport. *Sociology of Sport Journal, 20*, 127–146.

Safai, P. (2013). Sports medicine, the state and the politics of risk. In D. Andrews & B. Carrington (Eds.), *A Companion to sport* (pp. 112–128). Malden, MA: Wiley-Blackwell.

Thing, L. F. (2012). Docile bodies or reflexive users?: On the individualization of medical risk in sports. In D. Malcolm, & P. Safai (Eds.), *The social organization of sports medicine: Critical socio-cultural perspectives.* (pp. 187–203). New York, NY: Routledge.

Thorpe, H. (2012). Moving bodies beyond the social/biological divide: toward theoretical and transdisciplinary adventures. *Sport, Education and Society*, DOI:10.1080/13573322.2012.691092.

Ussher, J. (2004). Premenstrual syndrome and self-policing: Ruptures in self-silencing leading to increased self-surveillance and blaming of the body. *Social Theory and Health, 2*, 254–272.

Vertinsky, P. (1987). Exercise physical capability and the eternally wounded woman in late nineteenth century North America, *Journal of Sport History, 14*, 7–27.

Vertinsky, P. (1990). *The eternally wounded woman: Women, doctors and exercise in the late nineteenth century.* Manchester, England: Manchester University Press.

Vertinsky, P. (1994). The racial body and the anatomy of difference: Anti-Semitism, physical culture and the Jew's foot. *Sport Science Review, 4*, 1–24.

Warren, M. P., & Perloth, N. (2001). Hormones and sport: The effects of intense exercise on the female reproductive system. *Journal of Endocrinology, 170*, 3–11.

Wells, C. (2010). Diagnosing sex-gender verification and the IOC. In *Rethinking Matters Olympic: Investigations into the Socio-Cultural Study of the Modern Olympic Movement* (pp. 301–311). Retrieved from www.uwo.ca/olympic/files/downloads/2010_edition_collection.pdf.

Wheatley, S., Khan, S., Székely, A., Naughton, D., & Petróczi, A. (2012). Expanding the Female Athlete Triad concept to address a public health issue. *Performance Enhancement and Health, 1*, 10–27.

12 Ultrarunning

Space, place, and social experience

Maylon Hanold

While the marathon is precisely defined as 26.2 miles, ultrarunning refers to any running event over 26.2 miles. Typical ultrarunning distances are 50 km, 50-miles, 100 km, and 100-miles, but also include multi-day or timed running events such as 12 or 24 hours. Notably, over 85 percent of ultra races occur on mountain trails, forest paths, or dirt surfaces ("Year in review," 2013) with elevation gains and losses substantially more than most marathons. According to *Ultrarunning* magazine, there were 30,789 finishes in the US in 2008, but by 2012 that number more than doubled to 63,530 finishes. While participation is not on the scale of the marathon, the rapid growth of ultrarunning indicates a significant interest in this particular endurance experience.

In this chapter, I explore what it means to endure in ultrarunning. In particular, I am interested in the complex ways that participants make sense of endurance as moving bodies within ultrarunning spaces. While the strict definition of ultrarunning is simply comprised of the measured distance, physical space appears to figure prominently in the production of this social space and informs what it means to endure. In order to examine these interrelated meanings, I employ Lefebvre's (1991) "spatial trialectic," in which space is considered beyond its materiality. Namely, Lefebvre theorizes space as being produced through not only by the physicality of any given place, but also by how people understand those places and how they move within those spaces. In this way, Lefebvre's (1991) spatial triad helps us move beyond simple descriptions of space and facilitates an examination of the power relations within spatial productions. In other words, Lefebvre suggested that spatial productions are always imbued with cultural and ideological values, and that there are always those who benefit and those who are excluded. In particular, I consider ultrarunning spatial practices as visible markers of the ideal citizen in a neoliberal context.

At its core, neoliberalism positions individuals as unequivocally responsible for the consequences of their actions. Thus, ideal neoliberal citizenry is displayed by making individual choices among various economic and social options that satisfy their own needs and desires (Larner, 2000). Further, these desires often align with socially conscious values that become a form of individual empowerment. The heightened emphasis on the individual has unintended consequences. Namely, neoliberal logic "uses progressive social values while the consequences of these practices tends toward an increasing striation of society along both economic and social lines" (Erikson, 2011, p. 479). One outcome of this logic is the conflation of rational action and morality (Harvey, 2005). As a result, the neoliberal citizen becomes a desired position *because* progressive social values are overtly supported despite the fact that, paradoxically, these choices may reproduce inequalities. I am especially interested in the ways that "moving forward" in ultrarunning sustains such neoliberal sensibilities, becoming simultaneously a sporting site for empowerment, contradiction and marginalization.

A note on methods

My analysis is based on data from an ethnographic study of ultrarunning conducted from 2009 to 2013. Data collection consisted of interviews, participant observation, and observation. I also gathered media data comprised of blogs, websites, magazines, and 25 podcasts of interviews with ultrarunners. I conducted 32 semi-structured interviews, ran seven ultras, and volunteered at 12 races over the course of four years. Data analyses were ongoing. All interviews were transcribed and media content were analyzed via two processes. First, directed content analysis (Hsiu-Fang & Shannon, 2005) was employed to identify key elements of the spatial triad. Directed content analysis involves beginning with predetermined codes. As such, I began with the three definitions of the spatial triad, showing how each manifests in ultrarunning. Given that these moments of space are interrelated and interdependent, I engaged in an iterative process to confirm or disconfirm particular aspects of ultrarunning that fit within these theoretical constructs (Potter & Levine-Donnerstein, 1999). Second, I employed a dialectic approach, which focuses on the tensions and contradictions that emerge in the production of space (Lefebvre, 1991). This approach facilitated identification of the complex, often paradoxical, relationships between ultrarunners' everyday practices, beliefs, and values that arose from the synergistic relationships among the three elements. Finally, utilizing the dialectic approach, I conclude with implications of these findings within the neoliberal context.

Lefebvre's re-conceptualization of space

Lefebvre's (1991) consideration of space begins with a critique of the ways that space is constructed in the modern era. Namely, he shows how space becomes predominantly understood as a tangible, physical entity that can be measured, described, and categorized through scientific explanations. He observed that these ways of understanding space relegates all conceptions of space to "Euclidean space which philosophical thought has treated as an 'absolute'" (p. 285). Lefebvre argued that through this lens space becomes a static thing, only relevant enough to be described as where life occurs. Furthermore, static space becomes attached to specific socially constructed mental propositions about what that space means. For instance, ultrarunning spaces can be understood in terms of many physical aspects including distance, total elevation gain and loss, smooth terrain, rooty or rocky terrain, ascent and descent parameters in terms of gain/loss per mile, aid station locations, locations of easy access points, and descriptions of sections of trail that are remote. These scientific descriptions serve as the "absolute." In the case of ultrarunning, these concrete descriptions of ultrarunning spaces produce the mental representation that ultrarunning is about overcoming these absolute challenges. One outcome is that ultrarunning spaces described in this way positions "endurance" as an abstract concept. Lefebvre argued that this perspective is incomplete because it fails to take into consideration the physical and social realities of the lived experience, which leaves "our lived experiences estranged from the conceptions that purport to represent them" (Watkins, 2005, p. 210). Correspondingly, such considerations of space disassociate the lived experiences of ultrarunning bodies from what it means to endure in ultrarunning.

In order to understand more fully what it means to endure in ultrarunning, I drew on Lefebvre's (1991) reconsideration of space, which views space as a dynamic interplay of direct experiences and discursive constructions of space. Thus, space becomes a fundamental way in which we understand the world and, as living bodies in spaces, become key elements in (re)creating those fundamental understandings. In order to engage this dynamic, Lefebvre proposed a way of theorizing space that would render these relationships visible, the spatial triad. The triad is composed of three viewpoints: discursive constructions of space, everyday practices that are viewed as "normal" within spaces, and the ways that people actually act in spaces. Lefebvre's considered the triad a conceptual tool given that the interactions between the three positions are inseparable, continuously and iteratively informing each other. He further suggested that it was important "to pay critical attention to the ways in which spaces are produced and maintained through social conflicts that are inherently political and ideological (van Ingen, 2003, p. 202). In other words, to understand lived experiences requires understanding what each of these three concepts consists of in any given space and how these elements work together synergistically to both reproduce dominant power relations as well as provide opportunities to resist and reconfigure power relations. To this end, Lefebvre intended the spatial triad to be a practical entry into the complex relationships between the abstract and the lived experience. Elaborating on the significance of Lefebvre's spatial triad, Watkins (2005) noted,

> It is this process of creation and being, the production of present space rather than the privileging of a singular aspect of space, which needs to be apprehended as fully as possible if a richer understanding of the world is to be achieved.
>
> (p. 211)

In what follows, I employ Lefebvre's spatial triad as a practical approach to bridge the abstract and lived experience in order to gain deeper understandings of ultrarunning endurance and the ideological implications.

The spatial triad: conceptions and manifestations in ultrarunning

Lefebvre's (1991) first kind of engagement with space is called "representations of space" (p. 38). This concept refers to the "logic and forms of knowledge, and the ideological content of codes, theories, and the conceptual depictions of space" (Shields, 1999, p. 163). Lefebvre considered this aspect of space to be the most dominant form of thinking about space in the modern world. This form of space is the discursive construction of space. Specific forms of knowledge in ultrarunning include the logic of longer distances and knowledge about how the terrain, weather, and rules shape the experience. For example, the longer the race, the steeper the terrain, or the more technical the running surface, the more difficult the race is perceived to be. Extreme temperatures bring in other difficulties. An ultra taking place in mostly wilderness versus being highly accessible also affects how ultrarunners approach the undertaking. The detailed knowledge of distances between aid stations as well as rules around the type of and how much support from others is allowed also make up representations of space. More importantly, the ideological content of these representations of space shapes the meaning of challenge for ultrarunners.

The dominant mental representation (meaning) attached to these absolutes is that the greater the challenge, the more runners value the experience. They often constructed this experience as restorative as illustrated by one runner, who indicated, "It wasn't pleasant, but I bounced back renewed, awakened and rejuvenated" (Tim). Another runner reflected on why she finds a difficult race more satisfying than one that feels easy says, "people DNF [did not finish] from races all the time … it is always an option … but when we push through, we restore our faith in ourselves. We fill up our holes" (Sandy). Race directors shape these experiences by establishing races that take place on physically challenging terrain. As one race director said, "I go out of my way to have challenging races … I want them to go through a lot of different emotions out there" (Joe). The "conceptual depictions" of ultrarunning spaces position them as "absolute" physical difficulties, that when overcome, lead to an improved sense of well-being.

Lefebvre's (1991) second concept in his triad is spatial practice. Spatial practice consists of "commonsense" understandings about what activities happen within which spaces (Friedman & van Ingen, 2011; Simonsen, 2005). For Lefebvre, spatial practices are everyday routines, the movements and physical activities that occur automatically and unreflectively. While ultrarunning is not an everyday activity, there are specific practices that are considered routine within these spaces. The strongest practice considered routine in ultrarunning is that walking and power hiking are considered a normal part of "running." These particular practices become very apparent when newcomers from other types of distance running, marathon distance or shorter, take up ultrarunning. As one accomplished distance runner but newcomer to ultrarunning noted,

> I had to give up the idea that I was going to be able to run the whole time. That was the hardest thing because you just didn't do that [walk] in these other races, it was considered a failure, but in ultrarunning, it's a necessity. (Sam)

Many runners remarked that it takes time to learn both physically and mentally how to transition between running, walking, and power hiking, but that this skill eventually becomes second nature and is essential to success. As Sally noted, "I got really good at going between walking and running, which helped me be more efficient out there." Another common practice is carrying extra clothing, food, and water. Even though aid stations containing food, water, and electrolyte drinks are dispersed throughout ultra races, eating and drinking between aid stations is common. The extra clothing is carried because of the wilderness settings in which access to help is often many hours away. These practices are based on the common understandings that the amount of time between aid stations can vary significantly depending on the concrete, physicality of those spaces.

The third aspect of Lefebvre's (1991) spatial triad considers spaces of representations. These moments are those "as directly *lived* [emphasis in the original] through its associated images and symbols, and hence the space of "inhabitants" and "users"' (Lefebvre, 1991, p. 39). In other words, spaces of representation are those lived moments in which people simultaneously negotiate the representations of space and spatial practices, which produce "specific ways of knowing" (Collinson, 2008, p. 46). There are two important possibilities that arise out of this dynamic. On the one hand, it is the lived space that "forms, informs and facilitates the deviations, diversity and individuality that are a fundamental aspect of any social encounter" (Watkins, 2005, p. 213). Lefebvre was insistent upon the importance of this experiential aspect of space, noting that discursive constructions of space and commonly understood spatial practices do not account for all the ways that people live and move in spaces. It is attention to lived space that allows for identifying moments when conventional understandings of spaces are resisted or modified. On the other hand, it is lived space where unreflective movements and physical activities occur that become powerful reproductions of the power relations already present in any given space. It is the complexities and paradoxes that emerge from these two possibilities to which I now turn.

The problematization and privilege of pace

Ultrarunning spaces complicate traditional understandings of distance running that depend on the scientific measurements of time and distance (Bale, 2004). In most distance running training practices and racing aims are governed by minutes per mile. The goal for most distance runners is to run faster in terms of absolute pace. However, in ultrarunning, pace becomes much more fluid and relative. One contributor to the destabilization of pace as an absolute measurement of improvement or success is the physical space in which most ultra races take place. Given that over 85 percent of ultras take place on trails in parks or national forests, ultra races are subject to highly varied terrain, weather, trail conditions, and elevation gains/losses. Furthermore, despite there being four common distances in ultrarunning (50 km, 50 miles, 100 km, 100 miles), courses are never measured precisely. One outcome is that an advertised 100-mile race could be 103 miles in reality. An analysis of the spaces of representation (lived experience) of moving over ultrarunning courses reveals that high variability in the ultrarunning physical spaces results in high variability of pace. To illustrate the significance of this difference, I consider the average elevation gains/losses of marathons compared to ultra races.

According to a marathon pacing website (Maclin, 2014), most marathons do not exceed 1,000 feet gain/loss for the entire marathon. In contrast, 3,000–6,000 feet gain/loss for an entire 50 km (31 miles) would be in the normal range ("Year in review," 2013). This increase in total gain/loss in ultra races also results in either significantly steeper sections or hills that last significantly longer in any given race compared to the average marathon. As noted above, one spatial practice that facilitates moving over this terrain is varying pace from walking to running, resulting in pace difference averages from 8-minutes per mile to 30-minutes per mile. Other factors result in large differences in pace during any ultra race. For instance, rain produces muddy conditions that slow down runners. Extreme weather can mean bringing along clothing or other supplies in a pack that makes one go slower due to carrying added weight. In this way, pace becomes destabilized as an absolute measurement in ultrarunning.

Such destabilization opens up multiple meanings associated with endurance. Most importantly, endurance becomes the ability to complete the distance. The spatial practices of walking, power hiking, and running are engaged to make completing the distance more possible for more people. These spatial practices help produce the representation of space (meaning) that finishing an ultra signifies success. A second practice that emerges via the representations of space lens is that runners talk more about what their next challenge will be in terms of increasing the difficulty or attempting longer distances. Specifically, overcoming challenges (representations of space) combines with acceptance of widely varied pace (spatial practices) to produce the desire to engage in subsequent ultra races in which pace will inevitably get slower. As Holly noted when talking about her next ultra,

> I know I can run 100 miles, so I'm looking for something that will be harder because I don't know if I can do that. That's why I keep putting my name in for the Hardrock 100 [a race that takes place between 8,000–14,000 feet with a gain/loss of 66,000 feet].

More recently, 200-mile trail races are becoming more prevalent. Notably, the 205-mile Tor de Geants in Italy has been around since 1999, and there will be at least five 200-mile races in the United States in 2015. One ultrarunner remarked, "It's about seeing where your ceiling is and realizing it might be higher. Can I go farther? I don't know. It's pushed by a series of I don't knows." These questions are notably different from other distance runners where the question is more frequently, "Can I go faster?"

It is the lived experiences of ultra races that in turn shape the representations of space in an iterative manner. Specifically, the relationship between time and space is continually re-imagined. Amy's description about how she views success illustrates this nuanced troubling of time and distance. She commented,

> the mountains and trails don't really care about time. It will take what it takes to go up and down a trail and that trail will never change. In the long run, who cares? What does it matter if I finish a race in 32 hours or 28 hours? I've had this relationship with the mountains and my running and that's a beautiful thing.

Another runner confirms the idea that the experience is more valued than going fast when he stated that he had "extraordinary moments of elation for a million reasons, nearly none of which had anything to do with running quickly" (Sam). In contrast to the marathon, endurance in ultrarunning becomes the experience itself, which further relegates pace as much less relevant to abstract understandings of ultrarunning. The experience becomes another way of gaining a sense of well-being, a significant representation of space in ultrarunning. Thus, the three forms of space work together synergistically to produce ultrarunning spaces, that in turn shape ultrarunners' experiences and understandings of their practices. More importantly, the interrelationship of the triadic elements lead to a desire to increasingly experience greater challenges requiring more time on the trails, which is valued as an experience in and of itself.

While most ultrarunning bodies move within the abstract understanding that finishing and enjoying the experience equates to success, there are elite runners who aim not only to finish, but to finish ahead of other runners. The spatial practices during a race with respect to these faster bodies weaves additional, contradictory representations of space into the physical spaces of ultrarunning. Namely, slower runners always give the right of way to faster runners. Sometimes these practices become official stated rules, other times they are grounded on common understandings that privilege faster bodies. As such, the spatial practices of ultrarunning infuse these spaces with a representation of space aligned with dominant representations of space attached to most other forms of distance running. Because of these spatial practices, the trails become re-appropriated space during ultra races. Namely, forest trails were built for leisure, facilitating the movement of people through wilderness spaces for enjoyment of natural beauty. The representations of space of forest trails from this perspective results in trail etiquette for hikers that gives people moving uphill the right of way. However, during ultra races, the trails become a social space altered by the spatial practices of ultrarunners. Bodies move faster in these spaces and faster bodies are privileged regardless of direction. In this way, trails become sites for active personal achievement rather than for passive personal enjoyment.

Yet, even these faster bodies are shaped by the representations of space in ultrarunning. Specifically, the idea that the experience itself defines success manifests in how elite ultrarunners talk about what makes for a good race. Notably, winning does not always equate to a good race while feeling good during the race does. A common understanding of good races of elite ultrarunners is illustrated well in the following comment:

> A good race for me is feeling good, not performance. It's being able to have lows and highs, physically and mentally, but really, it's about staying out of those really horrible times. I'm feeling happy, dancing, enjoying the terrain, and being happy. It's this intense feeling that has nothing to do with performance. I've had races I've won and not wanted to talk about because I didn't feel like it was a good race because I pushed too hard. Those are not good races.
>
> (Ana)

Another runner confirms this idea, when he says, "It's really about staying out of the pain cave" (Justin). Thus, through the interactions of the three elements of spatial production, the complexity of ultrarunning spaces becomes apparent. While going fast is a spatial practice within ultrarunning by some runners, most remain unconcerned with pace as a definitive measure of success. In this way, the representations of space and spaces of representations (lived experiences) are mutually constitutive in unique ways for runners of varying paces. Runners draw on various representations of space specific to ultrarunning and from the larger distance running domain, combining them in individual ways. These complex intersections between ultrarunning specific representations of space, dominant social constructions of distance running, and spaces of representations (lived experiences) result in multiple, often contradictory spatial practices within ultrarunning.

"Do what works for you"

While Lefebvre (1991) suggested that representations of space and spatial practices work together to constitute the basic framework for moving within spaces, he asserted that spaces of representation (lived experiences) are equally important to the production of spaces. Common sense understandings of how to (not) plan for a race rely substantially on personal experimentation and in the moment judgments. In this way, ultrarunning practices challenge the priority of planning found in high performance distance running (Denison, 2010), recreational runners to a lesser extent (Bridel & Rail, 2007), and other sports (Heikkala, 1993; Shogan, 1999). For instance, although nutrition protocols and race strategies are shared among ultrarunners and specific ideas governing these practices exist, the dominant way to approach endurance is to "do what works for you" in training and in the moment determined by lived experiences. Ultrarunners at all levels talked about the need to draw from what other people are doing and experiment. When talking about nutrition, Alex observed, "There's a middle ground that everyone can start with, but in the end, you have to figure out what works for you. Everyone is so individual." The "middle ground" manifests as guidelines such as: eat early and eat often; optimum caloric intake is 200–300 calories per hour; keep electrolytes balanced; and, train the body to use fat as a fuel among others. Despite the prevalence of scientific knowledge that makes up some of the spatial practices in ultrarunning, lived experiences are essential to ultrarunning spaces. One runner sums up the methods in which ultrarunners engage in the following:

> After doing this for a while, I'm better about figuring out what's going on when I feel crummy in a race. Based on how I feel, I go through a list of things that I think it might be, like have I eaten enough, is it an electrolyte thing or do I just need to slow down. You never know what's going to happen in an ultra. I just do what seems right at the time.
>
> (Andy)

In the above comment, it is evident that prior lived experiences both shape the disruption, an issue in moving forward during an ultra race, as well as inform the spatial practices of ultrarunners in individual ways. Thus, responding to issues during a race requires an intuitive, highly flexible response, resulting in a new lived experience upon which runners can draw in any future moment. It is the balance of all these aspects working together that produces ultrarunning performances rather than the strict adherence to a specific plan.

Despite the fact that lived experiences inform divergent, individually based practices with respect to planning (Watkins, 2005), and position ultrarunning practices as different from other distance running, the increased emphasis on these experiences intensifies the importance of the individual. One effect is heightened self-surveillance and self-responsibility during races in order to avoid the DNF, did not finish (Hanold, 2010). Avoiding the DNF becomes the primary logic of competing in this context and often shapes spatial practices in ways similar to rigid protocols. For instance, one common spatial practice is setting watches to beep at regular intervals in order to remind runners about nutrition intake. Another practice is to carry information about location of aid stations, distances and estimated times of arrival at each, which regulate movement during races. Paying attention to lived experiences in order to better move forward reinforces ultrarunning's representations of space in ways that privilege bodies able to complete ultra distances. As Heikkala (1993) noted, such focus on performance, however it is defined, functions as power over bodies in ways similar to strict plans. Although the basic frameworks of ultrarunning need to be transcended by engaging what is learned during lived experiences in order to be successful, success is reinforced as an individual accomplishment. These practices complicate other common understanding of ultrarunning, to which I now turn.

Social support, success, and significance

Another significant finding that emerges from ultrarunners' lived experiences is relying on others for success. While social support during training runs and races manifests in many micro-level behaviors, these practices can be grouped into two distinct, interrelated types. First, runners overwhelmingly talked about moments during races in which they experience mutual encouragement in relation with another runner. David elaborated on the importance of social support during his first 100 km ultra.

> I was sitting on the side of the trail. I was really in the pain cave when a runner came up behind and said, "come on man, you can just walk with me." I thought, ok, I can walk. Was he a distraction from the pain? Was it because I realized that I wasn't the only one feeling this way? I'm not sure, but we talked and I learned a lot from him. Then, he took a dive the last five miles and within the context of one race, the tables were turned. When we finished, we knew it was because of helping each other out.

Similar to individual body knowledge, these experiences are talked about as occurring spontaneously, emerging from the experience itself. The lived experience of social support becomes part of ultrarunning spatial practices as evidenced when ultrarunners articulate the common understanding that people help each other. Alison illustrates this sentiment well when she commented, "When I'm in a race, even if I have a race goal, if I see someone having trouble, I'm gonna check in with them, you know, walk with them, make sure they're ok." Here, social support is part of the representations of space. The second way that social support emerges in races is through reinforcement of the eminence of the experience, a key representation of space in ultrarunning detailed above. Dan noted that at the start line of his very first 50-mile race, runners were saying, "Let's have some fun and enjoy this experience." Ultimately, social support can be viewed as a spatial event that is produced through the interaction of the triadic elements.

Social support takes on another meaning when examining ultrarunning lived experiences, which "allows us to identify the moments when conventions of moving through or knowing space are disrupted and new spatial practices and experiences of space become possible" (Jeyasingham, 2014, p. 1884). Further experiences of ultrarunning spaces that become possible are the development of significant social relationships, which are unequivocally framed as different from other types of distance running as well as everyday life. Runners agreed that the slower pace, induced by the length and terrain of ultras, facilitates these social relationships. Brenda illustrates this idea when she said,

> In road running, it always seemed like people were going fast, but in ultra, the nature of the training, the nature of the events lend themselves to really getting to know people. You're running slow enough that you can talk. It's amazing how intimate your conversations can be with other people. Something about being out there makes you more talkative.

In addition, the following comments illustrate how runners' lived experiences contribute to a complex web of mental representations in ultrarunning:

> During the race I never felt alone; a feeling quite different from that which I experience on a daily basis waiting for public transportation in the big city surrounded by lots of people.
>
> (Stewart)

> When in real life do you get to have a four hour conversation with someone? It leaves me feeling really connected.
>
> (Brenda)

In this way, previously understood ways of moving through distance running spaces, which entail a focus on speed and individual achievement (Bale, 2004; Chase, 2008; Denison, 2007), are disrupted. However, while the social relationships enhanced through ultrarunning provide unique opportunities for connection, these connections tend to strengthen relationships among like minded people, often bolstering prevailing economic and social divisions (Erikson, 2011). It is this issue that I take up next.

Spaces of (in)(ex)clusion

Lefebvre (1991) contended that social inequalities are often concealed in spaces due to who does and does not occupy those spaces. He noted, "there are beneficiaries of space, just as there are those excluded from it (p. 289). He further pointed out that spaces may be discursively constructed as inclusive or considered "open" to everyone, but fail to function as inclusive spaces upon examination of who occupies spaces. This move towards examining the production of space requires engagement with the tensions and contradictions of social space. As such, I consider the discursive constructions of inclusivity in ultrarunning as compared to which bodies occupy these spaces, noting which bodies are invisible or silenced.

Not only do ultrarunners construct their sport as an inclusive, supportive running space based on the social support they feel, they consistently express that ultrarunning is open to everyone because it does not require much gear or equipment. The framing of inclusivity as related to economic means is dominant throughout ultrarunning narratives. Runners frequently remarked that only shoes are required, race fees are cheaper than the marathon, and gear is cheaper than for triathlons. Nowak (2010) even summed up his study of Polish ultrarunners' opinions of whether or not ultrarunning is healthy by noting that, "Ultramarathons are egalitarian sports events open to everyone. They do not require any expensive sports equipment or special athletic skills" (p. 38). Furthermore, observations based on my personal experiences in ultra races and training reveals that social justice issues are part of the ultrarunners' public discourse. Open support for racial equality and gay marriage frequently emerged in conversations on the trail within the context of discussing current events. Despite the discursive production of ultrarunning spaces as inclusive, further examination of this social space reveals notable contradictions.

The bodies that take up ultrarunning spaces are predominantly white, well-educated, married men. Recent studies have shown that 80 percent of ultrarunners are men (Hoffman & Fogard, 2012), 70 percent are married (Knechtle, 2012), and nearly half of all ultrarunners have either undergraduate (43.6 percent) or graduate degrees (37.2 percent). As one runner observed, "It's a fairly homogenous group" (Anna). As van Ingen (2004) noted in her study of marathoners, "Whiteness conveys privilege and normalcy so pervasive that it's virtually invisible to its beneficiaries" (p. 264). Similarly, the dominance of white, heterosexual, middle/upper-class men in ultrarunning renders privilege invisible. Notable evidence of this invisibility is that there are no ultrarunning demographic studies that include race or ethnicity as a category. Further, diversity is a word that is practically non-existent in any ultrarunning media. I found only one blog post that talked about the lack of racial diversity in ultrarunning. Roes (2012) observed, "there just aren't that many non-white and/or lower economic class individuals taking part in this sport" (para. 2). Finally, I found only one ultrarunning website post about gay ultrarunners. The website host remarked, "From my perspective, there are very few–if any–elite LGBT MUT (acronym-palooza!) runners, and I can't figure out why" (Schranz, 2014). There were only two responses in the comments below regarding this comment. "Thanks for the video about Matt Llano. I'm a gay ultra runner, and wish there were more out athletes out there!" and "Hm, I thought I was the only one." These comments combined with the lack of commentary on this post and general non-recognition of LGBTQ ultrarunners renders this group invisible within ultrarunning spaces. Notably, I never encountered openly gay ultrarunners, and only one African-American runner along with a few self-identified Hispanic and Asian runners. I suggest that it is the un-remarkability of male, white, heterosexual, and middle/upper class bodies in ultrarunning spaces that sustains the invisibility and silencing of these groups despite discursive constructions to the contrary.

Conclusion

What does it mean to endure in ultrarunning? At the most basic levels, ultrarunning endurance is about moving over distances longer than a marathon. It is further understood as overcoming the difficulties that the physical spaces present. Yet, through Lefebvre's spatial triad nuanced understandings of what it means to endure in ultrarunning are possible. The synergistic relationship among representations of space, spatial practices, and spaces of representations reveals that common (Western) understandings of distance running are challenged while dominant ideologies and social power relations are sustained.

Consideration of ultrarunning's social space reveals that ultrarunning endurance is shaped by practices that emphasize flexibility rather than tightly monitored ways of moving forward. Ultrarunners rely on training and planning in order to be flexible on race day. This flexibility is evident at the individual and social level. Ultrarunners develop individual body knowledge so that they can be flexible in the moment and respond to how they are feeling. Training and race practices are guided more by "feel" and loose guidelines than by strict adherence to plans and scientific principles. In addition, they count on the norms in ultrarunning to engage social support for race success and for social well-being. These practices contrast prior understandings of running that reflect modern society's emphasis on planning, efficiency, and scientific perspectives such as pace and focused, efficient training (Bale, 2004, 2005; Denison, 2007). Such valuing aligns with Ong's (1999) notion of the "flexible citizen" who "respond[s] fluidly and opportunistically to changing political-economic conditions to accumulate power and capital" (p. 6). Ong posited that the flexible citizen is positioned as a key attribute within the context of late capitalism.

As van Ingen (2004) noted, "a Lefebvrean production-oriented approach to examining space would more clearly link the relation between identity and the spaces through which identity is produced and expressed" (p. 208). Here I consider the production of the "flexible" ultrarunner as a specific form of identity work particularly salient within the context of late capitalism. While flexibility as a practice for success distinguishes ultrarunning from prior practices in distance running, I propose that it reflects "a new type of capitalist production" (Kedhar, 2014, p. 25) that Harvey (1989) suggests is a result of and response to volatile, uncertain competitive environments in a more global marketplace. This new form of production revolves around flexibility (Harvey, 1989) and depends on the flexible citizen (Ong, 1999) who is able to employ creative strategies to adapt to new environments. Ong argues that more than simply a practical strategy, flexibility can be a way for the late modern individual to gain social and cultural capital. The reliance on flexibility as the foremost value and strategy for success in ultrarunning is not only a practical strategy as suggested by the runners' practices and mental abstractions of what it takes to succeed, but also provides a site in which flexibility helps them accumulate social capital. Through the demonstration of "successful flexibility" in increasingly more difficult ultra races, ultrarunners gain social capital not only within this running space but also in the larger social context. Specifically, ultrarunning endurance becomes a marker of the ideal citizen (Larner, 2000), who makes choices that result in success and satisfies individual desires. Individualism paradoxically grows stronger through the social relationships precisely because the social relationships support individual success.

Moreover, every social space has boundaries that become evident by "the 'properties' of a space" (Lefebvre, 1991, p. 289). A significant property of ultrarunning social space is the dominant visible demographic. Specifically, it is white, heterosexual, middle/upper class males who benefit from the mobilization of flexibility. While these boundaries do not appear to exist in discursive productions of ultrarunning spaces, they manifest in the relative *im*mobility of other identities to move into and be recognized in ultrarunning spaces. The spatial effect of who occupies space and who is displaced are imbued with power relations (Lefebvre, 1991; Taylor, 1998). The sociospatial effect of the *im*mobility of other identities is the ideological positioning of flexibility as a white, heterosexual, middle/upper class, masculine characteristic. I suggest that such effects contribute to the conceptual subordination of other identities as capable of flexible citizenry and position ultrarunning endurance as a cultural signifier of the ideal citizen both conceptually and materially.

References

Bale, J. (2004). *Running cultures: Racing in time and space*. New York, NY: Routledge.

Bale, J. (2005). *Roger Bannister and the four-minute mile: Sports myth and sports history*. London, England: Routledge.

Bridel, W., & Rail, G. (2007). Sport, sexuality, and the production of (resistant) bodies: De-/re-/constructing the meanings of gay male marathon corporeality. *Sociology of Sport Journal, 24*, 127–144.

Chase, L. (2008). Running big: Clydesdale runners and technologies of the body. *Sociology of Sport Journal, 25*, 130–147.

Collinson, J. A. (2008). Running the routes together: Co-running and knowledge in action. *Journal of Contemporary Ethnography, 37*, 38–61.

Denison, J. (2007). Perspectives on coaching pace skill in distance running: A commentary. *International Journal of Sports Science & Coaching, 2*, 217–218.

Denison, J. (2010). Planning, practice and performance: The discursive formation of coaches' knowledge. *Sport, Education & Society, 15*, 461–478.

Erickson, B. (2011) Recreational activism: Politics, nature, and the rise of neoliberalism. *Leisure Studies, 30*, 477–494. doi:10.1080/02614367.2011.594078.

Friedman, M. T., & van Ingen, C. Bodies in space: Spatializing physical cultural studies. *Sociology of Sport Journal, 28*, 85–102.

Hanold, M. T. (2010). Beyond the marathon: (De)construction of female ultrarunning bodies. *Sociology of Sport Journal, 27*, 160–177.

Harvey, D. (1989). *The condition of postmodernity: An enquiry into the origins of cultural change*. London, England: Wiley-Blackwell.

Harvey, D. (2005). *A brief history of neoliberalism*. New York, NY: Oxford.

Heikkala, J. (1993). Discipline and excel: Techniques of the self and body and the logic of competing. *Sociology of Sport Journal, 10*, 397–412.

Hoffman, M., & Fogard, K. (2012). Factors related to successful completion of a 100-mile ultramarathon. *Ultrarunning, 31*, 26–28.

Hsiu-Fang, H., & Shannon, S. E. (2005). Three approaches to qualitative content analysis. *Qualitative Health Research, 15*, 1277–1288. doi:10.1177/1049732305276687.

Jeyasingham, D. (2014). The production of space in children's social work: Insights from Henri Lefebvre's spatial dialectics. *British Journal of Social Work, 44*, 1879–1894. doi:10.1093/bjsw/bct053

Kedhar, A. (2014). Flexibility and its bodily limits: Transnational South Asian dancers in an age of neoliberalism. *Dance Research Journal, 46*, 23–40. doi:10.1017/S0149767714000163.

Knechtle, B. (2012). Ultramarathon Runners: Nature or Nurture? *International Journal of Sports Physiology & Performance, 7*, 310–312.

Larner, W. (2000). Neo-liberalism: Policy, ideology, governmentality. *Studies in Political Economy, 63*, 5–25.

Lefebvre, H. (1991). *The production of space*. Oxford, United Kingdom: Blackwell.

Maclin, G. (2014). Home of the "Pacing & Info" Spreadsheet. Retrieved from http://mymarathonpace.com/.

Nowak, P. F. (2010). Ultra distance running in view of health and amateur sport. *Human Movement, 11*, 37–41.

Ong, A. (1999). *Flexible citizenship: The cultural logics of transnationality*. Durham, NC: Duke University Press.

Potter, W. J., & Levine-Donnerstein, D. (1999). Rethinking validity and reliability in content analysis. *Journal of Applied Communication Research, 27*, 258–284.

Roes, G. (2012, October 3). Lacking Diversity … and how to change that. [Web log comment]. Retrieved from www.irunfar.com/2012/10/lacking-diversity-and-how-to-change-that.html.

Schranz, E. (2014, October 1). Daily news, Wed, Oct 1. [Web log comment]. Retrieved from http://ultrarunnerpodcast.com/daily-news-wed-oct-1/.

Shields, R. (1999) *Lefebvre, love and struggle: Spatial dialectics*, London, England: Routledge.

Shogan, D. A. (1999). *The making of high-performance athletes: Discipline, diversity, and ethics*. Toronto: University of Toronto Press.

Simonsen, K. (2005). Bodies, sensations, space and time: The contribution from Henri Lefebvre. *Geografiska Annaler Series B: Human Geography, 87*, 1–14.

Taylor, A. (1998). Ghetto girls/urban music: Jamaican ragga music and female performance. In R. Ainley (Ed.), *New frontiers of space, bodies and gender* (pp. 129–141). New York, NY: Routledge.

Ultrarunning 2012: The year in review (2013). *Ultrarunning*, 40.

van Ingen, C. (2003). Geographies of gender, sexuality and race: Reframing the focus on space in sport sociology. *International Review for the Sociology of Sport, 38*, 201–216.

van Ingen, C. (2004). Therapeutic landscapes and the regulated body in the Toronto Front Runners. *Sociology of Sport Journal, 21*, 253–269.

Watkins, C. (2005). Representations of space, spatial practices and spaces of representation: An application of Lefebvre's spatial triad. *Culture & Organization, 11*, 209–220. doi:10.1080/14759550500203318.

13 An interdisciplinary conversation about running between two academics who run

Marie-Josée Perrier and William Bridel

In 2014, a special issue of the *Sociology of Sport Journal (SSJ)* was published with the purpose of creating dialogue between sport sociology and sport psychology. The guest editors suggested that such conversations were important as an engagement between the two disciplines "has the potential to create change and stimulate new research directions that will make sport studies more relevant to the everyday 'doing' and 'understanding' of sport and exercise" (Thorpe, Ryba, & Denison, 2014, p. 134). Knowing from our years together in graduate school that we had a shared interest in researching the moving body but from different perspectives—sport and exercise psychology and socio-cultural studies respectively—we were intrigued by the suggestion of the potential for interdisciplinary work to contribute to sport and exercise studies. As such, the primary goal of this chapter is to add our own insights to what we think is an important line of inquiry. Given the centrality of the body in all its forms to our work as exercise and sport scholars, how might research that endeavors to address intersections of exercise psychology and sport sociology further our understanding of sporting or exercising bodies: specifically in this case, (our) running bodies? And what might such an inquiry reveal about the notion of endurance?

The starting line

From the outset we want to note that rather than providing any sort of conclusive argument, we consider this chapter the beginning of a larger project we plan to undertake on exercising bodies. We also envision it as a starting point for conversations between the two of us as well as with others about the challenges and possibilities of interdisciplinary work more generally. We are, of course, not the first interdisciplinary team to consider how sport and exercise psychology and sport sociology might be put into conversation with one another to offer new insights on sport, exercise, and health. In the special issue of *SSJ* mentioned in the opening paragraph, for example, two articles adopted a conversational approach to consider the challenges or tensions, as well as the possibilities, in doing interdisciplinary work.

Focused on their personal experiences working as academics at the nexus of sport psychology and sport sociology, Butryn, LaVoi, Kauer, Semerjian, and

Waldron (2014) wrote vignettes based on their positions as what they referred to as "boundary-dwellers." The group then discussed these vignettes, revealing common challenges such as academic politics, funding policies and practices, discipline-specific language, and traditional disciplinary rigidity. They also reflected as a group on the potentialities of meaningful work done at the boundaries of psychology and sociology. In the second article, Moola, Norman, Petherick, and Strachan (2014) chose a specific topic—obesity, health, and physical (in)activity in the Canadian context—as the starting point for their interdisciplinary conversation focused on both researching and teaching in kinesiology. From this latter group's discussions, similar concerns about disciplinary boundaries and resultant tensions emerged as did the challenges of, and possibilities provided by, teaching and researching beyond traditional notions of psychology and sociology as distinct academic disciplines.

While both groups of authors raised many important issues, disciplinary rigidity, which manifests in different ways, emerged as a key issue to be addressed in interdisciplinary work, especially since multiple paradigms are often (seen to be) at odds with one another. In general, the most commonly perceived weakness of psychology is the focus on the microsocial and goal directed, autonomous behavior. This focus can have negative moral implications such that lack of behavior change is constructed as a personal failure. In terms of sociology, a commonly stated limitation is that too much of a focus on power relations ignores or disavows the possibility of people's agency and desire for change. As a specific example, in the article by Butryn and colleagues (2014) it was noted by one of the scholars that good exercise programming (as a form of behavior change) can enhance the lives of older adults but pursuing this line of research also works to reproduce disciplinary bodily practices within a neoliberal social and political context.[1] As a group, these scholars also suggested that while cultural sport psychology is more critical than traditional sport psychology, a focus on performance enhancement—another key feature of sport and exercise psychology research—is at odds with more critical research from the sociology of sport that focuses on, for example, college athlete exploitation. How can one seek to help an athlete improve her/his performance without also contributing to the ways colleges benefit from an athlete's improved performance in ways the athlete does not?

The overarching goals (i.e., micro versus macro) that seem to, in traditional ways of thinking, define the boundaries of sport psychology and sport sociology have served then as a major obstacle to interdisciplinary work, thus producing tensions when attempting to do work that might attempt to blur or at the very least straddle the line between sport psychology and sport sociology. Yet as Moola and colleagues (2014) argued, it isn't simply about there being epistemological and ontological differences but the production and reproduction of knowledge hierarchies over time as a result: "Kinesiology is not by any means a homogeneous discipline … [and that] some ways of knowing (e.g., positivist, quantitative, and predictive) are elevated over others (e.g., qualitative, interpretative, and critical)" (p. 211). Thus, to open up space for a conversation between psychology and sociology, and perhaps blur the boundaries between the two, it must first be acknowledged that knowledge hierarchies exist in an academic context where evidence-based research is given primacy.[2] When aware of these hierarchies and the resultant tensions, however, collaborators can avoid reproducing these same knowledge hierarchies. Furthermore, this awareness can also help avoid the attempt to create one unique solution to a social problem that that doesn't acknowledge the messiness of human lives (Moola *et al.*, 2014), one of the positive outcomes of boundary-blurring work.

Beyond these broad stroke concerns about disciplinary rigidity and knowledge hierarchies, tensions also play out in terms of language, rhetoric, and the idea of "being current." With expansion and specialization, it is difficult to keep up to date on literature in both fields but we wonder if this is where collaborations are key, a point we address later in the chapter. In a similar vein, current teaching and training does not foster interdisciplinarity and as such language and rhetoric can prevent researchers (and students) from engaging in meaningful discussions. Moola and colleagues (2014) found that finding a common point such as the emotional aspects of obesity was one way to move out of their disciplinary silos and begin to engage with one another, issues of language and rhetoric aside (if only temporarily). That said, as Butryn and colleagues (2014) noted, it is paradoxical and problematic when the current academic context (funding, research, teaching) requires specialization but expects interdisciplinarity. As a response, they argued for a new epistemological, ontological, and physical space (e.g., interdisciplinary conferences) that can be accessed and shared between disciplines, with studies exploring both socio-cultural and political context, as well as personal experience at the level of the individual.

Cognizant of the cautions but also the potentialities outlined in the two collaborative, conversational articles discussed above, we embarked on our first interdisciplinary project together. There did, however, remain one challenge—the "doing" of the research. William had previously produced a conversational, transdisciplinary text with six colleagues, in which they, influenced by their academic disciplines, analyzed personal narratives written about physical activity and emotions (Avner *et al.*, 2014); his experience with that project influenced our work here to a certain extent. We decided we would use ourselves as the "research subjects" since we are both runners (albeit sometimes reluctantly):

MJ: For almost 20 years, I HATED running. During my undergraduate training, I began running to lose weight and to embrace a "healthy" lifestyle, though I would not have identified as a runner. In May 2008, I signed up for my first half marathon. I became hooked and continued progressively increased my distance from the half-marathon up to the marathon. After the marathon, I experienced a string of running injuries that sidelined me from endurance running and "competition." Eventually, I returned to running shorter distances for fitness.

WILLIAM: I LOVED running when I was younger and had been a member of the track and cross-country teams in elementary and high school and then again in my mid-20s to early 30s, completing several marathons and shorter distance road races. In 2007, I ceased to run altogether for various reasons. I now incorporate the activity as one aspect of my weekly workout schedule, with little to no interest in "racing" as an age group athlete again.

Using digital voice recorders, we documented runs on three occasions, twice on longer training runs and then while participating in a local road race, providing empirical materials from "the field" that would serve as the basis for our analyses and discussions. With respect to the race, on October 19, 2014 MJ ran a half-marathon in Toronto, Ontario and William ran a 10 km event in Calgary, Alberta. Both distances are popular with non-elite runners, adding another dimension to this collection on endurance running as many of the chapters focus more on elite runners and/or longer distances.

The goal of documenting our runs on the digital voice recorders was to comment on what we were feeling, seeing, smelling, thinking—in brief, experiencing—during the course of each run. We did not discuss any specific topics prior to recording our respective training runs and races, only the technicalities of recording ourselves while running. We exchanged recordings after each run in order to transcribe each other's running commentaries, noting points of interest as we did. We were surprised that we had noted similar themes but, of course, had already started to think about them differently. After some discussion and (friendly) debate, we felt it prudent to focus on the themes that seemed the most prevalent but that would also allow for the most fruitful interdisciplinary conversations. From there, the final step of our analysis was informed by theories from our respective academic fields.

William considered the main emergent themes through, primarily, a Foucauldian lens with a particular interest in thinking about the relationship between discourse, the body, and lived experience. Cognizant of assertions that poststructuralist interrogations of sport and the body ignore the materiality of the body and notions of "agency," he came to this project interested in the possibility provided by thinking about social life from a more "micro" perspective. *MJ* approached the data from the perspective of popular behavioral and motivational theories (e.g., social cognitive theory, self-determination theory, identity theory) to explore the motivation behind, and experience of, distance running events. In addition to traditional approaches in exercise psychology, *MJ* also approaches her research and data using a critical psychological lens. Given her primary focus on the individual, but with an acknowledgement of the broader social, political, and historical contexts in which people live, she approached this project interested in the possibility provided by a thorough consideration of broader discourses and their impact on bodily experience and behavior.

What we talked about when we talked about running[3]

It struck us that woven throughout our observations and commentary and our subsequent analyses were different ideas about "identity" and connections to motivation and experience. In the following sections we discuss individual and group identity, running clothing and accessories, and the theoretical/methodological challenges and potentialities that we experienced. Although presented in separate sections there is a great deal of interconnectedness between the topics.

Developing running identities

Our thoughts during our runs referenced ideas about running as an individual and (possibly) group activity:

> I just passed another guy running. Little bit of a head nod. It's not quite as friendly as it was in Ottawa but it's still nice to feel a little bit of a community. People get it, you know?
>
> (MJ's training run)

> People are taking pictures. This is interesting. Almost half way and I'm feeling okay still. I wish I had a camera just to take a picture of all the people. You know you're not alone.... The guy who I was running with was awesome.
>
> (MJ's race)

> I've mostly run on my own. A few exceptions: I ran with the Ottawa Front Runners when I lived there. Saturday mornings, it was a nice, easy fun run for the most part. I also for awhile, when I was trying to get really fast, maybe qualify for Boston, you know like around ten years ago, 2004, I trained with an elite group with the Running Room in Ottawa and I was definitely one of the slowest people there but I also improved my running quite a bit but I just didn't love the environment.
>
> (William's training run)

We know that running provides the opportunity to connect with other runners, to make friends with similar interests, to have others to train with—in short, the opportunity to be part of a community—which is a draw for many even if it is somewhat paradoxical. As Shipway, Holloway, and Jones (2012) noted, in running "individuals follow an individual pursuit within the social world of the distance running community—highlighting that the focus is on both the individual and the social" (p. 259). This in mind, we turned our conversation to running as an individual and/or group activity and how that might relate to notions of identity from our different academic perspectives.

MJ: I approach my research using both a cognitivist psychological approach as well as a critical psychological approach. In reading our transcripts, my first thoughts focused on *relatedness*, a central component of Basic Psychological Needs Theory (Deci & Ryan, 2000). According to Deci and Ryan (2010), when we engage in activities that enable us to form meaningful social connections with others, we are more likely to develop stronger, self-determined motivation for those activities. From an exercise psychology perspective, we are interested in self-determined motivation because of its association with long-term exercise maintenance (Teixeira, Carraca, Markland, Silva, & Ryan, 2012). As highlighted by the quotes above—my own in particular—even running alone as well as in a group can foster feelings of relatedness through verbal (e.g., conversation) and non-verbal encounters (e.g., head nods, waves). This led me to think more about the importance of other runners for the development and support of a "running identity."

Role identities, or the meaning that people attach to specific identities, are used during social interactions (Burke & Stets, 2009; Stryker & Burke, 2000). If others validate our identities, such as a nod from other runners on the road or inclusion in a group conversation, these identities will be strengthened (Stryker & Burke, 2000). From my perspective, strong exercise identities are of interest given that they are associated with exercise and running behavior as well as plans to overcome barriers to exercise (Strachan & Brawley, 2008; Strachan, Woodgate, Brawley, & Tse, 2005).

Although for this chapter my analysis was based solely on the recordings William and I produced while running, I would incorporate interviews in future research projects in order to further explore exercise identities. After asking participants broad "grand tour" questions (Sparkes & Smith, 2014), for example, I would follow up with specific questions about other runners' behaviors and perceived connections to the running community based on past literature and identity theory. That said, as suggested in William's earlier quote about the different running groups with which he has been involved in the past, not all environments will motivate running and support running identities. Self-efficacy, a situation specific form of confidence in one's ability, and the related construct, competence, are consistently associated with maintained behavior and running identities (Bandura, 1997; Edmunds, Ntoumanis, & Duda, 2006; Strachan *et al.*, 2005). Following from my previous comment about future research projects, in interviews I would also include questions that seek to determine how running environments can either enhance or inhibit self-efficacy and competence. For example, in a hypothetical scenario where William was one of my participants, I would ask him about his experiences connecting with members of the elite running group and his perceptions about his running skill in that particular group. When analyzing the transcript from his interview, I would likely use a dialogical narrative analysis to explore the relational nature of identities, with an interest in how competence and relatedness with others foster running identities (Frank, 2012).

WILLIAM: I do find the approach MJ has taken to analyze ideas about individual and group identity vis-à-vis running intriguing and as an individual who runs, the ideas she raises offer insights into relatedness in particular. But my academic interests push me to think about questions of identity from a broader perspective; how do people come to make meaning of their experiences in running in terms of, as MJ has discussed above, sense of community and the notion of a "running identity"?

Foucault's body of work focused on systems of thought, with a view toward challenging taken-for-granted "truths" constructed and maintained through discourse. His interest, as Fady and Nicholls (2013) explained it, was to "locate the historical conditions that allow us to think, speak, and act as we do now" (p. 25). Foucault (1972) defined discourse as, "the general domain of all statements, sometimes as an individualizable group of statements, and sometimes as a regulated practice that accounts for a number of statements" (p. 80) and contended that discourses are practices that both shape and constitute subjects. He argued that power/knowledge produced through discourses, "systematically form the objects of which they speak. Discourses are not about objects; they constitute them and in the practice of doing so conceal their own intervention" (p. 49). Dominant discourses of expertise, such as medicine, law, politics, religion, and ethics—Foucault was particularly interested in medical and scientific discourses—produce and disseminate knowledge that individuals take up and make use of as they create themselves as subjects (Foucault, 1972, 1980, 1988, 1995). Scientific discourses, for example, produce specific ways of knowing based on so-called objective and quantifiable measures. These measures are then used to create universal categories or classifications and "people come to recognize themselves as objects and subjects of scientific knowledge" (Markula & Pringle, 2006, p. 25). Foucault referred to this as the process of subjectivation.

According to Markula and Pringle (2006), there are two steps in the process of subjectivation. First, "the individual [is made] a subject to someone else by control and dependence, and second, it ties him/her in his/her own identity by a conscience or self-knowledge" (p. 138). Following the example from above, scientific knowledge operates as a discourse of expertise. As such, binary categories of normal/abnormal (for example, thin/obese) are created through the so-called objective measures of science and come to be seen as the "Truth" or the norm. Recognizing this, individuals shape themselves and their identities in relation to these contextually specific norms in any number of ways—their sexuality, their gender, their ability, or their health—mostly in accordance to ideas promoted through dominant discourse.

There is, in Foucault's way of thinking, no way of knowing one's experiences or oneself outside of discourse: "A person's account of themselves and their experiences cannot be seen as an origin for the construction of meaning, because the subject is constituted through discourse, and discourse provides the means of articulation and action" (Fady & Nicholls, 2013, p. 25). Specific to our conversation about running and running identity in this chapter, from a Foucauldian perspective then, the "running subject" is a discursive effect, resulting from powerful discourses that structure our reality (Foucault, 1972). Thus, although both MJ and I referred to other runners and running groups in the quotes featured earlier, and MJ made links to running identity from an exercise psychology perspective, any sense of identity would be fleeting. That is not to say, however, that there is not power/privilege connected to a running identity. This notion of power/privilege as connected to running identity is especially the case in a socio-political context where running is often connected to notions of healthiness, a highly valued trait in contemporary, neoliberal times. Furthermore, a "healthy body" reflects discipline, another highly valued trait in contemporary, neoliberal times. The Foucauldian paradigm helps us to understand running as a social phenomenon: one that does not operate outside of discourse but rather as a discursive field through which docile bodies are produced in line with contemporary constructions of bodily practices and performances.

Dressing the part

We also noted that clothing and accessories had a significant presence in our recordings, comments that led to further micro and macro conversations about identity, as well as enjoyment and pleasure.

> I really like these shoes. Every time I look down it's like a little bright orange pick me up. I'm actually digging my outfit. I picked something that would, I don't know, make me feel a bit more put together. A little bit more like a runner.
>
> (MJ's training run)

> There's a few more runners out. I like all their colorful shirts. Something to look at. A lot of the guys who are out … I've only passed one female … a lot of the guys look like they're pretty into this stuff. They have their Garmins out, you know, no music, very stern look on their face. It looks like they mean business.
>
> (MJ's training run)

> Energy wise, I still feel good. I also caved and bought new Lululemon for the occasion. I'm feeling pretty in that.
>
> (William's race)

WILLIAM: From my perspective, gear and accessories certainly help identify oneself as "a runner." But gear and accessories also serve to situate oneself as part of the larger running community, a community that is largely comprised of middle- to upper-class individuals and, more specifically, white middle- and upper-class men since traditional gender roles tend to allow men in this age-group and with this socio-economic standing greater access to the running community (Abbas, 2004; Serravallo, 2000) and simultaneously the related accouterments.

While scholars have pointed to a diversification of the running community through the introduction of, for example, weight divisions (Chase, 2008), there nevertheless remains a privileging of a certain body type in the running community. Despite the "running is for everybody" messaging that dominates popular texts, scholars have argued that the running community favors an idealized body type perhaps most appropriately labeled as the "distance running body" (Abbas, 2004; Bridel & Rail, 2007; Hanold, 2010; Smith, 1998) and clothing and accessories are designed more for those kinds of bodies than larger, heavier ones (Chase, 2008). Thus, it is not simply about clothing and accessories helping to constitute one's running identity but also about who might be excluded, or at the very least marginalized, by these same items, an exclusion that further solidifies often limited ideas about who *is* a runner.

It also seemed in some of our comments that clothing acted as a source of pleasure. Most of our references to enjoyment or pleasure throughout our recordings had to do with, as above, what others or we were wearing; I even went so far as to buy a new shirt for the day of the race. We also talked about other kinds of external rewards. In listening to the recording from my training run, MJ pointed out that over the final few kilometers I had begun negotiating with myself for a post-run reward:

> Alright, I'm about 2k from home. I've set a new goal. These last 2k, no stops and I actually run the full massive hill that's just past my house and back down and the glass of wine is back on the table 'cause I'm not training for the Olympics here.
>
> (William's training run)

Smith-Maguire (2008) has argued that the external rewards related to participation in physical activity (such as material goods, peer recognition, or the consumption of foods and beverages as reward for exercising) are promoted as the primary forms of pleasure, particularly in the fitness field. She contended: "Exercise itself is not pleasurable; but is a matter of discipline; pleasure comes from the effect one's fitter body has upon others" (p. 196). Certainly the "distance running body" fits the bill, at least as popularly promoted, but it was nevertheless startling, given MJ's and my academic interest in exercise and exercising bodies, to listen to our recordings and realize that not once did she or I mention the idea that we were actually enjoying the process of running. A lot of our enjoyment of running seemed to come, paradoxically, when the running itself was over. Not far into my 10k road race I made the following comment:

> I'm actually just not sure that I very much enjoy the process of running, the feeling of running. Maybe I'm just getting old and the relation to my body is continuing to change. But I'd way rather do yoga than run.
>
> (William's race)

Some scholars have suggested that what we find pleasurable is entirely dependent upon what we desire (Aho, 1998; Rose, 1999, 2001). But rather than thinking of desire as an intrinsic or inherent feeling that humans possess, a

Foucauldian-influenced analysis would position desire as a discursive construction imbued with and constituted by contextually-specific regimes of power. Rand (2008) argued in this regard that what we come to think of as "social norms" function in such a way to regulate our desires. She wrote: "Norms solicit our desires. They create, meet, and frustrate our needs with an intensity that is often challenging to explain and, as a result, crucial to explain" (p. 571). Desire—for "better" health, for products (like running clothes and accessories), for normalcy—is not constant or unchanging. What we want and what we strive for is discursively constructed. In times when great value is placed on health, for example, "healthiness" becomes a desirable norm for individuals; running is held up as one way to both achieve and demonstrate this. This leads to another observation that both MJ and I made during our events, the first which is a conversation that took place between MJ and another runner:

> MJ: I almost wore my Around the Bay[4] shirt today too. It's a good shirt, it's warm. It's perfect for this temperature!
>
> BOB[5]: It's not too thick and not too thin.... It's [weather] one of those things where you're always guessing, like do I wear shorts? Do I wear long sleeves? Do I wear a jacket? Do I wear two layers?
>
> MJ: Yeah, I changed about three times. It's [jacket] not very warm. So, I'm a little cold but it's easy to roll up and unzip.
>
> BOB: But you're always cold at the start!
>
> MJ: The only thing, I was running the other day and if it's windy, you get a hood to the face [both laugh].
>
> BOB: This year I did Around the Bay and I had a jacket and I regretted it, 'cause like, I was freezing at the start, even in the jacket but 2 k in, I took it off and I carried it for the remaining 28 k.
>
> (MJ's race)

> Lots of people are wearing finishing shirts from other races. Suppose that goes to show a lot about running identity.
>
> (William's race)

WILLIAM: Turning from Foucault for a moment, Pierre Bourdieu's ideas prove useful here in offering one interpretation of why runners might choose to wear finishing shirts from previous events, beyond simply being comfortable. Bourdieu (1984) contended that in some social spaces or fields, groups of individuals develop cultural peculiarities that distinguish or differentiate them from others. Simply put, they have distinct cultures, hence, "distinction" (Crossley, 2008). These differences can become a source of struggle, however, as the members of the distinct culture seek to legitimate their difference and, at the same time, assert their superiority. The struggle for distinction is a process through which distinct class habitus is formed. Crossley (2008) stated that, "groups form themselves, in some part, by cultivating distinguishing features and signs of 'superiority'. Note, however, that this already presupposes some degree of 'in group' identification and interaction" (p. 96). While running shirts and accessories such as Garmins serve to identify individuals as "runners," finishing shirts not only solidify this identification but also work to create distinction within the running community itself. This would be particularly true for someone wearing a finisher's shirt or jacket from the Boston Marathon, an event still considered by many to be the ultimate representation of one's running abilities since there are quite challenging qualifying times one must achieve in order to participate.

MJ: I would think about accessories in a similar yet slightly different way than William does. Narrative identity shapes my understanding of clothing and accessories. From this perspective, people are story-telling beings and identities are constructed through the stories that we hear and share with real or imagined others (Smith & Sparkes, 2009). As such, the stories we hear shape our understanding of who we are and who we may become and the stories we share with others allows us to construct identities (Smith & Sparkes, 2009). In addition to sharing stories verbally, identities are performed through the activities we engage in and the clothing we wear (Frank, 2010). Thus, from my perspective, clothing and other electronics are a component of performed identity and highlight the underlying "runner" narrative that William and I used to inform our behavior and moreover, to claim a running identity (Smith & Sparkes, 2009). As highlighted above, during our runs we performed in accordance with the expectations of these real or imagined others. As part of the dialogical nature of identities, others can have an impact on the stories we share and the identities we claim (Frank, 2010, 2012). Clothing, such as old race shirts, served as an indicator that these people would be open to hearing stories about running, and moreover, sharing running stories with these others will connect us to the "running community." This is highlighted by a quote from my race transcript where I claimed an identity as a runner through a conversation with another runner who was wearing an old Around the Bay race shirt. With respect to running identities and new runners, Griffin (2010) found that the Women's Running Network presented a narrative for running that could *hail* more women to running by expanding the running narrative to include women of all shapes and sizes. However, this type of network still presents women with a specific way of understanding their bodies and the importance of activity through a very specific visual and material culture. Thus, in interviews in future research, I would be particularly attentive to how runners think about real and imagined others, as well as the role these others play in identity construction and behavior on the course.

WILLIAM: Although you and I are looking at clothing and accessories and the concept of running identity from a macro and micro perspective, I think that when taken together, our differing approaches do shed some insights into the role of distance running in individuals' lives as well as the meaning of running in the larger context. In a sense, we have begun to embark on a collaborative, interdisciplinary journey that follows Markula's (2014) assertion that conversations between exercise psychologists and sport sociologists can shed greater insight into the process of subjectivation or self-identification. This is so primarily because the fields share similar interests in interrogating individual experiences in relation to the larger socio-cultural context and both fields have potential limitations that could gain from collaborative work. Specifically, Markula (2014) suggested that,

> psychological approaches might benefit from a more careful problematization of the different theoretical approaches to power and the socio-cultural approach might benefit from a more informed reading of the distinct meanings of psychologically derived concepts such as individual, subjectivity, identity, and self.
>
> (p. 155)

It is this point—individual experiences placed into conversation with the larger cultural context—where we both, I would offer, have been influenced to think at least a little bit differently. Considering the ways people make sense of their experiences and sense of self in their individual lives helps address what has been argued to be the discursive foundationalism in poststructuralist approaches to theorizing "identity." There are limitations when the "subject and her identity are considered entirely regulated by discourses" (Markula, 2014, p. 145). That said, as I commented earlier, according to Foucault nothing exists outside of discourse; there are always multiple discourses circulating in any given spatial and temporal context. This is where I get "stuck" but perhaps where future interdisciplinary research could help. Could collaborative work between exercise psychologists and sport sociologists help produce alternative discourses that might, for instance, promote behavior change without simultaneously disciplining the body in limited and potentially problematic ways?

MJ: My perspective, which is arguably more focused on individual experience, is that a more careful consideration of the socio-cultural contexts in which people live can further elucidate why people are drawn to specific behaviors and identities. Using the Bourdieusian concept "unchosen choices" Frank (2010) highlighted that the narratives that people draw upon to construct identities and interpret their everyday are just as often unchosen as they are chosen. That is, the narratives that circulate in people's environments are a product of the social, historical, and political context and thus, unchosen. Given that traditional psychological approaches tend to focus on the "chosen" aspect of identities and stories, could collaborative work provide more insight into the role dominant health discourses may have on the "choices" that people make?

Further discussion and concluding thoughts

Our primary goal in writing this chapter was to create dialogue between sport and exercise psychology and sport sociology, using distance running as our point of entry. Our analysis of our recordings led to conversations about identity and the notion of endurance as simultaneously an individual pursuit and a socio-cultural phenomenon. But even in making such a statement, we realize that we continue to reproduce the disciplinary boundaries that have been created between the individual (psychology) and the context (sociology). Thus, aware of and acknowledging the benefits and limitations of each of our academic perspectives and the conversations that occurred as a result, we can't help but wonder, where do we go from here?

In writing this chapter, we were faced with a challenge given that our language, research approach, and general understanding of identity and behavior are firmly rooted in our academic silos. Even still, we began our collaboration with similar questions about endurance running, the "whys" of it in particular. We also both were willing to acknowledge the advantages one another's perspective would bring to this analysis, as well as future analyses of endurance running and endurance running bodies. But yet we must ask, are these perspectives (e.g., macro versus micro) truly unique or perhaps is this knowledge being artificially relegated to academic silos for other purposes? Consider, for example, the distinction between William's understanding of discourse and MJ's understanding of narrative.

Narratives are framed and circulate in the broader socio-cultural environment (Frank, 1995) and therefore an argument can be made for narratives as being discursively formed. Yet, discourse itself is reproduced and operates through the narratives that shape individuals' understanding and interpretation of individual lived experience. So we must ask, aren't narratives discursively formed and aren't discourses so powerful because they operate as narratives? Much like the macro/micro divide we have alluded to throughout this chapter, is the narrative/discourse divide also an artificial one? And if so, how do we negotiate this divide in further interdisciplinary studies, particularly in fields that are already well established with their own conceptualization of knowledge that "counts"? Can we truly leave behind our silos and meet in the middle? If so, what would this partnership and its methodologies look like?

Perhaps one of the biggest "aha" moments we had in our collaboration for this chapter resulted from MJ's commentary (woven throughout this chapter) about the kinds of questions she would want to ask of participants in future research projects. Somewhere along the way William realized that he would ask exactly the same questions yet both of us were initially convinced that asking the same questions from our "own" perspectives would somehow lead to greater insight. Such is the influence, even with our critical awareness, of the way knowledge has been fragmented and hierarchized for all varieties of reasons and how that influence has played out in our training in our respective academic disciplines.

In navigating interdisciplinary research and partnerships, it is important to note that people, including us as researchers, are not blank slates but rather, they/

we are shaped by the broader socio-cultural context; we are also specifically influenced by the expectations and practices of our individual academic fields (Moola *et al.*, 2014). By narrowing our discussion to a specific focus (i.e., endurance), much as Moola and colleagues (2014) did in their discussion of physical (in)activity, obesity, and health, we were able to appreciate not only how our own "academic baggage" influenced how we approached our data but also the possibilities that interdisciplinary collaborations offer in terms of opening up our own individual analysis and contributing to a different perspective on running identities and the body.

We believe that continued discussions that draw from both of our academic perspectives—but that then challenge and blur these distinctions—will provide further insights into the ways people understand the role of endurance in their own lives, perhaps as part of their identity but in relation to contextually specific social norms and values. We hope that other scholars will follow suit and seek out and form interdisciplinary partnerships and teams in order to offer different and more complex or nuanced insights on the physically active, moving body in contemporary times. The imperative of undertaking such boundary-blurring research seems especially important given the neoliberal turn in academia and funding agencies that now encourage (require?) interdisciplinary collaborations with a view to "solving" issues related to, amongst other things, health. Truly interdisciplinary work cannot give primacy to one discipline over another but rather strive to acknowledge and chip away at disciplinary silos that seem to have a kind of endurance of their own.

Notes

1 At no point in the article by Butryn and his colleagues (2014) did they attribute specific quotes or ideas to anyone person in the group, thus our phrasing "one of the scholars in the group…"

2 Silk, Brush, and Andrews (2010) provided an excellent critique of evidence-based research, research that promotes empirical methods, objectivity and "proof" as the gold-standard for academic research, rendering subordinate other types of approaches to research.

3 The subtitle here is inspired by Haruki Murakami's book, entitled *What I Talk About When I Talk About Running*, in which the author philosophizes about his long-term interest and participation in long-distance running.

4 Around The Bay is a 30km race in Hamilton, Ontario, Canada and is among the oldest in North America, predating the Boston Marathon by three years.

5 "Bob" is a pseudonym we assigned to a runner who MJ met in the start corrals at the Scotiabank Toronto Waterfront Marathon.

References

Abbas, A. (2004). The embodiment of class, gender and age through leisure: A realist analysis of long distance running. *Leisure Studies, 23*, 159–175.

Aho, J. A. (1998). *The things of the world: A social phenomenology*. London, England: Praeger.

Avner, Z., Bridel, W., Eales, L., Glenn, N., Loewen Walker, R., & Peers, D. (2014). Moved to messiness: Physical activity, feelings, and transdisciplinarity. *Emotion, Space, and Society, 12*, 55–62.

Bandura, A. (1997). *Self-Efficacy: The exercise of control*. New York, NY: Freeman.

Bourdieu, P. (1984). *Distinction: A social critique of the judgement of taste*. Cambridge, MA: Harvard University Press.

Bridel, W., & Rail, G. (2007). Sport, sexuality, and the production of (resistant) bodies: De-/re-/constructing the meanings of gay male marathon corporeality. *Sociology of Sport Journal, 24*, 127–144.

Burke, P. J., & Stets, J. E. (2009). *Identity theory*. New York, NY: Oxford University Press.

Butryn, T., LaVoi, N., Kauer, K., Semerjian, T., & Waldron, J. (2014). We walk the line: An analysis of the problems and possibilities of work at the sport psychology-sport sociology nexus. *Sociology of Sport Journal, 31*, 162–184.

Chase, L. (2008). Running big: Clydesdale runners and technologies of the body. *Sociology of Sport Journal, 25*, 130–147.

Crossley, N. (2008). Social class. In M. Grenfell (Ed.), *Pierre Bourdieu: Key concepts* (pp. 85–97). New York, NY: Acumen.

Deci, E. L., & Ryan, R. M. (2000). The "what" and "why" of goal pursuits: Human needs and the self-determination of behavior. *Psychological Inquiry, 11*, 227–268.

Edmunds, J. K., Ntoumanis, N., & Duda, J. L. (2006). A test of self-determination theory in the exercise domain. *Journal of Applied Social Psychology, 36*, 2240–2265. doi: 10.1111/j.0021–9029.2006.00102.x.

Fady, J., & Nicholls, D. (2013). Foucault, the subject, and the research interview: A critique of methods. *Nursing Inquiry, 20*, 23–29.

Foucault, M. (1972). *The archaeology of knowledge*. New York, NY: Harber Torchbooks.

Foucault, M. (1980). *Power/Knowledge: Selected interviews and other writings 1972–1977*. New York, NY: The Harvester Press.

Foucault, M. (1988). Technologies of the self. In L. H. Martin, H. Gutman, & P. H. Hutton (Eds.) *Technologies of the self.* Amherst, MA: University of Massachusetts Press.

Foucault, M. (1995). *Discipline and punish: The birth of the prison*. New York, NY: Vintage Books.

Frank, A. W. (2010). *Letting stories breathe: A socio-narratology*. Chicago, IL: University of Chicago Press.

Frank, A. W. (2012). Practicing dialogical narrative analysis. In J. A. Holstein & J. F. Gubrium (Eds.) *Varieties of narrative analysis*. Thousand Oaks, CA: Sage.

Griffin, M. (2010). Setting the scene: Hailing women into a running identity. *Qualitative Research in Sport and Health, 2*, 153–174.

Hanold, M. T. (2010). Beyond the marathon: (De)Construction of female ultrarunning bodies. *Sociology of Sport Journal, 27*, 160–177.

Markula, P. (2014). Embodied subjectivities: Intersections of discursive and critical psychology with socio-cultural exercise research. *Sociology of Sport Journal, 31*, 139–161.

Markula, P., & Pringle, R. (2006). *Foucault, sport, and exercise: Power, knowledge, and transforming the self.* New York, NY: Routledge.

Moola, F., Norman, M., Petherick, L., & Strachan, S. (2014). Teaching across the lines of fault in psychology and sociology: Health, obesity, and physical activity in the Canadian context. *Sociology of Sport Journal, 31*, 202–227.

Rand, E. (2008). I wanted black skates: Gender, cash, pleasure, and the politics of criticism. *Criticism, 50*, 555–580.

Rose, N. (1999). *Powers of freedom: Reframing political thought.* Cambridge, United Kingdom: Cambridge University Press.

Rose, N. (2001). The politics of life itself. *Theory, Culture, and Society, 18*, 1–30.

Serravallo, V. (2000). Class and gender in recreational marathon running. *Race, Gender and Class, 7*, 96. Retrieved from http://proxy.bib.uottawa.ca:2078/pqdlink?did=494618281&sid=4&Fmt=3&clientId=3345&RQT=309&VName=PQD.

Shipway, R., Holloway, I., & Jones, I. (2012) Organizations, practices, actors, and events: Exploring inside the distance running social world. *International Review for the Sociology of Sport, 48*, 259–276.

Silk, M., Brush, A., & Andrews, D. (2010). Contingent intellectual amateurism or the problem with evidence-based research. *Journal of Sport and Social Issues, 34*, 105–128.

Smith, S. (1998). Athletes, runners and joggers: Participant-group dynamics in a sport of "individuals." *Sociology of Sport Journal, 15*, 174–192.

Smith-Maguire, J. (2008). *Fit for consumption: Sociology and the business of fitness.* New York, NY: Routledge.

Smith, B., & Sparkes, A. C. (2009). Narrative analysis and sport and exercise psychology: Understanding lives in diverse ways. *Psychology of Sport & Exercise, 10*, 279–288. doi: 10.1016/j.psychsport.2008.07.012.

Sparkes, A. C., & Smith, B. (2014). *Qualitative research methods in sport, exercise and health: From process to product.* London, England: Routledge.

Strachan, S., & Brawley, L. R. (2008). Reactions to a perceived challenge to identity: A focus on exercise and healthy eating. *Journal of Health Psychology, 13*, 575–588.

Strachan, S., Woodgate, J., Brawley, L. R., & Tse, A. (2005). The relationship of self-efficacy and self-identity to long-term maintenance of vigorous physical activity. *Journal of Applied Biobehavioural Research, 10*, 98–112.

Stryker, S., & Burke, P. J. (2000). The past, present, and future of an identity theory. *Social Psychology Quarterly, 63*, 284–297.

Teixeira, P. J., Carraca, E. V., Markland, D., Silva, M. N., & Ryan, R. M. (2012). Exercise, physical activity, and self-determination theory: A systematic review. *International Journal of Behavioral Nutrition and Physical Activity, 9*, 78. doi:10.1186/1479–5868–9–78.

Thorpe, H., Ryba, T., & Denison, J. (2014). Toward new conversations between sociology and psychology. *Sociology of Sport Journal, 31*, 131–137.

14 Hitting a purple patch

Building high performance runners at Runtleborough University

P. David Howe

In the past I have been involved in research which highlights the importance of Runtleborough, England, as a place for creating high quality running bodies that are co-constituted by the surrounding landscape and the effort put into the body in the act of running (Howe & Morris, 2009).[1] This current chapter builds upon this work by using phenomenological ethnographic methods to elucidate the embodied habitus that surrounds the middle-distance running squad at Runtleborough University. Having worked as a member of the cross-country and middle-distance coaching team, I have amassed detailed field notes of the culture surrounding this successful team. In this chapter, I further illuminate how, year in, year out, the student athletes at Runtleborough Students Athletics Club (RSAC) successfully develop into elite runners and regularly hit a purple patch. The expression "purple patch" takes on extra significance at RSAC as it is not only a statement about being in the personal best shape but the club vest is also a wonderful shade of African violet.

The pull of the elite running culture in and around Runtleborough is such that many club members stay in town, long after their student days, in pursuit of the fastest times their mortal engines can muster. Drawing upon a blend of the methodologies and theories of Merleau-Ponty and Bourdieu, this chapter offers an account of how an elite running culture can become sustainable through the formation of distinctive embodiment. The relationship between the physical and social environment fostered over several generations by the charismatic head coach is a distinctive balance of tried and tested science of running with the flair of humanism, which emphasizes the value and agency of the runners. Adopting a periodized program where patience, persistence, passion, and progression are all of importance in equal measure, the athletes develop the ethos required of elite runners. This chapter offers details of the RSAC training program in hope of illuminating how the embodied cultural habitus of the runners is created and sustained. To do this, this chapter highlights the importance of ethnographic methods to collect data on running culture. This is followed by an ethnographic vignette that illuminates a typical season for runners on the RSAC program. I specifically highlight how Ingold's (2000) conceptualization of taskscape is a useful tool for analysis before turning to issues of embodied training more directly.

Ethnography and running culture

Previous writing that nicely articulates key elements of running culture and in particularly the importance of place and space in its development (Bale, 2003, 2004; Bale & Sang, 1996) provides an important foundation for this chapter. I wish to, however, highlight the role that a detailed ethnographic account of a running culture can add to our understanding of this important physical practice. Running like all physical activities is a sensuous experience. Even if elite runners in the heat of training may only engage with the sensuous in passing, it is important for written ethnographic accounts to endeavor to capture this experience (see Howe, 2011). As Abram (1996) suggests:

> When we attend to our experiences not as intangible minds but as, speaking bodies, we begin to sense that we are heard, even listened to, by the numerous other bodies that surround us. Our sensing bodies respond to the eloquence of certain buildings and boulders, to the articulate motions of dragonflies. We find ourselves alive in a listening, speaking world.
>
> (p. 86)

Ethnographic accounts of sporting practice allow readers detailed insight into their sensuous nature. It is hoped that what follows will allow readers to engage with material as lived experiences of my informants. My ethnography at this club has been endorsed by the ethics committee at Runtleborough University where the runners, who are part of the training program, sign a consent form to participate in my research.

Many of the informants highlighted in this chapter have been part of the RSAC for over a decade. They have taken up employment in the town and/or are "permanent" students. This running tribe is a close-knit group that exhibits a blend of personal sacrifice to facilitate running fast with a collective desire for those in the program to achieve success. The data collected in this research is gathered during training sessions, at races and individual meetings that I have had with the runners. Nature of training at a club such as RSAC is seasonal in nature as is highlighted in the quote below:

> Hey coach will be hitting the roads for tempo runs at the start of the season like last year I really feel that allowed me to get to know the freshers in a non-threating way. The track can be a scary place to meet new and potentially faster recruits and I also feel the tempos allow me to build into the cross-country season gently.

The seasonality associated with the program that is led, through a consultation process by the head coach, affectionately known as the Guru, is by no means distinctive to the training at RSAC but has ensured the longevity of the success of this high performance program. Since the Guru's arrival in Runtleborough in 1971 the RSAC program has produced several hundred international senior middle- and long-distance athletes, almost half of who were personally coached by him.

When the athlete quoted above talks about the replicating last season's structure he knowingly is contributing to the continued legacy of the program. Whether runners arrive as junior stars who are simply in need of a "little coaching polish" from the program or whether their bodies are co-produced "from scratch" in this environment (Howe & Morris, 2009; Ingold, 1997, 2000), the longevity of the success of the training system at RSAC is exceptional. But what is the secret? According to one seasoned athlete:

> [The Guru] is always up for a laugh. The training has changed subtly since my arrival as a first year and now I am personally coached by him. I have being graduated for a few years now but opted to get a job in town so I could remain part of the RSAC program. The old adage is true—"Why fix it if it isn't broke?" I was not particularly good when I arrived—I hadn't even broken 4:05 for 1,500—but under the guidance of the Guru and one of the other coaches I am regularly making the 1,500 final at the nationals. In recent years some at the club have question whether the Guru still had it as a coach—his stories were a bit long winded but if you listen carefully there is so much to learn from him and his planning of my train program is meticulous. The combined with the fact he has time to chat with runners of all abilities should be a lesson to those who wish to establish long-term success in the sport.

This quote illuminates the coaching ability or rather charisma that makes the nickname *The Guru* appropriate. Over 40 years of experience has taught the Guru and the handful of coaches who have been closely mentored by him in the RSAC system that great running bodies can appear down at the track in all shapes and sizes. By harnessing the enthusiasm for the physical act of pushing the body in the act of running and related exercise RSAC has been able to continually produce high quality elite athletes from average student members.

In this chapter, the culture of middle- and long-distance performance running is described through one "fictional" running body (after Weber's ideal types in Runciman, 1978), a methodological device that is based on participant observation of the runners that are part of the RSAC program that has been and continues to be researched for over a decade. Following from Hammersley and Atkinson (2007), this is an "analytic construct. It does not, and is not intended to, correspond in every detail to all observed cases. It is intended to capture key features of a social phenomenon" (pp. 195–196). As Clifford (1986) suggested some time ago reality in as social construction and representational fictions of the kind I have written below can according to Rabinow (1986) be used illuminate social facts. In a sport-specific context, the representational ideal type has been utilized effectively by Klein (1993) in his construction of the *Olympic Gym*, a single fictitious gym that is used as a vehicle for representing four similar gyms in which he conducted ethnographic research on bodybuilding: "[E]ven though I dealt with four gyms, they were remarkably similar often sharing the elite competitors among themselves. Merging them into one posed no problem, and,

I thought, added to the placement of the reader into the gym setting" (Klein, 1993, p. 280). Such fictional representations have been celebrated in sports studies since the postmodern turn (Bruce, 1998). What follows is an ethnographic vignette that outlines a year's worth of training. It is designed to give the reader the essence of the program and leads to my analysis of its significance.

RSAC—a typical year

The academic year in the United Kingdom begins at the end of September or beginning of October, also the start for a typical training year.

In autumn and winter, RSAC training is focused on cross-country competitions as a means of strengthening the body with the aim of enhancing its performance in the more rationalized space of the running track in the late spring and summer. The first phase of training allows the runner's body to build up its capacity to run large mileage, starting with approximately 40 miles per week and increasing this by 10 percent each week until the runner is covering over 70 miles per week. The overall aim is to enhance the body's endurance capabilities as the mileage is increased each week. With this increase, the runner is advised to undertake 70 percent of his running "off road," in the semi-unrationalized spaces such as playing fields, canal towpaths, rural footpaths and parkland in and around Runtleborough. Such spaces, with their typically "softer" and gently undulating surfaces of grass, mud, and wood chips afford impromptu massage of his calf muscles that can become over tight with much running on hard tarmac surfaces. Every other day the runner will run a route that incorporates some hills, in and around a local park, where he will add effort on the uphill portion of the run, an exercise that helps build strength in his leg enhancing muscular consciousness.

There are two key training sessions a week in the second phase of the period which coincides with the cross-country season and runs from November to the end of March. Initially these key training sessions are "unstructured." The first session is a tempo run over approximately six and a half miles, run continuously at a steady pace that the runner can sustain for the distance on hard surfaces such as roads and pavements around the town. The run takes place on a Tuesday evening as part of the athletic club's training night. In each week of the initial month of training, the runner slightly increases the intensity of effort. The second session, in the early stages of this period, is a "fartlek" or speed play, run over rolling terrain off-road. This session is designed to allow the athlete to run "as he feels" while also increasing his strength and endurance capabilities through the presence of the inclines. The off-road location of this run means that it is typically undertaken on a Saturday morning, when the light is good: the temporality of this component affords the athlete to run in areas that are not illuminated with artificial light. In and around Runtleborough, this element of training often takes place in a woodland site, "Coronation Woods," a semi-natural woodland on a small ridge to the south-west of the town. The woods themselves afford a rolling dirt track (which winds its way through the trees) around their perimeter (approximately three kilometers) that is soft under foot. It is covered with bark chips in places and wooden planks in others, where the path is susceptible to being water-logged. It contrasts with the hard surfaces of the town's roads.

Some of the routes the athlete follows on his numerous weekly runs (up to a dozen per week for a seasoned athlete) will have been passed down to him by more senior members of his club. Other routes he will have established himself through trial and error. Local maps are also used to plan training runs. In addition to the numerous pavements within the town itself, these runs can incorporate the Country Park and Coronation Woods as well as smaller town parks, playing fields, footpaths on field edges, and canal towpaths. Over time some routes may become very well-known through use and reuse by the runner and may be given particular names such as "The French Loop."

Phase three in the clubs training lasts for approximately eight weeks and involves structured repetitions[2] on well-groomed and relatively flat playing fields on a Tuesday evening. This location affords better visibility for the runner at a time in the year when the days are short. It is also easier for the coaches to police the training. The grass surfaces of the playing fields afford the runner's legs a break from the unevenness and undulation of less managed terrain. These sessions are used to improve speed endurance. The Saturday morning session in this phase comprises structured hill repetitions[3] with each repetition emphasizing relaxed efficient running where the descent is as important as the ascent. On the ascent, the aim is for the hill to "do the work"; staying loose in the shoulders, relaxed, and at full stride (if a runner "works" up the hill his stride will be "chopped"). Saturday cross-country competitions, when scheduled, replace the hill session. These are run as if they were tempo runs with the focus upon building the body's ability to provide itself with oxygen while under stressful conditions. The cross-country races typically take place on various forms of publicly owned parkland (and not, therefore, "country" in a conventional sense) where the courses are undulating and have uneven surfaces, which can get boggy during the winter months. This uncertain footing helps to strengthen the runner's body. The courses are temporarily established for the races through the use of removable barriers. Some of these courses will be within the same space, year on year (although this will have changed often in an unnoticeable way), allowing the runner to become familiar with contours, routes, and muddy patches of the course.

The fortnight at the end of the calendar year is a period of consolidation in the runner's training schedule. The intensity of training does not increase but is maintained to allow the runner's body to recover and regenerate in preparation for the next serious phase. The second week of the new year marks the beginning of the fourth phase in training: a 12-week cycle that is distinctive from the previous three cycles. It has a series of four micro-cycles, each of which entails three weeks of activity where the training becomes progressively more intense, followed by one week with less intense work-load. Each micro-cycle is established to allow the runner to recuperate from the more intense training of this

12-week period. By this stage, weekly mileage should now be at its maximum: each week incorporates three key sessions, each of which is designed to have different "training effects" and each takes place in different spaces. An interval training session takes place either on a tarmac hill in Runtleborough town or on the running track. It is designed to tax the body and to increase the body's ability to supply itself with oxygen at intense levels of activity (stress the body's aerobic capacity). The adaptation of the body occurs during the breaks in training effort. A tempo run, the week's second session, takes place either on parkland or on the pavements around the town depending on the time of year. During the late winter and early spring there may not be enough light to make use of off-road running environments in the early morning and evening. The third session in this phase is specific cross-country preparation conducted on some of Runtleborough's playing fields and the grassy slopes around their perimeter, an environment within the taskscape that has been regularly used for local cross-country races. Importantly, the perimeter slopes are not as well groomed as the fields used for the Tuesday sessions prior to the end of the previous calendar year and as such, afford a different kind of running. The runner is forced to exaggerate his cadence by lifting his feet. Such positive stressing the calf muscles will benefit him when he returns to the more rationalized space of the track in late spring. The fourth week of the micro-cycle is to provide each runner with a small opportunity for bodily regeneration (but not a complete rest) by incorporating two sessions. The first of these is a 30-minute fartlek run within the urban environment of the town and the second is a 2,000 m time trial over the fields used on the Saturday sessions. This allows the runner and his coach to obtain an understanding of his relative fitness as he progresses through this 12-week period of training. The time trial takes place on playing fields rather than on tarmac because it is oriented to the typical environment of cross-country competition, the same environment as the competitive spaces during this training period.

In the springtime, around April/May, RSAC groups normally train away from home to begin the next phase of training. A popular destination for middle- and long-distance runners are spaces with favorable weather after the runners have all toughed up in the damp and cold English winter. These might include beach resort of Portugal or Spain at sea level or high altitude location in the French Pyrenees or Boulder Colorado. High altitude environments afford reduced oxygen. After acclimatization the athlete who trains in these conditions is believed to develop improved cardiovascular efficiency shortly after his return to sea level or much lower altitudes. Aside from the physiological advantages that are believed to accrue from training in these environments, training camps of this kind enable the athlete to focus exclusively on training as he is removed from his daily routines. The camps are by no means a holiday or respite from training. Furthermore, it is believed that they freshen and invigorate the athlete's running spirit by giving him a "break" from his usual training environments.

Training in the fifth phase of the cycle (8–10 weeks) begins while away at altitude or warm weather training. The mileage that was maintained through the winter is reduced by about 15 percent as the intensity of the three important weekly training sessions is increased. Because the focus has shifted towards the competitive track season, two of the three sessions in this period are conducted in the more rationalized space of the athletics track. The third of the key sessions at this time of year uses two distinctive spaces. The first entails running a series of hill repetitions on three hard surfaces at a point with a short jog from the RSAC track. The steepest of the hills is relatively short. It is run at the fastest pace so when the hills get longer and shallower the intensity is decreased.[4] *The second utilizes the closely trimmed grass surfaces of a playing field to provide respite from the rationalized track space but also the use of spiked training shoes that can cause over-use injuries in the lower leg. The runs in between each training session are less intense than previously and undertaken mainly on grassy undulating surfaces surrounding agricultural fields, parkland environments, and some woodland trails within and immediately surrounding Runtleborough. Often the Saturday session is replaced by an early season race: a "conditioning event" that prepares the body for the rigors of competition.*

The summer period represents the zenith of year. Like the other phases preceding it, it entails particular combinations of environments as highlighted above. On average the runner's mileage decreases and at times, there is only one weekly training session because of a race in the same week.[5] *It is accepted that the embodied habitus established during the winter and spring training carries the athlete through this phase. The need to rest between intense efforts associated with competition is paramount. Training sessions are often not completed, particularly in the lead up to national championships where two or three races may occur on subsequent days. Travel to races that are at a distance means that some of the running is done simply to keep the body at peak fitness. Uneven surfaces, sought out and celebrated at other times in the training cycle, are avoided to prevent twists to the ankle and Achilles tendon. Rationalized spaces take on a greater significance at this time on two levels. First, there are the athletics track of the competitive environment and second, the ideally closely cropped and regularly managed playing fields of the training environment that are likely to be more "forgiving" underfoot than tarmac.*

The taskscape of RSAC

The training that the runner above has undergone forms a single periodized (Coe, 1996) season during which his body has developed through the discipline and habit of training in the various environments of the running taskscape. This taskscape afforded distinct opportunities for the making of the elite running body. Regardless of the success or failure of the season the runner will take as much as four weeks of active recovery not only to give his body a rest but also to re-evaluate the successes and failures of the whole season with their coach. This period of reflection is required to determine what training habits need to become more embodied, be they focused on strength, endurance, or speed, within the next phase of training season. But how do we make sense of the training year?

Sticking to the task at hand requires a great deal of physical effort on the part of the athlete (and the investment of time by the coach). The task, to follow Ingold (2000), of co-producing a high performance running bodies is the act of the coach in harmony with his athlete. Ingold uses the term "task" to help describe the practices of work and defines it as "any practical operation carried out by a skilled agent in an environment, as part of his or her normal business of life. In other words, tasks are the constitutive acts of dwelling" (Ingold, 2000, p. 195). He defines the "taskscape" as follows:

> [I]t is to the entire ensemble of tasks, in their mutual interlocking, that I refer by the concept of taskscape. Just as the landscape is an array of related features, so—by analogy—the taskscape is an array of related activities.
>
> (Ingold, 2000, p. 195)

Ingold's understanding of task has been influenced by Merleau-Ponty (1962) and Bourdieu (1977, 1984, 1990a, 1990b) and as such, I believe, is particularly important in understanding high performance running bodies. An understanding of a running taskscape (Howe & Morris, 2009) at RSAC nicely articulates how we can we can make sense of high performance running in various environmental contexts. For example, a hill used for repetition running enters our "muscular consciousness" and at the same time movement becomes "embodied" "on the side of the landscape, in its network of paths and tracks. In this network is sedimented the activity of an entire community [runners and non-runners alike], over many generations. It is the taskscape made visible" (Ingold, 2000, p. 204). As a result of this contemplation, the taskscape may be altered very subtly within the subsequent training period as the emphasis on developing particular bodily characteristics may lead to certain sites, and their associated affordances, being sought out and utilized more than others.

As I described earlier, the training of high performance running bodies in the taskscape of middle- and long-distance running often unfolds over a period of training that is organized into six phases over the course of one calendar year. This format has been chosen because a period of training is broken into numerous phases that allow for the strengthening of embodied habit (Crossley, 2001; Leder, 1990; Shilling, 2005). Although a period of training may be as long as a year, some athletes might have several periods of training in one year as they may have more than one important competition on which to focus. The ability of the athlete and their coach to reach optimal performance several times in a season is referred to as periodization (Coe, 1996). During a period of training a runner utilizes all manner of environments (typically in association with advice from a coach) to work towards a peak performance (Howe & Morris, 2009).

Since the arrival of the Guru at RSAC, the work that the running body performs in the variety of environments within the taskscape enables transformation within any given year. Nature is not simply "there" to be uncovered or discovered (Castree, 2001, 2005) by the runner but actively emerges in a variety of forms through the habits, routines, and practices associated with the work of producing the high performance running body. As a result, a runner's favorite routes may eventually be passed on to other members of the club as the process repeats itself. Ingold (2000) refers to this "wayfinding" as the "life historical process of 'getting around'" (p. 232). It is a process that is distinct from map using and "more closely resembles story telling" (p. 219). It entails intimate knowledge of an environment that emerges through dwelling in and the building of a distinctive taskscape. The presence of the Guru in Runtleborogh for over 40 years has shaped the taskscape as has his mentoring of various coaches. These coaches in turn help to transform the taskscape in a manner that fits the purpose of RSAC.

Training mortal engines

To fully understand the blend of art and science of coaching associated with elite middle-distance running at RSAC, it is central to understand the concept of embodiment. Kimayer (2003) explains:

> The anthropological use of the metaphor of embodiment serves to maintain a place for the richness of bodily experience and significance of bodies as agents and areas of action. Embodiment works against the tendency to treat bodies simply as property (my body and yours) or as vehicles entirely subordinate to our will. The essential insight of embodiment is that the body has a life of its own and that social worlds become inscribed on, or sedimented in, body physiology, habitus, and experience.
>
> (p. 285)

From a methodological perspective, embodiment postulates that the body is not an object to be studied in relation to the cultural world but is the subject of culture or the existential ground of culture (Csordas, 2002). I adopt an embodied approach to explore the habits that are imposed upon the elite middle runners under the watchful eyes of the coaching team led by the Guru. Adoption of habitual training of the body can be seen to be central to much of the work that has been done, past and present, examining the body in the social world (Bourdieu, 1977, 1984, 1992; Leder, 1990; Merleau-Ponty, 1962, 1965; Shilling, 2005). The examination of habit illuminates the concept of agency as important to a practical and embodied praxis. In other words, the physical manifestation of culture through embodied action is fundamental to exploring the importance of the body in the context of training regimes within the sport of middle and long-distance running as practiced in Runtleborough (Howe & Morris, 2009).

Physical action that becomes embodied in certain situations may be seen as habitual. These acts are often drilled into runners through countless repetitions that lack imagination. Although Foucault might consider such training as disciplining the runners into docile bodies (Foucault, 1979; Markula & Pringle, 2006), I perceive running in between these directed training sessions as the habitual glue that holds the training program together. In this sense, I see

Bourdieu's concept of *habitus* related to Foucault's concept of discipline. From Bourdieusian viewpoint, habitus is a result of the social environment where it is learned: "the body is used (walks, carries itself) differently by different social groups, and sport is one of the most important ways that the body's *habitus* is learned" (Blake, 1996, p. 23).

Habitual acts that are further developed by improvisation can be considered dispositions (Ryle, 1949). A disposition is an underlying tendency or propensity to act in a certain way and is therefore more flexible than the habits that result from the learning of rudimental drills. Thus, the purpose of the running drills is to eventually develop an effective, unconscious running disposition. According to the Guru:

> When our athletes engage in running drills we are in essence trying to get them to relearn their bodies. Trying to get them to forget the bad elements of their distinctive running technique and to some degree get them all to run in the same efficient and fluent manner. Would it not be ideal if all your runners were as efficient as [Seb] Coe?

The use of running drills and weight training act as supplements to running training of a high performance runner (Gilmour, 1962; Lydiard & Gilmour, 1962; Martin & Coe, 1991) and these physical acts can go some way to re-setting the unconscious nature of dispositions. As one athlete suggests:

> Looking back at videos of how my body moved (while racing) when I started at RSAC it is a wonder I could run reasonable well at all. My body was all over the shop. My movement is so much more efficient and I put this down to not the fact that I am much fitter than I was three years ago but that over an extended period of time I have at times used weight and body mass training as well as dynamic running drills which allows me to maintain my form while running at pace for longer.

The disposition is the embodied ability to put the habitual training together in such a way that it can be quickly adapted to any situation. Our disposition suggests that we are likely to act in a certain way in a particular social situation. This distinction between habit and disposition usefully explores the notion of human intervention in the sporting environment. When an athlete goes through the training regime required of an elite middle-distance runner his or her body habitually knows what the "race-pace" is simply by the "feel" of the body. There is no need to rely upon a stopwatch (or GPS device) when running off a premeasure surface like a track. The ability to respond to changes that occur within a race in terms of the tactics of the other competitors is directly linked to the disposition or the ability to improvise that the athlete innately has developed through physical training and lived experiences more generally.

Merleau-Ponty's (1962) conceptualization of corporeal schema can help determine how middle and long-distance runners (and other actors) make the decisions without really thinking about them. When athletes make strategic moves in a race, they do not have to think about running or accelerating. In a sense, they "know without knowing." According to Crossley (2001), "the corporeal schema is an incorporated bodily know-how and practical sense; a perspectival grasp upon the world from the 'point of view' of the body" (p. 123). Corporeal schema, therefore, and the embodied knowledge that it entails, need to be excavated in order to establish how the coaches were able to train their athletes to perform at the highest level. This concept nicely articulates the embodied agency of a runner both as an individual and as a member of the RSAC training squad. The corporeal schema comprises the skills required for the performance and the practical understanding of the race that may be transformed depending on the action of other runners. A good runner reads a race without thinking. In other words, they explore the relationship between different levels of structure that constrict movement at a subconscious level. Commenting on the work of Merleau-Ponty, Crossley (2001) suggests:

> Habit involves a modification and enlargement of the corporeal schema, an incorporation of new "principles" of action and know-how, which permit new ways of acting and understanding. It is a sediment of past activity which remains alive in the present in the form of the structures of corporeal schema; shaping perception, conception, deliberation, emotion and action.
>
> (p. 125)

The emphasis on innovation (Merleau-Ponty, 1965) gives the runner the raw material to turn into habit. Merleau-Ponty (1965) conceptualizes improvisation as fundamental to an individual's disposition. In this research, elite middle-distance runners, although manipulated by the coaches to engage in repetitive training, also bent rules "to improvise." This improvisation is most noticeable in the context of racing. The coach and athlete plan racing strategies that play to the strength of the athlete but however meticulous the plan, there is always allowance for improvisation. While each athlete will go into a race with a plan, the winner tends to be the one who has the ability to improvise in the actual race. Over time these improvisations can become habitual and may be seen as a product of creative praxis result in a diachronic shift in the social world.

The running disposition, or more general forms of social competence, however, may be seen as a product of well-established social environment of the club. For example, Stampfl (1955) may have been describing disposition below:

> Training is principally an act of faith. The athlete must believe in its efficacy; he must believe that through training he will become fitter and stronger; that by constant repetition of the same movements he will become more skilful and his muscles more relaxed. He must believe that through training his performance will improve and continue to improve indefinitely for as long as he continues to train to progressively stiffer standard. He must be a fanatic for hard work and enthusiastic enough to enjoy it.
>
> (p. 37)

This is a philosophy that resonates with the culture of developing the disposition of elite runners at RSAC. For Bourdieu (1984), an athlete's habitus is the embodied sediment of every encounter they have had with the social world. It can be used to mould perception, thought, and action to play an important role in decisions that an athlete might make in future encounters.

Although not articulated this way by the Guru, it is safe to say that every action of a runner embodies a structure and logic that is distinctive to the habitus of elite distance runners. As such, the works of Merleau-Ponty (1965) and Bourdieu (1984, 1988, 1993) are useful allies. For Bourdieu, actors do not simply follow rules but also bend them in much the same way as Merleau-Ponty envisions improvisation as being fundamental to an individual's disposition. In other words, while society may be seen as shaping agents, individuals improvisation, routed in dispositions, impacts society and its power relations. Guru's own "improvisations" created a distinct social environment for the entire club. For example, one well-known international runner commented on the Guru's influence:

> [The Guru] is the coach and driving force behind the university athletics and cross-country squads. He has been the man responsible for making the [RSAC] teams the "Liverpool" of student sport. In recent years there have been innumerable student sport victories making [Runtleborough] the most respected, and in some quarters the most reviled, athletic university in the country.
>
> (Buckner, 1989, p. 44)

In other words, the Guru, through shaping the taskscape and the culture of RSAC, has been instrumental in creating a club habitus.

Therefore, in the world of middle-distance training, it is as important to see the body as much a product of the self, as it is of society. The self improvises by drawing upon the sediment of previous social encounters. This is evident when a sporting contest is observed. While the event is run within a set of rules (any transgressors ideally are penalized) a sporting performance is full of improvisation. Some sports are more dependent than others on improvisation. In middle-distance running, improvisation entails a change in racing strategy. The ability to improvise is an important quality to embrace when an athlete is being educated in the embodied habits of an elite middle-distance runner. Abrahams, already in the early 1950s, suggested that, "training is that process of education of the body which prepares it to meet with safety exceptional and extreme demands upon its energy" (Abrahams, 1952, p. 25).

Summary

Training methods for elite high performance athletes have not changed too much over the last 40 years at RSAC. Technology has improved to the point where some athletes—shall we say the GPS generation—struggle to tell whether they are running hard without looking at their watches. While technological developments have improved performances, the basic skills required to run fast have not changed. Increasingly the coaching staff at RSAC needs to re-train new recruits to understand their bodies in a more primal way. The Guru maintains that: "Progress year on year comes not simply from new technologies and ideas but from embracing of what the body can do and having the passion and persistence to teaching it what it currently can't do!" It is this simple philosophy of giving runners the physical literacy that has shaped the distinctive taskscape of RSAC. It continues to make the program successful and allows a wide variety of runners to hit their own purple patch on a regular basis.

Notes

1 Runtlebourough is a pseudonym for a market town in middle England that has been used in previous work (see Howe & Morris, 2009).
2 Sessions may be structured as follows: five minutes of effort followed by a 90-second break, repeated five times; or two minutes of effort, followed by a 60-second break, repeated ten times, or one minute of effort followed by a 60-second break 20 times. The rests are kept short enough to allow the runner's body to recover enough to complete the session without over-stressing it. In essence the rest period is directly related to the intensity of the effort.
3 A hill of approximately 1,000 m in length within the Country Park affords a 30-degree climb. The training phase begins with three repeats and gradually builds towards six repeats during the eight-week period, enabling runners to improve their strength.
4 This is then followed by two times 400 m at his 1,500 m pace. The reason for doing this is that the exertions on various hills tire the body but do not drain it completely and so the athlete is able to step on the track and perform better than expected over the 400 m distance. This session is an indication to Richard that the perception of fatigue can be an issue of mind over matter.
5 This session may be short sprints of 100–300 m in length with long, almost full recoveries between efforts.

References

Abrahams, A. (1952) *Fitness for the average man.* London, England: Christopher Johnson.

Abram, D. (1996) *The spell of the sensuous: Perception and language in a more-than-human world.* New York, NY: Vintage Books.

Bale, J. (2003). *Sports geography* (2nd Ed.). London, England: Routledge.

Bale, J. (2004). *Running cultures.* London, England: Routledge.

Bale, J., & Sang, J. (1996). *Kenyan running: Movement culture, geography and global change.* London, England: Frank Cass.

Blake, A. (1996). *The body language: The meaning of modern sport.* London, England: Lawrence & Wishart.

Bourdieu, P. (1977). *Outline of a theory of practice.* Cambridge, England: Cambridge University Press.

Bourdieu, P. (1984). *Distinction: A social critique of the judgement of taste.* London, England: Routledge.

Bourdieu, P. (1990a). *The logic of practice.* Cambridge, England: Polity Press.

Bourdieu, P. (1990b). *In other words: Essays towards a reflective sociology*. Cambridge, England: Polity Press.

Bourdieu, P. (1993). *Sociology in question*. Cambridge, England: Polity Press.

Bruce, T. (1998). Postmodernism and the possibilities for writing "vital" sports text. In G. Rail (Ed.), *Sport and postmodern times* (pp. 3–20). Albany, NY: SUNY Press.

Buckner, J. (1989). *Running the distance: An athlete's year*. London, England: Heinemann Kingwood.

Castree, N. (2001). Socializing nature: Theory, practice and politics. In N. Castree, & B. Braun (Eds.), *Social nature: Theory, practice and politics* (pp. 1–21). Oxford, England: Blackwell.

Castree, N. (2005). *Nature*. London, England: Routledge.

Clifford, J. (1986). Introduction: Partial Truths. In J. Clifford & G. E. Marcus (Eds.), *Writing culture: The Politics of politics of ethnography* (pp. 1–26). Berkeley, CA: University of California Press.

Coe, P. (1996). *Winning running: Successful 800m and 1500m racing and training*. Marlborough Wiltshire, United Kingdom: Crowood Press.

Crossley, N. (2001). *The social body: Habit, identity and desire*. London, England: Sage.

Csordas, T. (2002). *Body/meaning/healing*. New York, NY: Palgrave Macmillan.

Daniels, J. (2005). *Daniels' running formula: Proven programs 800m to marathon* (2nd Ed.). Leeds, United Kingdom: Human Kinetics.

Foucault, M. (1988). *Technologies of the self*. In L. H. Martin, H. Gutman, & P. Hutton, (Eds.), *Technologies of the self: A seminar with Michel Foucault* (pp. 16–49). Amherst, MA: University of Massachusetts Press.

Gilmour, G. (1962). *A clean pair of heals: The Murray Halberg story*. Auckland: Reed.

Hammersley, M., & Atkinson, P. (2007). *Ethnography: Principles in practice* (3rd ed.). London, England: Routledge.

Hannigan, J. (2006). *Environmental sociology* (2nd ed.). London, England: Routledge.

Howe, P. D. (2011). Sporting bodies: Sensuous, lived, and impaired. In F. E. Mascia-Lees (Ed.), *Companion to the anthropology of bodies/embodiment* (pp. 102–116). Oxford, England: Wiley-Blackwell.

Howe, P. D., & Morris, C. (2009). An exploration of the co-production of performance running bodies and natures within "running taskscapes." *Journal of Sport and Social Issues, 33*, 308–330.

Ingold, T. (1997). Life beyond the edge of nature? Or the mirage of society. In J. Greenwood (Ed.), *The Mark of the social* (pp. 231–252). London, England: Rowman and Littlefield.

Ingold, T. (2000). *The perception of the environment: Essays on livelihood, dwelling and skill*. London, England: Routledge.

Kirmayer, L. J. (2003). Reflections on embodiment. In J. M. Wilce Jr. (Ed.), *Social and cultural lives of immune systems* (pp. 282–302). London, England: Routledge.

Klein, A. (1993). *Little big men: Bodybuilding subculture and gender construction*. New York, NY: SUNY.

Latour, B. (1993). *We have never been modern*. Hemel Hempstead, United Kingdom: Harvester/Wheatsheaf.

Lear, C. (2003). *Running with the buffaloes*. Guildford, CT: Lyons Press.

Leder, D. (1990). *The absent body*. London, England: University of Chicago Press.

Lewis, N. (2000). The climbing body, nature and the experience of modernity. *Body and Society, 6*, 58–80.

Lydiard, A., & Gilmour, G. (1962). *Run to the top*. Auckland, New Zealand: Reed.

MacNaughton, P., & Urry, J. (2001). Bodies of nature: Introduction. In P. MacNaughton, & J. Urry (Eds.), *Bodies of nature* (pp. 1–11). London, England: Sage.

Markula, P., & Pringle, R. (2006). *Foucault, sport and exercise: Power, knowledge and transforming the self.* London, England: Routledge.

Martin, D. M., &.Coe, P. (1991). *Training distance runners: The art and science of optimal Training.* Leeds, United Kingdom: Human Kinetics.

Merleau-Ponty, M. (1962). *Phenomenology of perception.* London, England: Routledge and Kegan Paul.

Merleau-Ponty, M. (1965). *The structure of behaviour.* London, England: Methuen.

Rabinow, P. (1986). Representations are social facts: Modernity and post-modernity in anthropology. In J. Clifford, & G. E. Marcus (Eds.), *Writing culture: The Politics of politics of ethnography* (pp. 234–261). Berkeley, CA: University of California Press.

Runciman, W. G. (1978). *Weber: Selections in translation.* Cambridge, England: Cambridge University Press.

Ryle, G. (1949). *The concept of mind.* London, England: University of Chicago Press.

Shilling, C. (2005). *The body in culture, technology and society.* London, England: Sage.

Snell, P., & Gilmour, G. (1965). *No bugles no drums.* Auckland, New Zealand: Minerva.

Stampfl, F. (1955). *On running.* London, England: Herbert Jenkins.

Turnbull, S. (1982). *Steve Ovett: Portrait of an athlete.* London, England: Star Books.

Williams, S. J., & Bendelow, G. (1998). *The lived body: Sociological themes, embodied issues.* London, England: Routledge.

15 Digging in

The sociological phenomenology of "doing endurance" in distance-running

John Hockey and Jacquelyn Allen-Collinson

In this chapter we draw on a theoretical and methodological approach to the study of endurance and the lived distance-running body: sociological phenomenology, which to date has been relatively under-utilized in sports studies generally. Given the highly embodied nature of endurance running as lived experience, the phenomenological quest to uncover and explore the essential structures of embodied experience seems highly applicable. Here, for those unfamiliar with its tenets, we introduce a "sociologized" variant of the phenomenological approach and situate our own research within the context of a literature we have been developing on the sociological phenomenology of distance running (Allen-Collinson, 2009; Allen-Collinson & Hockey, 2011, 2013; Hockey, 2005; Hockey & Allen-Collinson, 2007). We then describe the autoethnographic and autophenomenographic project on distance-running, from which our data derive. The project's findings are subsequently theorised, drawing upon insights from sociological phenomenology, and phenomenologically-inspired work, such as that of Leder (1990). Leder's (1990) notion of corporeal "dys-ease" is particularly apposite in exploring "doing endurance" in distance running, where the body is at times brought acutely and forcibly to the forefront of consciousness in training and racing, during experiences of "intense embodiment" (Allen-Collinson & Owton, 2015). Enduring, as a particular mode of being-in-the-world is not just an individual phenomenon, but is shared by and communicated between distance runners, constituting an interactional subcultural practice.

Sociological phenomenology and the lived sporting body

Modern-day phenomenology developed from the philosophical work of Husserl (1900/1901, 2001), and provides an umbrella term for a diverse set of theoretical and methodological frameworks (Allen-Collinson, 2009). Derived from the Greek *phainomenon*, phenomenology is the study of phenomena—things as they appear to our consciousness. Husserl sought to address the "things themselves" (*den Sachen selbst*), devoid from presuppositions and preconceptions regarding these things. He thus advocated utilizing the phenomenological method in an attempt to suspend or bracket (via the technique of *epochē*) the "natural attitude," that is our everyday, taken-for-granted assumptions and presuppositions about a phenomenon. Phenomenology and sociology thus share common ground in seeking to challenge the taken-for-grantedness of everyday life and to uncover the assumptions and presuppositions that often go unacknowledged and un/under-analyzed. Of further note is phenomenology's interest in lived experience (*Erlebnis*), and the "lived body" (*Leib*) that is, the experiential ground of the body as subjectively lived in everyday life. This stands in contrast to the "object body" (*Körper*), the objectified and reified body often construed in much of sports science. In phenomenological thinking, mind, body, and world are fundamentally interconnected and intertwined; a relationship exemplified post Husserl in the work of Merleau-Ponty (2001) and his focus upon embodied habitual action.

With regard to the sociology-phenomenology nexus, phenomenology was adopted and applied within North American sociology by Schütz (1967) whose sociological imagination was particularly captured by the concept of the everyday lifeworld (*Lebenswelt*). Combining elements of Husserlian thought with a Weberian focus upon *Verstehen* and social action, Schütz (1967) emphasized the need to address social actors' lifeworlds as embedded within social structure and cultural milieux. As we have previously argued (Allen-Collinson & Hockey, 2011), adopting a more "sociologized" form of phenomenology encourages researchers to acknowledge the "structurally, politically and ideologically-influenced, historically-specific, and socially situated nature of human embodiment and experience" (p. 332). This responds directly to criticisms of phenomenology as positing some kind of universalist vision of human beings, devoid of social-structural influence.

Bringing a sociological lens to bear on insights drawn from phenomenology, we argue, allows us to analyze the considerable impact of social-structural forces upon our lived sporting experience. Utilizing phenomenology's insistence on questioning and problematizing the taken-for-granted world of everyday, Garfinkel (2002) created ethnomethodology, the study of the ways in which social actors go about "doing" everyday life. "Doing sport" has only relatively recently been analysed at the phenomenological level but promisingly there is now a small but developing literature (see Allen-Collinson & Owton, 2015; Hockey & Allen Collinson, 2007; Sparkes, 2009). We now proceed to consider distance running specifically, and how endurance constitutes a fundamental state of mind and of general *Dasein* or "being-in-the-world," for those of us who "do distance running."

Digging in: endurance and the embodied mind

A substantial sports science literature examines distance-running endurance from a physiological and biomechanical stance, much of which has found its way into "how to" training guides for runners (e.g., Fallowfield & Wilkinson, 1999). There is also psychological literature on "mental toughness" in endurance sports, such as long-distance walking (Crust, Keegan, Piggott, & Swann, 2011). Of direct interest to the phenomenological concern of this chapter is sociological/anthropological work on enduring pain as a subcultural practice in extreme and/or endurance sports (e.g. Atkinson, 2008; Reischer, 2001), a practice that valorizes stoicism in the sporting embodied mind. Stoicism can be defined as the exercising of endurance in the face of adversity (Moore, Grime, Campbell, & Richardson, 2012). Within the distance running subculture, the desire and ability to endure, to keep running in the face of fatigue and pain, as Reischer (2001) notes, is often juxtaposed with the practice of "dropping out" of races where the individual ends up in the category of DNF (Did Not Finish)—a stigmatized categorization, unless there are substantive extenuating circumstances. "Doing endurance" is thus highly valorized by the distance-running community.

Racing distances *seriously* (and certainly not "for fun") to completion, let alone to achieve targeted times, demands huge volumes of training at a certain intensity of pace. This endeavor results in physiological changes that develop physical endurance, whilst simultaneously a certain kind of embodied mind develops, in which the capacity to endure becomes a central feature that also validates athletic identity. The practice of enduring is encapsulated in United Kingdom subcultural argot by the phrase "digging in." The phrase is arguably of military origin, given that "digging in" is a practice undertaken by troops when facing enemy threat, using entrenching tools to dig into the ground and construct defensive positions. In a distance-running context, "digging in" means setting one's "enduring consciousness" (i.e., an enduring frame of mind) to defend the athlete from her/his own frailties in the face of fatigue, discomfort, pain, and a gamut of geographic and climatic stressors. Distance runners exhibit "habituated action" (Merleau-Ponty, 2001), which is mindful, not just in terms of its cyclical activities of respiration and leg cadence which demand intentionality, no matter how routine, but also in terms of the motive power to sustain those activities. So, whilst physiological and muscular-skeletal endurance is built through physical training, so also is a kind of stoic consciousness, which learns to endure the rigors of training (and racing). This stoicism of consciousness is never total or complete, however, in the sense that vulnerability is always liable to emerge, as one inevitably has "bad days" in both training and racing. What emerges is then a provisional, contingent confidence, based on an ongoing assessment of one's fitness levels and what has been endured before. Confidence—or the lack of it—is also proportionate to the specific terrain and conditions. For example, the first author was an experienced cross country and road running athlete, but the first time he undertook an 18-mile group training run over the North West English fells (upland hills) on a lowering, winter Sunday morning, the self-asked question was: "can I finish this session with this bunch of fell rats?"

When training/racing is experienced as optimal, there is a *relative ease* to movement. This is often characterized by runners, both to themselves and to running-peers, in the phrase "going well." That categorization is established by an ongoing sensory monitoring, with a main focus on the lower legs and respiratory system. So when "going well," the runner's breathing will be rhythmic, muscles relatively pliable, tendons responsive, movement light, tempo tolerable, and posture aligned. At the other extreme are runs in which the running-body protests the effort of enduring from the very first stride to the last. Not a pleasant mode of being. There are also those in-between sessions that combine what athletes often term "little good patches" and "little bad patches" in which the mind's bodily focus fluctuates in intensity, depending upon how much or how little the body "complains" or "dys-appears" (Leder, 1990) to the mind. The greater the degree of running-ease, the more the body "disappears" (Leder, 1990) from the forefront of running-mind, receding into a background presence. In contrast, when the body "dys-appears," as a result of pain, fatigue, and so on, it is encountered as "that which stands in the way, an obstinate force interfering with our projects" (Leder, 1990, p. 84). The relativity of "disappearance" should, however, be emphasized. Corporeal awareness is actually perpetual, and any diminishing of corporeal awareness is a matter of degree and duration. Runners thus develop a particular "somatic mode of attention" (Csordas, 1993, p. 148) which is perpetually focused on how they are managing to endure. Via the variety of types of runs (Hockey, 2013) the "enduring body" as a "project" is "worked at and accomplished" (Shilling, 2003, pp. 4–5) resulting in the building of a stoic, athletic self-identity.

The empirical research

In this section, we portray the two-year research project, from which our findings are drawn. Before describing this collaborative autoethnography/autophenomenography of distance running, we first provide some running-biographical information so as to situate ourselves as researchers and to explain the basis of our "insider" perspectives on the distance-running subculture. Both of us have been involved in that United Kingdom subculture for decades, currently the first author for 47 years and the second for 29 years, sustaining a commitment to training six to seven days a week, with racing experience ranging from five miles to marathons. We now both occupy "veteran" status under the United Kingdom athletic classification system. To date both of us remain highly committed, "serious" runners, who: "regularly (run) further and faster than fitness for health would demand" (Smith, 2000, p. 190). Furthermore, our running coheres with two of Bale's (2004) forms; these are: (1) welfare running, pursued for health and fitness aims; and, (2) performance running, pursued in order to improve and sustain performance (although perhaps unsurprisingly at our "advanced" age, "performance" is not what it once was!). Our training for running is commensurate with Bale's (2004) conceptualization of running as *work* rather than leisure, for although it is not professional work, it nevertheless demands highly disciplined, regular, and routinized engagement. In this regard, Howe and Morris (2009) describe the running "taskscape," which requires disciplined and routinized activity, and is typically experienced in a somewhat functional manner as a means of *producing* a running body. This, then, is the running-biographical information, which provides the backdrop to the study.

The research was primarily a collaborative autoethnographic project, which also incorporated strong autophenomenographic elements. Whilst autoethnography is now a widely accepted and utilized research methodology within the social sciences, for those unfamiliar with autophenomenography, this is similarly an autobiographical genre, but where the researcher focuses on her/his lived experience of a phenomenon or phenomena, rather than on a particular *ethnós* or cultural group (for a discussion of autophenomenography, see Allen-Collinson, 2011b), although inevitably there will be some overlap, given that embodiment is experienced through culture. The autophenomenographic researcher thus subjects her/his own lived experience to sustained and rigorous forms of phenomenological analysis. We initiated the collaborative research, when, having run together for many years, by coincidence some years ago we both sustained relatively severe knee injuries. We subsequently decided systematically to document our engagement with the injury and rehabilitation process, which we did for two years. As part of our data collection, we each constructed our own individual "injury logs" (John Log 1; Jacquelyn Log 2), and a third "reflective log" was used to analyse the research process itself. In this third log, we interrogated, reflected upon and synthesized our emergent data themes. Our relatively extended careers in running help address Garfinkel's (2002: 175) phenomenologically-derived "unique adequacy requirement" for the researcher to "be *vulgarly* competent to the local production and reflexively natural accountability of the phenomenon or order he *[sic]* is 'studying'" (p. 175). In other words, we were competent at "doing running" and "doing endurance."

The phenomenology of endurance

We now proceed to portray the phenomenology of endurance, and for heuristic purposes have separated our data into three sections addressing, respectively: fatigue, pain, and the inside/outside sensory dimension. In our lived experience, however, these elements are strongly intertwined and interwoven.

Fatigue and fire

Ingold (2000) argued that "locomotion not cognition must be the starting point for the study of perceptual activity" (p. 166), and we argue that a fundamental corporeal dimension of athletic experience is the sensory assemblage that is invoked from the very first running stride. For, as Leder (1990) observed, the "body is always a field of immediately lived sensations … (its) presence fleshed out by a ceaseless stream of kinaesthesias, cutaneous and visceral sensations" (p. 23). Learning endurance is a process in which the individual runner internally experiences a particular set of sensations, interprets those sensations so as to make them meaningful and then learns how to deal with them. There are positive sensations, for example feelings of lightness, energy and flow, and sensual pleasures, but overwhelmingly the practice of "digging in" means encountering negative sensations and learning how to cope with these. The most prevalent of these is leg fatigue, in which the legs and particularly the quadriceps muscles begin to tire during the course of a run/race. There is then a sensation of pressure, thickness, hardness, and heaviness, which is often described as "dead quads," there being no "spring" or *élan* in the muscles. The quads feel as though they are almost dragging the runner down and backwards, rather than propelling her/him forward, as the second author describes vis-à-vis one difficult training session:

> Totally duff 8-mile session today. Right from the start the quads like iron bars, dead weight, no push at all in them. Heavy, torpid, rigid. By the third mile I just knew it was not going to get any better, the quads weren't easing at all. On the hills, hip flexors achy too. Everything heavy and "no oomph," just dragged all of myself around the route. No power in the legs whatsoever. Just hope tomorrow a bit of the spring returns.
>
> (Log 2)

Encountering the above kind of fatigue becomes routine for distance runners, particularly if they are running high training mileage preparing for races or doing sessions such as hill repetitions. This sensation then becomes familiar, normalized, and the learnt response moves from a novice's perception that it just is not possible to run with such fatigue, to an experienced perception where runners know they can indeed keep running, perhaps not at the tempo to which they aspire, but nevertheless, they can continue training under the burden of heaviness. Moreover, whilst there are "dead" quads or calves or whatever bodily part feels that dead weight of fatigue, there are also subtle variations of these states that are learnt through much practice. Runners become experienced in and attuned to these variations, assessing them by the nuanced degrees of heaviness they feel. Between the two of us, the shorthand phrase "not so bad" was used to categorize and communicate to each other lesser states of fatigue, where there was a kind of background level of tiredness. These were then contrasted with more difficult states where the term "dead" was used, amongst other epithets. Ultimately runners work with what somatic resources they have at hand, or rather at foot, however depleted these resources may feel:

> We have given the concept of "head down, keep going" when running quite a lot of attention in our individual logs. What we have both agreed on is that it is a process of adjusting to the feeling of fatigue. In a way it is about staying with the feeling of being weighed down by the body and working with the little one has got in the moment. So we work with that sub-optimal source of energy and thus keep going. You learn that you can do that, however much of a struggle it feels in the moment, and that creates confidence and then in the next bad run or race that helps sustain the momentum. You learn you'll get through it, however unlikely it at first seems.
>
> (Log 3)

As runners, we—as do other athletes—develop a memory of "digging in," which is not only cognitive but also somatic, a lived corporeal experience. Phenomenology emphasizes this mind-body nexus, and the development of embodied remembering. Merleau-Ponty (2001), for example, considers the body memory of a typist, who first has consciously to think about how to type. Then as the action of typing becomes habituated, the typist can type spontaneously, almost automatically, without conscious reflection of where s/he should place fingers on keys. Other researchers similarly discuss this bodily memory (e.g., Brown & Jennings, 2013; Fuchs, 2012; Samudra, 2008). For us, it is as if the muscles themselves hold a memory of this tired, fatigued mode of being-in-the-world, and so "know" they will be able to keep going, and get through the session. Whatever the physiological "facts" of such muscle memories, the lived experience is that of deeply engrained memory in the body. Samudra (2008) described analogous feelings in relation to practitioners of martial arts who develop "memory in our body" that can be used almost instinctively. Commensurate with our experience, she also noted the difficulties in putting into words, of translating into writing, these kinds of kinaesthetic experience.

Distance-running training embraces a combination of aerobic and anaerobic work. The former consists of runs at a relatively steady pace for a specific duration/mileage and is designed to produce endurance. The latter is often called "interval work" and is composed of shorter, much more intense "efforts," which generate the capacity to run at speed. Runners evaluate their respiratory performance via the fluency of inhalation and exhalation at any particular juncture. So, breathing might be rapid, and deep during anaerobic work, but if the session is going well there will be a "flow" to one's respiratory pattern; a rhythm of respiration (Goodridge, 1999). Conversely, a lack of flow is signalled when breathing is "ragged" or disjointed. Runners routinely do "auditory work" in an ongoing assessment of their own performance (Allen-Collinson & Owton, 2014; Hockey, 2006). Breathing, however, is not just an auditory phenomenon, especially when moving anaerobically, but is also "felt" proprioceptively in the chest cavity and sometimes an intense burning feeling in the throat and thorax occurs (Allen-Collinson & Owton, 2015). As the first author portrays:

> We have not done any speed work for a long time, being very cautious after our knee problems. This week we started and it has been interesting to say the least. What I felt took me back to the first time I did intervals when I was living in Belgium. I felt if I was going to die! Well this week was like that, bent over after each session, sucking in the air, lungs like napalm has been dropped on them. The only reason one can tolerate this kind of training is that it is limited. One knows that the fire in the chest will stop and there will be respite in the brief recovery phase before the next effort.
>
> (Log 1)

When interrogating our data, our "endurance response" to uncomfortable muscular and respiratory sensations appeared to be located in the capacity of our mutual "enduring consciousness" to tolerate those sensations in the lived moment of inner time, or *durée* (Schütz, 1967). The temporal intervals of toleration differ with the more intense anaerobic work being smaller, and often the end point of this form of endurance-time is perceptible. For example, during such anaerobic sessions, we could espy the top of the slope, the end of the path, the finishing straight of a track, and this end-in-sight assisted our toleration.[1] As the second author noted at the end of one session: "I know I just have to hang on to there!" During aerobic work, which constitutes the principal component of distance-running training, the level of respiratory discomfort is relatively reduced, but the extended duration of effort means muscular fatigue and discomfort increase. Consequently, our consciousness seeks to convince itself that it will tolerate the physiological effort via a stream of sequential moments: up to the top of the next hill, down to the end of the next valley, and so on. When the going gets tough, we might focus visually on the ground as it *emerges* before us. If the terrain is already known, it is known as a series of oncoming sensory markers, each requiring degrees of particular physiological effort which are "remembered" as each marker approaches. Whilst the approaching place(s) are visually comprehended, they are also understood multi-sensorially (Grasseni, 2009):

> Where I run down to the bottom of the route there's a path—flat for a while, through some trees, then a little slope—but it's sharp, very steep for a short distance, before it flattens out at the top. To get to the top I have to drive suddenly with the quads, arms pumping, and lean into it, so as to generate a surge of momentum. I know just what the effort will feel like even before I get there. I mentally prepare just a few seconds before, drawing on some kind of muscle memory already there. Just now and again, my mind wanders elsewhere and that sharp little slope takes me—and the muscle memory—by surprise.
>
> (Log 2)

Moreover, even if the exact terrain is not known, the likelihood is that analogous terrain has been covered before, and that embodied knowledge helps generate confidence that what is emerging before the athlete *can* be run. In these various ways, as Schütz and Luckmann (1973) noted, "the stream of consciousness (of inner duration) intersects with the rhythm of the body" (p. 47) as the space-time of the run is endured.

Pain and persistence

Whilst the athlete's "enduring consciousness" has to deal with fatigue and fire, it also has to confront other physical problems generated by the combination of intensity and volume of training/racing, together with its repetitive nature. Within the running subculture the presence of injury and pain is normalized (Hockey, 2005) as perennial. From the runner's perspective, enduring some kind of "dys-ease" is routine, and the issue is: how much pain and in what form? In the main, serious running injuries are caused by trauma, chronic overuse, or biomechanical problems that eventually hinder or prevent running, and sometimes require medical intervention, knee injuries being a classic case. Far more prevalent, however, are the niggling, annoying, minor problems such as tendon inflamation, pulled or strained muscles, twisted ankles, or back muscles with a tendency to spasm. In effect, if distance runners manage any degree of longevity in their sport, their bodies become actual and symbolic maps, etched with these injury sites. The first author for example, has endured (wearisomely) the following minor-injury sites: back, gluteals, knee, adductors, hip flexors, hamstrings, calf, soleus, shin, ankle, Achilles' tendon, plantar fascia, etc., and the second author has an analogous list. Prolonged exposure to running results in the development of a somatic understanding of the various kinds of "dys-ease" that the panoply of running injuries can force into the athletic consciousness. The axiomatic question runners ask of themselves when suffering from these minor afflictions is "what can I get away with?" In other words, is running still possible with the problem, for how long, at what intensity? To answer that question an understanding of the differing degrees and sensations of pain and discomfort, and their import, must develop.

Our data revealed a series of contingent self-diagnoses and understandings pertaining to the enduring of such pains. The first focused upon the forms of the discomfort. Was it sharp, or stiff, or tight, or sore, or aching? Was there swelling, or heat? Was it twinging or pulling? We developed our own categorization and labeling system. Really acute, sharp pain and/or considerable swelling, for example, were prime indicators for our stopping to endure, as the physical action of trying to stride proved impossible to tolerate, risking more serious pain and injury. With other forms of pain, running generally proved possible, albeit on occasion with reductions in volume and/or pace. The second understanding pertained to the process of pain development during the actual training session. If the pain increased in severity through the session, again this was a prime indicator to desist. If it eased off during the run, however, we generally would "run through" the pain. If the pain came and went intermittently, this was again taken as positive encouragement to keep running. The third contingent understanding focused upon what we conceptualized as "what it (i.e., the injury) likes" and "what it hates." This pertained to the relationship we *felt* between the injury and the terrain being traversed. So for example, ankles that are twinging dislike rough ground, Achilles tendons when inflamed hate hills, and shins similarly inflamed are miserable when encountering hard surfaces with cambers. Having undertaken such reification, the strategy we adopted was to run on what "it" liked. The toleration of discomfort was then linked to these contingent somatic understandings, which are at root sensory. There was consequently a perpetual sensory monitoring of the afflicted part (or parts, as unfortunately these were often multiple!) as running sessions progressed, and contingent forms of decision-making, together with a bit of "body-bargaining" emerged:

> Today I ran from my campus office. Half way around the route I started to feel the bulk of my right calf tightening. So immediately I am giving it lots of focus. Am I going to get around the route with this? Can I afford to

> still run with it? At the back of my mind was a big left calf pull I had years ago running up through Galgate village, which stopped me dead for about a month. That came on insidiously—gradually spreading its evil tentacles, it even reached my soleus, until it was one big hard ball and then bang! So today I ran watching it, watching and running cautiously. It did not start to spread until I reached the converted pub, where I stopped immediately. Stretch it out gently against the wall, repeat three times and luckily it did not jam back up on me and I ran the remaining one hundred yards safely.
>
> (Log 1)

Such persistence is a practical, mundane but necessary strategy, given the perennial nature of minor afflictions, for without this insightful enduring, distance runners would never complete the training required, including for racing; indeed, many a time races are commenced when knowingly carrying these afflictions. Whilst such injuries arrive in the runner's body-world in the immediate present, some are unwelcome return visitors from the past; previous injuries that, having healed imperfectly, return periodically—old adversaries in the game of endurance. Having engaged in previous encounters with such recalcitrant "bits," experienced runners develop a deep somatic understanding of their injury-enemies:

> I have a developed sensibility or perhaps it is a sensitivity to my running body. Over the years via lots of injuries I now have ghosts. So one of these are my peroneals (tendons in the lower leg), which are OKish most of the time, but then they will emerge again. I know exactly what they are like in my head, it's a different kind of pain from say Achilles pain, kind of a longer pulling, grumbling away at me all of a sudden. It's like "ah you swine, you are back in all your perfidy, I know how to sort you out!"
>
> (Log 1)

"Sorting it out" means careful management during running, via the aforementioned sensory-based somatic knowledge, and also subsequently doing self-help remedial work (Hockey, 2005) on the afflicted part, so as to banish the ghost once again, at least temporarily. The distance-running "enduring consciousness" is then one that accumulates somatic experience of habitual pains, formulates contextual strategies to deal with these, and thus develops confidence in the possibility of further enduring in the face of future minor afflictions.

Outside and inside

Distance running is an outdoor activity and its participants are inevitably subjected to the vagaries of the elements. Montagu (1971) has portrayed how the skin provides the largest area of touch in the human body, and runners are touched perennially by heat, wet, cold, and wind as the elements bombard them (Allen-Collinson & Owton, 2015). The activity per se is difficult enough, but when this is compounded by climatic vagaries, the enduring becomes more arduous, and at the extremes runners can fall prey to heat exhaustion or hypothermia. Runners learn what conditions they can run in effectively and also not so effectively. For example, the first author is able to run effectively in high temperatures even in high levels of humidity; very cold and wet conditions, however, impact much more negatively on him. Exposure to the latter has over the years induced a particular kind of somatic understanding:

> I know now what I have to watch for in bad conditions. I can have aching hands and arms, and windburn on the face, freezing quads or feet and get away with those peripheral things. What I am much more alert to is if the core gets wet and cold. That feels like particularly the head, sort of inside it, when my thinking can then get a bit confused. And also inside my middle when that gets cold inside. I know if that starts to happen, I had better think about how far I am going to run, maybe cut it short and run a bit longer the next day.
>
> (Log 1)

In contrast for the second author, this kind of somatic discomfort is more apparent in relation to heat and high humidity, which for her render running-endurance more difficult, but also generates similar sensory-based knowledge:

> Heck, that was a hard evening's work. The workday left my quads heavy, lethargic and dead, no "whack" at all, and it's that awful, heavy, hot-humid weather. I know by now, after all these years, that this *might* mean cutting short the run (as absolute last resort). I'm rubbish in this kind of weather, and I'm furious at having to sacrifice hard-won running-time to waste-of-time work. The fury assists the first 20-mins of the run, but after that, as my body-core starts to heat up relentlessly, I'm beginning to sink. Not even the energy to seek out the slightly cooler air under the trees. The heat bounces up at me mercilessly—off the tarmac and even off the torpid grass. Angrily had to stagger home after just 40-mins today, the heat and humidity compounded by hotness of hayfever. Horrid.
>
> (Log 2)

Exposure to extremes of weather produces an understanding amongst runners that whilst the outside of their body is impacted so also is their inner-core, and it is this to which they have to pay most attention in endurance situations. Alongside the aforementioned somatic awareness and knowledge develop other forms of sensory knowledge, generating lived understanding that high ground is generally cooler than low-lying ground, that buildings, forests and sheltered canal tow paths all diminish wind chill, and that welcome shade is provided by tall structures, natural or otherwise. These understandings then inform the choice of training routes in the face of meteorological conditions that threatens to diminish runners' capacity to endure.

Other experiential, somatic learning revolves around hydration and food intake, for without adequate water and energy intake, running becomes problematic. Lack of hydration signals itself to athletes principally via the major running-muscle groups (hamstrings, calves, quadriceps) beginning to tighten, and the impact of the terrain then tightens them further. The body's elasticity begins to diminish and movement becomes, to use our own term, "jerky." This somatic way of knowing leads us, especially prior to undertaking running in hot weather, visually to evaluating our urine via its colour; the darker it is, the less hydrated we are. The remedy here is to hydrate as much as possible prior to the run. As noted in the above extract from Log 2, however, this may be difficult when opportunities to consume fluids are restricted, for example in the workplace. Similarly, opportunities to eat may be restricted during the workday, and as many a runner will testify, devouring a meal or snack too close to a training session can generate all sorts of unpleasant digestive problems. This can give the runner constrained by work demands a difficult decision: (1) eat something and risk indigestion or sickness on the run; or, (2) set off for the run hungry and with low glycogen stores. The latter state results in "running on empty."

> Today lots of teaching and lots of meetings—all a bit mad, so a really rubbish training session tonight. Got out there and felt hollow all the way round, empty core, no push, a proper "nothing in the tank" run. No time for lunch, and brought half my sandwiches back home uneaten, could only snaffle a few bites late pm. Angry at the session, angry at the University for making me overwork!
>
> (Log 2)

Runners thus learn, over time, an intimate awareness of the complexity of factors impacting upon their enduring. They come to understand that there is a mutually influencing relationship between the external climatic and social environments (often occupational work) and the running-body, in relation to both the body's external surface and also the internal tissues and organs. Indeed, as phenomenology highlights, the internal-external distinction is often blurred in lived experience (Allen-Collinson, 2011a).

Conclusion

In this chapter, we have sought to provide a flavor of some of the key elements in our lived experience of endurance, and the ways in which the running-mind and running-body inter-relate and mutually influence. For us, "doing endurance" lies at the heart of our everyday *Lebenswelt*, and also constitutes a core component of our athletic "identity work" (Allen-Collinson & Hockey, 2007) required to substantiate inhabiting the distance-running subculture—both to ourselves, and to our running peers. Doing endurance is not just part of the activity of running itself, but also becomes a central component of athletic consciousness and of general being-in-the-world. Furthermore, other corporeal manifestations become interpreted vis-à-vis their impact upon the capacity to endure. So for example, when runners catch sight of themselves in the bathroom mirror, if they have been training hard and well, the lean torso they glimpse is valorized functionally, as well perhaps as aesthetically, for the less "surplus" weight a runner carries, the easier it is to endure the mileage. In contrast, waking up to the "dys-appearance" (Leder, 1990) of a "creaky," stiff Achilles' tendon signifies not only that the body is not in a state of perfection, but that imperfection might seriously jeopardize the ability to endure the day's training session(s). In this way, enduring permeates not just the physiology of running but also the embodied habitual consciousness of the distance runner even when not running; the mind-body nexus holds strong.

Using the autoethnographic and autophenomenographic data, what we have portrayed above is a series of sensory-based practices that constitute, in Merleau-Ponty's (2001) terms, habituated embodied actions. In this way, the habit of enduring is built. From Merleau-Ponty's position, however, habit is not an automatic phenomenon, but rather, as Crossley (2001) notes, it is an essential practical "principle" that comes into the social world via the construction of meaning, intention and appropriate action. Together these constitute what Schütz (1967) has called the "stock of knowledge at hand." This is used by distance-runners to accomplish the mundane "doing" of endurance. Utilizing this stock of knowledge, runners construct what Schütz conceptualized as *typifications*; commonsense constructs which individuals use to order the social world on a moment-to-moment basis, to organize and structure experience (Benson & Hughes, 1983). The first and most directly autophenomenographic typification is when runners typify themselves, via the kinds of sensory practices depicted above. They thus experience and understand themselves to be an athlete who can and does *endure*, a conception of self that permeates their identity and being-in-the-world. The second form of typification, drawing upon autoethnographic as well as autophenomenographic insights, occurs when runners draw upon the same stock of knowledge to evaluate their training partners and race competitors, and come to categorize them also as enduring (or not). In this way, enduring becomes a shared subcultural practice: done, achieved, known, perceived, commented upon; a lived experience shared amongst a community of practitioners and *Lebenswelt* inhabitants.

In our own case, we had a strong co-training partnership for nearly two decades, as part of which we constructed elaborate typifications of each other as athletes who could/can and did/do endure. These typifications encompassed our various physiological strengths and weaknesses, and how these impacted upon our individual and mutual capacity to endure. As described above, for example, the impact of heat and cold differentially affected that capacity, as did other features, such as one being a stronger hill climber than the other, with the latter being more nimble on hill descents. Also typified was an intimate knowledge of the other's breathing, posture and demeanor and how these features indicated relative ease or "dys-ease" (Leder, 1990) when "doing enduring." The typifications held about competitors against whom one races frequently, and who are thus "known" vis-à-vis enduring, may not be quite so rich and complex, but in our direct experience they are similarly constructed and put into practice. Stoicism is tested under competitive conditions during races, scenarios in which the objectives of times, positions, or just finishing, assist and encourage the practice of enduring. Arguably, however, it is within the more routine, mundane context of regular training—which does not directly provide such objectives and encouragements—that enduring is habitually learnt and relearnt, and the motive power to keep going is repeatedly tested.

Note

1 The term espy means "to catch sight of."

References

Allen-Collinson, J. (2009). Sporting embodiment: Sports studies and the (continuing) promise of phenomenology. *Qualitative Research in Sport & Exercise, 1*, 279–296.

Allen-Collinson, J. (2011a). Feminist phenomenology and the woman in the running body. *Sport, Ethics & Philosophy*, *5*, 287–302.

Allen-Collinson, J. (2011b). Intention and epochē in tension: Autophenomenography, bracketing and a novel approach to researching sporting embodiment. *Qualitative Research in Sport, Exercise & Health*, 3, 48–62.

Allen-Collinson, J., & Hockey, J. (2007). "Working out" identity: Distance runners and the management of disrupted identity. *Leisure Studies*, *26*, 381–398.

Allen-Collinson, J., & Hockey, J. (2011). Feeling the way: Notes toward a haptic phenomenology of scuba diving and distance running. *International Review for the Sociology of Sport, 46*, 330–345.

Allen-Collinson, J., & Hockey, J. (2015). From a certain point of view: Sensory phenomenological envisionings of running space and place. *Journal of Contemporary Ethnography, 44*, 63–83.

Allen-Collinson, J., & Owton, H. (2014). Take a deep breath: Asthma, sporting embodiment, the senses, and "auditory work". *International Review for the Sociology of Sport, 49*, 592–608.

Allen-Collinson, J., & Owton, H. (2015). Intense embodiment: Senses of heat in women's running and boxing. *Body & Society, 21*, 245–268.

Atkinson, M. (2008). Triathlon, suffering and exciting significance. *Leisure Studies, 27*, 165–80.

Bale, J. (2004). *Running cultures*. London, England: Routledge.

Benson, D., & Hughes, J. A. (1983) *The Perspective of Ethnomethodology*. London, England: Longman.

Brown, D., & Jennings, G. (2013). In search of a martial habitus: Identifying core dispositions in Wing Chun and Taijiquan. In R. S. García & D. C. Spencer (Eds.), *Fighting scholars: Habitus and ethnographies of martial arts and combat sports* (pp. 33–48). London, England: Anthem Press.

Crossley, N. (2001). *The social body: Habit, identity & desire.* London, England: Sage.

Crust, L., Keegan, R., Piggott, D., & Swann, C. (2011). Walking the walk: A phenomenological study of long distance walking. *Journal of Applied Sport Psychology, 23,* 243–262.

Csordas, T. J. (1993). Somatic modes of attention. *Cultural Anthropology, 8,* 135–156.

Fallowfield, J. L., & Wilkinson, D. M. (1999). *Sports performance in middle and long distance running.* Chichester, United Kingdom: John Wiley.

Fuchs, T. (2012). The phenomenology of body memory. In S. C. Koch, T. Fuchs, M. Summa, & C. Müller (Eds.), *Body memory, metaphor and movement* (pp. 9–22). Amsterdam, Netherlands: John Benjamins.

Garfinkel, H. (2002). *Ethnomethodology's program: Working out Durkheim's aphorism.* New York, NY: Rowan & Littlefield.

Goodridge, J. (1999). *Rhythm and timing of movement in performance.* London, England: Jessica Kingsley.

Grasseni, C. (2009). *Developing skills, developing vision: Practicalities of locality at the foot of the Alps.* Oxford, England: Berghahn.

Hockey, J. (2005). Injured distance runners: A case of identity work as self-help. *Sociology of Sport Journal, 21,* 38–58.

Hockey, J. (2006). Sensing the run: The senses and distance running. *The Senses & Society, 1,* 183–202.

Hockey, J. (2013). Knowing the "going": The sensory evaluation of distance running, *Qualitative Research in Sport, Exercise & Health, 5,* 127–141.

Hockey, J., & Allen-Collinson, J. (2007). Grasping the phenomenology of sporting bodies. *International Review for the Sociology of Sport, 42,* 115–131.

Howe, P. D., & Morris, C. (2009). An exploration of the co-production of performance running bodies and natures within "running taskscapes." *Journal of Sport & Social Issues, 33,* 308–330.

Husserl, E. (1900/1901; 2001). *The shorter logical investigations, Volume 1.* London, England and New York, NY: Routledge. Originally published 1900/1901 in German, as *Logische Untersuchungen,* M. Niemeyer, Halle.

Ingold, T. (2000). *The perception of the environment.* London, England: Routledge.

Leder, D. (1990). *The absent body.* Chicago, IL: University of Chicago Press.

Merleau-Ponty, M. (2001). *Phenomenology of perception,* trans. C. Smith. London, England: Routledge & Kegan Paul.

Montagu, A. (1971). *Touching: The human significance of skin.* New York, NY: Columbia University Press.

Moore, A., Grime, J., Campbell, P., & Richardson, J. (2012). Troubling stoicism: Sociocultural influences and applications to health and illness. *Health (London), 17,* 159–173.

Reischer, E. L. (2001). Running to the moon: The articulation and construction of self in marathon runners. *Anthropology of Consciousness, 12,* 19–34.

Samudra, J. K. (2008). Memory in our body: Thick participation and the translation of kinaesthetic experience. *American Ethnologist, 35,* 665–681.

Schütz, A. (1967). *The Phenomenology of the social world.* Evanston, IL: Northwestern University Press.

Schütz, A., & Luckmann, T. (1973). *The structures of the life world, Volume 1.* London, England: Heinemann.

Shilling, C. (2003). *The body and social theory, 2nd ed.* London, England: Sage.

Smith, S. L. (2000). British non-elite road running and masculinity: A case of "running repairs"? *Men and Masculinities*, *3*, 187–208.

Sparkes, A. (2009). Ethnography and the senses: Challenges and possibilities, *Qualitative Research in Sport and Exercise*, *1*, 21–35.

16 Enduring ideas

William Bridel, Jim Denison, and Pirkko Markula

While writing this book three major motion pictures were released that focused on distance running and endurance: *4 Minute Mile*; *McFarland, USA*; and, the Oscar-nominated *Unbroken*. Each film, in its own way, reflects what seems an ongoing fascination with people who choose to push their bodies physically and mentally through different sorts of endurance challenges and, maybe even more so, what—in a neoliberal social and political context—can (or should?) ostensibly be learned from such quests.

In *Unbroken*, the true story of American Olympian Louis Zamperini, human endurance is highlighted in two utterly contrasting ways. The first is his rise to national and international prominence as a distance runner. The second focuses on his ordeal during World War II. After his fighter plane was shot down, Zamperini survived 47 days at sea only to be captured by the Japanese military and imprisoned in a POW camp, where he remained until the war ended in 1945. It is to say the very least, a powerful tale of the human capacity to endure in the most drastic of circumstances. One cannot help but speculate that unpacking the meanings of endurance in Zamperini's life would reveal a close parallel to those of "Lost Boy" Lopez Lomong, as elucidated by Walton-Fisette in Chapter 9 of this book.

Distance running factored into the public imagination in several other ways as well over the course of writing this book. Several videos on YouTube went viral, the most popular of which was the short documentary about long-distance runner Kayla Montgomery, with well over ten million views. Montgomery, an 18-year old high school student, was diagnosed with multiple sclerosis (MS) at the age of 14. Despite that, she has gone on to become one of the best young long-distance runners in the United States. A significant part of her documentary, *Catching Kayla*, focuses on the end of each one of Montgomery's races. It is here that her coach has to catch her, has to hold her up as she crosses the finish line devoid of any feeling in her legs, a lasting impact of her MS.

It wasn't just movies and videos about distance runners that continued to place endurance into public discourse during the writing of this book; it also seemed that people were finding different ways to run. While running groups are certainly not a new development in the running community, an article in the December 2013 issue of *Runner's World* highlighted emergent types of running clubs. In New York City one can join a "bridge running club" and in Boston there is a group called the November Project; "At their free workouts, hugs and positivity awards are the norm. So are F-bombs and spray-painted T-shirts. They stage their own guerilla street races, with the finish line a local watering hole" (p. 66). The popular explanation of the emergence of these different kinds of running clubs wrests in the group most represented in them—25 to 35-year-old members of "Generation Y" who "want to be seen as unique and to be part of something special" (Daniloff, 2013, p. 66).

The birth and growth of events like Tough Mudder, the Warrior Dash, the Neon Run series, and new and more challenging ultramarathons, along with new forms of running clubs, speaks to the fascination people have with running and the way that new means of testing human endurance are produced. That said, what one might refer to as "anti-endurance" events also appeared on the running circuit in the last two years: the Instant Gratification Zero Mile Fun Run held in California in which participants walked 10m past the start line and collected their finisher's t-shirts, is one such example. But apparently even 10m seemed too much for organizers of the 0.0 Instant Gratification Run held in Philadelphia in February 2014. In that event, one step was all that was required to complete the course ... at a cost of $20 to $35. In both events, the after-party seemed to be where participants intended to truly test their endurance, a kind of pleasure reflective of the popular notion that running is most fun when it's over, even when the race is really over before it begins.

Beyond the popular

What seems an almost constant advent of new ways to test human endurance led to the idea for this book. Given the popularity of running, the birth and growth of different types of distance running challenges, and interest in these kinds of activities within the physical and mind sciences and health promotion, a compilation of texts written by some of the leading scholars in the field of sports studies seemed especially timely and important. The structure we chose for the book—categorizing the authors' contributions in three sections (running beginnings, running because, running bodies)—was more than just an organizational strategy. While each chapter in each section makes unique contributions to socio-cultural knowledge about distance running and endurance, when the sections are taken as a whole we also gain new and fresh insights about running histories, the meanings behind why people run, and the relationships between running and the body.

Running beginnings

The chapters in this section covered over 200 years of endurance history and in so doing have re-emphasized the importance of looking to the past to understand the present. More than just historical accounts, however, the authors have, in different ways, theorized the relationship between distance running (and walking) and contextually specific ideas about endurance. As Adams stated, analyzing endurance challenges (in her case, two specific pedestrian events) allows for an interrogation of the "shifts in the meanings of endurance and the kinds of ideological work that performances of endurance might have accomplished" (p. 22). When placing these early constructions of endurance vis-à-vis pedestrianism into conversation with the other explorations of running beginnings, however, perhaps not all that much has changed.

Examining over 70 years of distance running training practices, Mills and Denison argued that scientific knowledge and dominant notions of individual responsibility and self-sufficiency circulating in the larger social context limited ideas about how coaches train distance runners to endure. As they questioned: "Were all of these coaching icons just doing variations of the same thing: more science, more discipline, more toughness?" (p. 58). How might present-day coaches step outside of these traditional approaches to endurance training to find a way to do things differently and enhance athlete development? Weedon similarly called into question the "newness" of mud runs, events that while appearing relatively recently in the endurance sportscape seem to reproduce the principles and values aligned with physical cultural movements of the nineteenth century: most notably a desire to "return to nature" and more arduous physical practices as a way for people to create new senses of self in post-modern times.

Chase reminded us that one must always be conscious of whose history is being told and why. While undoubtedly Kathrine Switzer is an important figure in the development of women's involvement in distance running in the United States, it is imperative that the stories of individuals such as Roberta Gibb, Merry Lepper, Fred Lebow, and others be told and understood. The same is true for key events that have resulted from and contributed to the increased participation of women in elite and non-elite distance running. In her work here, Chase has produced an historical narrative about distance running while simultaneously highlighting the way that the sport and notions of endurance have been shaped by and resisted dominant gender ideology.

As a collective, the four chapters expose the relative consistency with which endurance has been considered a valued trait and the different ways people have set out to achieve that in different spatial and temporal contexts. These four chapters also highlight the ways in which social and political norms and values have shaped the understanding of endurance in the larger context generally but also in distance running challenges specifically. As such, people's experiences of endurance are also shaped by social and political norms, a theme affirmed and contested by the authors contributing to the second section of the book.

Running because

Oprah Winfrey once proclaimed that, "running is the greatest metaphor for life, because you get out of it what you put into it." Authors contributing texts to *Running Because* explored quite varied topics but with a common goal—to explore the meanings of distance running and endurance beyond popular explanations and understandings. These explorations mostly played out in two ways.

On the one hand, Giardina, King-White, and Bunds along with Peers turned to running events to consider the effect the narratives about these events had on the public at large. While their foci were quite different—the Boston marathon bombings and cross-Canada marathons undertaken by three "inspirational" endurance athletes—Giardina, King-White, and Bunds and Peers provided complex and nuanced understandings of endurance challenges in relation to neoliberalism, colonialism, racism, and ableism. Both chapters, thus, provide critical readings of popular narratives that relied on stereotypical and problematic constructions of "others" that worked, no matter how "well-intentioned," to reify a normalized (and enduring) identity at the center of North American-ness, a center that is white and able-bodied.

On the other hand, Pringle and Walton-Fisette turned more to the meanings individuals make of or ascribe to their involvement in distance running. Typically in popular and critical considerations of running, suffering, hurt, and pain articulate with senses of self and identity. Walton-Fisette used Lomong's life story to consider the central role of the body in subjectivation, but also the various meanings that endurance had held for Lomong throughout his life, oftentimes a source of joy, hope, and inspiration. Pringle sought to complicate the notion of "running=pain" idea by considering running-related enjoyment and pleasure through the analysis of textual representations and embodied experiences, while also challenging traditional notions of identity categories reproduced through existing running-related research. As he compellingly noted,

> By thinking of runners by what they do and their affects/emotions, there are possibilities for disrupting running identity categories so that runners do not just conceive of themselves, for example, as "white-runners" or "gay-runners" or "aged-runners" or "male-runners": identity categories that possibly constrain what individuals think they can or should do.
>
> (p. 108)

Finally, Markula—by focusing on the (perhaps fluctuating) popularity of the minimalist running movement—placed the very physical experience of running (i.e., the foot striking the ground and the resonant impact throughout the rest of the body) into conversation with capitalist agendas, scientific knowledge, and running shoes themselves to chip away at an emergent popular meaning of running—the "naturalness" of it for all bodies.

As a collective, the five chapters move beyond popular, celebratory accounts of the role of running in individual lives and public life. Following from *Running Beginnings*, they also either directly or indirectly explicate the way historical and ideological conceptualizations of endurance continue to influence contemporary understandings of distance running challenges and life in general. Finally, the chapters all contribute to understandings about the relationship between running and both individual and cultural identities, an idea that also gets some consideration in the final section of the book.

Running bodies

The scholars contributing research to this section of the book had a common starting point: the running body. Perhaps not surprisingly given the previously published literature on the topic, the "running body" meant different things to the different authors. These differences simply demonstrate the complexity of the body when it is considered a product (to greater or lesser extents) of cultural context. Three chapters sought to place different theoretical approaches to the body into conversation: Hockey and Allen-Collinson turned to their own experiences of running to consider the running body as both sensorial and discursive. Thorpe also adopted a dualistic approach to the body by considering both the biological and sociological, providing important insights about women who run recreationally, their lived experiences of amenorrhea, and notions of agency. And Perrier and Bridel used their own bodily experiences of running to both understand and then blur the ways identity has been theorized within exercise psychology and sociology (which are perhaps not that different after all) with a particular focus on the ways experiences of the body are shaped (physically and discursively) by the spaces in which ultrarunning takes place. Hanold turned to ultrarunning bodies to augment the socio-cultural literature on that sport and understandings of the relationship between the body and space (or nature) more broadly. Similarly, Howe (using representational fiction) considered the production of elite distance-running bodies in relation to space, time, and disciplinary training practices (similar to the ones critiqued by Mills and Denison in Chapter 4) ultimately arguing that despite (or in spite of?) technological "developments," runners must be connected to their corporeality in order to be successful.

In the introductory chapter of this book, my co-editors and I noted that there has been a call for the inclusion of the biological, sensorial nature of people's bodies in socio-cultural investigations of running. By examining running bodies in the way that they have, the scholars contributing to *Running Bodies* have, in varied ways, contributed knowledge to sociological considerations of the body writ large. With individual efforts and collective outcomes, the authors have in a sense demonstrated how we might gain greater insights on the body and embodied experiences by making more permeable the otherwise rigid boundaries created and maintained between theoretical paradigms and academic disciplines.

What next?

In its many forms, running—as a popular leisure pursuit and high-performance sport—continues to contribute to contextually specific social norms about bodies and identities, as well as the way we think about, experience, and maybe even politicize, endurance. Outside of the running context, cross-country skiing, show shoeing, speed skating, marathon swimming, orienteering, and multi-sport events like duathlons and triathlons continue to be popular for elite athletes and "weekend warriors." But endurance challenges of different sorts have also cropped up. CrossFit, for example, has become popular in the past few years as both a type of exercise and formal competition (i.e., the CrossFit Games).

According to CrossFit founder Greg Glassman, the program he created is "a magic formula, which improves ten areas of fitness including cardiovascular/respiratory endurance, stamina, strength, flexibility, power, speed, agility, coordination, balance and accuracy" (quoted in Edgley, 2015, para. 5). Other types of high intensity interval training (HIIT) such as Jillian Michaels BodyShred™ and Les Mills GRIT™ are also gaining in popularity globally. The former is promoted as a "a high intensity and endurance based 30-minute workout."[1] Whether CrossFit and these other programs are endurance activities is certainly up for debate, but one cannot argue their popularity and, in the case of CrossFit in particular, the close connection to other popular activities like run/obstacle races and the successful television show *American Ninja Warrior*. The main point here is that there are other ways beyond distance running that endurance factors into public discourse. This should make endurance a topic of continued interest for socio-cultural scholars in particular when one considers how these activities and others like them as well as "endurance narratives" filter into the public imagination in mostly celebratory (and, thus, unproblematized) ways.

Bordo (1999) contended that, "cultural interpretation is an ongoing, always incomplete process, and no one gets the final word" (p. 29). In the spirit of her suggestion, would an investigation of activities beyond distance running reveal different conceptualizations of endurance and/or reaffirm endurance as a valued physical (mental and emotional) trait? Might constructions of endurance emerge that challenge what some scholars in this book have pointed to as an intricate connection between scientific and political discourse and endurance? In short, what different kinds of questions can be asked about different sports and physical activities and with what outcomes?

Beyond endurance, we also hope that the three-pronged but interconnecting analytic structure we have created here—beginnings, because, bodies—may prove useful to scholars wishing to investigate topics from multiple perspectives. What about speed? Strength? Power? Flexibility? And how might explorations of these other kinds of movements/traits/behaviors be put into conversation with the different constructions of endurance that have emerged in this book? Collaborating with other scholars on a project where such an analytic framework is established from the outset (and thus framing the research, analysis, and writing) may just provide new and interesting insights on physically active and moving bodies historically and in contemporary times.

Note

1 Definition as it appears on the company's website: https://www.jillianmichaels bodyshred.com/about.

References

Bordo, S. (1999). *The male body: A new look at men in public and private*. New York, NY: Farrar, Straus, and Giroux.

Daniloff, C. (December, 2013). Running rogue. *Runner's World*. Emmaus, PA: Rodale.

Edgley, R. (April, 2015). What is Crossfit? The sport, science, and state of mind. Retrieved from: www.gq-magazine.co.uk/entertainment/articles/2015-04/08/what-is-crossfit-crossfit-games-crossfit-london.

Garris, M. (Executive Producer), Jashni, J. (Executive Producer), & Jolie, A. (Director). (2014). *Unbroken* [Motion picture]. United States: 3 Arts Entertainment.

SportsWriter100. (2014, November 20). *Catching Kayla* [Video file]. Retrieved from www.youtube.com/watch?v=kpA-FsKLA6A.

Index